mind games

the assassination of John Lennon

David Whelan

Publisher:
Orwell Books Ltd
25 Margaret's St
Ipswich
Suffolk
IP4 2AT

ISBN Number: 9798866748273

Mind Games – The Assassination of John Lennon
is dedicated to John Lennon and anyone else who
has dared to speak truth to power

Contents

Our society is run by insane people for insane objectives. I think we're being run by maniacs for maniacal ends and I think I'm liable to be put away for expressing that.
John Lennon

Men never do evil so completely and cheerfully as when they do it from religious conviction.
Blaise Pascal

Background

Ever since Oliver Stone's 1991 *JFK* movie first opened my eyes to the possibilities of grand conspiracies, I have always been interested in famous assassinations.

In my professional career as a writer and producer for television, I have worked alongside many excellent researchers who validated claims or sought to disprove them by dint of sheer hard work and dogged insistence on evidence. I am schooled in this practice. It is second nature to me. Sometimes, like the proverbial gold digger, research leads to small gems which are rich in value, but nothing in my experience comes near the shock of the discovery I experienced over the past three years working on this project about the assassination of John Lennon. It took my breath away, to the extent that I ate and slept the causes and the consequences of John Lennon's untimely death. Note the difference here: I started on a *murder* and found an *assassination*. I need to share this with you for it contradicts the received wisdom from that era and still today. This book will unearth the truth of a seismic historical event. Lennon's death is undoubtedly one of the most infamous celebrity killings of our time – in fact, of any time. It has, until now, never been fully investigated. Never been forensically examined. And the world seems set to have accepted that. I have consumed everything that has been published on the subject. I have studied newspaper articles from 1980 onwards; I have spoken to people who found themselves witnesses; and I have gained access to official documents, many of which were kept locked away from the public eye. Sadly, some still are. Each was laboriously studied, analysed and cross-checked.

I began to realise that there was something very wrong with

several claims which were recorded and reported. What the New York Police Department (NYPD) saw as a simple, straightforward closed murder was nothing of the kind. After all this intense research and hundreds of hours of interviews with numerous people close to and connected with Lennon, the alleged killer Mark Chapman, the NYPD, the Dakota and witnesses to the murder itself, I have uncovered overwhelming evidence to the contrary. My work will prove that Chapman, like Lee Harvey Oswald and Sirhan Sirhan before him, was not just a stereotypical "lone nut"; that the murder was far from the straightforward open and shut case which vested interests want the world to believe; and that we have been fed a lie.

In my research, I gained access to numerous notebooks and files from the NYPD "investigation" into John Lennon's killing. These long-hidden files reveal much that has never been seen by the public before – until now. Important material from the FBI had previously been prised open through the insistence of the author Jon Wiener. His long struggle to obtain these reports was eventually successful thanks to the Freedom of Information Act. A successful researcher must dig deep and have the iron will to stay the course. The reader also must battle against the comfort of all the received wisdom to look afresh at the myriad of lies and deception which have circulated about John Lennon's death since December 1980.

What is incredible about the assassination of one of the most famous men of the twentieth century is the disturbing fact that, to this day, specific details about what precisely happened in the Dakota driveway at 10.50pm on 8th December 1980 remain unknown. Sure, we know that the New York DA's office, the NYPD and, shamefully, the world's media at the time were all happy to confirm that Mark Chapman shot John Lennon and admitted his crime – case closed. Just another one of the "lone nuts" who want a place in history. What more is there to say? Trust me on this one: there is much more to say, and it is all in this book. We have been consistently told who, where and when with regards to John Lennon's death but we have never been asked to critically analyse the questions why and how. This book will explore the why and how – in depth.

The only way one can understand John Lennon's assassination is to study all the various eyewitness accounts and the (superficial) police "investigation" that took place. Now, finally, the world can do this. I must warn the reader that many accounts are tainted by embellishment and the passage of time. First-hand accounts given (in some cases, again) forty years after the event do provide useful source material, but only by matching those accounts with the evidence from the time can we come to a factually accurate conclusion. It is a journey. A long trek which we are still only part the way through. Believe me, critical evidence remains hidden from the public's gaze. I'm hoping this book will help change that.

My aim is to give John Lennon the respect he deserves by investigating his killing properly. New evidence uncovered while writing this book points to a conspiracy of many facets. This fresh proof allows the reader to reconsider the known facts and evidence surrounding Lennon's assassination. Please read the book and make up your own mind about what really happened on that fateful night in December 1980. Like all great true crime stories, the reader must become the investigator. This is no easy task because, in essence, this is one of the twentieth century's most notorious assassinations, covered up and buried. Until now.

Nowadays, as never before, truth is often shredded into tatters. We are lied to. Constantly and repeatedly. Duplicity has become an industry in itself. The media struggles to differentiate between what really happened and what a vested interest wants you to think happened. And a lie repeated time and again has every chance of being regurgitated as a truth. History books are crammed with the simplicity of ages, written or repeated by those whom it benefits.

A convenient solution has now become accepted common parlance. No matter the complexity of an assassination or even an attempted assassination, "a lone nut did it." There is an older generation which genuinely believes that President John Fitzgerald Kennedy was shot dead in his Dallas cavalcade by one man: Lee Harvey Oswald. No matter the evidence of other sightings or the potentially dangerous evidence Oswald could have given if he defended himself in court, the myth of the "lone nut" persists.

We are asked to put aside Oswald's repeated insistence that he did not shoot John F Kennedy. Close your mind to the convenience of Oswald's public murder, silenced by a bullet inside the basement of the Dallas Police Department. Forget the oft cited and dubious relationship of Oswald's murderer, a violent Jack Ruby who was a mob associate and a figure known to the Dallas police. Despite the serious reservations of the circumstances in which Oswald was "removed", despite the Warren Commission's conclusion that Jack Ruby's path to the police basement was greased by unlocked doors and absent guards, the world was assured that the murder was Ruby's emotional reaction to the president's death to protect Jacqueline Kennedy from prolonged pain. It had nothing to do with silencing Lee Harvey Oswald, they said. Both the assassination of JFK and the slaughter of Oswald was the independent work of the "lone nut" perpetrator. Impossible. Two lone nuts together? Absolutely ridiculous.

The Nobel Peace Prize winner, Dr Martin Luther King, was allegedly assassinated by a "lone" sniper in April 1968. He was an international figure and a political activist of the highest moral order and a figure of sheer hate for some in the wider community. His life was dedicated to liberal causes including equality, an abhorrence of war and civil rights for all in America. Dr King was fatally shot by James Earl Ray at precisely 6:01pm on Thursday, April 4, 1968, as he stood on a second-floor motel balcony.

The assassin was a convicted robber and fraudster. According to the FBI, he killed Martin Luther King with a single shot from his Remington rifle. Given that Ray was seen minutes later running away from the incident, how he managed to escape to Canada and then England beggars belief. But he did, and was eventually arrested in Heathrow airport, London and sent back to the USA. Years later, Dr King's widow openly blamed a conspiracy of the Mafia and local, state and federal government for her husband's assassination. In a civil suit, the jury accepted overwhelming evidence that identified an alternative culprit, not James Earl Ray. They also agreed that Ray was the fall guy, set up to take the blame. So, despite the media frenzy, he wasn't a "lone nut" after all. Pity, really. It is more comforting to deal with lone nuts than corporate assassinations.

A second Kennedy, the popular Robert Francis (known to many as Bobby) was assassinated at close range by Sirhan Sirhan (a Palestinian-Jordanian) as he left a Democratic Party Primary rally at the Ambassador Hotel in Los Angeles, in June 1968. In recent years, Sirhan's lawyers have stated that Sirhan was framed and he himself has said that he had no memory of his crime. Claims were also made that ballistic evidence pointed to a second gunman. Yes, these are merely "allegations made in court". So, discount them; put aside any doubt. The lone nut struck again. Didn't he? It's easier to accept that notion. But you have to think beyond such claims.

Indeed, these "lone nuts" appear to be very dangerous people.

The human rights activist Malcolm X was shot in New York by assassins in 1965 and although three members of a group called The Nation of Islam were jailed, rumours abounded that the assassination was conceived of and aided by leading members of the Nation of Islam and by law enforcement agencies. The allegation persisted for decades. This earlier assassination was not the malignant work of one "lone nut". This time, it was seemingly a bag of nuts.

Looking back at these assassinations in the 1960s, a circumspect reader will find a number of common threads. The dead are all persons who had upset the Establishment or insulted the right-wing of American politics. Often, they were damned as "activists". With the exception of Malcolm X, their killers allegedly acted alone. The evidence I will present here makes a mockery of that claim. Political and religious overtones also coloured these villainous actions. Lee Harvey Oswald was deemed to be a communist, a label which the FBI and a pliant press then attached to most civil rights leaders. Church goers from many different branches of Christianity were encouraged to despise the Beatles, and in particular, John Lennon, because of a casual remark about the Beatles being bigger than Jesus which offended their beliefs. Worse still, state and federal agencies supported a myriad of highly suspicious practices which made a mockery of the Constitution. All for the political advantage of the Establishment. They had a use for "lone nuts".

There is a catch-all. A magic get-out-of jail card which can be thrown into the mix to confuse issues and blind discerning observers when argument and detailed proof challenges them. Use the word "conspiracy". This term has unfortunately grown into a monster of gross proportions. Even the most obvious crime can be misrepresented in the media and challenged in court, including the court of public opinion, by the use of that wild and much-abused word: conspiracy. It's as if the Spanish Inquisition has taken on a new life form in the later years of the twentieth century and the ever-constricting millennium, to replace truth with the great lie called conspiracy. Consequently, she or he who is accused of being a conspiracy theorist is condemned to be silenced and (in more modern parlance) cancelled. And it is very difficult for the reader to abandon what they previously thought they knew, in the face of allegations which test their belief. Hold on to your independence. Please interrogate the evidence I am about to present.

The truth is far more complicated and disturbing. For Beatles fans and Lennon aficionados this will be heart-breaking. I was and remain shocked. As a veteran producer of TV programmes, I thought I was immune to such feelings. John Lennon's murder was never officially categorised as an assassination (considered to be a murder perpetrated for political purposes). The official line is that Lennon was murdered by Mark Chapman, a crazed Beatles fan who killed because he was insane or because he wanted to be famous – case closed. Like most people, I bought this version of events for many years. There was precious little alternative opinion. I believed it to be true by default for nearly forty years until one day in 2020, I received, out of the blue, some interesting information: that the doorman at the Dakota, the residence in Manhattan where Lennon was shot, might have been a CIA operative. From that day onwards, my life changed forever.

I started to analyse and research John Lennon's killing – which I am now convinced was an assassination. The holes, the inconsistencies, the downright lies I found in the official investigation became ever more painful. I felt obliged to take my investigation away from the computer screen, and onto the road. My aim? To talk to everybody who was connected to the case and question their previous testimony. It turned out that the possible smoking gun viz. the doorman being a CIA agent was probably untrue. However, other aspects of the case were deeply troubling. There were clear indications that the official story of John's death was deeply flawed. In fact, as the months rolled on, it became clear that much of what we have been told isn't even close to the truth. The more I uncovered, the deeper I plunged into the case. The initial ten pages of research quickly turned into three hundred. Many witnesses and observers opened up for the first time and some people, even after all these years, deliberately and systematically lied.

Here are the basic reported facts: John Lennon was fatally shot at around 10.50pm outside his apartment block, the Dakota, on the Upper West Side of Manhattan, New York City on the 8th of December 1980. As soon as the police arrived on the scene, they arrested Mark Chapman. Following the shooting, Chapman had remained on the scene (where he appeared to be) reading a copy of *The Catcher in the Rye*. The suspect was apprehended without a struggle. The American media and New York police officials immediately began describing Chapman as a "local screwball", after he confessed to NYPD officers that he had just shot and killed one of the world's most famous men. He was quoted by the NYPD as saying, "I'm sure the big part of me is Holden Caulfield, who is the main person in the book. The small part of me must be the Devil."

There were various inaccuracies in this early description of Chapman. Firstly, Chapman wasn't a New York local. He grew up in the American South and was living in Hawaii just prior to the time of his arrest. He also wasn't a "screwball" (taking this arcane and derogatory term to mean "clinically insane"). Mark Chapman, according to no less than six court-appointed experts, who concurred with the prosecution's examiners, was delusional, but the authorities ruled he was sufficiently competent to stand trial.

Having eventually pleaded guilty to the charge of murder, Chapman was sentenced as a legally sane man. He was given a 20 years to life sentence. After a 32-year stay in Attica prison, he is currently being held captive in Green Haven Correctional Facility in New York. Neither jail has any facilities for the criminally insane. Chapman has now spent over forty years in prison, mostly in isolation. His alleged insanity has long been an issue, as has his strange life before Lennon's assassination. Numerous motives for committing the crime have been aired and his reported actions after the crime have become part of the folklore of John Lennon's legacy. These "facts" have proved to be a desert of shifting sands, constantly changing, swirling around to blind us from the truth for the last forty years.

And so there it was, and there it remained, until eventually, encouraged by family, friends and colleagues, I decided that the only way to do justice to this story was to put the investment of the hundreds of hours of research into a book. This book is an attempt to make sense of what really happened on that fateful December night in 1980 because what my investigations uncovered are deeply troubling.

There are, of course, many different accounts of the assassination *outside* the Dakota Building… or was it *inside*… on the 8th of December 1980. If you believe one side of the story, the other suddenly seems to make no sense at all. This book will offer you every side, allegation and counter-allegation. I can only ask the reader to decide for themselves how, and by whom, John Lennon was assassinated. This book will present the official story, the alternative theories and all the witness testimony and forensic insight currently available. I will regularly highlight crucial points of interest you may have missed. In this vile assassination, sometimes the smallest detail reveals the largest clue.

One thing is certain: The official murder narrative surrounding John Lennon is impossible to square with the actual evidence to hand. I hope that through the publication of this book, the case will be re-opened and investigated afresh. For it was not a murder. It was a pre-meditated assassination.

This book will clearly prove that Mark Chapman could not have killed John Lennon in the way that it is currently presented, and, crucially, in the way Chapman thought he did. At the time, the world's most hated and reviled man (the "jerk of jerks" as Paul McCartney once described him) is, in my considered opinion, likely almost entirely innocent of the crimes with which he has been charged. I say almost because there is still crucial evidence and crime scene ballistics that have yet to be revealed to the public. For the present, let's just say that the new evidence which has come to light, and is laid out in this book, makes it clear that Mark Chapman did not do what we have been told he did. Mark Chapman, to this very day, over forty-two years after the assassination, still thinks that he murdered Lennon in a way that is physically impossible.

George Orwell famously wrote that he had found the power to face unpleasant facts. I must warn you now, there are many unpleasant and disturbing facts in this book, but if you care about truth and justice, I trust you will find the power to face them with me.

CHAPTER 1 | John Lennon and his Beliefs

This is not a biography of John Lennon.

Plenty of other authors have written about John's amazing life with the Beatles and beyond. However, for the purposes of a proper investigation into John's assassination, it is important to consider a few key influences in his life – beginning with his strong views on religion.

John Lennon was born in Liverpool, England, on 9th October 1940. His Catholic, sailor father married his Anglican mother on 3rd December 1938. Shortly after Lennon was born, his father disappeared from his life. There is no concrete proof that Lennon was ever baptised in his mother's local Anglican church of St. Peters, Woolton. He attended church as a child and apparently even sang in the choir. His mother gave John over to be raised by her sister Mimi from the age of five and he developed a unique bond with the woman who never let him down. In 1955, at the age of 15, John was confirmed, "of his own free will", Mimi proudly stated. One thing is for certain, by the time John Lennon was a teenager, conventional Christian practices and Catholic doctrine were not particularly on his radar. But he had fallen in love with music.

In 1957, Lennon formed a band called the Quarry Men with some friends, and shortly thereafter he met a local musician called Paul McCartney at a village fete. I'm sure you know what happened next. Hard work, subsistence level survival and dedication moulded them into one of the greatest rock and roll bands ever. It wasn't easy or predictable.

Before John, Paul, George and Ringo went on to conquer the music world as the Beatles, John's mother, Julia, was tragically killed in a road accident, a traumatic event that left John scarred by deep rooted issues of anger and abandonment. An off-duty police officer had killed Julia, just at the point where John and his mother were starting to have a more solid relationship. It was Julia who encouraged John's musical ambitions and her death was a crushing blow for him.

John had been blessed, or cursed – you decide – with a capacity to speak his mind. At first, he was hailed as the "cheeky chappy" in the Fab Four. He was quick of wit and the media couldn't get enough of his smart ripostes. The first impression most people had of John was that he was a free spirit, a co-writer of wonderful songs and a representative of new thinking. But sometimes his mouth ran ahead of his brain. He spoke openly and honestly, without fear, without realising that as a rock and roll superstar he had a growing cohort of critics who would happily crucify him. And dangers lay ahead.

The Beatles

The Beatles were a cultural phenomenon, not just because they made beautiful music, but because they were not afraid to push the boundaries of what was considered acceptable when it came to approaching contentious subjects such as politics, sex, drugs and God. They were seekers and they were seeking in a time when, unlike today, open minds and new ideas were encouraged and lauded by their own generation. But older generations nursed contempt for the changes and attitudes which many young people embraced. The Beatles single-handedly shaped the agenda of 1960s culture across the globe. How could the youth of that time not fall desperately in love with them? Accordingly, there was also an inevitability that their *action* would cause a *reaction*.

On the flip side, the Beatles were seen by the older, post-First World War generation as a moral affront and a spiritual danger to the impressionable younger generation, who were desperate to move away from the grey and depressing world in which their parents had been forced to live. Parents, whose living grandparents could remember kneeling at the feet of Queen Victoria, were worried by lax standards. Rock and Roll in all its guises was perceived by older observers as a dangerous and subversive cult. They didn't listen to the lyrics. Young people did. They were told that popular music was just a phase that they would go through. It wasn't.

A band of Christians across the globe, who thought that rock and roll music was the very work of the devil, began to criticise this new era in which youth demanded the right to have a different opinion; to challenge inequality; to protest against war; and to reject convention. How dare they? Such a backward thought process played well particularly in the southern states of America, where some Christians (especially the purveyors of pointy white hoods) believed that any affinity with "rock and roll" was akin to endorsing black music and black culture. Reason enough for the bigots to despise its creators.

By 1965, the Beatles had moved on from their original "boy meets girl" trademark music. They had created great tunes, clever lyrics and beautiful harmonies. The world all sang them and still does. But the conquerors of European and American culture graduated to darker more contentious issues. Sex, drugs and rock and roll was the banner headline to their new lifestyle. The band moved into more challenging, psychedelic music. They had often taken uppers in their early performances, but by 1965, the band were avid marijuana users – especially John Lennon. The Beatles' 1965 album, *Rubber Soul,* was their first masterpiece in this era, with more sophisticated music and thrilling left turns when least expected. Their lyrics tackled edgier pop subjects laced with introspection and social commentary. One Lennon song, the breathy "Girl", seemed on the surface to be about his infatuation with the opposite sex. On one level, this is true, but a single line stood out to the attentive listener: "Was she taught when she was young that pain would lead to pleasure, did she understand it?"

Lennon explained five years later in *Rolling Stone* magazine, that this line was a veiled attack on Catholicism, stating:

"I was trying to say something about Christianity, which I was opposed to at the time because I was brought up in the Church. I was pretty heavy on the Church in both of my books, but it was never picked up, although it was obviously there. I was talking about Christianity, in that you have to be tortured to attain heaven. That was the Catholic Christian concept: be tortured and then it'll be all right; which seems to be true, but not in their concept of it. I didn't believe in that: that you have to be tortured to attain anything; it just so happens that you are."

These thoughts had lain deep in his subconscious mind since childhood. But John was a thinker, a seeker, a man who wanted to understand; to find the ultimate truth. His first jab at Christianity slipped under the radar. In years to come, John Lennon would ensure this did not happen again.

In the same year that Lennon started experimenting with marijuana, the Beatles press officer, Derek Taylor, gave an interview to the Saturday Evening Post, a British magazine where he first alerted fundamental Christians that the Beatles were never going to be *their* band by stating:

"They're COMPLETELY ANTI-CHRIST. I mean, I am anti-Christ as well, but they're so anti-Christ they shock me which isn't an easy thing. Each time we arrive at an airport, it was as if the messiah had arrived. Cripples threw away their sticks. Sick people rushed up to the car, as if a touch from one of the boys would make them well again. Old women watched with their grand-children and as we'd pass by, I could see the look on their faces which was as if some saviour had just arrived and people were happy and relieved, as if things were somehow going to be better now."

I can understand what Derek Taylor meant. The boys brought a sense of fresh hope to millions, expressed through a music so original that each new album was a landmark in itself. But to liken their arrival to that of the messiah was loose if not downright stupid.

Popular wisdom suggests that any publicity is good publicity. Press officer Taylor should have known better, but this kind of statement enraged every Christian on the planet. Taylor was haunted by his quote for the rest of his life. At every press conference he attended, journalists brought it up, to his enduring embarrassment.

Over the ensuing years, journalists and commentators didn't have to look too far for more anti-Christian rhetoric from the Beatles. The band, and especially Lennon and George Harrison, constantly attacked religion. All four Beatles were brought up with some degree of Christian doctrine in their young lives but had forsaken their faith by the time they became famous. Always a cerebral and insightful group, the band often used their post "fab" years press conferences to take a dig at Christianity and what they perceived as its outdated and repressive teachings. Below are just some of their musings on religion, spirituality, and especially, Christianity:

1963

McCartney – *"Religion doesn't fit in with my life. None of us believe in God."*

Lennon – *"We are not quite sure what we are, but I know that we're more agnostic than atheistic."* (Trust John to show off his theological know-how)

1964

Lennon (on being asked about his views on religion and politics) – *"We are not interested in either."*

McCartney – *"I believe in the supernatural. I've got hung up on séances and the tarot."*

1965

Ringo Starr – *"See that idol* (Ringo was pointing at a statue of a fictional God prop called Kaili, used in the film *Help*), *if you'd been brought up to believe in that, you'd believe in it instead of God, wouldn't you?"*

Starr – (Talking to *Playboy*) *"The Beatles are anti-Pope and anti-Christian."*

Harrison – *"99% of people who go to church on Sunday think that if they don't go, God will get them."*

Harrison – *"The Catholic trick is that they nail you when you are young and brainwash you. Then they've got you for the rest of your life."*

1966

Harrison – *"There are a lot of people who like us and they are influenced by us. So, you know, in a small way, I may be able to influence them in another direction."*

Harrison – (while visiting Bombay) *"The religions that they have in India I believe in much more than anything I ever learned from Christianity. Their religion is not something which Christianity seems to be, which is you turn it on Sunday morning and go to church because you are supposed to go, rather than because you want to go."*

Harrison – *"Our music is our religion. We are giving a lot of happiness to a lot of people. I'm sure that we've given a lot more happiness to people than some of those priests."*

Harrison – *"If Christianity is as good as they say it is, it should stand up to a bit of discussion."*

Much of this overt criticism was lost in the plethora of interviews with the Liverpool lads, often in response to loaded questions. In March 1966, John Lennon gave an interview, which later started a chain reaction of Christian fundamentalist hate. I strongly believe it influenced his brutal death at his New

York apartment block 14 years later. I use the word "influenced" rather than "caused". You will appreciate why later.

In the original interview for the London *Evening Standard*, Lennon was talking to Maureen Cleave at his new mansion in Weybridge, seventeen miles southwest of central London. Cleave was a smart, stylish and attractive journalist who had slowly worked her way into the Beatles' confidence through her sharp writing and honest approach. There have always been rumours that Cleave and Lennon had an affair, and the classic song "Norwegian Wood" is cited in evidence of that affair. Paul McCartney dropped a classic deadpan hint when he recalled, "John used to know Maureen Cleave... quite well."

Back in 1966, when Cleave interviewed a 25-year-old Lennon, he was a bona fide global music superstar. He was also very bored and did not enjoy playing house husband with his first wife Cynthia and their young son Julian. John admitted, "I'm just stopping here like a bus stop. I'll get my real house when I know what I want. You see there is something else I'm going to do, only I don't know what it is. All I know is this isn't it for me" – I bet his wife Cynthia must have been thrilled to read that. Overweight and dropping LSD on his cornflakes, Lennon was in the mood for mischief and decided to bait the Christians in a similar vein as his comedy heroes Peter Cook and Peter Sellers did on a regular basis. Lennon was reading about world religions voraciously around this time, including Timothy Leary's interpretation of *The Tibetan Book of the Dead* and Hugh Schonfield's highly controversial *The Passover Plot*, which stated that Jesus was a mortal man, who faked his miracles with the help of his witless disciples. With all this alternative religious opinion floating around his acid-fuelled head, Lennon uttered the following statement:

"Christianity will go, it will vanish and shrink. I needn't argue about that; I know I'm right and I will be proved right.

We're more popular than Jesus now. I don't know which will go first – rock & roll or Christianity. Jesus was all right, but his disciples were thick and ordinary. It's them twisting it that ruins it for me."

John barely remembered saying it at the time. The interview, titled "How does a Beatle live?" was published in London's *Evening Standard* without any initial reaction. Lennon reflected on the UK's indifference to the article in 1974, declaring "Nobody took any notice in England, they know this guy is blabbing off". The *Evening Standard* editors did not use the quotation as a headline. The article was syndicated globally. Again, no one raised an eyebrow. It was a comment lost in a million words… until it came across the desk of a radical teen magazine in America, called *Datebook*.

Datebook pushed the boundaries of its time, and its editor, Arthur Unger, was committed to publishing stories about social justice and equality. The Beatles and their manager Brian Epstein were admirers of *Datebook* and the magazine was given exclusive access to the band on multiple occasions. Their press officer, Tony Barrow, sent Cleaves' interview to Unger saying: "I think the style and content is very much in line with the sort of thing *Datebook* likes to use." Unger agreed and the interview was published in *Datebook's* July 1966 issue. On the cover, Unger placed Lennon's "I don't know which will go first" quote next to a Paul McCartney diatribe about America, "It's a lousy country where anyone black is a dirty nig**r." I'm not sure that copy of *Datebook* would have sold particularly well in the deep American south. But the die had been cast. Enter Tommy Charles.

Charles was a shock-jock of his day, working in Alabama on WAQY Radio station. He liked to scour magazines and tabloids looking for salacious stories. When he picked up July's *Datebook,* he knew he had struck gold. Together with his partner, Doug Layton, he trumpeted his outrage at the article and launched a "ban the Beatles" campaign. He refused to play the Beatles music on-air and shortly afterwards, encouraged listeners to come in and put their Beatles albums and singles through a tree shredder. Charles took the moral high ground, stating:

> "Because of their tremendous popularity throughout the world, especially with the younger set, they have been able to say what they wanted to without any regard for judgment, maturity, or the meaning of it, and no one has challenged them to any degree."

Matters escalated. Multiple (mostly southern) radio stations, banned the Beatles' music. Before you could say "Nazi Germany", young people from across the southern states of America were burning their Beatles records and memorabilia on large bonfires. Fundamental Christians were horrified to hear their saviour equated to a pop act. The Ku Klux Klan didn't want to miss out on all the rampant intolerance in their own backyard, so they started to nail Beatles records to wooden crosses and set them on fire, at what they called "Beatles Bonfire" events. The Klan's then leader, Imperial Wizard Robert Shelton, accused the Beatles of being brainwashed by communism and he predictably criticised them for supporting black civil rights. In Rome, Pope Paul VI added his voice to the controversy, condemning the Beatles "profanity". The Ku Klux Klan and the Pope apparently singing from the same hymn sheet. Did no one see the irony?

Multiple death threats flew into the Beatles' mail boxes and security was tightened on their American tour. Pastor Thurmond Babbs of Cleveland, Ohio, threatened to excommunicate any member of his congregation who dared attend a Beatles concert, and KZEE radio in Weatherford, Texas, "damned their songs eternally." Predictably the fascist governments of South Africa and Spain also issued official condemnations. One can only wonder what the American intelligence agencies of the time thought. Agencies stuffed to the rafters with veterans who were currently fighting the Cold War against communism in the name of their Christian democracy. If some of those intelligence agency men were also men of the cloth, they must surely have been some of the angriest and most dangerous of Lennon's detractors. John being John, initially he failed to apologise.

The Beatles bonfires had begun to blow themselves out, and the right-wing Christian communities congratulated themselves that decent Christian values had taken some form of revenge on liberal agnosticism. Then, a few weeks later, it reignited again. In a spectacular instance of bad timing, the Beatles started their American tour. The burnings, condemnations and death threats returned, and John Lennon was forced to face the press. Like a man condemned to death, an ashen-faced Lennon apologised in front of 30 members of the American press. Ironically, it was the media which had fuelled the storm in the first place. The experience did not stop further criticism of religion from John Lennon and the Beatles. It did not stop his reckless streak.

1967

McCartney – *"God is in everything. God is in the table in front of you. For me, it just happens that I realised all of this through acid."*

Harrison – *"Everyone is potentially divine. It's just a matter of self-realisation before it will all happen."*

Lennon – *"The youth of today are really looking for some answers, for proper answers the established church can't give them, their parents can't give them and material things can't give them."*

1968

Lennon – *"We are all Jesus and we're all God. He's inside all of us and that's what it is all about. That's the whole bit. Jesus wasn't God come down on earth any more than anybody else was. He was just a better example of a good guy."*

John couldn't stop himself. He couldn't let his personal philosophy be silenced. But his endless search for truth continued.

George Harrison thought he had found the truth. In February 1968, the group travelled to Rishikesh in India to stay at a retreat (ashram) run by a proponent of transcendental meditation, Maharashi Mahesh Yogi. Basing his doctrine mostly in Hindu philosophy, the Yogi believed that people could reach higher levels of consciousness through meditation. George and Pattie Harrison, her sister Jenny, John and Cynthia Lennon, and Mal Evans, the Beatles' long-time roadie and personal assistant, arrived hot and bothered in India on February 16th. Paul McCartney, Jane Asher, Ringo Starr and his wife Maureen came on the 19th. Ringo, according to Harrison, brought "fifteen Sherpas carrying Heinz baked beans" because of his allergies. Donovan and The Beach Boys' Mike Love also travelled out to find some Eastern wisdom. Actress Mia Farrow and her sister Prudence and brother John were already at the ashram when everyone arrived. It read like the cast of Top of the Pops. Deep meditating didn't play too well with Prudence Farrow's mind, prompting her to stay in her room for most of the trip. This gave John the opportunity to write one of his most endearing songs, "Dear Prudence". Lennon also wrote a biting song about the Yogi, which was eventually called "Sexy Sadie", to avoid litigation. Unlike Harrison, Lennon was not overly impressed with Eastern spirituality after Rishikesh. "Sexy Sadie" explicitly laid out John's anger at what he eventually perceived as a waste of time.

It certainly wasn't a complete waste of time. While the Beatles were in India, they independently wrote several of the iconic songs that comprised much of the brilliantly eclectic *The White Album*. Bored after a few weeks, they all began to slip home. When the yogi asked Lennon why they were leaving, Lennon quipped, "Well, if you are so cosmic, you should know."

Not long after John Lennon and Yoko Ono got together as an official couple in late 1968, Yoko Ono apparently introduced

John to the Process Church in London. I have been told by a reliable Beatles source that Ringo's wife Maureen introduced Ono to the Process Church, which was comprised of radical Christians and was started by two former scientologists. The group were considered Satanists by some in the British media because they promoted the worship of the devil as well as Jesus. Filled with Process Church rhetoric, Lennon famously called a meeting at Apple Records in May 1968 and declared "I am Jesus Christ". The three other Beatles believed it was a drug psychosis episode. Tony Bramwell, Apple's head of films (who was at the meeting) thinks the outburst was due to John's recent Process Church activities. Lennon asked for his "I am Jesus" revelation to be announced in a press release. Wisely, John's band mates and their team chose to ignore his request.

On August 9th and 10th in 1969, seven horrific murders in Los Angeles took place. The perpetrators were all later found to be members of a cult run by a failed musician, drug addict and thief called Charles Manson. Manson seemed to have an almost hypnotic power over the young waifs and strays he cobbled together as his personal sex and drug-fuelled "family", living together on a disused ranch. His thesis was that there was going to be a race war between black Americans and white Americans. Once this imminent race war was over, all humanity, except a few victorious blacks, would eventually be wiped out. To save themselves from being killed in the upcoming war, Manson and his followers would hide out in caves in the desert and emerge again when he believed the blacks would lose interest in governing and Charlie and his crazy crew would take over and govern.

The problem was, Manson was impatient for the war to start, so he decided to murder some rich white people, feeling that people would blame it on some black perpetrators and the race war would start. This warped lunacy was embraced to the hilt by Manson's LSD fuelled young followers, and actress Sharon Tate was one of their victims, brutally murdered while heavily pregnant. The world was shocked, and the flower power optimism of the sixties was finally extinguished, at its bloody end. Writer and journalist Tom O'Neill discovered a link between Manson and a CIA brainwashing expert called Dr Jolyon (Jolly) West. O'Neill argues there was a strong possibility that West was teaching Manson how to brainwash people for nefarious purposes. We will return to Dr Jolly West in due course. This is all laid out in O'Neill's brilliant book, *Chaos*.

Charles Manson became a problem for the Beatles and yet another excuse for "people of faith" to accuse them of being in league with dark forces because Manson obsessed about the Beatles' *White Album*. Deluded by his constant use of acid, Manson thought certain songs on the *White Album* spoke directly to him. According to Manson, "Blackbird" was urging black radicals to start becoming active. "Piggies" was a veiled attack on rich white people and "Happiness is a Warm Gun" was a call to get armed. Manson believed secret messages were being sent through the *White Album's* songs. When Sharon Tate and her friends were ritually slain at her home in Beverly Hills, Manson's murderers wrote in blood the Beatles song, "Healter Skelter" (sic) and also "Death to Pig" in the house and "Pig" on the door. The Beatles were understandably outraged that their songs were used in this horrific way. Far right supporters and fundamental Christians saw it as more proof that the Liverpool Lads were in league with the Devil.

In 1969, John and Yoko started a peace movement with the slogan "War is Over – If You Want It". They conducted bed-ins, where they spent all day in bed in cities like Amsterdam and Montreal and asked the press to join them. They released a song to highlight the campaign and we can safely assume that the staffers in the Pentagon and CIA never bought a copy. "War Is Over" posters were slapped on walls in ten cities across the globe. Lennon, a previous vocal critic of the Vietnam War, was becoming a major problem for the military industrial complex.

After the Beatles split, Lennon's solo career began in earnest in 1970 and he was soon back to his Christian-baiting form of old. He simply refused to back down.

His first official solo album, *Plastic Ono Band* was a hard but riveting listen. Lennon sang about isolation and loneliness, with an absent father and the death of his mother foremost in his mind. Three of the songs were expressly about religion and Lennon's new strident atheism. The brilliant "Working Class Hero" stated that "Religion in general was a drug". "I Found Out" claimed that "Krishna was pie in the sky" and most controversially, "God" was "a construct by which we measure our pain". The song "God" listed fifteen concepts in which John Lennon had lost faith. Nine of the fifteen were related to religion. He concluded that the only people whom he believed in was himself and Yoko.

John's next album, *Imagine,* not only took his regular pop shots at religion but appeared to some to promote atheism and communism. The famous title song "Imagine" began with the words "Imagine there's no heaven". He then stated, "no religion too." What? Cried the faith peddlers and fervent believers, if there was no heaven or hell, what bloody use was religion? Sacrilege. Burn that man at the stake. They knew how to deal with such recalcitrants in the Middle Ages. And his song promoted a world without fear, hatred, war and greed. My goodness. What were the international armaments industries for? Many right-leaning Christians believed the song as an anti-religious communist manifesto – many still do. Lennon argued that an existentialist doctrine about the notion of heaven and hell hinders people from "living for today." He admitted that it was anti-religious, anti-nationalistic, anti-conventional and anti-capitalistic. John assumed that his song was successful because "Imagine" was sugar-coated in a memorable melody. And there is truth in that. It is a beautiful anthem to hope. An aspiration without individual threat. A plea to everyone to think of the potential freedoms all societies might embrace. But, come off it, "imagine all the people sharing all the world." For many fundamental Christians with capitalist instincts and anti-communist sentiments, "Imagine" was a very scary pill to swallow. Moreover, it merged the power of music with the potential for political change.

John later reflected that "religion was an outlet for my repression" and "religion was directly the result of all that superstar shit." Unfortunately, his contempt for religion, and his inability to find truth in religion, marked him as an enemy to some very dangerous people. For all that he was loved, his stance against religion was hyped into the mark of the Devil. It followed him like a dark shadow. Forgiveness may be a Christian tenet, but that did not apply to the fundamentalist zealots who saw John as a target for their extremism.

Lennon and Faith – Recap

The Beatles highlighted the unholy alliance between industry, politics, the military and religion. Organised religion unequivocally endorsed and strengthened the pillars of the establishment – and helped to prop it up. The Vietnam War raged throughout the Beatles years, bringing with it a scale of devastation and disgust. The Western military powers endorsed it. In fact, many religious "leaders", were deeply embedded in the military-industrial sphere. Many still are. Young people were rightly sceptical of the church in the sixties. Attendances plummeted. In 1940, the year Lennon was born, 36 per cent of British children attended a Christian Sunday school. In 1960, it was 24 per cent. In 2000, it was 4 per cent. Young people from the sixties onwards looked elsewhere for guidance. It is ridiculous to blame the Beatles for this trend. There were many other influences, but as the writer Al Aronowitz stated in *The Saturday Evening Post*, "the Beatles had become role models for the youth of the entire Western world." They were. Perhaps it was inevitable. Their message was unequivocal.

The potent ingredients of love, peace, and truth offered a secular alternative to Christianity. The established church hated the influence which people like the Beatles had on the young. The far-right, hell-fire Christian teachers, predominantly found in the southern states of America, embodied in organisations such as the Southern Baptists, proved a very dangerous bear to poke. And the Beatles rattled their cage. Baptists in the south preached with a disturbingly righteous fire and fury. Alongside the Baptists in the South, the Ku Klux Klan stood firm in its racist prejudices. The Klan were one example of a far-right cult which detested not only the Beatles and their anti-Christian views, but also their insistence on playing to unsegregated audiences. John, Paul, George and Ringo would not budge on that issue either.

The Beatles' journey from (lapsed) Christianity, to more esoteric and spiritual occultism, was a mirror of Western culture throughout the sixties and, I would argue, it continues into the present day. George Harrison almost single-handedly exposed the West to eastern religions and philosophies after 1968. The Hare Krishna movement, embodied by chanting groups walking up and down every main street in every major city, was funded by Harrison. Fundamental Christians saw this as a serious assault on their beliefs (and for some, livelihoods). The Beatles were not shy of dabbling with the occult. I believe that they deliberately looked to tease religious organisations with their occult appropriations. John wanted to include Jesus on the iconic cover of the *Sgt. Pepper* album, but it would have been too controversial. But John certainly knew how to rub salt into a wound. He included a picture of Aleister Crowley, the infamous Satanist and self-declared anti-Christ. In his 1965 book, *A Spaniard in the Works*, Lennon wrote a fictional scene where a clergyman is asked by an African man why there is so much disease and starvation in the world. The clergyman replies with a surreal metaphor about people "being like bananas swaying in the wind, waiting, as it were, to be peeled by his great and understanding love." John cleverly highlighted the religious nonsense that is often presented as deep theology.

Fundamental Christians were always uneasy about the Beatles and were not shy in saying so. Elvis was a threat to them, but he eased their fears by singing Gospel songs and strongly identified himself as a Christian. The famous evangelist and friend of President Nixon, Billy Graham, broke with his strict anti-television stance and watched the Beatles' seminal 1964 *Ed Sullivan Show* TV performance. Graham predictably lamented that their performance was "symptomatic of the uncertainties of the times and the confusion about us". When the Beatles landed in San Francisco in 1964, placards were held up by Christian protestors, stating "BEATLES WORSHIP IS IDOLATORY. THE BIBLE SAYS, CHILDREN KEEP YOURSELVES FROM IDOLATRY".

These right-wing influencers moved in high places amongst powerful politicians. And the politicians feared that the rejection of their values would translate to younger voters and threaten the old order. They set the tone. It was like an Orwellian nightmare. Old values = good; new thinking = bad.

One of the most high-profile early Christian critics of the Beatles was a young pastor called David A. Noebell, the author of the 1965 and 1966 books *Communism, Hypnotism and The Beatles* and *Rhythm, Riots and Revolution*. He was also an associate of Billy James Hargis, a notorious right-wing preacher who was a member of the John Birch Society (an organisation that strongly favoured segregation and was vehemently anti-communist). Noebel claimed that rock 'n' roll sucked the moral fibre from the young, while subsequently enabling the revolutionary aims of the "Left". He claimed that "the Beatles in particular have a special significance to the disrupters of society for their promotion of drugs, avant-garde sex and atheism. The revolution, though sometimes veiled, is fundamentally against Christianity and Christianity's moral concepts. Karl Marx sought to dethrone God before he set out to destroy capitalism."

Note the constant drive to equate the Beatles with communism.

I believe that Noebel represented the views of the most fundamental Christians of the time. He was fairly harmless, but if some of the far-right Christians who shared his views had access to nefarious intelligence and military capabilities, the threat would be more than real to anyone whom they despised. Be assured – John was a figure of hate in such circles. And it was to get worse.

CHAPTER 2 | John Lennon: The Final Decade

Key People

Yoko Ono

Mike Medeiros (Lennon house gardener)

Jack Douglas (record producer)

Fred Seaman (Lennon assistant)

May Pang (Lennon personal assistant/John's girlfriend)

President Richard Nixon

Senator Strom Thurmond

J Edgar Hoover (FBI Chief)

Att. General John Mitchell

After volumes of legal wrangling and months of petty in-fighting, the Beatles decided to split up in 1970. Many fans blamed Yoko Ono for this sad event but, in my eyes, it was inevitable. Having spent so many years together in their fish bowl world, the lads genuinely had to move on. At the end of the day, they had created the greatest body of work in popular music history and by 1970 were mentally exhausted. Anyone who has seen Peter Jackson's *Get Back* documentary might find themselves annoyed by Yoko's constant presence and assumed influence on John while the Beatles struggled to find their mojo again. Strangely nobody seemed concerned about the presence of Paul's girlfriend and wife to be, Linda, or Ringo's wife, Maureen. So why all the fuss about Yoko?

In late 1970, John Lennon and his then new wife Yoko Ono started to campaign in earnest for global peace. Lennon quickly became the figurehead for anti-war protest and rebellion. Yet he carried his own demons. After the peace "bed-ins", John and Yoko attended primal scream therapy sessions with Arthur Janov. This well-known psychologist developed a strategy to treat psychological trauma through primal screams and psychodrama. The discipline, like a lot of other cathartic, expressive therapies, focused on the idea that people can bring all their repressed pain to the surface and solve it by acting out the problem and expressing the pain that comes up because of it. John later claimed that Yoko didn't buy into Janov's therapy, stating she only went along with it from the start to satisfy him and that in her heart, she felt John was only searching for another "Daddy". For sure he carried the scars of rejection caused by his own upbringing. Even superstars must hurt. The father who walked out on him. The mother who gave him away to her sister. Thank goodness for Aunt Mimi. John needed to find answers to his own fears and confusions. Religion had failed him.

Yoko sat in on all of John's recording therapy sessions, gaining a unique insight into his secret fears and phobias – two of which were dying an early death and cremation. She rarely left his side.

According to long-time friend Tony Bramwell, John Lennon considered himself Irish (as apparently did McCartney and Harrison). Sometime in mid 1971, he became an Irish Republican sympathiser. The "troubles" in Northern Ireland seemed unsolvable. Internment had been introduced to take known members of the IRA and its counterpart, the UDA, off the streets. This special power allowed the British army to arrest, detain and imprison suspected terrorists indefinitely without trial or access to legal representation. Arrests were sectarian by design and the policy caused a huge surge in support for Irish Republicanism in Northern Ireland and further afield. During this time, a total of 1,981 people were interned: 1,874 were from an Irish nationalist background, whilst 107 were from a unionist background.

In America, many people of Irish descent gave generously to the IRA in the 1970s. In August 1971, John Lennon went on a march in London to protest about British involvement in Northern Ireland. He was pictured carrying a poster that boldly declared: "The IRA Against British Imperialism". The British state and their numerous intelligence agencies were deeply concerned about Lennon's defiant and very public support for the IRA. When John was asked later how he reconciled his support of pacifism and the IRA, he declared, "If it's a choice between the IRA and the British Army, I'm with the IRA. But, if it's a choice between violence and non-violence, I'm with non-violence. So, it's a very delicate line". It was also a very dangerous line. He didn't flinch. In Britain, the internal security service, MI5 would surely have been keeping a close watch on John Lennon's activities.

In late 1971, John and Yoko moved to New York. Around this time, the FBI started to monitor his movements and used his 1968 London drug bust as an excuse to try and deport him from America. Certainly, John had been fined £150 with 20 guineas costs at Marylebone Court in London, having admitted possessing cannabis. It was no big deal but John's many political enemies sought to use it as a reason for deportation. Lennon rigorously fought every deportation attempt for the next five years and used every available opportunity to criticise President Nixon. Dan Richter, a close friend and associate of the Lennons in 1971, told me that "men in black" were constantly following them and they in turn were convinced that their phone lines were being tapped.

Soon after moving to New York, John and Yoko wrote "The Luck of the Irish" as a blatant criticism of what Lennon perceived as British Imperialism in Ireland. In early 1972, British soldiers shot dead thirteen unarmed Catholic men during a demonstration in Derry in protest against internment. Lennon took to the streets in New York after Bloody Sunday and sang "The Luck of the Irish". He proclaimed to a boisterous crowd that he was proud of his Irish roots and Liverpool was the uncrowned capital of Ireland. Not long after this, Lennon wrote the song "Sunday Bloody Sunday" and offered (in secret) to perform a concert in Dublin and Belfast for the Republican cause. The concert never took place because Lennon was concerned that if he left America, he wouldn't be allowed back in again.

The reader may not be aware that the constant surveillance on John Lennon by the FBI, though sometimes juvenile and crass, was a burden he had to carry. Its motivation was entirely political and vindictive. But John was never going to bend to the repeated attempts to have him deported. In December 1971, John Lennon and Yoko Ono performed at a "Free John Sinclair" concert at Michigan University. Sinclair was a local peace activist who had been sentenced to ten years in prison for allegedly selling two joints of marijuana. It was nothing less than absurd. Unredacted FBI documents eventually revealed that their informers in the audience were closely monitoring the event. Sinclair was released from prison the very next day. Lennon intended that the concert would be part of a national anti-Nixon tour, on which he aimed to bring together rock 'n' roll and politics in a dozen US cities. At each stop, local organisers would give anti-Nixon and anti-war speeches and young people would be urged to vote against the war. Lennon had talked about ending the tour at a giant protest rally outside the 1972 Republican National Convention, where Ricard Nixon was due to be renominated.

A series of concerts for peace then ensued throughout 1972. Further FBI documents released in 1997 showed that the Nixon administration was trying to stop Lennon from setting off on the tour, to silence him as a voice of the anti-war movement and critic of the president.

As I write this in 2023, the FBI, CIA and MI5 are all still withholding documents on Beatle John Lennon – "in the interest of national defence or foreign policy" in the case of the FBI. Some documents were eventually released under the Freedom of Information Act in America, but many have been heavily redacted. What could they possibly reveal? Clearly John Lennon, the ex-Beatle, is still a problem for American and British national security, over forty years after his death. Or might the redacted documents prove that the FBI could have worked in collusion with other parties involved in the assassination? Are they waiting for everyone named and involved to die?

In 1972, Senator Strom Thurmond of South Carolina, the man who tried to stop the passing of the United States Civil

Rights Act, sent a secret memo to Attorney General John Mitchell outlining Lennon's supposed political plans and suggesting that he be deported. Thurmond was precisely the kind of southern politician who considered John an evil influence. He tried to filibuster the proposed act by talking non-stop for twenty-four hours and eighteen minutes on the floor of the Senate. He failed. *Rolling Stone* magazine printed a copy of this secret memo in 1975, prompting Lennon to sue former Attorney General John Mitchell. After a further year of constant government surveillance, John Lennon told the writer Paul Krassner "If anything happens to Yoko and me, it was not an accident". Remember that.

Life was not smooth for John Lennon in 1973. Yes, he was a multimillionaire, but he was not happy. The next album he produced, *Mind Games,* was arguably his least inspiring. Artistically, he was all over the place. Amid numerous court appearances, where he battled the American Immigration and Naturalization Service, Lennon tried to produce some new music. The FBI were monitoring him, and Lennon knew it. The jumbled *Mind Games* album summed up his disturbed state of mind. John wrote all the songs for the album within a week. It was unworthy of his incredible back catalogue. Just as the sessions for *Mind Games* were about to begin in June 1973, John and Yoko split up.

John then embarked on an eighteen month "lost weekend" retreat to Los Angeles, with various drinking buddies such as Ringo Starr, Keith Moon and Harry Nilsson. Yoko Ono agreed that a young assistant who worked for the couple, May Pang, should accompany Lennon to Los Angeles to "look after him". According to Pang, Ono told her that Lennon found her sexually attractive and inferred she should sleep with him. Pang was reluctant, but Ono said she would "arrange everything". Soon after arriving in LA in October 1973, Pang and Lennon started a physical relationship. During their time together, Pang encouraged John to see more of his son Julian and she even managed to arrange a brief reunion with Paul McCartney.

At some point in 1974, Yoko Ono hooked up with a tarot card reader called John Green and invited him to stay at the Dakota. Green called himself Charlie Swan in those days and he was initially recommended by a girlfriend of Harry Nilsson to help Ono exorcise the ghost of the previous owner's wife. Ono was convinced that the ghost had a constant presence in the apartment. Some Lennon insiders have alleged that John Green was also advising Ono on how to get John back from May Pang. Green stayed for six years, and the Lennons rarely made a decision without asking his advice. Green consulted his tarot cards first. Ono has often remarked over the years that she had no problem with John and May being together and she always knew John would come back to her. Green's view that his employment by Ono was to try and help her win John back, if true, somewhat negates the credibility of her confident opinion.

In 1974, John and May left Los Angeles and moved back to New York. John stopped drinking and started recording his tepid *Walls and Bridges* album. According to Pang, the day before the Lennon and McCartney reunion, Yoko Ono rang John up and asked him to come and see her because she had found a new hypnotherapy cure to quit smoking. John went to the Dakota building and did not return the next day. John had been scheduled to visit the McCartneys with May Pang. When Pang rang, Ono told her that John was too exhausted to see her after a hypnotherapy session. Two days later, May and John were reunited at a joint dental appointment. May was deeply concerned that John appeared befuddled and confused, leading her to conclude that he had been brainwashed. Shortly after, Lennon told Pang that he was reconciled with Yoko Ono and his relationship with May was finished.

Over the ensuing years, it is alleged that Pang and Lennon met up from time to time. According to Pang, such arrangements were agreed with Yoko Ono. In her memoir *Loving John: The Untold Story* Pang claimed that she and John remained lovers until 1977 and stayed in contact right up until his death. Ono always refuted May's assertion that hypnosis snared John. She argued that it appeared to have no effect. John smoked every day until the end of his life. In 1975, John and Yoko had a son, Sean. Ono said she allowed the pregnancy to go to full term on the condition that Lennon retired from music and became a "house-husband". He agreed. Perhaps John was trying to compensate for being an absent father to his first son Julian or perhaps he was mentally exhausted after fighting the American government for nearly five years. Either way, Lennon dropped out of the public realm and retreated to his bedroom.

American politics was in crisis in the mid 1970s. A combi-nation of a youth culture, which was determined to assert itself, and a growing awareness that the Vietnam War had become a scourge on the nation changed the public perception of President Richard Nixon. Backed as he was by J Edgar Hoover, head of the FBI, Nixon, who was famously paranoid, saw potential enemies around every corner. He cast himself in the role of the victim and was prepared to endorse illegal activities like wiretapping and unlawful surveillance. John was one of those who was closely followed by the agents of the state in this period, though he was by no means the prime target. Nixon's second term in office self-imploded after his re-election campaign was caught in the act of bugging the Democratic Party headquarters at the Watergate complex. In 1974 he resigned as President because he was certain to be impeached by Congress. But the FBI files on John grew thick with allegations of his political involvement with left-wing activists in the USA.

In 1976, Democratic Party candidate Jimmy Carter was elected President of America, and in June Lennon received his provisional green card. This was a permanent residence permit which allowed the holder to live and work in the USA with a five-year probation period. In January 1981, Lennon was sched-uled to become a full US citizen and could never be deported.

His death in December 1980 ended that possibility. Convenient some might say.

A 1976 FBI document regarding John Lennon (released to the public via a 1987 FOI request) reveals he was still under official USA government surveillance at that time. The main body of text on the document was entirely blacked out – except for one small inked phrase in the margin that indicated that a copy had gone to the CIA. In the Summer of 1976, three and half years before his murder, the FBI and the CIA were still interested in John Lennon. The world wouldn't see much of the former Beatle for the next four years – according to numerous reports, the self-imposed "house-husband" was baking a lot of bread and smoking a lot of dope.

Speaking to me in early 2022, the Lennons' house gardener, Michael Medeiros, gave a highly revealing interview which provided many insights into life at the Dakota from 1977 to 1980. Medeiros was nicknamed "Mike Tree" by John and was very much a privileged insider at the Dakota. Medeiros got the gig as an indoor gardener (self-styled as a *plant decorator*) in March 1977 through meeting John Green at a party. Green introduced Medeiros and he quickly became a regular fixture at the Dakota, watering plants and recommending new foliage for each room. Later, Medeiros also became an archivist for the Lennons and helped them organise their extensive film and tape collection of movies and music.

Mike Medeiros believed Lennon was deeply depressed between 1977 and 1979. John seemingly spent most of his days stoned, writing partly-finished songs in his bedroom with his acoustic guitar. Ono was also seeing more and more of a flashy New York art dealer called Sam Green and Lennon thought they were having an affair. People working for the family noticed Ono wearing make-up in this period, which she apparently never did, and pregnancy kits were also allegedly seen in the Dakota bathrooms. John Lennon accused Sam Green of being a "people collector". It is alleged that one of Green's assistants was providing Ono with heroin, which she confessed had been a major problem for her in the latter half of the seventies. In fairness, we must be careful when dealing with allegations, but observers felt that John and Yoko lived inside an unhappy marriage.

As 1980 heralded a new decade, John badly needed a break and change of scenery. He found it in a sailing holiday in Bermuda where his spirit was rekindled. He was happy. Back in touch with his muse. It was as if he had been swimming in soup and the tide had turned it back to the refreshing sea. Sean came to spend time with his dad in Bermuda. He too was happy. Even more so because he didn't have to stay in what he called the "spook house". The prison called Dakota. When Yoko eventually arrived to join John and Sean, she said that she felt it was "too hot". Despite – or perhaps because of – the warmth around her, she returned to New York after two days. What was really happening? This reaction caught the deterioration in their relationship in a single cameo moment. John in Bermuda; Yoko back in New York. A fresh approach to new circumstances versus a retreat to the safety of Fort Dakota. Freedom versus incarceration. Bermuda brought John back to life. Did this challenge Yoko?

While in Bermuda, Lennon ingested lots of mushrooms and inspired by the McCartney song "Coming Up", he started to write more solid numbers which would eventually appear on the *Double Fantasy* album. Lennon saw "Coming Up" as a direct message to him from Paul McCartney and his rivalry with his old song-writing partner was a challenge to which he responded by writing a response song called "I Don't Wanna' Face it" (eventually released on the posthumous *Milk and Honey* album).

By the time John returned to New York in July 1980, Yoko had decided to record an album with him called *Double Fantasy*. She had previously taken record producer, Jack Douglas, by private plane to their home on Cold Spring Harbour to play him her demos, under the instructions to "not tell John". Someone must have told John because throughout August and September, he and Ono recorded their double album together, half comprising

Lennon songs and the other half, Ono's.

Geffen Records released the album in November 1980 – to mixed reviews. John was officially back, musically. He also planned a political revival. He was scheduled to attend a rally for Asian workers in San Francisco on December 13th. He never made it.

Fred Seaman, John's personal assistant in Bermuda, was sent back to New York to check on Yoko Ono. Clearly John harboured suspicions. Fred recalled in his book *The Last days of John Lennon: A Personal Memoir* that he and John had concocted a plan, or more accurately a ruse, whereby Fred was instructed to bring a large suitcase of clothes, which John had purchased in Bermuda, back to the Dakota. When Seaman arrived back in New York, he struck up a conversation with Luciano Sparacino, an associate of Ono's. It could hardly have been a chance meeting and a chance conversation. Sparacino told him shocking news. Yoko planned to divorce John. As a first step, she intended to move into an adjacent apartment at the Dakota on his return. What was going on? Was it a childish ploy to draw John back to New York where he would be under her control? After all, they had effectively gone their separate ways – again. It didn't happen. But Seaman stood by his story. He alleged that Yoko Ono abandoned her plans when John returned from Bermuda.

In the months leading up to his death, John Lennon seemed to sense that he would die. Soon. He also seemed to know that his would not be an accidental death. He talked about his fears in late July 1980 when still in Bermuda. Towards the end of the vacation, he started to discuss his legacy with Fred Seaman. John talked about "weird recurring dreams" where he "suffered a violent death". John confided in Seaman. They appear to have had a trusting relationship. John fantasised about getting shot, which he thought was a modern form of crucifixion and a rather elegant means of moving on to the next life with a clean karmic slate. The most pertinent Lennon comment Seaman could recall after his assassination was John's insistence that "there are no accidents".

John could not shake off this premonition of death. How did that come about? Who could have put such a notion in his head? In his last days of recording, John repeatedly talked about death with producer Jack Douglas. The last conversation they had on the 8th of December 1980 was so strange and disturbing for Jack that he destroyed the tapes on which they were recorded. Naturally this caused wide speculation. What was so contentious that the tapes had to be destroyed? Given their value in terms of understanding John's state of mind, surely they were priceless?

While working for Yoko Ono in 2010, Douglas almost revealed all when he said:

"If I told you what he said you'd think I was a nutter. There's been a lot of speculation over the years that it was something personal about Yoko. But it wasn't, it was about his death. I destroyed the tape after his murder."

So, thirty years on, Yoko and Jack Douglas remained bonded by their work. It should be noted that Douglas had been involved in litigation with Ono over unpaid royalties from *Double Fantasy*, so it was not always plain sailing.

On Friday 5th December, Lennon booked plane tickets for himself and his family to fly to San Francisco the following week to attend a rally by the Teamsters union and to march through the streets in support of Japanese workers and wage equality. Lennon then called his Aunt Mimi in the UK and told her he was coming home for a visit soon. John, revitalised and confident, appeared to stand ready to do what he did best – make music and stand up for the downtrodden. John Lennon never made it back to the UK. He would not march through the streets of San Francisco. A young man called Mark Chapman had a date with infamy and John Lennon. But who exactly was Mark Chapman and did he really assassinate John Lennon at the Dakota?

Recap

John and Yoko sought to establish their careers in America. They eventually settled in New York at the exclusive Dakota buildings in 1973 which became a place of self-confinement which stifled John's creativity. Both he and Yoko immediately involved themselves in American politics supporting several activities to "dump Nixon" and defend political causes which the establishment considered "left wing". His arrival coincided with the drive by the Republican Party to re-elect President Richard Nixon, a man who found enemies – real and imagined – on every street corner. The most powerful man in the world was fed information by his secret services, the FBI, the CIA and prominent Republican Senators about an Englishman who was considered a danger to his re-election campaign. The former Beatle became the target of regular surveillance and ludicrous reports from the FBI. Many of these reports remain heavily redacted or are still deemed too sensitive to let the public have sight of them on the grounds of national security. National security? A singer and songwriter? What devious allegations or government plans lie locked from public view? I believe that there must be something hidden in these files. J Edgar Hoover referred to John as a former member of the Beatles singing group. How little he knew about youth culture and he was head of the Federal Bureau of Investigation. But ignorance breeds its own intolerance. In the murky depth of the Bureau's paranoia, what were they or their unknown associates possibly concocting to deal with the troublesome singing man?

And John's relationship with Yoko became strained beyond sanity. He was never a man who could embrace boredom. We know they fell out. John's infamous lost months in Los Angeles and his relations with May Pang suggest deep and lasting personal problems for John and Yoko's relationship. Would they have lasted the course beyond 1980 if John Lennon was not assassinated?

CHAPTER 3 | Mark Chapman

Key People

Pastor Ken Babbington
Pastor Arthur Blessitt
Pastor (and Special Agent) Charles McGowan
Preacher Fred Krauss
Minister Paul Durbin (retired Brigadier)
Cortez Cooper (Senior Analyst, Joint Intelligence)

Young Men's Christian Association
Harold Adlerberg (Lawyer)
Kim Hogrefe (Assistant DA)
Jack Jones (writer)

If Mark Chapman grew up as a lonely nerd, sitting alone every day in his bedroom listening to Beatles records backwards while raging against a world that hated him, I would be more comfortable with the Chapman persona that the media have sold to us over the years. You are probably familiar with the media's representation of this kind of persona —Chapman was a "lone-nut" loser who was obsessed with John Lennon and wanted to become famous by murdering the former Beatle.

However, having spoken to Mark's friends and acquaintances, what becomes clear is that Chapman was considered a very sociable guy who had many friends and interests. As for obsessing over the Beatles or John Lennon records, this is not true. Chapman liked all kinds of music throughout his life, including (but certainly not limited to) the Beatles – no music-loving kid growing up in the 1960s could not like the Beatles. In fact, Todd Rundgren was Mark's main musical hero. There are very many questions to be answered about Mark Chapman. One which caught my attention centres on his finances. For a young man of limited means, he had a strange and rather rich globetrotting life, with seemingly limitless supplies of money on hand when he needed it.

Throughout his young adult life, Chapman was surrounded by Southern Christian Baptist figures who enjoyed strong ties to the military and intelligence services. These aspects of Chapman's life have never been fully explored or acknowledged before now, but they do give us strong clues about who Chapman was and what, or who, may have driven him to be at the Dakota in New York on 8th December 1980.

Mark Chapman was born on May 10th, 1955, in Fort Worth, Texas, to a middle-class family. His father was David Curtis Chapman, originally of Connecticut, then an air force sergeant stationed at Carswell Air Force Base. His mother was Diane Elizabeth Pease Chapman, a nurse from Massachusetts. Mark's father left the air force and then worked for an oil company and then a bank. The family eventually settled in Decatur, Georgia, where Mark first went to school.

Mark also had a younger sister and was a well-adjusted and happy boy. His mother Diane, was, by most accounts, a loving person with a kind heart. His father had a proclivity for violent outbursts which were taken out on Chapman's mother. Although it was far from a perfect family set-up, both of Chapman's parents stayed together and were nearly always present when Mark was growing up.

By the time Chapman was 14, he was tempted, like many other teenagers, to get involved in drugs. At first it was limited to marijuana but soon developed into frequent use of LSD. 1970 marked a peak in drug taking amongst the youth movement in America. Mark and his best friend (who has spoken to me at length but wishes to remain anonymous, therefore I will call him "G") took LSD tabs together every weekend for many months. They listened to Mark's Todd Rundgren albums and dreamed of being in a rock band. It was a mainstream habit in those times. Hardly unusual.

One of Mark's friends, Vance Hunter, revealed the full extent to which Mark took LSD, claiming that he regularly took whole tabs of a potent batch called LSD-25 and, according to his friends, would disappear for days under its influence. After tripping on LSD-25, Mark told a friend that Jesus came down and spoke to him. It is unclear whether this visitation was during Mark's "Jesus Freak" phase, but this is likely.

Mark told writer Jack Jones in his 1992 book, that he discovered the "wonders" of LSD from a 16-year-old neighbour. This was probably "G". They both believed the drug instigated self-reflection and insular thought processes. Mark regarded "G" as a "mentor and big brother". Chapman saw his LSD period as "the first chance in my life to be a group player, a part of something". Tripping on acid throughout the summer of 1969, Mark's mother recalled that the family came to consider Mark a stranger in their house. An "alien creature" that she and her husband could no longer control or understand. Diane Chapman said she grew to fear her own son and to believe that he held a "mysterious power" over their family. Mind altering drugs can have such dangerous effects. Mark's mother told journalist Jim Gaines, in a 1987 *People* magazine article, about the concern she felt at the time:

"During spring vacation that school year [1970], Mark ran away. We were frantic. The police wouldn't even pay attention—they had thousands of these cases. Finally, his friend told me Mark had gone to California to join the hippies, I made him tell it all—that Mark was on drugs. I just couldn't handle things like that."

Strange. How could he have gone all the way across America to join the hippies? According to Gaines, when Mark finally returned home two weeks later, he bused in from Miami. Diane Chapman had been fed a lie.

Five years later, in 1992, the mysterious writer Jack Jones relayed a different take on "runaway Mark" in his book on Chapman, based on hours of Attica prison interviews. Jones inferred that Mark lied to his friends about going to California and he only went to Florida. When in Florida, he then met an anti-Castro hippie "friend", who apparently put Mark up for a few days. Pastor Ken Babbington added further implausibility to the Florida story in his book, also written around his conversations when Chapman was in prison, called *Not My God*. Babbington stated that by 1970, Chapman was going by the name "Mark the Freak".

According to Babbington, a 15-year-old Chapman flew all by himself to Miami. (I'm guessing Mark's pocket money from his parents stretched a long way in those days.) When Chapman arrived at Miami airport, "Mark the Freak" instructed an airport taxi driver to take him to the "freaks". The taxi driver was (thankfully) aware of where the "freaks" lived, and drove Mark to meet the "freaks" – I promise you that I am not making any of this up. Mark then apparently found a group of people in a "circus-carnival-environment" and in true Pinocchio style, Mark hung out with the circus freaks for a few days. The circus leader then decided that little lost boy Chapman should go back home to his mother in Georgia and he paid Chapman's bus fare home. Chapman's golden opportunity to live a life as a circus freak had gone forever.

In speaking with me in October 2020, his childhood friend "G" insisted that Mark never ran away at all in 1970 and that "G"'s mother allowed Mark to stay at their house to escape Mark's "tyrannical" father. Gaines can be forgiven for believing Mark's mother's story of a bogus Californian trip, but where Jones and Babbington got their fantastical Florida, anti-Castro, circus freaks story from is a total mystery.

Then things got weirder. When we examine Chapman's pre-trial hearing, which occurred shortly after Lennon's assassination, Manhattan Assistant District Attorney (ADA) Kim Hogrefe embarrassed himself and his office by claiming in court that Chapman had convictions dating back to 1972, and that there was an outstanding warrant for Chapman's arrest for armed robbery and abduction. Clearly, Hogrefe's desire to nail Chapman as a cold and calculated killer, who murdered John Lennon for fame, meant he wasn't too concerned about checking facts. Thankfully, Hogrefe's boss, Allen Sullivan, *was* interested in checking details, and within an hour Sullivan released a press statement stating that law enforcement officers in Florida had given the New York police the wrong records.

Interestingly, when these 1972 Florida charges were read out in court, Chapman did not bat an eyelid. He was totally unfazed by the accusations. This disturbed Chapman's first lawyer Harold Adlerberg so much that he was convinced from that point onwards that Mark Chapman must be mad.

I have now obtained the Florida court document and the man named was a "William Allan Chapman". William had the exact physical characteristics of Mark Chapman regarding weight, height and eye colour. Amazingly, their dates of birth also exactly matched up. *This* Chapman was wanted for multiple felonies. The actual William Allan Chapman from that time appeared to be a state trooper with the Georgia patrol. William Allan Chapman also served in the US Navy from 1969 till 1976 when these alleged offences took place. He therefore could not feasibly have been the Chapman who committed these misdemeanours in Florida. But the coincidence of the birth date, matching surname and physical features is troubling.

The court document below also fails to mention armed robbery and abduction. Where did Hogrefe get this extra criminal information from? Much more research is needed on William Allan Chapman and the "Chapman" in 1972 Florida, who was allegedly committing multiple offences.

Mark Chapman's possible pathway to God requires close attention in this story. According to Chapman, while he was in first or second grade, he "somehow got to know the local pastor", and this unidentified pastor made Chapman the guardian of the local church. Mark apparently took the job very seriously and

Florida Chapman Court Document © David Whelan

would walk around checking the church grounds daily, acting as a kind of juvenile security guard. Chapman eventually drifted away from his religious security activities, but clearly someone in his local church had their eye on him from a very early age.

By the Spring of 1971, a 16-year-old Chapman, still heavily using LSD, rediscovered God.

These two facts sound like cause and consequence. "Jesus Freaks" were a new popular craze in American culture and Mark Chapman would have been attracted to the "tune into Jesus" drug/god amalgamation, used by many of the on-the-make preachers of the day, looking to garner a young audience. One of these dubious preachers was called Arthur Blessitt (I'm imagining his last name may have been a stage name). Blessitt emerged on the hippy Christian scene in the late 1960s, when he became known as the "psychedelic evangelist". Was Blessitt's drug reference nickname an attempt at appearing hip with the kids, or was it perhaps a reference to a more sinister practice of administering drugs to young kids to help them "find god"? Blessitt based himself on the seedy sunset strip in Hollywood, where he made a name for himself by preaching at a local strip club.

He then founded a Christian nightclub/coffee house called "His Place". Blessitt used popular counter-culture sayings to gain further attention, by preaching clever soundbites such as "turn on to Jesus" and comparing finding Jesus to an "eternal rush". All this talk of drugs and Jesus didn't go down too well with local businesses, and they managed to have "His Place" shut down in the summer of 1969. Upset by the shutdown, Blessitt looked again into his well-worn bag of tricks and decided to chain himself to a 12-foot wooden cross, which was attached to the front of his former nightclub. He allegedly fasted for 28 days and lo, yet again, his stunt bore fruit and he was allowed to open another nightclub further down the strip. Blessitt decided to raise his profile to a higher level once again. This time, Blessitt picked up his ever-useful 12-foot cross and decided to walk across America carrying it on his back, just as Jesus did before he was crucified. Moving from town to town, Blessitt was given sustenance and accommodation and he even managed to squeeze in a visitation from Jesus, who apparently glided across a lake on his fantastical journey. Eventually, in early 1971, the psychedelic preacher wound up in Mark Chapman's home town.

Blessitt initially spoke at Chapman's school and Chapman and his best friend "G", agreed to go along to a local church, where Blessitt promised he would introduce the spirit and power of the Lord by blessing the youngsters. Chapman and "G" had planned to make fun of Blessitt and his followers. Inside the church, an orderly queue line duly formed at the altar. Locals were touched on the forehead by Blessitt. Most, apparently struck dumb by the apparent power of Jesus omitting from Blessitt's divine hand, fell back in to a waiting catcher's arm behind them. Some, like "G", thought this was all a great joke. "G" remembers falling back laughing as he pretended to be struck dumb by Blessitt's righteous powers. Chapman also duly fell back into a catcher's arms. The joke was seemingly a great success. "G" did all he could to not collapse into fits of laughter as he returned to his wooden pew. But, when Chapman returned to his seat, he informed "G" in awed tones, that "something happened to me up there". From that day onwards, Chapman embraced Jesus.

I believe Chapman's fast-track Christian conversion is instructive. It indicates that from a very young age, Chapman had the kind of malleable mind that could be convinced to believe anything, very quickly. The kind of mind that could possibly be used for nefarious purposes if accessed by the wrong people or organisations. We also must consider whether it was just a coincidence that LSD loving Chapman converted to Jesus so quickly via a preacher who was known as the psychedelic evangelist? Just exactly what did Blessitt put in his holy water and wine?

It was around this time in 1971, that Mark Chapman declared to his friends that he no longer liked John Lennon, citing Lennon's claim that "the Beatles are more popular than Jesus" quote from five years earlier as one of the main reasons why. John had just released "Imagine", with its anti-religion lyrics. For a newly converted zealot like Chapman, these lyrics could have been seen as blasphemous. He did not have to look far in the southern states of America at that time in history to have those anti-Lennon thoughts confirmed by hell-fire preachers. Hell-fire southern preachers like Charles McGowan.

Chapman continued practising his newly discovered Christian ideals, by volunteering to work at his local YMCA and attending a local Baptist church, called Chapel Woods Presbyterian. This church was run by Pastor Charles McGowan, who later eulogised how Mark morphed from a guy who was a frequent drug-taker and listened to psychedelic music, to a young man who embraced Christianity to the hilt. From one drug to the other some might say, or perhaps, one fed into the other?

McGowan is a very interesting character and will play a central part in Mark Chapman's journey. Before he became a pastor, McGowan served in the U.S. Army and in the office of naval intelligence as a "special agent" in counterintelligence. He would have been fully aware of the raging Cold War of the early 1960s and all the nefarious intelligence activities that were happening at that time.

As I write this in 2023, McGowan is in his eighties, so he was probably born just before the Second World War. He attended Davidson college between 1954 and 1958, so he would have been too young to have served in the Korean War. As the sixties dawned and the Beatles were about to take off, McGowan was in his early twenties. There is a window of five years between 1958 and 1963, during which McGowan effectively disappears. There is no military record covering his activities. Five years is a relatively short time to serve in the army and naval intelligence and become a special agent, but McGowan clearly excelled in his work.

He appears to have found God in 1963, studying at the Columbia Theological Seminary between 1963 and 1966. We know he became a well-established pastor at Mark Chapman's Southern Decatur church. Was he still working undercover for his intelligence paymasters while working as a pastor? Did his intelligence work carry on beyond his earlier pastoral work? There is a theory that once a person is a spook, they are always a spook, so I'm going to periodically refer to Pastor McGowan as Special Agent McGowan. Doing so helps us understand what his motives were at times, when he was perhaps working under a less than spiritual guise.

Throughout his career Special Agent McGowan morphed into a pastor who spent a considerable amount of time placing pastors all over the world. It is well documented that the CIA have used Christian missionaries as cover for placing agents abroad. Could Special Agent McGowan have assisted his old intelligence colleagues in further intelligence work throughout his global preaching spiritual work placement career?

I believe you can tell a lot about a person by the type of people they have as friends. One of McGowan's "very, very close friends", was a man called Cortez Cooper. The "fraternity brothers" met in Davidson College in the 1950s. Cooper, now deceased, was, like McGowan, a busy, globetrotting pastor. Like McGowan, Cortez

Cooper also had a serious side hustle in intelligence. Cortez was actually a spook titan. He served in the US Navy Executive Service and was a senior analyst for the joint intelligence centre Pacific command.

His biography states that he had an unspecified assignment in Hawaii. Cooper was also a senior analyst at CENTRA Technology Inc. CENTRA was a notorious cutout company for the CIA. Its executive ranks were filled to the brim with former intelligence officers. Cooper's intelligence career reached its apex, when in 2005, he became a director at the Rand Corporation. Rand was basically the Pentagon and CIA's number one think-tank. Rand was considered by many to be the very epitome of the deep state. A covert shadow government working exclusively for the military industrial complex. I'm sure Jesus would have wholeheartedly approved of their work. One can also only wonder what Cooper would have thought of John Lennon and his consistent affiliation with socialism and anti-Christian views? I'm sure he would have absolutely detested him.

Another one of McGowan's interesting friends was Joe M. Rodgers. Rodgers was an Alabama-born businessman who was very much on the intolerant right of the political spectrum. The first thirty years of Rodgers' life are a mystery, but in 1966 at age 33 he became part of a successful construction business focusing on building hospitals. In 1973, at aged forty, he had a near fatal heart attack on a plane. This led Rodgers into the arms of Jesus. No doubt Charles McGowan entered his life at this time. Ronald Reagan then publicly entered Rodgers' life three years later in 1976, with Rodgers becoming an early backer of the former California Governor's failed candidacy for the presidency. Rodgers served as Tennessee finance chairman for Reagan's primary campaign against President Gerald Ford. Despite Reagan losing against Ford, Rodgers was identified as a man who could get his hands on lots of financial support. He swiftly became Reagan's chief money man, serving as finance chairman of the

Republican National Committee from 1978 to 1980. The committee raised an astonishing $75 million. Rodgers ensured Reagan had the financial war chest he needed to take on and beat Jimmy Carter to the American presidency in 1980. Ronald Reagan would not have had a more powerful and passionate supporter than Joe M. Rodgers. After Reagan took office in January 1981, he appointed Rodgers to the Foreign Intelligence Advisory Board. Rodgers continued to raise funds for a variety of Republican related causes, and in 1984 he served as finance chief for the successful Reagan-Bush re-election campaign. To put it simply, Joe Rodgers, Charles McGowan's "dear friend" as he once called him, was the Republican party's all-powerful financial chief from 1978 until 1984. I wonder if he was a John Lennon fan.

We will return to Special Agent McGowan many times in our story. For now, please ponder what McGowan and Cooper must have spoken about together in private, when they donned their pastoral robes and roamed the world preaching the word of God. Apparently.

While deeply embedded in his new Christian circles, Mark met the first love of his life, Jessica Blankenship, at a Christian retreat in 1971 when she was also 16. Jessica noted that Mark had a difficult relationship with his father, but Mark's mother was a lovely person whom Mark tried to protect from his father's violent episodes. Jessica and Mark got together for a few months as "boyfriend and girlfriend" and the relationship seemed platonic. When they eventually broke up, Mark, by all accounts, took it badly.

In 1971, Mark and Jessica were encouraged by persons unknown at McGowan's Chapel Woods to attend an Evangelical Christian prayer group. This group was conducted by a psychologist preacher called Mr. Krauss. Krauss and his wife opened their home for young people to attend and listen to the Christian teachings of Krauss, all infused with charismatic ramblings.

Chapman recalled the fundamental prayer group often involved the laying on of hands and speaking in tongues. "Miraculous healing" was also involved, alongside the gift of prophecy and "deliverance from demons". Chapman remembered that "at times, I'd be on my back and five or six people will be laying on hands". Chapman even recalled the famous Christian singer Pat Boone ringing in to wish them all good luck in their demon scrubbing activities.

Was this a form of exorcism being performed on Chapman and is this where Chapman's future affliction of talking to inner demons was first manifested? The key question is whether this was a deliberate ploy, or just the actions of a Christian zealot who had gone too far? Chapman recorded later that there were "manifestations of demonic power" occurring at the house of Krauss. He remembered one man barking like a dog and then bizarrely assuming a karate position. He also recalled that they talked about demons more than they did about Jesus. Mark's girlfriend, Jessica, also attended and confirmed the demonic exorcisms by Krauss. She also remembered the laying on of hands and speaking in tongues. So, who exactly was this Krauss person?

We only know that the fundamental prayer groups Chapman and Jessica attended were conducted by a "Decatur psychologist" because this information was obtained by the journalist Jim Gaines. I later discovered that this man was called Krauss. Decatur, Illinois, is where a Reverend Fred Robert Krauss operated in the early 1970s. This Fred Krauss was not a psychologist, but he was a preacher. Crucially, preacher Fred Krauss was also interested in hypnosis. Preacher Fred was a special speaker at the National Association of Clergy Hypnotists (NACH). In 1997, the NACH joined up with the National Guild of Hypnotists as a "clergy special interest group".

In an address to the NACH congress, Reverend Fred R. Krauss said:

"Religion has traditionally used hypnotic techniques in a variety of ways. The atmosphere of the religious service is geared to the induction of the trance state. The architecture, décor, and religious symbols have a profound spiritual effect on believers. The alter, cross, and flickering candles provide a fixation point for concentration and meditation. In prayer, most Christians bow their heads and close their eyes which can be a similar experience to hypnosis."

Rev. Krauss continued to say that prayer and meditation were the best hypnotic inductions of all. Everything is there that should be, including a harmony of body, mind, and spirit that enhances communication by God. By assuring the appropriate posture, closing your eyes, bowing heads, listening, and responding with an amen. In the sermon, the pastor uses voice inflections, modulations, and repetitive ideas with anecdotes, Bible stories, and other illustrations.

Paul Durbin was a United Methodist minister, Chaplain (Brigadier General) in the United States Army (retired 1989), and Director of Pastoral Care & Clinical Hypnotherapy, Methodist Hospital, New Orleans, LA (retired 2001). His CV also declared that Durbin was Director of Clinical Hypnotherapy, MHSF, affiliated with a Methodist Hospital (retired June 30, 2005). Durbin had this to say about the Krauss speech to the NACH congress:

"Prayer and meditation are traditional Christian disciplines that parallel what we call auto-suggestion. Of course, the auto-suggestions are not the only aspects of prayer for through prayer, we are able to open our minds to God. When we are open and responsive, prayer is basically communication with God. If I understand Reverend Krauss, he is pointing out that the use of hypnotic procedures in worship and Christian experience is blessed by God."

To add another layer of intrigue, preacher/hypnotist Fred Krauss was a pastor in the United Church of Chicago denomination. The very same church organisations where former president Barack Obama was a member. Preacher Krauss also served at an aid programme for Vietnamese refugees, which may have put him in direct contact with Mark Chapman who was engaged in the same kind of work. Krauss the preacher/hypnotherapist advocate died in 2021.

Fred Krauss was an important and currently unknown central figure in the Mark Chapman story. Chapman confessed that he often prayed to demons and the devil throughout the 1970s. It's not hard to assume that Chapman's issues with personal demons were fostered by his sessions with Krauss. I believe they were. The key question is, was Mr. Krauss acquainting Chapman with his inner demons deliberately and was there a hidden agenda outside of Christian hell-fire fundamentalism?

Recap

Mark Chapman, like millions of young Americans dabbled in the new drug culture. He graduated from marijuana to LSD. When he found God, he was surrounded by pastors, ministers and preachers who realised that the young Mark had a malleable mind which was perfect for suggestion. Look at them. Preacher Arthur Blessitt the stunt-loving psychedelic Evangelist, Special Agent Pastor Charles McGowan formerly of naval intelligence, psychologist preacher Krauss, the exorcist Paul Durbin, minister, formerly of the US Army. Such a gallery of rogues, some might say. The young man absorbed the favour of these men and trusted in them. There can be no doubt that if the CIA or any other agency was looking for a candidate, the Dakota candidate, here he was. Susceptible, malleable, trusting and eager to please. Perfect.

CHAPTER 4 | The Travelling Wannabe

Key People

Michael MacFarlane (friend)

Lynn Watson (school friend)

Dana Reeves (Mark's dubious friend)

Gloria Abe (later Chapman)

Pete Anderson (preacher)

Dennis Mee-Lee (psychiatrist)

Judy Herzog (psychologist)

Judy Harvey (therapeutic nurse)

David Mair (YMCA)

Jack Jones (writer)

Jessica Blankenship (girlfriend)

By most accounts, Mark was a popular figure in his "Jesus Freak" phase. According to his friends, Chapman did not have a particular interest in the Beatles, John Lennon or *The Catcher in The Rye* book, at least not around this time in his life. In May 1973, Chapman and a Christian friend called Michael MacFarlane, whom he met while at Special Agent McGowan's church in Decatur, decided to move to Chicago and live in a small apartment. By day, the friends would work in the mail room of the "Youth for Christ" organisations and by night, they attempted to be Christian comedians, performing at a "Christian nightspot". The holy jokers apparently didn't wow the crowds and Chapman left MacFarlane in Chicago and returned to Georgia where he tried, unsuccessfully, to date a school sweetheart called Lynn Watson. Chapman would later describe Lynn as his "first true love". He drifted back to the YMCA in Georgia, working in a summer camp at South De Kalb in 1974. The local De Kalb YMCA executive director, Tony Adams said that whenever Mark was feeling down, he always returned to the "Y for pumping up again." Unfortunately, the YMCA have apparently lost all their records regarding Mark Chapman and his work for them.

Tony Adams employed him as a summer camp counsellor

and Mark was befriended by a local "Rambo-type" called Dana Reeves. Reeves was two years his senior and, according to Chapman's parents and girlfriend at the time, he was a bad influence on Mark. None of Chapman's original high school friends knew Reeves. He appeared out of the ether. By all accounts, Chapman always changed his demeanour whenever Reeves was around. Dana Reeves offered his new young friend a room at his house, and they remained friends for years to come. Why a rough-edged stranger like Reeves wanted to befriend the meek and mild-mannered Chapman has never been explained. Their personalities were hardly a fit. Reeves worked as a security guard at a hospital before he became a police officer, and he encouraged Chapman to take over the job he was vacating.

Mark's girlfriend, Jessica Blankenship, immediately took a dislike to Dana Reeves. Reeves encouraged Chapman to shoot guns with him and they often took pictures of each other posing in tough-guy stances at the gun range. Blankenship felt Reeves was dangerous and violent. Every friend of Chapman I've spoken with has told me that Dana Reeves was a very dark and dangerous individual who constantly exuded an aura of menace. What Chapman saw in this individual can only be imagined. What attracted Reeves to Chapman? That's the interesting question.

Dana Reeves and his sister, Jan, play important roles in the official Mark Chapman story. We should consider their impact and wonder how and why this happened – if indeed it is true. Firstly, our mild-mannered Christian was enticed into the gun culture in which Reeves revelled. Secondly, while working as a sheriff in Atlanta, Dana Reeves supplied Chapman with the five hollow bullets which were allegedly used to kill John Lennon. Thirdly, he took Chapman out into the woods for firing practice, weeks before John was shot. Why? Jan Reeves was the first person to suggest that Chapman told her brother that "there would be nothing worse than going through life and die without anybody remembering your name". Jan's claim became the origin of the

Dana Reeves (Left) and Mark Chapman. Circa 1974 © Unknown

oft repeated story that Mark Chapman killed John Lennon so that his name would be remembered. To thrust himself into the hall of infamy by assassinating a world celebrity.

From 1980 until 1992, Chapman made no mention of personal fame. His immediate actions post 8th December 1980 backed this up. Chapman eventually claimed in a TV interview in 1992 that he "killed john Lennon to acquire his fame". To my way of thinking, these were hollow words, awkwardly staged, repeated by a man saying what he thought people wanted to hear. After twelve years of incarceration, had someone whispered to him that such an admission might help him gain his freedom? Jan Reeves also claimed in 1992 that Chapman, when aged 18, "talked to me about *The Catcher in the Rye*... He wanted a much deeper understanding of it." How convenient. A second-hand and unproven allegation blossomed into an answer which fitted the profile of "the lone nut", *Catcher* obsessive – all twelve years after the event.

Consider what was being claimed. A former acquaintance of Mark Chapman suddenly remembered incidents which allegedly took place and retold them to a questionable journalist. We should be aware that Reeves' stories about Chapman's desire to become famous and his love of *The Catcher in the Rye* were initially revealed to the mysterious "journalist" Jack Jones, and laid out in his 1992 book, *Let me take you Down.*

In 1975, a 20-year-old Mark Chapman applied to become a foreign councillor for the YMCA. His first choice of the Soviet Union was turned down. Why a deeply religious and anti-communist southern state Christian wanted to go to the Soviet Union has never been explained. Chapman, like President John F Kennedy's alleged assassin, Lee Harvey Oswald, even wanted to learn Russian to secure the trip. Undeterred, Mark Chapman then decided he would go to work for the YMCA in Beirut in the summer of 1975. Beirut was the war-torn capital of the Lebanon, rumoured to contain CIA training camps for assassins. It was also an established base for US Navy intelligence. Chapman barely stayed a month in Beirut and on his return, friends remarked that he had "fundamentally changed". There is little credible information about Mark's activities in Beirut, but we know he spent a lot of time in his hotel room recording the sounds of the violence going on outside on a tape recorder. It was as if he was being trained to accept and acclimatise himself to violence. Once back from Beirut, Mark was invited by Charles McGowan to speak about his experiences in Beirut at the local church. Mark and Jessica got back together and they became engaged. According to Blankenship, they sort of "fell into" the engagement.

On returning from the bizarre trip to Beirut in 1975, Chapman continued to be involved with the YMCA. He hooked up with David Moore, a YMCA director working at a Vietnamese refugee resettlement camp in Fort Chaffee, an ex-military base in Arkansas. Moore was a pastor with side-lines in other areas – areas that involved the highest echelons of government. Moore allowed Chapman to travel with him and meet government officials. Mark was even introduced to President Gerald Ford at Chaffee and the president shook Chapman's hand. Moore made the twenty-year-old Chapman an area co-ordinator for the refugee camp. By all accounts, Chapman excelled in his new role which mostly involved recreational activities with children. Moore described him as "one of the most compassionate staff members we had". He took a real shine to his young protégé, even cooking dinner for Mark's girlfriend, Jessica Blankenship, when she came and visited Chapman at the camp.

Many have speculated that the Christian organisation World Vision were involved at the Chaffee camp. President Reagan's would-be assassin, John Hinckley, was linked to World Vision through his father. Cue furious dot-connecting online. World Vision were involved at Chaffee, but only through helping with adoption. They were not working at the camp with Chapman or the refugees. World Vision and Mark Chapman is a red herring that needs to be put aside.

In December 1975, Fort Chaffee was closed down. The Vietnamese refugees had found American homes. On Chapman's last day, Dana Reeves turned up at the Fort to drive Mark home to Atlanta on what would have been a 1350-mile round trip. Reeves showed a long-barrelled, six-shooter gun to Chapman and his co-workers, who all observed that the older and "rougher" Reeves had a strange effect on Mark. Reeves seemed to "excite" him somehow and Chapman astonished his co-workers by proudly showing off Reeves' gun and telling them how well it held in his hand. A Fort Chaffee co-worker told Journalist Craig Unger that Mark would do anything for Dana and remained infatuated with his friend. According to the co-worker, Chapman "cleaned his nails, put on clean clothes and made numerous telephone calls" for Dana.

The same colleague also observed the non-violent Mark sitting in the office of the YMCA Chaffee centre with Reeves "playing with his gun, looking at it, talking about it, and rough housing each other". How odd. "It just wasn't like Mark" he observed. Finally, the co-worker observed that Reeves "gave Mark this 'look' and Mark just froze". Going by these accounts, Reeves clearly held a powerful psychological control of Mark Chapman. Some might say he was Chapman's handler.

In early 1976, Mark Chapman enrolled with Jessica Blankenship in a strict Presbyterian Covenant College in Tennessee, where Chapman attempted to gain a four-year degree which would allow him to qualify for a lifetime career with the YMCA. He couldn't cope and quit after a single semester. He abandoned any hope of gaining the theological degree that would have helped further his YMCA career. Mark also parted company with Jessica Blankenship and, according to some sources, went into an emotional tailspin.

By the summer of 1976, Mark was yet again sharing an apartment in Atlanta with his old friend Dana Reeves. He tried to return to work at a YMCA camp but was fired after a few weeks due to an argument he had with a parent of one of the campers. Dana Reeves found a solution. A job for Mark as an armed security guard. The previously non-violent Chapman was sent on a pistol-training course as part of his training. Out of a 100-point score, novice Chapman notched up a surprisingly good 88. Chapman's former girlfriend, Jessica Blankenship, and her family noted a significant personality change in Mark, saying, "he [Chapman] became quickly angry – just a trigger! He could just explode". It was as if his father's behaviour had crept into Mark's psyche. His demeanour grew darker and Dana Reeves was constantly by his side. It was no co-incidence.

In early January 1977, Mark surprised everybody who knew him by selling his car and all his belongings and flying to Hawaii. Chapman's old YMCA boss, David Moore, had apparently often eulogised about the "serenity" and "calmness" to be found in Hawaii, a paradise island with a multitude of military bases and secret facilities. Mark subsequently told his security guard colleagues that he "had always wanted to go to Hawaii". Chapman relayed a different reason for going to Hawaii to his estranged girlfriend, Jessica, telling her that he was going to go to Hawaii to kill himself there "as it was so beautiful".

Hawaii in 1977 held no less than seven major military and naval bases including, of course, Pearl Harbour. On arrival, Chapman booked himself into the expensive five-star Moana Hotel. After a splurge of drinking and expensive tours, Chapman ran out of money and ended up in the Honolulu YMCA hostel. Strange behaviour indeed. Was this to be his final blowout?

Chapman started to have suicidal thoughts and began seeing a psychological social worker called Judy Herzog. She worked for the Waikiki Mental Health Clinic, a state psychiatric facility in downtown Honolulu. Chapman told Herzog that he was depressed about his unsuccessful career, his failed relationship with Blankenship and his drug-taking school days. But Mark also mentioned, Herzog remembered vividly, the fact that he was "very proud" of his brief time working in Beirut. He thought that was a period when he had "done well" and "people thought well of [him]". This is a bizarre claim when you consider he apparently spent most of his trip in his hotel room. But if this is what he thought, the question is – under what influence was he operating? And who with? Judy Herzog put him on some unspecified medication.

Chapman then played the ultimate manipulation card. He rang Jessica to tell her that he was going to kill himself. She begged him to fly back to her and when he did, he quickly realised she was not interested in their getting back together. Dejected, he flew back to Hawaii and allegedly tried to kill himself with a vacuum hose attached to a car exhaust. His explanation to Herzog was that the vacuum hose burned off and a local Japanese fisherman found him alive and confused in his car. Herzog thought the suicide attempt was a cry for help. Chapman wasn't serious about killing himself. But where did all this money for expensive flights to and from Hawaii come from?

After his abortive suicide bid, Judy Herzog told him that

a hospital on the other side of the island called the Castle Memorial Hospital had opened a new psychiatric unit, with merely three patients residing there. That was at best unusual. Castle Memorial was a strange destination for Herzog to recommend. Normal procedure for attempted suicides under Waikiki care was that they were taken to the nearby Queens Hospital for treatment. Why Judy Herzog took Chapman to Castle Memorial on the other side of the island remains a mystery.

She drove Chapman to the hospital herself on June 21st, 1977. Some might say she delivered him. They spoke about their joint love of music on the long drive to the hospital. Interestingly, Chapman never once mentioned the Beatles or John Lennon. Castle Memorial was run by the Seventh Day Adventist Church, where a large proportion of its staff were practising Adventists. Yet again, Mark Chapman found himself with people who mixed psychology and religion. The Adventists are firmly in the "conservative" Christian camp. They believe in Creationism and they oppose LGBT rights. They sprung up in 1844 when their prophet, Ellen G. White, started having religious visions as a child after she suffered a traumatic brain injury.

In the 1950s and 1960s, the Adventists made an alliance with the military whereby they supplied Adventists, who didn't want to enlist and fight, as human guinea pigs. The volunteers were shipped off to Fort Derrick where they were given experimental pathogens to help in research on biological weapons. Having discovered this, I asked myself – did the Adventists also help the military in MK-Ultra mind control activities? We will return to this important link in the chain because of its relevance to Mark Chapman's behaviour, but if they did, their Castle Memorial hospital offered numerous candidates including Mark Chapman.

Castle Memorial was a private hospital, but Mark's fees were paid for by state welfare. According to the writer Jack Jones, Chapman claimed that within two weeks of being at Castle Memorial, he was confined to a doorless room and slept for almost three days straight. He was given plenty of food to eat after his slumber and Judy Herzog said she saw a dramatic improvement in his condition. According to his new psychoanalysts, Mark was suffering from severe depressive neurosis and not from a psychosis condition. He was not classified as a "mental patient". Chapman apparently told a therapist that he had a recurring fantasy of wanting to be in prison, where he could rest and read. In just three years' time, "Chapman's fantasy" would come true. Something concerns me here. Where did the notion that prison was an experience like a Christian retreat come from? As in, I want to go to prison and it will be a relaxing experience? Had this idea been planted by someone with another agenda?

Chapman was assigned a psychiatrist called Dr. Ram Gursahani to work on him. Dennis Mee-Lee was a Director of Mental Health Services in Hawaii and a senior psychiatrist at Castle. Mee-Lee subsequently confirmed that Gursahani did work on Chapman many years later. Strangely, the specific psychiatric work Gursahani performed on Chapman was not known by Mee-Lee. We do know from an early reported assessment on Chapman by someone at Castle Memorial (almost certainly Gursahani), which was given to Allen Sullivan at the New York Manhattan District Attorney's office, that Chapman was assessed as suffering from severe depressive neurosis. They did not find him to be suffering from a mental illness. This firstly begs the important question, why was Chapman consistently portrayed as an ex-mental patient after Lennon's assassination? And secondly, if Chapman was not a mental patient, what was Dr. Ram Gursahani doing with him?

Thankfully, one of Gursahani's colleagues, Dr. Barnett Seymour Salzman, decided to tell the world about what Gursahani might have got up to with Mark Chapman, and what Salzman revealed lies at the very heart of John Lennon's assassination. In 1981, Salzman gave a sworn affidavit to the Citizens Commission on Human Rights, a mental health watchdog organisation which was established in 1969 by the Church of Scientology. Dr.

Salzman's affidavit stated that in the late 1970s, the hospital was engaged in a "behavior modification program" headed up by Dr. Ram Gursahani. Salzman characterized this programme as "brainwashing." Salzman stated that the programme "would use mind-altering drugs to enforce compliance similar to brainwashing techniques used in prisoner-of-war camps." Salzman believed that it is likely that somebody like Chapman, with suicidal low self-esteem "would come to Dr. Gursahani's programme, which demanded compliance to authority through covert techniques of subliminal approval and disapproval." We now know from Dennis Mee-Lee, that Gursahani did work with Chapman. Mee-Lee claimed that he personally only had contact with Chapman "in the corridors." It is claimed, though, by an unnamed Memorial worker that Mee-Lee covered for Gursahani when he was away. When contacted at the time, Gursahani declined to comment on Chapman's treatment. He did say, "I was just one of the psychiatrists who treated him. There were more." Strangely, Gursahani claimed not to know who the other psychiatrists were. When further pressed about his work on Chapman, Gursahani declared: "You won't be any wiser from me."

The programme led by Gursahani consisted mainly of the abundant administration of psychiatric drugs. These drugs were linked to conditioning techniques intended to modify verbal and motor behaviour. The patients were "verbally abused" in order to assess the response of their changed behaviour. It was claimed by Salzman that the programme undermined a patient's ability to control their actions and will and was convinced that it did more harm than good and increased psychopathic behaviour. He opined, "Patients with extreme anxiety and guilt were unable to cope with the stress that the treatment caused, which was actually like brainwashing." Among the means used to break the individuality of the patients were potent drugs, mockery and pitting patients against each other. Violent outbursts were common. "Someone who has fully completed the program," he continued, "will sooner or later see that the therapy has further alienated him from himself; however, such an infringement has already been committed that help is impossible. From that moment on, that person will vent his envious despair on someone whom he considers to be free and happy and who, in the eyes of the patient, has succeeded in mastering his personal problems."

The drug Thorazine was often used at Castle Memorial. This was a favourite drug for the CIA in developing mind control. Interestingly, Thorazine is a reddish/orange colour. This will become important later. The Memorial programme could treat 10 to 12 patients simultaneously and lasted at least three weeks. The records show that few patients completed the programme. Those who could not withstand the systematic name-calling and other "verbal abuse" were usually transferred to another institution on the island.

Salzman's allegations regarding drug-use and mind-control programming at Castle Memorial are a game-changer in the theory that Mark Chapman was a "Manchurian Candidate". The fact that Salzman's allegations were given to a commission established and funded by Scientology has allowed some to dismiss his affidavit. But Salzman was not a Scientologist. He was an ex-US Navy Lieutenant Commander who served in Vietnam. He was also a fully qualified psychiatrist who worked at Castle Memorial when Chapman was there under Gursahani's care. Salzman had no particular axe to grind. He merely wanted the truth to come out about Gursahani's work. It will not surprise you to know that Castle Memorial refused to release any files on Mark Chapman and Dr. Ram Gursahani, and still to this very day cannot recall what kind of procedures and drugs Gursahani was using on Mark Chapman.

While being treated at Castle Memorial, Chapman moved into a small apartment nearby. His given address was 112 Puwa Place, Kailua. After John Lennon's assassination, Chapman's driving license had this as his address, issued on 29th July 1977.

The Honolulu Star Bulletin newspaper investigated Chapman's driving license address. They were perplexed when the landlord told them that a Mark Chapman lived there with a woman and three young children, possibly the woman's sister's children. The apartment at 112 Puwa Place had been rented by the woman's mother and everybody skipped out of the apartment in April 1980, leaving the rent unpaid and a $2000 cleaning bill. The mystery of who these people with whom a "Mark Chapman" was apparently living has never been resolved. *The Honolulu Star* deduced it must have been another "Mark Chapman". Not feasible. None of this makes sense.

In late 1977, Chapman settled down in Kailua, though he rarely settled for long, and was given a job at a local gas station. All arranged by the ever-helpful Castle Memorial staff. Chapman then started volunteering to work at Castle Memorial. According to his supervisor, Leilani Siegfried, Chapman "was delightful to work with. He tried to please us so. And he was so sympathetic to the old people. He would play them Hawaiian songs on his guitar and pay attention to them when nobody else would. Some of them hadn't spoken to anybody in years, but they started again when Mark showed them some attention." Delightful Chapman charmed everyone at Castle Memorial to such an extent that he was offered a job in maintenance at the hospital. In just a matter of two short months, Chapman had gone from patient to worker at the facility.

Around this time, Chapman struck up a platonic friendship with a therapeutic nurse at Castle called Judy Harvey. Bizarrely, Harvey claimed she was the illegitimate daughter of Oliver Hardy from Laurel and Hardy fame. By most accounts, Harvey was the spitting image of the comedy star. Harvey and Chapman became close, sharing dinner and wine at Harvey's apartment. Another friend from the hospital, George Kaliope, often joined them. Kaliope came from a military family and had previously served in Vietnam.

Mark's blossoming friendships were curtailed when he was introduced by Castle psychiatrist Dr Dennis Mee-Lee to yet another Southern pastor with a military background, Peter Anderson. Anderson was building a church in Kailua and, like Special Agent McGowan, he went on to help build Christian communities across the world. Presbyterian preacher Anderson, in the words of the *Honolulu Star Advertiser*, "placed emphasis upon the infallibility of scripture, Christian education and evangelism." I bet he was wonderful at parties.

Anderson offered Chapman the use of his house, as you do to a complete stranger, and for many months Chapman stayed with Anderson and his family. Judy Harvey thought Anderson deliberately curtailed their friendship and, under Anderson's orders, Chapman went out of his way to avoid her and others in their social group at the hospital. Harvey noted in her diary that after moving in with Anderson, Chapman was acting weird and moody. Closeness to God seemed to have that effect on Mark Chapman. By the summer of 1978, Chapman had apparently stopped living at Anderson's house and moved into his own house in Kailua. Chapman continued to act cool towards Judy Harvey at work. According to Kaliope, Chapman allowed the minister (Anderson) to get to him because of his "sinful ways".

In April 1978, Chapman decided he wanted to travel around the world – a feat few people even in comfortable retirement could achieve. Apparently, this fantastical idea came to him while he was mopping the floor at Castle Memorial hospital. Mark secured a letter of introduction from his old YMCA World Alliance boss, David Moore, which would allow him to stay and potentially work in YMCAs around the world. Chapman told Moore that he "loaned" the money for the trip. He told journalist Jim Gaines in 1987 that the loan money came from the hospital's credit union. And yet, why would a hospital want to finance an expensive global trip for one of their ex-patients turned junior maintenance man? With no collateral, how did they even know that Chapman would come back from his trip and repay them? Why would the Adventists apparently fund this global trip? Following Lennon's assassination, Detective Hoffman added a further twist to Chapman's world tour in his notebooks, stating that his father paid for it. If true, why would Chapman say something else seven years later?

In June, Chapman wandered into a Hawaiian travel agency called Waters World and asked a Japanese travel agent working there to organise his unlikely round the world trip. Gloria Abe duly arranged the whole tour for Chapman, taking in Tokyo, Seoul, Hong Kong, Singapore, Bangkok, Delhi, Israel, Geneva, London, Paris, Dublin, Atlanta and then back to Honolulu. A millionaire's trail indeed.

What Chapman did and who he met on this fantastical global jaunt, has never been discovered. Chapman told the writer Jack Jones that he witnessed a lot of "putrid filth" and poverty on his travels. He witnessed children sleeping on the streets and while in India, a man apparently stared at him with "voodoo eyes" before trying to steal his camera. In Geneva, Chapman said that he met up with David Moore and bizarrely attended a United Nations session with his old boss – as you do.

After his global jaunt, Chapman flew back to Atlanta, hoping to renew his relationship with Jessica, but when she told him that she only wanted to be friends, he decided to check in again with Dana Reeves, before flying back to Hawaii. To add another layer of improbability to this period in Chapman's life, Gloria Abe was apparently waiting for him at the airport terminal gate, ready to run excitedly into his arms. He immediately started dating Gloria. The Japanese travel agent was six years older than Mark and was brought up a Buddhist. She also dabbled in the "occult and witchcraft" and admitted having led a previous "promiscuous life" traveling abroad as a travel agent.

Gloria's so called immoral lifestyle was immediately dropped when Mark came into her life and she converted to Christianity for Chapman in late 1978. He converted Abe via a Christian "discipleship process" through a religious Christian group called The Navigators. You will probably not be surprised to discover that The Navigators are strongly linked to military bases, where they first came to prominence and gained a lot of ongoing support. Peter Anderson was a pastor with a military background, so the Navigators' influence probably came from him, but Hawaii was awash with military bases, so I'm speculating here.

In January 1979, Chapman proposed to Gloria on a Hawaiian beach, and they were married in June at a large United Methodist Church in Kailua, which was just two miles down from Castle Memorial Hospital. Peter Anderson was allowed to officiate, despite the fact that his own fledgling church had only 27 members and was run out of an old school classroom. By this time, Mark's mother had divorced his father and followed the newly-weds to Hawaii, where, apparently, she constantly vied with Gloria for her son's attentions and engaged in embarrassing romantic entanglements with local beach bums who were much younger than her. Shortly after their wedding, the newly named Gloria Chapman went to work at the Castle Memorial Hospital in the accounts department. This cosy arrangement was further cemented when the lovebirds commuted together to work every day from their new and very expensive $425 a month apartment in Honolulu. Gloria was now with Mark almost 24 hours a day. In September 1979, Mark discovered a sudden love of art and bought a Dali lithograph for $5000, using money allegedly borrowed from Gloria's father. Mark tired of the Dali and traded it in, buying a Rockwell for $7500, this time using $2500 from his mother's divorce settlement. In today's money, Mark's art purchases would be worth over $40,000. Being a $4 dollar an hour maintenance man at Castle Memorial was clearly a very lucrative gig.

Scepticism aside, the question of Mark and his access to money needs serious attention. His 1978 world tour had to be funded through a generous loan, of which there is no record. The concept of this religious enthusiast purchasing thousands of dollars' worth of artwork is inventive. When did he fall in love with art? It's an expensive hobby. How would a young working-class lad from the South know which artwork might have future potential? To whom did he sell the valuable work? Was the money held in cash? Did he have a bank account? If so, the police would have been able to trace the flow of money into and out of his account. As the celebrated fictional detective, Jimmy McNulty, regularly advised in the hit TV series, *The Wire*, "follow the money."

In December 1979, Mark had an argument with the rather benevolent Castle Memorial Hospital over a promotion he expected to win, and walked out. Whether Mark paid the hospital back the money they had given in advance to travel the world is unclear. Desperate to have money over Christmas, Mark took a job as a security guard at a holiday apartment complex. His fellow employees found him a dependable employee, who now and again talked about his past problems with drugs and his involvement with an unnamed "religious organisation". One colleague visited Mark's home in Kailua and they listened to some music in his apartment. No Beatles or John Lennon records were to be found in Mark's collection.

Recap

Take a step back and consider the evidence: The drug years, the God years, and the weird bond with Dana Reeves. Mark was born into a household where his mother suffered physical abuse at the hands of his father, a staff sergeant in the Air Force. No doubt he had his own violent demons. His school years were unremarkable. His talent, yet unproven. He tried to find relief in drugs, as many in his generation did. He ditched drugs for religion and found himself gravitating towards preachers and pastors who appeared to offer the one route to salvation. The YMCA began to play an important role in his life. He worked on summer camps and was at one point a foreign counsellor. He spent time in Beirut, worked at a camp for Vietnamese refugees and sought a lifetime career in the YMCA. Nefarious types began to circle him. He was vulnerable, susceptible and willing. Specifically, Pastor McGowan and the southern evangelist, Peter Anderson, were with him at vulnerable times. He became infatuated by Dana Reeves whom others saw as a bad influence on Mark. Reeves introduced Mark to guns. Reeves is also said to have – while serving as a police officer – provided the hollow bullets which allegedly killed John Lennon. Mark's relationship with girls tended to be short. He had access to money for travel, yet his background and work life suggested that would be unlikely. The "psychiatric work" on Mark by Dr Gursahani at Castle Memorial is tantamount to abusive brainwashing. Could this be where Chapman was first given the seed to assassinate John Lennon? Mark was a conundrum. Easily led down the path of fantasy or was he deliberately led? How could a man like Mark Chapman assassinate John Lennon?

CHAPTER 5 | The Catcher in the Rye

Key People

Mark Chapman

J.D. Salinger (author)

Jan Reeves (sister of Dana)

Gloria Chapman (Mark's wife and travel agent)

Fenton Bresler (writer)

Anthony Fawcett (writer)

Albert Goldman (writer)

If you attempt to analyse John Lennon's assassination logically, it becomes very clear that the official narrative is marred by dubious evidence and riddled with anomalies. Lennon's murder is a highly emotive subject and has been heightened by the careful packaging of the Lennon narrative over the last 40+ years. The packaging has been focused on emotions rather than facts. The subliminal message is clear: don't think about John Lennon's assassination, just feel the impact that it has had on you. Don't think, just feel – surely a motto for our times if ever there was one.

Mark Chapman's alleged obsession with the J.D. Salinger book, *The Catcher in the Rye*, was used to capture the imaginations of every newspaper and documentary filmmaker who attempted to cover Lennon's assassination. But slowly, over time, Mark Chapman's *Catcher* prop has been carefully, and tellingly, airbrushed from Lennon's assassination.

J.D. Salinger's novel *The Catcher in the Rye* is narrated in an appealingly subjective style. It's the kind of book that speaks directly to the people who "get it", as if it was written specifically for them and them only. Holden Caulfield, a 17-year-old teenager, narrates the story from a mental hospital. Released in 1951, *The Catcher in the Rye* has now sold over 70 million copies. From the 1960s onwards, *Catcher* became the de facto bible for disenfranchised western young men who saw themselves on the periphery of society, sniping at the "phoneys" of the world, just like the book's self-obsessed main character.

Before we get into Mark Chapman's obsession with the book in the months leading up John Lennon's murder, let's explore who Salinger was and try to put the book into context.

According to a 1988 unauthorised biography *In Search of J. D. Salinger*, by Ian Hamilton, Salinger worked for Defence Intelligence during World War 2 and served with the Counterintelligence Corps, an early precursor to the CIA. His main duties apparently involved interrogating captured Nazis. In 2013, *The Daily Telegraph* newspaper published an article headlined: "JD Salinger's five unpublished titles revealed, and how Second World War shaped his thinking." According to the article, one of Salinger's unpublished books was "about his time interrogating prisoners of war when he served working in the counter-intelligence division." The book's title, *A Counterintelligence Agent's Diary* sealed the deal: J.D. Salinger was a spy. Ian Hamilton's book also mentions that as the war ended, Salinger was an active participant in the "de-nazification of Germany". Some people have come to believe that Salinger was perhaps more involved in the business of the resettling of German Nazis and he could have been part of Operation Paperclip. Paperclip involved smuggling hundreds of Nazi experts into America. Some have estimated over 1600 Nazis and their families, incredibly, made the top-secret trip.

The freshly imported Nazis were mostly used to "enhance" the USA's intelligence and scientific communities. The top-secret mind control programme, MK-Ultra, would have been top of their to-do list. Much more on this later. Declassified files have revealed that much of America's efforts in de-Nazifying Europe did, indeed, amount to resettling the Nazi regime's top scientists and the scientific technologies in America. The post second world war American government were more concerned about beating the Communist Russians in a technology race, than the ethics of working with ex-Nazi war-criminals.

Interestingly, Operation Paperclip (named after the paper-clips used on the Nazi files the Americans collated) will enter the mainstream public conscience in 2023, with the release of the Indiana Jones film, *The Dial of Destiny*. In this fifth Indiana Jones instalment, the main antagonist is a Nazi scientist working for the Apollo programme in 1969. Jones is understandably uneasy about Operation Paperclip thanks to his previous clashes with the Nazis.

Salinger was always uneasy about dealing with the general public and remained a recluse for much of his mysterious life. Actual hard evidence on what he really got up to is difficult to ascertain. We depend for any personal insight on accounts from his ex-wives and they all bring an understandable bit of baggage to the discussion. Disturbingly, we do know Salinger had a bit of a predilection for young women. Salinger never published another novel in his lifetime and, despite some claims to the contrary, he was clearly a misanthrope after 1945, with deep psychological problems that almost certainly emanated from his Second World War experience.

Apart from Mark Chapman's obsession with the Salinger book for a short period of time, there are also reports that the book was on the bookshelf of JFK patsy, Lee Harvey Oswald. The book was also definitely in the hotel room of Ronald Reagan's would-be assassin, John Hinckley. That's three of the 20th Century's most infamous alleged assassins on *The Catcher*'s fan club list. That's quite a coincidence.

Taking Salinger's interesting war and post war years into account, *The Catcher in the Rye* could easily be seen as a perversely sentimental favourite of the CIA and intelligence communities. I don't believe the book has any special powers to warp young and impressionable minds into committing illegal acts, as some people have claimed. But its pages clearly have dark intelligence matter coursing through its very DNA. This is not just a story of alienation from a bygone age, it's a book whose author has a troubling backstory. It's a book that I am certain could potentially be used as a device, to help program impressionable and malleable young minds.

The Mark Chapman *Catcher in the Rye* story seems straightforward at first glance. According to some, Chapman was always obsessed with the book since childhood and strongly identified with the lead character, Holden Caulfield. Chapman related to Holden Caulfield's dislike of phoneys and this somehow morphed into Chapman wanting to kill phoney John Lennon. An impulse apparently instigated after Mark read a book on John Lennon in the Summer of 1980, where the former Beatle's great wealth was discussed in detail.

From the interviews I conducted with Chapman's friends who knew him before his "Jesus Freak" phase in 1970-71, no one has ever mentioned the Salinger book, not once. However, in 1992, Jan Reeves claimed that the eighteen-year-old Chapman "talked to me about *The Catcher in the Rye*". As I explained earlier, I don't believe her account. Why would Mark disclose this to her? The inference of Mark's obsession with the book was introduced later to satisfy the rising tide of sceptics, who picked holes in the official assassination narrative.

Writer Fenton Bresler, who examined John Lennon's assassination in a 1989 book, noted that in the weeks after the killing, hordes of journalists descended on Chapman's hometown of Decatur and questioned Mark's friends and teachers about the Salinger book. Not one of them ever said Chapman identified with the main character or even said he read it. In a 1988 documentary by Kevin Sim, a YMCA worker called Vince Smith, who apparently knew Chapman "quite well", said that "the Catcher business was one of Mark's passions". The controversial writer Albert Goldman believed Chapman saw *Catcher* as his "private bible". Bresler rightly pointed out that Holden Caulfield was very close to his younger sister Phoebe and wanted to protect her from the world's "phoneys". Chapman was not close to his younger sister who, like his parents, chose never to visit Mark in prison.

Chapman's identification with Caulfield, if we are to believe Mark's wife Gloria, started sometime at the beginning of 1980. The same year that Chapman became fixated with John Lennon – almost as if one fixation fed into the other somehow. In January 1980, Mark bought a copy for himself and one for Gloria and allegedly started calling himself "the Catcher". By late August 1980, Mark Chapman was still apparently obsessed with the book. In September, Mark wrote to a friend and told her "I'm going nuts". Mark drew a picture of Diamond Head Mountain with the sun, moon and stars above it. He signed the letter "the Catcher in the Rye, Mark".

In August 1980, Mark became obsessed with a new book and subject matter, Anthony Fawcett's *John Lennon: One Day at a Time*. According to Gloria, Mark would read this book and "get angry that Lennon would preach love and peace, but, have millions". The "phoney Lennon" appeared now to firmly be fixed in Mark's mind. Some of his friends claimed that Chapman requested that the state attorney general of Hawaii change his name to Holden Caulfield. There is absolutely no proof of this. As Chapman's obsession with *Catcher* and Lennon was beginning to reach boiling point, in August 1980, two other events were occurring on the world stage simultaneously. Ronald Reagan emerged as the front-runner for the upcoming USA elections and John Lennon was back in the studio recording his new comeback album, *Double Fantasy*. For these events to coalesce at exactly same time was disturbingly prescient.

After eight months of obsessing over Holden Caulfield and his dislike for "phoneys", Mark, we are told, focused solely on a "phoney" John Lennon. Chapman appeared to be losing his own identity and morphing into that of Holden Caulfield. The key question we must ask ourselves is – was this part of

Mark's deteriorating mental illness, or was this a persona shift in Chapman's mind implanted by the hypnotists we know Chapman was seeing in Hawaii? I strongly believe *Catcher* was used as part of a programme to make Chapman believe he was morphing into the central character, and he was led to believe that he had to eradicate one of the world's most famous men, whom Chapman was conditioned to believe was one of the world's ultimate "phoneys", John Lennon.

Recap

The story of Mark Chapman's obsession with *The Catcher in the Rye* was hailed originally as evidence of his deteriorating mind. The book was given special attention and assumed to play the role of a trigger to fire Mark's purpose. As theories swirled around as to what caused Mark Chapman to assassinate John Lennon, the net effect diverted attention away from individual suspects with military connections, to a novel. But was it actually as important as has been claimed? In the years that followed, the significance of J D Salinger's book to the narrative of John's assassination began to wane. At one stage, as will be shown later, Mark threw the book away as if resenting whatever was inside which conditioned his intentions. But in the long run, given the evidence that we have to date, it has been relegated to a sideshow, of which there are many. You could easily lose yourself down that rabbit hole for one very important reason: It might have appeared to be a cause, but it was not. It was an effect. The significance which it held for Mark was implanted by those who played with his mind, and it is they who organised or assisted the assassination.

CHAPTER 6 | Countdown to Dakota

Key People

Dana Reeves (Mark's friend/police officer)
Jessica Blankenship (Mark's former girlfriend)
Gloria Abe (Mark's wife)
Pastor Charles McGowan (special agent)
Jack Douglas (record producer)
Make Snyder (cab driver/ student)
James Taylor (recording artist)
Michael Medeiros (Lennon indoor gardener)
Bert Keane, Laurie Kaye, Dave Sholin (radio team)
Ron Hummel (radio producer)
Rabiah Seminole (receptionist at The Record Plant)
José Perdomo (Dakota doorman)

Paul Goresh (photographer)
Kenneth Anger (satanist)
Mark Snyder (taxi driver)
Ed Opperman (podcaster)
Daniel Schwartz (psychiatrist)
Wesley Nunn (special agent)
A. Louis McGarry (psychiatrist)

From December 1979 until the 3rd October 1980, Chapman worked as a security guard and maintenance man in a holiday apartment complex. While there, Chapman apparently found himself entangled with a Scientology centre that was across the road from the complex.

Scientology is another group that is often linked to Lennon's assassination and Mark Chapman. This link occurred because Chapman was reported to have harassed members of the cult and even visited the Scientology centre himself. Two Scientology members were interviewed by the media after Lennon's murder. Diane Kay and Dennis Clarke both described a manic and crazed Chapman threatening them at the centre. Another member, who wishes to remain anonymous, described Chapman declaring that he was the "Real" John Lennon, and the other John Lennon was a fake. This member also described Gloria being with Mark when he visited the centre. A personality test performed on Chapman in a private room resulted in Chapman being told that he had to work on areas of his "communication". This assessment apparently led to Chapman attempting to attack the Scientology worker, whose screams led to other workers entering the room and escorting Chapman out of the centre. While he was being led out, Chapman apparently threatened the centre and its staff. This bizarre Scientology visit appears staged to me. It was almost as if somebody wanted to portray Chapman as a crazed John Lennon obsessive who was somehow linked to Scientology. Scientology was an organization viewed with much suspicion in 1980. Seen by some as a dangerous cult, Chapman connecting himself to them would be a cast iron red herring for the future. I am still asked today whether John Lennon's assassination is connected to Scientology. Mission accomplished.

In late October 1980, Mark realised that he urgently needed money and decided to sell all his artwork. Meanwhile, on Thursday 23rd October, John Lennon released his comeback single "Just Like Starting Over" and on that same day, Chapman walked out of his job as a security guard. He is said to have signed off by writing "John Lennon" on the ledger, but he allegedly scrawled it out with two thick lines. Chapman's manager at the time, Joe Bustamante, was interviewed by the TV news after Lennon's assassination. Bustamante's sly grins to somebody off camera as he described the alleged signature leads the viewer to conclude that this was probably a prank to garner attention. The apparent prank worked. The Chapman signature story was always featured in every Lennon documentary and book that was subsequently produced.

Thereafter, matters started to escalate:

Monday, 27th October – Mark Chapman buys a gun from J & S Enterprises in Hawaii. It was a .38 Charter Arms Special with 5 Shots. On that same day, he also bought a one-way plane ticket to New York.

Tuesday 28th October – Republican Ronald Reagan outper-forms President Jimmy Carter in a pre-election television debate, watched by 100 million viewers.

Wednesday 29th October – Mark flies to New York with his new gun in the hold of the plane. Mark checks into the Waldorf and calls Gloria. Wait a minute! The Waldorf Astoria Hotel? One of the most expensive and iconic hotels in the world. The Park Avenue symbol of wealth. Mark Chapman stayed there? How could he afford such blatant luxury, you know, the kind of luxury which his alleged bête noire enjoyed?

Thursday 30th October – Mark discovered that he could not buy ammunition for his gun in New York because he didn't have a New York gun permit. This cold and calculating killer, as he was subsequently depicted, could not even figure out how to buy ammunition for his weapon. Chapman needed help and Dana Reeves was the person to whom he would turn.

For the next four days, Chapman's whereabouts and activities in New York are unclear. There are reports he went to see some Broadway shows with a girl he had befriended. Other reports mention a helicopter ride and an Empire State Building visit. Again, money appears to not be a problem for the security guard from Hawaii. Some reports had Mark moving to a YMCA and according to psychiatrist, Danial Schwartz, Mark said he was upset with the homosexuals there.

Monday 3rd November – Mark checks into the Sheraton Hotel.

Tuesday 4th November – On this day and on the following day, Chapman called the Henry County Sheriff's office, where Dana Reeves worked. I have accessed the Sheraton Hotel phone records that prove that Chapman made these calls. It is highly likely that Chapman contacted Dana to ask how he might get hold of bullets; or did Dana offer them? Reeves has always stated that Chapman asked him for bullets for "protection from muggers" for an "upcoming" New York trip. Clearly Chapman and Reeves discussed bullets while Chapman was already in New York, hell-bent on fulfilling his "mission" as he described his desire to kill John Lennon. There is a very high probability that Reeves knew exactly why Mark Chapman wanted bullets for his .38 charter arms gun.

(Also, on 4th November, Ronald Reagan is elected as the fortieth president of America, beating Jimmy Carter in a landslide victory).

Wednesday 5th November – Mark checks into The Olcott Hotel.

Friday 7th November – Mark flies down to Atlanta to meet up with Reeves. Being a police officer, Reeves has no problem accessing and supplying his friend with hollow-point bullets. Hollow-points are popular with US police officers because they break up inside the victim and do not often follow through and exit the victim, potentially hitting an innocent person. This detail will become very important in John's assassination investigation. After supplying Chapman with hollow-point bullets, Reeves then took his friend out into the fields for shooting practice. No doubt using the local trees as substitutes for the "muggers" whom Chapman was apparently so afraid of.

Later, after John Lennon's assassination, a special agent in Georgia, called Wesley Nunn, was tasked to look into Dana Reeves. However, Nunn revealed that his investigation was limited in scope, stating:

"Apart from wanting me to go to check on where he [Reeves] got his bullets from, the primary thrust of my enquiries was into his background. What sort of guy he was, that kind of thing. I got the impression the DA in New York was more concerned with fighting a defence of insanity at the trial than anything else. I never got into conspiracy. No one mentioned anything to me about the possibility and I certainly didn't get into that area."

While being assessed at Rikers Island Jail in New York after his arrest, Chapman was still concerned about Reeves. Southern Pastor Charles McGowan revealed to writer Fenton Bresler, in 1985, that one of the most important things Chapman asked him to do on his first visit to Rikers Island was to communicate with Dana Reeves and tell him that he (Chapman) was "alright". McGowan told Bresler that he contacted Reeves, but Reeves didn't want to talk to him for fear of being implicated. That makes sense. Chapman wanted to talk to his friend and mentor, the man who provided the ammunition but was blanked by him "for fear of being implicated".

And then Dana Reeves was allowed to drift into obscurity. When Fenton Bresler wrote his book about the John Lennon assassination in the 1980s, he bizarrely decided to give Dana Reeves the pseudonym, Gene Scott. In my early discussions with the assassination's lead NYPD detective, Ron Hoffman, he initially tried to keep Reeves' identity a secret. When I informed him that I knew Reeves' identity, a somewhat surprised Hoffman replied, "Oh, you know about him do you?" Why would Hoffman do that? Had Reeves been granted immunity from prosecution or reallocated as part of a deal?

As of 2023, Dana Reeves is currently serving time in jail for child molestation offences. His brief police decertification record details are below:

Decertification No. 1633978368 - 819219226
Individual:
Reeves, Dana P Reason:
Criminal Conviction Employer:
Henry County Sheriff's Office
Official Statement:
CHILD MOLESTATION

So, who hired a child molester to be Mark Chapman's mentor? Did it have some bearing on the assassination? Was he blackmailed by other parties? What kind of relationship existed between the two men? I don't know, but it is exceptionally strange.

Back to the timeline:

Saturday 8th November – Mark decides to see his old girlfriend, Jessica Blankenship, one more time. In a brief visit, feeling depressed, he told her that he thought he was a failure.

Sunday 9th November – Mark flies back to New York with his "loaded" gun in the hold. Airport security still apparently not a problem.

Monday 10th November – Mark waits outside the Dakota hoping to see John Lennon in the morning. Mark asks a "senior" doorman whether the Lennons were out of town. The reply was "yes, they were out of town". Chapman goes to the cinema to watch the feel-good film, *Ordinary People*. Inspired by the film's sentimental tone, he returns to his Olcott Hotel room and calls his wife Gloria. He told her that he has "won a great victory", and that he is "coming home and would tell her all about it when I get there".

Mark checks out of the Olcott Hotel and flies from New York that very night. We should again consider the advice from Jimmy McNulty to "follow the money". Where did it come from? Flights, expensive hotels and sustenance in New York all cost a great deal. If he had been paying from his own pocket, his wife, Gloria, would have been furious. Surely? But what if it wasn't from the family bank account?

Wednesday 12th November – Mark arrives back in Hawaii. Mission aborted or was it a successful dry run?

In mid-November, a "depressed" Mark Chapman apparently confessed to Gloria that he went to New York to kill John Lennon, but her "strong love" saved him. According to the writer Albert Goldman, Mark threw his gun and hollow bullets into the ocean. There is no further evidence of this. Gloria declined to tell the police about her husband's bizarre claims.

Mark told his Gloria-confession story to prosecution psychiatrist, Dr A. Louis McGarry. He also told McGarry that he threw away his copy of *Catcher* at this time. Clearly Chapman equated his mission to kill John Lennon with *The Catcher in the Rye* book. By throwing the book away, was Chapman trying to throw the mission away?

In the interim before Chapman flew back to New York, he met Kenneth Anger at a film festival in Hawaii. Anger was a cult film director and writer who had an unhealthy interest in Satanism and the weirdos who followed it. Anger was also an avid fan of British black magic tsar Aleister Crowley and he had dubious friendships with Anton LaVey, the founder of the Church of Satan and Bobby Beausoleil, one of the Manson family. This is the guy Chapman decided to approach and according to Anger, "handed me a fist full of bullets and said these are for John Lennon". Anger then further explained that Chapman gave him two .38 caliber live bullets – hardly a fist-full – but I digress. According to Anger's biographer, Bill Landis, Chapman sent Landis a letter confirming that there were three parts to his meeting with Anger. Chapman also allegedly asked Landis for a

Koran and some money. I personally find this so-called letter to Landis very hard to believe. Chapman could have easily obtained a copy of the Koran in prison and he had never shown any sign of wanting to make money from his infamy.

This connection with Kenneth Anger spawned a whole wave of Chapman and devil worship gossip when Anger's new film *Lucifer Rising* was shown in New York, a few days after John Lennon's murder. Anger gave an interview about his encounter with Chapman and people instantly, and perhaps understandably, started to connect Yoko Ono's interest in the occult with Anger and Chapman. People started to speculate whether John's death was somehow connected to devil worshipping cults. Once the internet arrived in the late 90s, speculation increased when people discovered Gloria Chapman's past interest in the occult. I have also spoken to people close to Lennon who have told me that they believe that the Process Church, a sixties cult linked to Satanism, was somehow linked to John's death. There is no proof of this.

I didn't put much faith in the validity of the meeting between Chapman and Anger until I managed to obtain some official police records. One of the NYPD property vouchers from 18th December 1980 clearly states that Kenneth Anger gave Detective Ron Hoffman two "WW .38 cal bullets". The voucher also notes that the "finder" (Anger) stated that they were given to him by Mark Chapman.

Remember that a "crazed" Chapman visited a Scientology centre and a famous Satanist in the weeks leading up to John Lennon's assassination. Both times, crazy Chapman mentioned John Lennon. If someone wanted to associate a crazy John Lennon obsessive with two organisations that were often feared and viewed with great suspicion in 1980, they wholly succeeded.

While awaiting his trial in 1981, Mark Chapman said that he resented the fact his wife didn't tell the police when he showed her his gun and bullets and announced he was going to kill John Lennon. He told a psychiatrist:

"I laid out the gun and I laid out all five bullets, she [Gloria] had never seen a gun before. And then I said this is what I am going to do. My God, I still have a deep-seated resentment that she didn't go to somebody, even the police, and say look, my husband's bought a gun and says he is going to shoot John Lennon."

On the 10th December, two days after Lennon's murder, Gloria and her lawyer, Brook Hart, called a press conference. Incredibly, Brook Hart and Chapman's lawyer, Jonathan Marks, were childhood friends. Hart said: "She [Gloria] knew he was going on an airplane. She knew he was going somewhere, but she didn't know precisely where he was going". That was untrue. More on this later. Gloria Chapman has stuck to this story ever since. I strongly believe that Gloria Chapman should have been prosecuted for failing to report her husband and his desire to kill John Lennon. That Gloria avoided the attention of the police after Lennon's assassination indicates to me that she must have had friends in very high places.

Back to the timeline again:

Friday 21st November – Mark tries to see a psychiatrist but not at his old clinic. According to Fenton Bresler, he fails to show up for an appointment on the 26th of November. This raises the question, what did he do during this key week? When he did emerge on 28th November, he seems to have had a clarity of purpose. He was decisive and prepared. It was as though he had had a refreshment week with a minder who turned him back into the would-be assassin.

Friday 28th November – Mark allegedly buys a United Airlines "special fare" ticket for a flight from Honolulu to New York via Chicago for Tuesday 2nd December, with a return flight from Chicago to Honolulu on 18th December. The dates were confirmed by a Hawaiian private detective, Captain Louis Souza. On

10th December 1980, the *New York Post* printed a story quoting Gloria Chapman in which she stated that Mark left for New York from Hawaii "eight or ten days ago". This would mean that Chapman flew out of Hawaii around the 1st or 2nd of December and not the 5th of December, as the official version claimed. But there is a flaw in Gloria's version of events – one which we will return to later. Her original position was that Mark had booked the flight. But it was Gloria who had been the travel agent and later evidence will confirm that lies were told.

Tuesday 2nd December – Gloria drives Mark to the airport. It is reported by Gloria that Mark was in good spirits on the drive. Mark flies to Chicago on his way to New York. Some reports have stated that he dropped his grandmother off in the windy city. Wow. In the depth of a Chicago winter, consumed by his personal crisis, he allegedly took his grandmother to Chicago. Why? Surely investigative journalists or the Chicago police would have found an answer. Apparently, Mark stayed in Chicago for the next three days. His whereabouts and activities in Chicago for these lost days and nights are unknown and remain a mystery. Journalist Fenton Bresler obtained a copy of a plane ticket from the New York police. Mark Chapman had laid it out in his New York hotel room on the day he shot John Lennon. The ticket was for a flight from Honolulu to Chicago, but the date of departure states the 6th December. The date of departure the Hawaiian detective discovered was the 2nd December and this was further confirmed by a December 10th press statement by Gloria Chapman. Bresler believes this ticket may have been forged. Mark Chapman did not leave his Chicago to New York plane ticket in his room. Apparently, he lost it. Bresler asked Assistant New York District Attorney Allen Sullivan (the man who prosecuted Mark Chapman) to find a 16-page official "Chapman movements" report, to help to get to the bottom of Mark's itinerary. Sullivan told Bresler that the file "could not be located".

Saturday 6th December – Mark Chapman flies from Chicago to New York. His three-day break in Chicago has never been explained. He initially stays at the YMCA West Side Branch at 5 West, 63rd Street. Mark would later tell the journalist Jim Gaines that he was bothered about "two fags across the hall talking about hairy chests and things like that". In 1980, YMCAs were well known as establishments for homosexuals to meet up – how could Mark not have known this? Or perhaps he did. Writer Fenton Bresler speculated that Chapman was a closet homosexual who was too scared to come out because of his Southern Christian upbringing.

There is another interesting issue which also needs to be considered. Followers of the JFK assassination will be aware that there was a fascinating theory regarding two Lee Harvey Oswalds. The real one, who was framed as the patsy for Kennedy's assassination, and a fake one, who kept popping up in various locations in the weeks leading up to the foul deed. The theory is that unknown parties sought to build up a fictitious profile of Oswald to place him in locations where they wanted him to be seen acting suspiciously.

While the real Lee Harvey Oswald was elsewhere, fake Oswald was seen at a shooting range firing an unusual weapon which, according to witnesses, garnered great attention because his gun shot a ball of fire out of the barrel when it was used. This occurred two weeks before JFK's assassination on November 9th, 1963. A week later, fake Oswald returned to the rifle range and shot at another person's target causing an argument. He also shot bullseyes on each visit, laying down a legend that Oswald was a great marksman. Everything was designed to ensure fake Oswald drew as much attention to himself as possible. More fake Oswald stunts were reported in the same time frame. At a car dealership, fake Oswald boasted that he would be coming into some money soon. He then recklessly drove a car on a test drive. The real

Oswald was verifiably elsewhere when this was happening. And he couldn't drive. On and on this went, with further fake Oswald sightings being reported. The author Richard Popkin wrote a fascinating book in 1966 that addressed the issue, called *The Second Oswald*.

What has all this got to do with Mark Chapman? Well, interestingly, there appears to have been a fake Mark Chapman running around New York before the real one allegedly shot John Lennon. Upon arrival in The Big Apple on 6th December, Chapman checked into the West Side YMCA. Perhaps his money was draining away. Later, at approximately 7:00pm, he took a tortuous taxi ride through Manhattan, making stops here and there, all the while holding a large mysterious black bag. The cab driver, a law student named Mark Snyder, later described Chapman's mood as "very agitated" in an extensive *New York Post* article about the incident.

According to Snyder, Chapman angrily demanded that Snyder drive him around different parts of New York. Chapman would then get out and appear to drop items off in random buildings before continuing onwards to the next random drop-off point. First off, Chapman disappeared into a building on West 62nd Street for about five minutes. Then, the taxi driver was instructed to drive across Central Park to the corner of East 65th Street and 2nd Avenue where he disappeared for another few minutes. They then drove to Greenwich Village on the other side of town where Chapman got himself dropped off at the junction of Bleecker Street and 6th Avenue. Between the drop-offs, Chapman frantically flipped through a notebook and bragged about being a record producer who was working with the Rolling Stones. He also mentioned that he had just got back from a recording session with The Beatles at a time when the Beatles hadn't worked together for over ten years. Bizarre.

Chapman then allegedly offered Snyder some cocaine, which Snyder tested with his fingertip and declined. It wasn't cocaine at all. To raise the implausibility factor one more notch, Mark Chapman exited Snyder's cab for the last time saying: "My name is Mark David Chapman. You'll remember my name."

After Lennon was slain, Snyder saw Chapman on television news. He was certain it was the guy who was in his cab a few days earlier. He went to the police and the media, both of whom whole-heartedly embraced his story without question.

I conducted a lengthy interview with Mark Snyder about his experiences and he was certain that the man in the back of his cab was Chapman. I seriously doubted the validity of Snyder's story when he told me that Chapman shape-shifted in the back of his cab like a chameleon. I asked him if he meant that Chapman's mood changed, but Snyder was adamant that Chapman's whole face changed, multiple times, like an alien. Snyder then told me that as a teenager, while he was stoned smoking hash and listening to a Bob Dylan record, he had a premonition of a voice in the song saying "Mark David Chapman will assassinate John Lennon". That must have been some very good hash.

It wouldn't be a John Lennon assassination story without another strange twist. Not long after Snyder thought he had a *shape-shifting* Mark Chapman in the back of his cab, he was appointed as a court attorney in the New York City legal system. While working in court, Snyder saw Chapman's second lawyer, Jonathan Marks. Snyder approached Marks and told him about his taxi experience with Chapman, and asked Marks to ask Chapman if he remembered the taxi ride. Marks agreed to do so, but the answer was negative: "Yeah, I asked him. He said there was no taxi driver." Confusion reigned. Perhaps it was meant to.

The next Chapman doppelganger story is perhaps the most famous. Singer James Taylor alleged that Chapman accosted him in the New York subway on 7th December 1980. A day before John Lennon was assassinated. Taylor recalled:

"Chapman pinned me to the wall, glistening with maniacal sweat, and tried to talk in some freak speech about what he was gonna do, and stuff about how John was interested and how he was gonna get in touch with John Lennon. It was surreal to have contact with the guy 24 hours before he shot John."

It is worth remembering that Taylor was a recovering heroin addict at the time, and he was heavily into Methadone when he allegedly met Mark Chapman, well before Chapman became world famous and easily recognisable. That said, the Chapman whom Taylor encountered sounds like the same aggressive Chapman who Snyder said was in the back of his taxi. Both encounters also mentioned the Beatles and John Lennon. If you were trying to enhance the legend of Mark Chapman's obsession with John Lennon, this would be the way to do it. At first, I didn't give James Taylor's story much credence, but considering the other reports, I think Taylor was sincere in his recollection of his troubling encounter.

There is a third reported "Mark Chapman double" encounter in New York. Private investigator and podcast host Ed Opperman has added further credence to the Chapman lookalike claims by stating that he met someone who looked like Chapman at the Youth International Headquarters (Yippie) in Bleecker Street, New York. The same Bleecker Street where Snyder said he dropped off his "shape-shifting" Chapman. The Bleecker Yippie hang-out was the HQ of an influential left-wing collective, with members openly dealing dope and offering a safe place to hang out for anyone who embraced counterculture and anti-Republican beliefs. Opperman was attracted to the radical socialism on offer and was, by his account, working the door at the Yippie HQ because of his large physique. He, too, said that his Mark Chapman was as menacing a figure as Mark Snyder and James Taylor had described.

Taking all this into account, there clearly was a Mark Chapman lookalike running around New York in the days leading up to John Lennon's killing. The fact that Chapman has never said he was in Mark Snyder's taxi or at the Yippie headquarters is very revealing. For a 1970s pop music fan not to remember harassing James Taylor is doubly strange. Why would Chapman try and conceal this kind of activity after he was convicted? There may be two feasible explanations. Either a Mark Chapman double was employed to run around New York (and possibly Florida as well as Hawaii) in a chaotic and suspicious fashion to build a profile that would fit an unhinged killer. Or the real Mark Chapman was hypnotised into acting out these bizarre encounters in a pro-grammed, aggressive mind-set that was wholly different to his own docile demeanour. Either way, the result would have been the same. Mark Chapman was being portrayed as an aggressive and highly suspicious character who was obsessed with John Lennon. A fake legend of a crazed man obsessed with John Lennon was being created for the whole world to consume. The whole world bought it.

Sunday 7th December – Chapman waits outside the Dakota all evening. Later he dines alone at the Sheraton Hotel. He allegedly calls a prostitute to visit him in his room. Sex was not on the menu. Mark just wanted to massage the call-girl and talk. This bizarre encounter echoed a similar incident with a prostitute for Holden Caulfield in *The Catcher in the Rye*.

The next day would be the last day of John Lennon's life.

When Chapman was arrested on the evening of 8th December for the murder of John Lennon, he told the NYPD that he had left a "layout" in his hotel room which would explain who he really was. Cue frantic court orders issued from the New York District Attorney's office to gain access to Chapman's hotel room. This was officially denied, but the police eventually gained access and discovered his "display". Over the years, the media have repeatedly covered the items laid out in Chapman's hotel, but they did not know (or perhaps did not want to tell) the whole story. I have now seen a full inventory of the items Chapman chose to leave in his hotel room at the Sheraton Hotel.

The public were officially told that Chapman had laid out the following articles:

1. A pocket Bible inscribed "Holden Caulfield" with "Lennon" inscribed in a passage from the Gospel of St John.
2. His multi-stamped old passport and the letter of introduction David Moore gave him from the YMCA.
3. A Todd Rundgren tape.
4. A photo of Mark at Fort Chaffee with Vietnamese children.
5. A photo of an old car he used to drive in high school.
6. His Honolulu-Chicago-Honolulu return plane ticket in its folder with the baggage tag attached (but no ticket from Chicago to New York).
7. And finally, and most bizarrely, a movie still from *The Wizard of Oz*, showing Judy Garland as Dorothy, wiping away the cowardly lion's tears. Mark allegedly inscribed this picture with "To Dorothy".

In examining the official police inventory, the fully itemised list from the Sheraton is in fact as follows:

1. Pocket Bible (no mention of any inscription).
2. U.S. Passport (expired).
3. Four photos. (Car, self, four persons, three persons – writing on back of each).
4. One Tape – Ballad of Todd Rundgren.
5. Airline ticket United – issued 11.28.80 (with holder). Honolulu to Chicago/O'Hare 5th December – Return Honolulu 18th December 1980 – $459.86.
6. Letter of introduction to the YMCA.
7. One place mat (*The Wizard of Oz*) (The is no mention of inscription and it is not a movie still).

Now the eagle-eyed amongst you will notice straight away that the authorities took it upon themselves to conceal the fact that there were inscriptions on the back of the photographs. We have also been told that there were only two photos: one of Chapman's car and one of him with Vietnamese children. What about the other two photos and who were all the people whom the authorities didn't want us to know about? Why omit them? As mentioned before, writer Fenton Bresler believes the airline dates were forged on the tickets to conceal when Chapman left Chicago to fly to New York. The redacted picture below, issued by the District Attorney's office on an FOI request, carefully hides the airline ticket dates.

Concealing the additional photographs was serious enough, but I have seen another official police voucher listing other items found "in the room of Mark Chapman".

Here's what the voucher lists:

1. Bottle of Vaseline intensive care lotion.
2. 50 pills, apparently aspirins.
3. 55 white pills, apparently vitamin C.
4. 17 red pills, apparently vitamins.

So, that's 122 unidentified pills which Chapman had left in his room. And the NYPD omitted to make this public. Surely

A redacted FOI released Image of some of Chapman's Hotel "layout" ©
Manhattan DA Office

aspirins and vitamins would be marked as such. According to the police voucher, these mysterious pills were sent to "the lab for content analysis". If they were vitamin pills, why would Chapman be concerned about his health and nutritional intake when he was hours away from allegedly killing John Lennon? Would his personal health be uppermost on his mind at this time? I have a strong feeling that if they were vitamin pills and aspirins, the NYPD and the DA's office would have revealed their existence. Interestingly, the drug Thorazine, which was often used by the CIA as a hallucinogenic, is reddish in colour. And the bottle of Vaseline? What an unusual item to have in your possession.

The NYPD and DA's office ensured that knowledge of these medical accoutrements was kept from the public for over forty years. Why the evasion? What were these mysterious pills and what did the lab discover? Something tells me we will never get to know. This was a cover-up. Plain and simple. Which inevitably leads us to an important question – what else did the NYPD and New York District Attorney's Office conceal? What else are they still concealing?

The clock kept ticking as the timeline to disaster raced on:

Monday 8th December, 8am – For most of the morning and early afternoon, John Lennon and Yoko Ono are engaged in a photo-shoot and radio interview in their Dakota apartments.

Monday 8th December, 11am – Mark Chapman walked to the Dakota building in the late morning sunshine. Despite the oft repeated insistence that he was obsessed with *The Catcher in the Rye* for the whole of 1980, Mark strangely didn't have a copy of the book with him when he flew to New York in early December. On the morning of Lennon's assassination, Chapman rectified that and bought a copy in a local book store on his way to the Dakota. We were told he wrote these words:

To Holden Caulfield from Holden Caulfield. This is my statement.
I have now seen a copy of this inscription and it says:
Mark David Chapman [signed] The Catcher in The Rye.
This is my Statement.

Mark's Catcher Inscription © David Whelan

He was at this point identifying himself as "The Catcher in the Rye" and not "Holden Caulfield". To my mind, the book was a device – a trigger to push Chapman into positioning himself outside the Dakota. Chapman was on his way to kill John Lennon. That was his mission. It filled his head. After shots rang out in the Dakota driveway at 10.50pm that night Chapman allegedly dropped a gun on the ground, though Mark speaking in 1992 said doorman José Perdomo shook it out of his hand. In an almost robotic fashion, Mark took off his coat and neatly folded it on the ground. He then opened *The Catcher in the Rye* and tried to read the pages, but he recalled: "The words were crawling all over the pages. Nothing made any sense".

It was as if Chapman's brain had imploded, and the *Catcher* programme had run its course. It was no longer working as a prop. Once arrested, Chapman gave a statement.

"This morning I went to the bookstore and bought *The Catcher in The Rye*. I'm sure the large part of me is Holden Caulfield who is the main person in the book. The small part of me must be the devil. I went to the building, it's called the Dakota."

More on this to come. Back once more to the timeline:

Monday 8th December – That morning Lennon and Ono played out their infamous *Rolling Stone* photo-shoot, where a naked Lennon wrapped his body around a diffident looking Ono who is staring off into space.

At 12 noon, back at the Dakota, an upbeat Lennon chatted with Michael Medeiros about releasing *Double Fantasy* and in doing so, was "opening the door to see if anybody was still out there". It was a charming and vulnerable side of John Lennon that Medeiros found endearing. Lennon also told Medeiros how happy he was that the critics appeared to like him again after the Beatles split.

During the afternoon, Chapman chatted to an amateur photographer and Lennon obsessive, Paul Goresh. Five-year-old Sean Lennon arrived at the Dakota with his nanny. Two regular Dakota Lennon female fans, Jeri Moll and Jude Stein, allegedly introduced Mark to the young boy, whose small hand he apparently shook. Mark then went with Jeri and Jude to a local restaurant to eat and apparently charmed them with his tales of global travel and Hawaii. I have seen the NYPD detective's notebooks where Jude and Jeri relayed the following facts to Detective Hoffman about their meal with Mark. They observed:

They spoke about the Beatles. "Mark was not well informed about the Beatles."

The idea that Chapman was a Beatles super-fan, which we were consistently sold, was clearly a lie.

Mark did not have the new Lennon and Ono Double Fantasy album. He only had the single.

Ditto the above. The Lennon-obsessive Chapman didn't even have his new album, released just a few weeks earlier.

He seemed excited about the possibility of getting the new album signed by Lennon.

He talked mostly about Hawaii and his global trip.

They discussed the food they ate. Jude observed that he was so nice, she would have dated him. He dressed nicely, was well groomed and polite.

According to the girls' statements to Detective Hoffman, after their meal, Mark went off to buy the new album, or so they thought. Jeri and Jude told Mark they would be back at the Dakota at 5.30pm and would see him then. The girls arrived back at the Dakota early at 5.15pm. They observed that Chapman was not initially there. He turned up shortly after with the new album in hand. Mark now seemed very concerned about getting Lennon's autograph. He told the girls that he had other Beatle's autographs but didn't say who.

When Lennon came out at 5.30pm, the girls noticed John was in a good mood.

Chapman subsequently claimed that he asked Jude Stein for a date that evening and he later wondered if this was a subconscious attempt to self-sabotage his desire to murder John Lennon. Stein later refuted Chapman's claim, stating, "No way, not in a million years. That whole story has to be fabricated in his own mind. Never. First I'm hearing of it."

The Lennons' self-styled "house plant decorator" Michael Medeiros explained an episode to me. One I had never heard before. He said that during the afternoon of Monday 8th December, he had been introduced to Mark by Jeri and Jude.

He described Chapman as odd, and was uncomfortable when Chapman asked questions about the Lennons. Medeiros also noticed that Chapman was carrying a blue canvas bag and had a pale, waxy face.

This is the first time anyone mentioned a blue canvas bag. What was in the bag and where it ended up remains a mystery. Such specific detail, and it hangs there unexplained. Medeiros was an "insider". He was standing beside Mark Chapman. He shook his hand. He had no known purpose to invent the story. His second claim about Mark's appearance is interesting because experts have regularly shown that people under hypnosis, appear to have a waxy, pale complexion.

Monday 8th December, 5.30pm – Lennon and Ono exited the Dakota with record executive Bert Keane; two radio reporters, Laurie Kaye and Dave Sholin; and a radio producer, Ron Hummel. The radio team were heading to the airport to fly home after conducting an earlier interview in the Dakota. It was the last interview John Lennon ever gave. Lennon and Ono were waiting for their limousine to take them to the Record Plant to work on a Yoko song. The limousine failed to turn up and John and Yoko accepted a lift with Sholin, Hummel and Keane.

Chapman is said to have walked up to Lennon without a word and thrust his *Double Fantasy* record and a pen towards him. John Lennon signed the record and handed it back asking Chapman, "Is that all you need?" Lennon, Ono, Sholin, Hummel and Keane then climbed into the limo and drove away. There was no room for Kaye, and she was left to make her own way back. An amateur photographer named Paul Goresh took a picture of the infamous signing which he sold to a New York newspaper for $10,000 the next day. The reason why the pre-booked limousine failed to show up has never been explained or investigated.

But who was this Paul Goresh who stalked John Lennon with the sole intention of profiting from his association? His main interest in life was collecting pop culture memorabilia, especially Beatles merchandise, and reselling it in the collectors market. After John's death, and in all subsequent Lennon documentaries, Paul Goresh took great delight in telling people that he became John Lennon's "friend" and that John allowed him to accompany him on some of his New York walks. There may be some truth in John placating his shadowy pest and allowing Goresh to accompany him for short walks to the shops. Lennon's assistant, Fred Seaman, told me John used to refer to Goresh as that "fat f**k" and Seaman considered Goresh a very real threat to John's safety. Another Dakota insider told me that Lennon thought Goresh might be taking pictures of him for the FBI. The "friendship" claim made Goresh a legend in his own head. Nothing more.

His most important contribution was the picture he took of John Lennon signing a copy of *Double Fantasy* for Mark Chapman, six hours before Lennon was gunned down. Chapman said subsequently that Lennon signed an album for him with a black Bic pen and this almost certainly happened. Chapman added an interesting detail about that moment, telling Larry King, the TV presenter, that Paul Goresh pushed him forward to get his record signed, saying "here's your chance". Chapman asked Lennon to sign his album and Goresh took the iconic photo.

When Paul Goresh heard about Lennon's murder on the following day, he rang the New York City Police Department to tell them he may have captured an image of the killer on his camera. "I told them it could be used as evidence to prove the guy was there," he claimed. This begs the question – how did the photographer know he had captured the killer on film? Mark Chapman's identity was concealed by the NYPD in the days after the shooting. Goresh said he knew it might be Chapman because he recognised Chapman's light brown scarf on the TV screen when the coat-shrouded accused was paraded by NYPD detectives past reporters and photographers.

The Police officer who answered Paul Goresh's first telephone call at the city's 20th Precinct police department hung up on him. Ever the obsessive, he tried again and again. On the final call, the same police officer angrily shouted, "You've called here three times now in the last hour, if you call here again, I'm going to trace this call and I'm going to charge you." Perplexed, Goresh the obsessive went to his local police station. Joe Zadroga was a sergeant in the North Arlington Police Department, and he recalled "we contacted the *New York Daily News* for him,". "The New York police probably didn't see any value in the photo," Zadroga added. "They arrested the guy [Chapman] right away, so they probably didn't need it." More evidence, if any more were needed, that the NYPD did not properly investigate John Lennon's assassination.

The local cops did a great job promoting Goresh and his undeveloped photos. *The Daily News* sent a limo over for Goresh and his film. Having verified that the man in Goresh's picture was Chapman, the paper bought the photo for $10,000 and helped the amateur photographer secure a syndicated deal which eventually earned him a fortune.

I have always found it strange that Chapman never went into any detail about where he bought the infamous *Double Fantasy* album, which John signed for him. I managed to gain access to NYPD evidence vouchers, specifically for items collected around the murder. One of the items is for "one LP record album by singer John Lennon (Double Fantasy) bearing autograph of John Lennon". The finder of this property was a Phillip Michael, who went on to sell the album at auction. According to people at the Dakota, a man (supposedly Philip Michael) found the album in a plant display, which stands next to the doorman's golden booth by the Dakota driveway. Strangely though, you would need a ladder to reach the plant-pot and place the album in it, but that is where it was apparently found. Or so he claimed. Was Philip Michael ever interviewed by the NYPD? It appears not and how could this album be claimed to be his? Chapman did allegedly try

Double Fantasy NYPD Evidence Voucher © David Whelan

and legally gain possession of the album in the eighties, claiming he wanted to sell the ghoulish item and give the profits to charity. It didn't happen. The album went on to be sold a couple of times since Philip Michael gained its bizarre possession. In 2020, it was up for private auction again. It was expected to sell for at least two million dollars.

There is one more mystery surrounding Goresh, Chapman and the signed album. Looking through the police inventory vouchers, I discovered that another *Double Fantasy* album was handed into the NYPD on the 11th December. This one came from Paul Goresh. Paul even handed in the "yellow Vogel Records and tapes" bag in which it had been allegedly purchased. The voucher stated that "this album was surrendered by the owner [Goresh], so that it could be processed for latent prints" (of Chapman). Why did Goresh have a copy of *Double Fantasy* and why were Chapman's fingerprints allegedly on it? Mark Chapman apparently had his own record, so why would he need to look at the Goresh album? Could Paul Goresh have given a copy of *Double Fantasy* to Chapman without his purchasing one, or did Goresh bring a job-lot of albums to the Dakota that day? That was his modus operandi. Get his merchandise signed and reap a fortune. That Chapman had his copy signed by John Lennon was very lucky for Goresh. He made a fortune from selling and licensing his picture. Like so much in John Lennon's death, it's all very strange and disturbing.

The limo driver who turned up late and failed to pick up the Lennons was called Bill Christian. Detective Hoffman spoke to him and recorded the following in his notebook:

5.30 – 6pm – "I arrived and the photographer told me that they had already left with people that were with him. About 15 mins later, someone told the doorman to tell me to return to garage. 10–15mins later, I had conversation with 2 people, photographer and Chapman. Conversation at the Dakota. Chapman mentioned a plaque on the building. They called Chapman 'that creep standing over there. I'm afraid of him'. An unknown male, Paul, Chapman and me, had a conversation.

Paul was the talker. Chapman appeared normal in all aspects. We thought Paul and Chapman were intimate friends. He was a bit shy. He appeared to be a friendly type who would make friends easily. He looked like a genuine autograph seeker. He got his autograph about 12.30. why did he wait around?"

Goresh has always stated that he first got talking to Chapman on 8th December and instantly disliked him. Yet Bill Christian thought they were "intimate friends". Also, Chapman was supposed to get his famed autograph at 5.30pm. Did Chapman get two autographs? Why did Christian think it was at 12.30? Finally, who was the unknown male talking with them?

Goresh often appeared on John Lennon documentaries claiming that he instantly felt there was something odd about Chapman and that he wished he could have changed history by staying at the Dakota and somehow stopping the awful deed. There were rumours in the late 1980s, that Paul Goresh intended to make a documentary with the involvement of José Perdomo, the doorman, but sadly this never came to pass. Perdomo decided to continue to stay in the shadows until his death. Goresh died in 2018 from an unspecified illness. His cousin posted news of his passing on Facebook to Goresh's 265 followers. His family have flatly refused to give anyone an interview about him or the whereabouts of his famed memorabilia. On news of his death, the Lennon twitter account simply tweeted "Rest in Peace, Paul Goresh."

Continuing the timeline:

Monday 8th December, 6pm – The doorman, José Perdomo, started his evening shift at the Dakota's front security. At 8.30pm, Paul Goresh left the Dakota. Chapman allegedly begged him to stay. Chapman later confessed that he thought that if Goresh had stayed, he wouldn't have gone through with his "compulsion" to kill John Lennon. Goresh later implied that he thought Chapman wanted him to stay there to photograph the murder. What conceit.

Monday 8th December, 9pm – According to music producer, Jack Douglas, John discussed something so troubling that he deleted the recording one day after John's murder.

Monday 8th December, 9.30pm – According to Mark Chapman in a 1985 interview with journalist Jim Gaines, Mark engaged in a discussion with José Perdomo about Fidel Castro, the Bay of Pigs and JFK's assassination. For a man who apparently had a poor grasp of the English language, Perdomo could hold a high-level conversation on multiple topics without a problem.

Monday 8th December, 10.30pm – Lennon and Yoko were about to leave the Record Plant. As they depart, John told Jack Douglas and studio staff he intended to stop off at a fast-food delicatessen called The Stage Deli to grab a bite to eat. For some reason, their rented limousine drove them straight back to the Dakota.

I managed to interview the Record Plant receptionist who was working that night, a lovely lady called Rabiah Seminole. Rabiah said that no phone calls came into the Record Plant for John or Yoko that fateful night. It seems they both wanted to eat and they were apparently very happy together in their last hours.

Rabiah also revealed that she had a business breakfast scheduled for that morning of 8th December 1980 at the Dakota, with one of its other residents, record executive Steve Gottlieb. When they exited to head off to the Record Plant in the morning, Rabiah remembers a strange person (almost certainly Chapman) hanging around the entrance to the Dakota. Gottlieb told Rabiah that the stranger had been seen hanging around the Dakota entrance for the past two days. Which begs the questions: why didn't anyone move Chapman away or call the police? Why was this stranger tolerated for so long?

One positive aspect from the dreadful evening of 8th December 1980 was the fact that John signed an autograph for Rabiah, which she subsequently sold at auction, using the money to set up a horse rescue and retirement centre. This was the last autograph John Lennon ever gave.

In 2007, while on BBC's *Desert Island Discs*, Yoko Ono added a new slant to the "going to The Stage Deli story". Ono claimed: "I said, 'Shall we go and have dinner before we go home?' and John said, 'No, let's go home because I want to see Sean before he goes to sleep.'"

The Stage Deli is exactly halfway between the Record Plant and the Dakota and it is on the route between the two. It would have been very easy for the hungry Lennons to stop there and grab some food. They didn't.

Monday 8th December, 10.50pm – The Lennons' limousine pulled up outside the Dakota.

Mario Casciano, John's and May Pang's assistant, verified to me that the Dakota driveway was too narrow for most limousines to enter and leave easily. It was normal procedure for John and Yoko to get out of limousines (Yoko's favourite form of transport) or cabs (John's preferred mode of transport) on the sidewalk. They would then walk through the Dakota driveway and into the lobby doorway on the far right.

The identity of the limousine driver was not verified at the time. He simply disappeared from history. He may have been Bill Christian. NYPD Detective Hoffman doesn't specify. If it was Christian, it would be ironic that the epitome of the devil, as far as the southern protestant fundamentalists were concerned, was driven to his death by a *Christian*. If it wasn't so distressing, it might be deemed laughable.

Waiting for Ono and Lennon, standing outside the gates on the kerb to the left side of the entrance was Mark Chapman. Moments later, gun-fire rang out from within the Dakota driveway.

Recap

The diary dates of events in this chapter speak for themselves. What I want to know is, who pressed Mark Chapman's button in October? Why did his mission to kill spark into life? Look again at the people to whom we know he turned. Dana Reeves, at that point, a police officer, providing the bullets. Gloria Chapman who knew what Mark intended to do, but did nothing stop him. I will also challenge her statement about her not being involved with Mark's return to New York in a future chapter. The three days in Chicago represents a worrying black hole in our understanding of Mark's whereabouts. Parasites like Paul Goresh were motivated by personal gain and fortune certainly smiled on him. But can his testimony be trusted? How much is it worth? And the whole issue of the Lennons' change of mind about stopping at The Stage Deli begs the question, why? Was there a previous appointment secretly scheduled into their itinerary about which they knew nothing? Or, as Yoko claimed, did he simply want to see Sean?

CHAPTER 7 | Enter the NYPD

Key People at the Scene

NYPD	Dakota
Officer Stephen Spiro	José Perdomo (Doorman)
Officer Peter Cullen	Joseph Many (Elevator Operator)
Officer Tony Palma	Jay Hastings (Concierge)
Officer Herb Frauenberger	Victor Cruz (Dakota workman)
Officer Jimmy Moran	Joe Grezik (Dakota workman)
Officer John Elter	
Officer Richard Cronin	Mark Chapman
Chief of Detectives James T Sullivan	
Assistant DA Kim Hogrefe	

History records that the first two police officers attending the Dakota crime scene after John Lennon was assassinated were NYPD officers Stephen Spiro and Peter Cullen. Disturbingly, Officer Spiro told his partner earlier in the evening that he thought "something big" was going to happen that night. The same officer wrote three letters to Mark after his imprisonment. Why? How often does an arresting officer write to a criminal and involve himself in a discourse? Stephen Spiro's Nostradamus premonition caught the attention of Mark Chapman, who in reply to a letter from the officer stated:

> "Thank you for your letter. I never saw that Daily News article about you. Send me a copy if you like. When I heard about your comments on the fact that you KNEW 'Something big was going to happen on that night', was from YOU, on that night! You just don't remember it due to the tremendous events going on. The reason I asked you about this is that I am investigating many such 'unusual' occurrences surrounding the death of John Lennon. It is

incredible, Steve. I am labelling it a phenomenon although I am still not sure what to call it. Someday you will know all the facts and 'see' all of this and we can write of it then."

Look at the expressions Mark Chapman used. "Unusual occurrences", "phenomenal" and "incredible" even calling the assassination "the death of John Lennon" rather than "my killing John Lennon". What exactly did Spiro say in his original letter to Chapman? We don't know. There is no known copy. But regardless, the pertinent question remains, why was a police officer writing to a convicted murderer in prison and bragging to him about being published in a newspaper? Chapman's reply to Spiro also indicated that he clearly thought something "unusual" was happening when Lennon was murdered.

Spiro was a very busy man after December 8th, 1980. He made it his mission to befriend John Lennon's friends and associates. On one occasion, he took May Pang and her friend and former assistant, Mario Casciano, out to lunch. A lunch where Spiro deliberately spread misinformation. Spiro also kept in contact with people at the Roosevelt Hospital and, of course, he kept in contact with Chapman. For what reason?

Like many of those who knew Mark Chapman, Officer Spiro, in his former life, served in the US Navy from 1968 until 1973.

Let's get back to the night of John's assassination. Spiro and Cullen arrived at the Dakota somewhere between three and four minutes after John Lennon was shot. There are many characters in this section, but each has an important role to play.

(1) Statement: Officer Steve Spiro: (From unedited notes – 8th December 1980)

"Upon exiting the car, a male in the street is yelling pointing toward the driveway archway. He's pointing toward the left hand saying, 'He's the one that did the shooting!'"

This account differs from that of other witnesses. Spiro knew José Perdomo and, by most accounts, Perdomo was the person who identified Chapman as the shooter. Spiro doesn't mention Perdomo; he only says that a male in the street identified Chapman. The mysterious male whom Spiro mentioned has never been identified. Forget the notion of a nameless male in the street. Here was a key witness. A vital cog in the wheel. The man who, by Spiro's own words, could identify "the killer" and he was allowed to disappear.

Spiro continued:

"I draw my revolver pointing it towards the man in the shadows. As I point my gun at suspect, a male, white, starts to put his hands up towards the top of his head. 'Put your hands on the wall and don't move'. Suspect does as he is told. 'Please don't hurt me' says the suspect. Put the gun to the subjects back. I see two males to my left, I don't know who they are. I place my left arm around suspect's neck, using him as a shield. Turning towards my right, I see the doorman, another male and at least three bullet holes in the glass door. The Doorman who I've seen before while working, yells that the man I have is the only one involved. I put the suspect up against the wall. Suspect says 'I acted alone! Don't hurt me'. 'No one is going to hurt you'. I hear José the doorman yell 'He shot John Lennon'. I ask suspect, did you shoot John Lennon? No response. Pete Cullen yells 'Steve put cuffs on him'. As I get cuffs on the suspect he again says, 'Don't hurt me'. I see police officers Palma and Frauenberger carrying John Lennon face up, shoulder height high, blood on Lennon's face, towards RMP [radio motor patrol car] I yell to Pete, 'let's get this guy to the precinct right now'. I ask suspect if clothing on the ground are his, he says, 'Yes. The red book is mine too'. I pick them up. I now see PO Blake carrying a gun using a newspaper in order not to disturb any prints."

Spiro has often stated that the first thing Chapman said to him was "I acted alone". Writer Jack Jones then added years later that Chapman also apparently said "I'm the only one". Why would Chapman say this? It is as if his responses were programmed to make the police's job as easy as possible.

Spiro confirmed that only officers Palma and Frauenberger carried John's body out to a police car. This has been disputed by Dakota concierge, Jay Hastings.

Lift operator Joseph Many, who we will discuss later, had made sure that any prints on the alleged gun would be disturbed and the chain of custody on the gun was broken. Spiro continued:

> "I put suspect into RMP. I put his belongings in the front seat. On way to car, he says again 'Don't let anyone hurt me'. I yell to oncoming officers to set up a crime scene. I see PO Moran in RMP 2123 turn on lights and take Lennon in back seat to Roosevelt hospital. I inform hospital there's a RMP incoming with a shooting victim, John Lennon. In the car, I turn to suspect and ask, 'Do you know what you did?' No answer."

Steven Spiro and Peter Cullen got in their RMP with Mark Chapman and drove him to their 20th Precinct station. The following alleged exchange in the patrol car is revealing (if true):

Chapman: "I'm sorry, I didn't mean to give you a hard time and ruin your night."
Officer Cullen: "You're apologising to us? You know what you just did? You screwed up your whole life. What the hell is the matter with you?"
Chapman: "I didn't have anything against him. I don't know why I did it."
Officer Cullen: "Then what did you do it for?"
Chapman: "The big man inside of me is Holden Caulfield. The small part is the Devil. And tonight, the small part won."

Steve Spiro's written account is the most complete police report we have from the night of the Lennon murder. All other police recollections are either undisclosed, fragmented or collated through notes from journalists and subsequent books and TV documentaries.

The British journalist Fenton Bresler managed to get access to Spiro's report for his book *Who Killed John Lennon*. Bresler also managed to talk with Spiro in 1985 and the officer observed:

> "We could see he was rational, not listening to voices or anything like that. He was not a wacko. And he said much the same to the New York press immediately after the murder. Mark seems to have got crazier with the years."

A potential murderer was claiming that a small part of him was the Devil yet Officer Spiro "could see he was rational". At the most basic level, Chapman was claiming to be two people – the fictional Holden Caulfield and the Devil. Rational?

When Chapman arrived with Spiro and Cullen at the 20th Precinct station, he refused to speak to anyone without Spiro by his side. The officers did a strip search on Mark and found his driving licence, Visa credit card, the receipt for his gun from J & S Enterprises in Hawaii and $2,201 in cash. In today's money, this would equate to over $8,000. Why the unemployed Chapman was carrying such a large amount of cash has never been explained. Once the police had possession of Mark's Visa card, surely they could have found out precisely how much he had spent and on what? It was vital information in the highest profile assassination for years. A New York judge would have insisted. But apparently, it didn't happen.

The receipt for Chapman's gun was very convenient for the NYPD. Clearly the "cold and calculated" Chapman wasn't too bothered about covering his tracks regarding the purchase and ownership of his gun. This has distinct echoes of Lee Harvey

Oswald ordering the rifle with which he allegedly shot JFK. He had used a traceable mail order.

(2) Officer Peter Cullen

Over the subsequent years, Spiro's partner, Officer Peter Cullen, gave his account of what happened.

> "When we got to the Dakota, Spiro shifted the car into park. I noticed someone running from the building. But this wasn't a perp. This was an honest citizen, frightened by what he just witnessed. 'Officer be careful,' the man yelled, 'there's a guy in the alleyway there, shooting a gun.'"

What inspiringly observant officers. One could determine that Mark Chapman was rational while the second instantly knew he was being advised by an honest citizen. Cullen confirmed Spiro's recollection that a mysterious man was seen running from the Dakota building when they arrived. The key question is – how did the mysterious, running "honest citizen" know the "guy in the alleyway" was shooting a gun? By the time Spiro and Cullen arrived, the shooting had ceased for at least four minutes and the lift operator, Joseph Many, had apparently taken the gun away. What did this man see and who was he? Could this have been a second shooter? Disgracefully, the NYPD never bothered to find out.

Cullen continued:

> "Everyone's frozen standing there. We don't see anyone on the floor. We don't see signs of anything. I see a fella with a shirt and tie on [presumably Chapman] and I see José the doorman, the only guy I knew. 'José what's going on?' I ask. José pointed and said, 'He shot John Lennon'. The Conservative guy, appeared to be embroiled in some type of disagreement with a Hispanic man in dirty clothes. The Hispanic guy was agitated, speaking

in some hybrid of Spanish and English. I pointed my gun at the man. 'No', José corrected, 'not him, that's our handyman', he [José], gestured at Chapman, 'him'. 'Where's Lennon?' I asked José, 'The bullets pushed him through the door' José said. He [Perdomo] motioned at the security station, 'Over there' he then added, 'that's the father of a five-year-old kid'."

Joseph Many was clearly billed as the elevator operator in his witness statement. Many was of Irish descent and did not look Hispanic. The same goes for Jay Hastings. Neither Many or Hastings spoke Spanish. Joe Many did have two co-workers, Victor Cruz and Joe Grezik, who went with him to get the gun and followed Many after he hid the gun. The Hispanic man whom Cullen described arguing with Chapman was almost certainly Victor Cruz.

Cullen went into the lobby and observed Lennon "face down" on a rug, bleeding from the mouth. Lennon wasn't moving. Cullen then returned to the driveway and confirmed to his partner that there was a shooting and told him that he needed to handcuff Chapman. By all accounts, this is what Spiro did. Asked who was in the driveway when he first arrived at the Dakota, Cullen confirmed that the doorman José Perdomo was there with a couple of witnesses who were, presumably, Dakota staff. Cullen did not say who the witnesses were but it was likely Grezik and Cruz. Cullen also stated that Yoko was in the driveway when he first arrived on the scene. This does not equate with Ono's statement and that of other witnesses regarding her immediate reactions – i.e., that she followed her husband into the Dakota.

(3) Officer Tony Palma and (4) Officer Herb Frauenberger

Officers Tony Palma and Herb Frauenberger then arrived at the Dakota crime scene. They both heard on their radio that shots had been fired at 72nd Street and Central Park West. There was very little traffic and the officers arrived at the Dakota within a few minutes. As they arrived, Officers Spiro and Cullen were dealing with Chapman. Someone, presumably Perdomo, shouted that a man had been shot in the "back of the building". The unidentified man was pointing towards the vestibule.

Guns drawn, Palma and Frauenberger then entered inside the building and went into the concierge's office area. The officers both agreed that the stricken man looked terrible but was apparently still alive. Frauenberger claimed that John had a pulse, but it was faint. This is disputed by all medical staff who treated John. They all claim that Lennon must have died almost immediately after being shot. If Palma and Frauenberger arrived a couple of minutes after the shots, John must surely have already been dead. Yet the myth was set that John was still breathing.

Officer Palma, apparently a Lennon fan, suddenly realised that his hero was dying or dead in front of him. "I turned him over, red is all I saw," he said. He turned to his colleague and added "the guy is dying, let's get him out of here".

Officer Palma confirmed to me that Lennon was lying face down when they discovered his body. Officer Frauenberger also told me that when they first came across John, he was lying face down, with his arms outstretched like a child who had fallen flat on their face. Surely it is basic medical common sense to turn a dying person onto their side when they have been shot and breathing may be difficult. Why was Lennon left to die on his front?

Officer Palma told me that he didn't know who the dying man was until somebody in the Dakota office told him and Frauenberger that it was John Lennon. Jay Hastings, the Dakota concierge, has confirmed to me that he thinks it was him who informed them.

Palma and Frauenberger, hearing that an ambulance was eight minutes away, then made the decision to take Lennon to hospital right away instead of waiting for the ambulance. Palma grabbed Lennon's head and arms and Frauenberger grabbed his legs and they carried him out of the building and towards the gathering patrol cars on the sidewalk. Today, this breach of protocol would possibly result in suspension or worse for a New York cop. In 1980, regulations in these matters were less clear-cut. Later, Cullen would remark, "You had a life to save here. Without an ambulance there, what are you going to do – stand over him and start praying."

Speaking to me in early 2022, officer Frauenberger did not mention that either Concierge Jay Hastings or Yoko Ono were present when he came across John's mortally wounded body. Hastings initially said that he put his jacket over Lennon and took his glasses off before running off to ring for help, so perhaps Hastings was off somewhere, running for help. Frauenberger alleges that neither Hastings nor Ono were present when the two officers first encountered John's shattered body – so if this is true, where exactly was Yoko? Why would she leave her dying husband? It's worth considering that if either Ono or Hastings were with the dying Lennon, neither Frauenberger or Palma would have had to wonder who the dying man was.

In March 2022, when I spoke to Officer Tony Palma, he contradicted his partner by stating that he saw a woman "straddling" her husband when they first found Lennon's body. He then said he brushed her aside and started examining Lennon. Palma said he did not know who Ono was until they arrived with her at the Roosevelt Hospital. Over the years, Palmer has often said that he was a John Lennon fan. It is hard to believe he did not recognise Yoko Ono at the Dakota murder scene or when she rode in his car to the hospital. Palma told me that when he walked out with Frauenberger carrying John's body, he swore at Mark Chapman, who was sitting handcuffed in another car, as he passed him.

Frauenberger told me that he and Palma carried Lennon out "like a sack of potatoes" to the police cars outside. Palma grabbed his arms and Frauenberger grabbed his legs. Their plan was to put Lennon in their squad car and drive him to hospital, but when they got outside their car was pinned in. Fortunately, another police car had just pulled up, driven by Officer James (Jimmy) Moran.

(5) Jimmy Moran

Frauenberger told Moran to take the stricken Lennon to Roosevelt Hospital as quick as he could. They laid Lennon face down on Moran's back seat and with lights glowing red and blue, he sped off. Officer Moran has said that he exchanged a few brief words with the dying Lennon in the back of his car, with Lennon affirming his name. Considering the condition of Lennon and the testimony of the medical people who saw his wounds and the people who saw his condition before being placed in Moran's car, it is highly unlikely this occurred. Another Lennon assassination lie was enshrined as a fact.

Jay Hastings was adamant that he had helped the two police officers carry John Lennon's body out to a police car. Dakota workers and staff who worked in the building have all stated that John Lennon was borne away only by police officers. Palma confirmed that Jay Hastings did not help either himself or Officer Frauenberger carry John's body out to the police car. He also told me that when they put Lennon into the back of Officer Moran's police car, there were no bystanders that he can recall at the scene. If true, this puts into doubt some witness statements from members of the public. Secondary statements that were lapped up by the media at the time. They were desperate for copy. Mark Chapman, speaking to broadcaster Barbara Walters in 1992, said he vividly recalled two police officers carrying Lennon's body out to a police car, while he was in a police car waiting to be taken to the police station. Chapman said the officer who was carrying John's head and arms swore at him profusely. Tony Palma confirmed to me that this was him. Chapman did not say anyone else was carrying Lennon's body out to the car. All the evidence points to Hastings lying about doing this. The pertinent question is why did he feel the need to lie about this?

Some reports said that Lennon was put into a police car that was blocked in by other police cars and could not get out before being transferred into another police car and being driven to hospital. Frauenberger didn't go that far, but he hinted to me that this might have happened. I don't believe it did. It was a stressful time but Frauenberger and Palma surely wouldn't have placed Lennon in a police car that they would have seen was blocked in. Frauenberger also confirmed to me that Jay Hastings didn't help them carry John Lennon out to the police car.

Though Officer Palma contradicted Frauenberger's claims of Yoko Ono's absence, Officer Frauenberger was adamant that he thought Ono was not beside Lennon's body when they found him dying on the Dakota office floor. Frauenberger also said Ono was absent when they were assessing John's condition and when they carried his body out to the street. He only saw her when Moran's car sped off to towards the hospital.

I put the "absent Ono" anomaly to Jay Hastings and he told me that she might have moved over to the side of the wall and out of the way by the time the two cops arrived on the scene.

Officers Frauenberger and Palma drove Yoko Ono to the Roosevelt Hospital. She seemed to be in total shock and said very little to them in the car. Officer Palma told me that he and Ono were first directed to the general-public waiting area of the hospital. A few moments later, Yoko was given a private waiting room. Palma said that in the thirty minutes or so he spent with her, there was an awkward silence between them both. Not unreasonably, he put this down to shock. When Palma did ask Ono what had happened, she seemed "unsure and confused". Yoko's varying statements that night and in the subsequent days to follow would bear this out.

(6) Officer John Elter and (7) Officer Richard Cronin

In December 2022, some forty-two years later, the names of two new police offices emerged as potential candidates for being first on the scene at the Dakota. Officers John Elter and Richard Cronin were working for the NYPD's Emergency Services Unit on 8th December 1980. Elter died in May 2020, but at his funeral Cronin told Elter's grandson the details:

"We heard the call over the air that said 'shots fired'. We happened to be a block away, block and a half away, and we went to back up the unit that got the call, which we usually did. There was a body, and we didn't realise it was John Lennon at the time. We looked at the scene, and there was nobody else around."

If true, this all begs the question – where was Yoko Ono and Concierge Jay Hastings? Cronin continued:

"They wanted us to do the search for anything we could find that could help identify whoever shot him. We did the job. When a cop needed help, he called us."

Another source has confirmed to me that NYPD emergency officers (police officers who were specially drafted in to help in "emergencies") were tasked to look for bullets at the Dakota crime scene. Officer Elter can be seen with a torch at the Dakota in a famous Associated Press photograph of detectives and police officers inspecting the Dakota driveway around the vestibule doors.

Though rarely mentioned, non-forensic officers standing in a crime scene were actually destroying evidence. UK police procedure requires that "a common approach path" is established at a crime scene. This is the least likely route taken by an assailant to ensure a crime scene is not contaminated before forensic officers arrive. Clearly, in December 1980 at the Dakota, this important procedure was not followed.

Officer Stephen Spiro died in 2013. Before he died, he sought to sell the letters Mark Chapman sent to him from prison for a fixed price of $75,000. It was never revealed how much Spiro eventually got for the letters. Clearly, befriending Mark Chapman was a highly profitable move for Officer Spiro.

Officer Cronin has not responded to my requests for an interview. If it were to be established that he and Officer Elter were first on the scene at the Dakota, this would put the integrity of Officers Spiro and Cullen's testimony into great doubt.

Speaking a few days later, Chief of Detectives James T Sullivan gave the official police statement to the press:

> "The Lennons returned to the Dakota at about 10:50 pm, alighting from their limousine on the 72nd Street curb although the car could have driven through the entrance and into the courtyard. Three witnesses – a doorman at the entrance, an elevator operator and a cab driver who had just dropped off a passenger – saw Mr. Chapman standing in the shadows just under the arch. As the couple walked by, Mr. Chapman called, 'Mr. Lennon'. Then the assailant dropped into a combat stance and emptied his pistol at the singer. According to the autopsy, four shots struck Mr. Lennon, two in the left side of his back and two in his left shoulder. All four caused internal damage and bleeding. According to the police, Mr. Lennon staggered up six steps to the room at the end of the entrance used by the concierge, said 'I'm shot' then fell face down."

In the early hours of 9th December 1980, the NYPD top brass held a press briefing at which many perceptive questions were posed. It is riddled with inaccuracies. Sullivan appeared to be in a big hurry to promote the official narrative to the media. In so much of a hurry, in fact, he forgot that a few hours earlier whilst speaking to WNEW-FM outside the Dakota (just a couple of hours after John Lennon was assassinated), he had confirmed that Lennon went into a vestibule and as he was walking though the vestibule, an individual fired five shots and Lennon was struck. What came next was a game-changer. The New York Police Department had radically altered their story. Why?

At three o'clock in the morning, well past the deadline for the morning newspapers papers, a large group of journalists were taken to the basement of the 20th Precinct police station. John Lennon had been declared dead for barely three hours. Chief of Detectives Sullivan began by giving the routine facts. Mark Chapman had been arrested and charged with homicide. He was a resident of Hawaii and visited the Dakota buildings on Saturday, Sunday and Monday afternoon. The non-controversial facts were laid out as explanation. According to Sullivan, the Lennons walked into the archway area of the Dakota at the front and turned into the vestibule which has a glass doorway. Chapman came up behind John Lennon and "emptied" a .38 calibre gun into him. John Lennon went up six steps, into the guards' area and collapsed in an office space at the rear of that area. (Really? John could still walk?) He was taken to the Roosevelt Hospital. The responding officers were Officers Stephen Spiro and Peter Cullen. They apprehended Chapman and made an arrest. He was standing there waiting. When he dropped the gun, it was kicked away by one of the doormen so the elevator man, (he did not use Many's name) took it away to keep it safe. Journalists fired question after question at the Chief Detective. Below I have itemised a selection:

Press: "How did he behave? Did he behave rationally?
Sullivan: He behaved very calmly.
Press: "Has he made a full confession?"
Sullivan: I can't go into that.
Press: "Was he represented by an attorney upstairs?"
Sullivan: "He was questioned by the District Attorney " (Not an answer)
Repeat question: "Was he represented by an attorney?"
Sullivan: "He was given his rights? Of course he was."

And again: "Was he represented by an attorney?"(the persistence did not abate.)

And again: "So he was not represented by an attorney."

Sullivan: "I don't think so." (At last. Mark Chapman was not represented. Is this not contrary to his civil rights?)

A change of tack:

Press: "How many shots were fired?"

Sullivan: "The gun was empty. Five shots"

Press: "Who told you he went into a combat stance?"

Sullivan: "Did I say that?" (He knew he had said so previously)

The whole room: "Yes!" (He knew he couldn't deny the fact in front of this "mob".)

Sullivan: "Well it must have been one of the doormen."

He corrected a journalist to say "He [John] was not in the doorway."

Press: "Had he been in psychiatric care?"

Sullivan: "I can't talk about that."

The New York District Attorney's office surprised everyone by choosing a young assistant district attorney to head up the New York State's prosecution of Mark Chapman. Like Chapman's main defence lawyer, Jonathan Marks (more on whom later), the man chosen to legally represent the State of New York, Manhattan Division, was clearly too inexperienced to do the job properly. Assistant district attorney Kim Hogrefe had only 3 years' experience as an assistant trial lawyer for the DA's office when he unexpectedly received a telephone call from a senior police officer late in the evening of 8th December 1980. At that time, Hogrefe was on what was termed a "Homicide Shift" for the DA's office. This meant he was the first port of call for any homicides that happened in Manhattan on that particular night. Hogrefe was required to authorise the arrest and prosecution of any homicides that occurred on his shift.

The caller told Hogrefe that John Lennon had been shot and taken to the Roosevelt Hospital. Hogrefe was asked to talk to the Lead Detective on the case, Ron Hoffman, at the 20th Precinct station. Hoffman told me that he became good friends with Hogrefe on the Lennon assignment. The fact that both men investigated the case together was a clear conflict of interests. How could Detective Hoffman remain impartial in his investigation, with the prosecuting district attorney always by his side? In the early hours of 9th December 1980, Hoffman told Hogrefe that a man had been arrested and charged with Lennon's murder and that the defendant had made a statement. Hogrefe quickly discovered that the high-profile case was, understandably, being assigned to the chief prosecutor in the Manhattan DA's office, Allen Sullivan. Hogrefe must have thought his involvement in one of the crimes of the century was over, as it should have been for an inexperienced trial lawyer in his early twenties. Allen Sullivan had other ideas and offered to work together with Hogrefe on the case. Sullivan wanted to stay in the background and he decided that young Hogrefe would be the media representative for the prosecution. Sullivan was still the senior prosecutor, but from a media perspective he deliberately stayed in the background. Hogrefe did the opposite. Like many others keen for the limelight, he made it his mission to be featured in every documentary which was produced thereafter. He relished telling the world that Chapman was an evil narcissist who killed John Lennon for fame. So narcissistic, in fact, he left a display about himself in his hotel room. Chapman, he claimed, was also so evil he used hollow bullets to kill Lennon when he shot him four times in the back.

Hogrefe was selective about the information he regularly gave for over 40 years. He failed to mention the 122 unidentified pills found in Chapman's hotel room. He failed to tell the world about the non-hollow bullet found in John Lennon's body. And finally, he also failed to tell the world about contrary medical testimony from the Roosevelt Hospital. Understandably, Hogrefe never again mentioned that he had identified a wrong Mark Chapman, who had multiple felonies, when Mark first appeared in court on 9th December. Hogrefe was out of his depth. A state of affairs that I believe was engineered to ensure he would be compliant and sufficiently ambitious to look no further than the areas he was instructed to. Years later, Assistant DA Hogrefe claimed that he never interviewed Chapman in the early hours of 9th December 1980 at the 20th Precinct. His reasoning was that he couldn't legally interview the defendant because Chapman had asked for a lawyer after his wife had called into the station. However, Sullivan revealed to the press briefing on 9th December that Hogrefe *had* questioned Chapman that night (thereby breaking protocol). Hogrefe was covering his own back.

When, at the 9th of December press briefing, the questions turned to the bullet numbers, Sullivan was evasive and the press didn't like it, but it was barely four hours after the assassination. He claimed that there were seven wounds (which could be possible since these might include entries and exits). Sullivan was relaying the information that Dr Lynn at the Roosevelt Hospital had given the press, a few hours earlier, about John's "seven wounds".

Everyone, and I mean everyone, was being rushed into a version of events which suited the NYPD and the government. The official narrative was being sown at warp speed.

On 8th December 1980, the 20th Precinct police station in New York was recovering from a gruelling case earlier that year called the "Metropolitan Opera House Murder". Christmas was looming and the last thing the station wanted was another high-profile case. When Mark Chapman was apprehended at the Lennon murder scene and apparently confessed, the crime became a "grounded case" in most officers' eyes. This was a blessed relief for many officers eyeing their much-needed Christmas break in a couple of weeks. To counter this narrative somewhat, Detective Hoffman insisted that they were determined not to allow a "Jack Ruby" situation to happen, with Chapman being assassinated in their custody. They were aware of how the Dallas police were criticised after the JFK assassination and they were determined not to have the same level of criticism thrown at them. Lead Detective Ron Hoffman stated unequivocally, "We knew that when this case went to trial, no matter what happened, we were gonna be criticised for years, for generations to come. We did our best. There was nothing too insignificant to go into." After numerous discussions with Detective Hoffman and being allowed to see his case notebook and documents, I can categorically confirm that there were numerous areas that the NYPD did not go into.

The following timeline includes some of Mark Chapman's recollections of what happened before and after he was convicted:

11.30pm, 8th December 1980 – Officers Spiro and Cullen drove a fully compliant and docile Mark Chapman back to the 20th Precinct police station

According to Cullen, Officer Spiro was very excited, exclaiming, "I told you, I felt it. I told you something big was going to happen tonight, this is History." It was almost as if Officer Spiro had forewarning that John Lennon was going to be shot.

11.40pm, 8th December 1980 – Chapman arrived at the 20th Precinct station. He is quickly bundled into a holding cell.

12.00am, 9th December 1980 – Chapman is strip-searched by Officer Spiro. Just after midnight local time, the NYPD officially had Mark Chapman's name. It would not be leaked to the press for another three hours.

12.20am, 9th December 1980 – Mark Chapman gave a full statement to the NYPD. A high-ranking detective, Peter Mangicavallo, wrote down Chapman's words for him. In my opinion, this is the most important and truthful statement that Mark Chapman ever made. It has been misquoted and embellished over the years, but I have now accessed this document and I can reveal the original written statement.

This is exactly what Chapman said:

> "I never wanted to hurt anybody, my friends will tell you that. I have two parts in me. The big part is very kind, the children I worked with will tell you that. I have the small part in me that cannot understand the world and what goes on in it.

> I did not want to kill anybody and I really don't know why I did it. I fought against the small part for a long time. But for a few seconds, the small part won. I asked God to help me but we are responsible for our own actions."

We have been told multiple times that Mark Chapman shot John Lennon to make himself famous. If this was the case, why didn't Chapman just say so when he made his initial statement? Why the evasion? Why the confusion?

He continued:

> "I have nothing against John Lennon or anything he has done in the way of music or personal beliefs. I came to New York about five weeks ago from Hawaii and the big part of me did not want me to shoot John. I went back to Hawaii and tried to get rid of my small part, but I couldn't."

There is no mention of killing Lennon for being "phoney". *The Catcher in the Rye* trigger to murder had not yet been fixed in Chapman's mind in the early hours after Lennon's murder. It would soon surface when other "experts" were permitted to interfere. Some interested parties have commented that Chapman killed Lennon to "become him" or to "acquire his fame". It has been suggested that Chapman was jealous of John Lennon's success. None of these claims hold weight or stack up against Chapman's possible motive, immediately after his arrest. If Chapman had a grudge against Lennon, why didn't he declare it, there and then?

The one item which Chapman tried to rid himself of when he went back to Hawaii in November 1980 was his copy of *The Catcher in Rye*. He clearly saw it as a device that provoked his "mission" to kill John Lennon.

He continued:

> "I then returned to New York on Friday 5th December 1980. I checked into the YMCA on 62nd street, I stayed one night. Then I went to the Sheraton Center 7th Avenue. Then this morning I went to the bookstore and bought The Catcher in The Rye. I'm sure the large part of me is Holden Caulfield who is the main person in the book. The small part of me must be the devil. I went to the building, it's called the Dakota. I stayed there until he came out and asked him to sign my album. At that point, my big part won and I wanted to go back to my hotel, but I couldn't. I waited until he came back. He came in a car. Yoko past first and I said hello. I didn't want to hurt her. Then John came, looked at me and printed me. I took the gun from my coat pocket and fired at him. I can't believe I could do that."

The phrase "printed me" has often been mistaken for "past me". Printed is a bizarre word to use and it can only logically mean "stared at me".

> "I just stood there clutching the book. I didn't want to run away. I don't know what happened to the gun. I just remember José kicking it away. José was crying and telling me to please leave. I felt so sorry for José. Then the police came and told me to put my hands on the wall and cuffed me."

It has often been reported that Chapman dropped a gun or that the doorman, José Perdomo, shook it out of his hand. Ninety minutes after Lennon was assassinated, Chapman has no clear idea about what happened to "his" gun. The gun that he saw being kicked by Perdomo could not definitively be connected to Chapman. It is incredibly strange that after he allegedly shot John Lennon, all Chapman recalled was holding *The Catcher* book. Is this possibly all he had in his hand, and he imagined he was shooting John Lennon through a "hallucination command"? Years later in 1992, Chapman would unconvincingly declare on TV that Perdomo shook his gun out of his right hand.

Chapman later revealed that he didn't recall pulling the hammer or aiming his gun. He also was amazed that the bullets were working and that immediately after he allegedly shot Lennon four times in the back, John just wasn't there. How can a man you are shooting four times in the back just not be there? Surely if you shoot someone four times, you would remember holding and aiming the gun and you would remember the person being there when you did this? You should also recall what the person was doing while you were shooting them four times in the back. Mark Chapman had no idea.

Does all this strike you as the recollections of a cold and calculated killer who ninety minutes earlier had expertly shot John Lennon four times in what would later be described as a "tight professional grouping" above his heart?

Police Lieutenant Arthur O'Connor had his own thoughts on the matter. The chief of 20th Precinct, O'Connor, had plenty of time to assess the Lennon murder suspect. O'Connor was also the first person to interrogate Chapman. O'Connor's comments on Chapman and the case are invaluable. Speaking to writer Fenton Bresler in 1988, he noted:

"The case was a grounder. In any kind of criminal investigation, a case is considered 'grounded' when a case is solved. This case was solved with the arrest of Mark Chapman. He remained on the scene voluntarily. He was not physically restrained. Nearby was an entrance to the subway on 72nd street. Had he so wished, he could have gotten clean away. He had a 75 per cent chance in my book of a clean escape. But he wanted to get caught. Now, had he run off, there would have been one hell of an investigation! As it was, there was no extensive investigation, there did not have to be. We had our man!"

O'Conner was absolutely frank. Why Investigate a possible conspiracy? Whatever for? Nobody cared to pursue the line. When a case is grounded, it's grounded – and this one was from the start. Mark acknowledged his guilt that first night at the precinct. What more was there to do? You don't go looking for a conspiracy. O'Conner stated, "I had no information about one – and I did not look for it. Look! I had only 20 detectives in my precinct for an area in which a million people lived. We did not test him for drugs, it was not normal procedure."

It should be said that had the 122 unidentified pills in Chapman's hotel room been made public it may have given O'Connor and the NYPD a very interesting result. Had they tested Chapman for drugs, it might have been a different story.

But the hounds were already at the door. The news had leaked. Bad news always does.

As Police Lieutenant Arthur O'Connor said:

"I had never seen anything like it, not even in the met case and that was big enough. I never saw the amount of international interest in a case that I saw then. Within two hours of the murder, there were literally 150 press reporters at the station-house. It was like we were under siege.

I saw him [Chapman] within half an hour of his arrest. I was the first one to interrogate him. He was in a daze. He was composed, yet not there. He gave me the impression he had done something, it was something he had to do and he'd done it. But he was very uncommunicative. He wouldn't speak, talk. I had to use different things to get to him.

Finally, I got to the family and that worked. Until then he would not vocalise, he would not speak – at least, not to me. But I said, 'Are you married?'. I got an acknowledgment. So, I said, 'You know your wife's going to be pretty upset about this?' and his answer was: 'I had to'. That was about the only statement: 'I had to do it.'"

Lieutenant O'Connor gave a clear indication that perhaps the real reason why the public had never seen the investigation details or a crime scene report is because they never took place.

As for Mark Chapman's first recorded statement? This gives me a clear indication that he had no idea why he apparently killed John Lennon. He also had no idea how he did it. These are not the words of a cold and calculated killer and they are not the words of someone who killed a celebrity to become famous. If a hypnotised Manchurian Candidate was asked to give a statement about a crime he believed he had committed but had not, I'm convinced this is exactly the kind of statement he would have given.

Remember that a Hawaiian detective, Captain Louis Souza, was tasked to make local enquiries for the New York Police. He was told to investigate only "background information" on Chapman. Gloria Chapman refused to see him because she was "too upset". The NYPD surprisingly did not want Souza to press Gloria. Souza was astonished at this, saying, "To my mind this is amazing. She could have given vital first-hand information, not only as to Mark's state of mind in the days and weeks before the killing, but also his associates and the actual mechanics of his getting to the mainland – and the finance for it". Yes, indeed she could.

When Souza asked the Castle Memorial Hospital to reveal their Mark Chapman account details to him, they refused on the "basis of confidentiality".

At the start of his court hearings, six months after his arrest, Chapman gave some insight into what happened that fateful night:

> "I fired five shots and hit John Lennon with four of them. I was standing twenty feet away from Lennon when I fired the shots. He was approaching the door that would lead up to the security area. I never spoke a word to Mr Lennon."

Remember that – "I never spoke a word to Mr Lennon."

In 1988, some seven years on, the following was broadcast by British TV producer Kevin Sim from Jim Gaines' audio tapes: Chapman said:

> "There was no emotion, there was no anger, there was nothing, dead silence in the brain, dead cold quiet. He walked up, he looked at me. I tell you the man was going to be dead in less than five minutes and he looked at me, I looked at him. He walked past me and then I heard in my head – Do It, Do It, Do It, over and over again, saying Do It, Do It Do It, like that. I pulled the gun out of my pocket, I handed over to my left hand, I don't remember aiming, I must have done, but I don't remember drawing the bead or whatever you call it. And I just pulled the trigger steady five times."

In 1992, Mark Chapman gave further insight into the murder to the mysterious journalist, Jack Jones, for his Chapman book, *Let Me Take You Down*:

> "I aimed at his back. I pulled the trigger five times. It was like everything had been stripped away. It wasn't a make-believe world any more. The movie strip broke. I took the *Catcher in the*

Rye book out and started reading it. I took my coat off to make sure the police knew I wasn't hiding a gun inside my coat. I was anxious, I was pacing. I tried to read the book, but the words were crawling all over the pages. Nothing made any sense. I just wanted the police to come and take me away from there."

Does this sound like the words of a clear-headed individual? Why oh why was everything rushed? Why were proper procedures not followed? Mark was arrested and interviewed without an attorney. He clearly had problems. So many questions were unasked because people in high places did not want his answers. So little investigation took place. But worse, much worse, was to come.

Recap

Right from the start this killing was treated differently. Procedure was casually discarded. It stinks. Officer Spiro claimed that he could see Mark was rational when he arrested him. I have no idea how many killers Spiro arrested in his lifetime – but I'll wager not one of them stood still awaiting arrest. Would you call it rational to commit a crime and wait patiently for the law to arrive? The rational killer would have taken to his heels and disappeared into the New York night. Indeed, Officer Spiro's action was more irrational that Mark's. Spiro treated him with kindness, took him to the precinct, sat with him like a proverbial wet nurse and developed a pen-pal relationship with the convicted killer. "Nothing made sense," Mark had said. How right he was.

One thing is also now crystal clear and deeply disturbing. Three police officers all stated that they found John Lennon bleeding out in the back office, face down on a rug. If Jay Hastings and Yoko Ono were tending to John, why did they leave him face down by the time the police arrived?

CHAPTER 8 | Gloria Chapman and her Time Machine

Key People

Mark Chapman
Gloria Chapman

Lt. Arthur O'Connor (20th Precinct)
Officer Stephen Spiro (20th Precinct)
Kim Hogrefe (Assistant DA)
Jim Gaines (journalist)
Fenton Bresler (writer)

2.55am, 9th December 1980

In the early hours of Tuesday 9th December, and just under four hours after John Lennon's assassination, the phone rang in the NYPD 20th Precinct station house with a call from Honolulu for Mark Chapman, the man who had been arrested four hours earlier for John Lennon's murder. The time was roughly 2.55am.

Head of the NYPD station, Lieutenant Arthur O'Connor, explained the call:

> "It was the detained man's wife [Gloria Chapman] on the line. At first I thought, hey, what's all this about? How did she know he was here, and at this time of night? I thought for the only time, it might be a conspiracy."

Officer Spiro took the call from Gloria Chapman. He made some notes, some of which he underlined:

> "Chapman's calm rational thinking amazes me under the circumstances."

"Chapman asks his wife if she is OK. Tells her not to talk to the press. Don't open the door. Call the police to protect you. (Wife says something about Mark's mother.) Mark tells wife to call a doctor for her. Mark tells wife maybe she should call a lawyer, that they had once used for guidance. Towards end of conversation, Mark gets teary eyed, fights them back. He says he still loves her. Phone call ends. Go back into interview room – silence. He says he was praying."

The Gloria Chapman phone call was broadcast for the first time in a Lennon murder TV documentary. The full transcript as used and broadcast is below. It is very revealing.

NEW YORK CITY: Yes, Twentieth Detective Squad, Detective Hoffmann speaking. Who am I speaking to, please?
GLORIA: Mrs. Chapman. [Choking, she clears her throat.] Excuse me.
NEW YORK CITY: Mrs. Chapman?
GLORIA: Yes. I'm his wife.
NEW YORK CITY: You're whose wife?
GLORIA: Mark Chapman's wife.
NEW YORK CITY: Mark Chapman's wife? Yeah, may I ask you how you found out about this, Ma'am?
GLORIA: A reporter from the Advertiser here called me.
NEW YORK CITY: From the Advertiser?
GLORIA: Yes, I don't know how he found out, but he found out way ahead of everybody.
NEW YORK CITY: What's the Advertiser?
GLORIA: Uh, it's one of the two major newspapers here in Honolulu.
NEW YORK CITY: Okay, a reporter called you and told you.
GLORIA: Yeah.

Mark Chapman on a call to his wife Gloria at the Police station. Note the time – 02.59 © NYPD

So, a reporter from Hawaii found out that Mark Chapman was John Lennon's alleged assassin and that he had a wife in Hawaii, way ahead of the baying pack outside the 20th Precinct. Really? How did that happen? Gloria does not say how the alleged reporter knew in which police station Mark Chapman was being held and what its contact details and call protocols were.

When Gloria made this phone call, the NYPD had only been able to verify Mark Chapman's name for just under three hours and it had not yet been made officially public. Chapman's name was given to the press at roughly 3am; Gloria called the NYPD station at just before 3am. We are being asked to believe that in a pre-internet age, sometime just before 3am, Gloria had been contacted twice – firstly, by the telephone company and then by an unnamed reporter who gave her information about her husband's arrest. Mark Chapman's name and Hawaii address were detailed at the 3am press briefing in the 20th Precinct base-ment by Chief Detective Sullivan. This then allegedly made its way to the *Honolulu Advertiser* in Hawaii, who figured out how to find Mark Chapman's wife. They then found Gloria's con-tact details through the telephone company and they called her, directly. Somehow, they knew which New York police station Gloria needed to contact in order to speak to her husband, and what number was best to use. Gloria must have climbed into a time-machine and used it to go back to 2.55am, when she then called her husband.

NEW YORK CITY: Okay, What could I do for you, Ma'am?

GLORIA: Well, is there any way I could speak to my husband?

NEW YORK CITY: Okay, we'll see if we can find out. Okay.

GLORIA: Okay, thank you.

NEW YORK CITY: Okay, hold on a second please.

GLORIA: Thank you.

NEW YORK CITY: Okay, well, uh, one second, Ma'am.

GLORIA: Thank you. [Long pause and click.]

NEW YORK CITY: Hello, Gloria?

GLORIA: [Breathlessly] Yes!

NEW YORK CITY: Yeah, this is Police Officer Spiro in New York. I'm here with your husband.

GLORIA: Yes! Is he all right?

NEW YORK CITY: He just wanted me to get you on the phone first and tell you that he's all right. And that he's, uh, that I'm here with him, and that I'm, uh, I'm more or less taking care of him, making sure that everything's all right. He's gonna talk to you now, okay?

GLORIA: Okay, umm, please.

NEW YORK CITY: You want to ask me anything?

GLORIA: Well, I just don't want somebody to, to hurt him.

NEW YORK CITY: NO, nobody's going to hurt him. I told him that. I will be with him, and there'll be nothing the matter with him. Okay? I promise you that.

GLORIA: Thank you.

NEW YORK CITY: All right. You're quite welcome.

MARK CHAPMAN: Hi.

GLORIA: Hi, Mark. I love you.

MARK: I know. I love you too.

GLORIA: Oh. [She starts to cry]

MARK CHAPMAN: Are the police with you?

GLORIA: NO! The first call I got was a reporter. Well, he didn't call me directly. But the phone company called me.

MARK CHAPMAN: Oh no! Are the police with you now?

GLORIA: NO, the police don't care.

Two points to consider here. Firstly, why was the arresting officer promising to take care of Mark, saying explicitly that everything would be alright, that he'd be with him and promising that nobody's going to hurt him. It's a conversation more akin to an emergency care nurse trying to reassure a mother that her child would be fine; that she would stay with him, that no harm would come to him. Had the NYPD taken a special course in prisoner care? It really doesn't add up. The NYPD is not overfull with caring hearts. Secondly, Mark's reaction to the news that it wasn't a reporter who first called is problematic. It was the phone company. That concerned him more than the caller being a journalist. What was he concerned about? Was a plan falling apart?

MARK CHAPMAN: Are you at home?

GLORIA: Yeah. Your mom and Greta [Mom's friend] are here and Jean [wife's sister] is gonna
stay with me tonight.

MARK CHAPMAN: Okay. Well, I don't want to talk to anybody else.

GLORIA: I know.

MARK CHAPMAN: But I don't want you crying 'cause they can hear me.

GLORIA: Okay.

MARK CHAPMAN: Why aren't the police there?

GLORIA: I don't know. UPI's been trying to get me.

MARK CHAPMAN: Don't answer the phone.

GLORIA: The operator called back. She says, "You don't want any more calls." She says, "I just feel like these are all newspapers."

MARK CHAPMAN: Yeah, please. You didn't say anything did you?

GLORIA: Well, I might have said too much to the first guy since you weren't here. But, you know, Mark.

MARK CHAPMAN: Call. Get the police over there.

GLORIA: Why?

MARK CHAPMAN: Please.

GLORIA: What can, uh.

MARK CHAPMAN: Call them.

GLORIA: Just what would—would I tell them?

MARK CHAPMAN: Just that you want them to come over. To keep the press off of you.

GLORIA: Oh, they're not harming me. They're not it, you know.

MARK CHAPMAN: Are they knocking on the door?

GLORIA: No. No one is.

MARK CHAPMAN: Well, they're gonna do that and I want to protect you from that.

GLORIA: Yeah, but you don't want me to go there then?

MARK CHAPMAN: Go where?

GLORIA: To New York.

MARK CHAPMAN: NO, no, no. You just stay where you are.

GLORIA: Okay.

MARK CHAPMAN: I love you and just call the police. I mean the police know, right? And they won't come over to your place?

GLORIA: No, I don't think they know.

MARK CHAPMAN: Well, they told me here that they called you. They called you?

GLORIA: No, they didn't. No one did.

MARK CHAPMAN: IS everybody else all right?

GLORIA: Well, no, I don't think your grandmother knows or anybody like that on the mainland knows.

MARK CHAPMAN: I'm not talking about that. I'm talking about my mom.

GLORIA: NO, she's worse off than me, I think.

MARK CHAPMAN: Well, you need to call her a doctor and call the police. You should call a lawyer or somebody.

GLORIA: [Starting to cry] Well, I don't know. You know, I can't afford anybody. I can't afford a lawyer. Has it hit you yet—what you've really done?

MARK CHAPMAN: I'm gonna have to go.

GLORIA: I love you.

MARK CHAPMAN: I know and I love you too. And.

GLORIA: I always will love you.

MARK CHAPMAN: I know and I love you too and I need your love, and I, everything will be all right. You'll see.

GLORIA: What do I tell people?

MARK CHAPMAN: You don't talk at all.

GLORIA: Okay.

MARK CHAPMAN: You don't tell nobody nothin'. It's not your position to do that. You just trust me. Don't talk. Especially the press. Don't let them bug you. That's why I say call the police. Tell them to keep the press away from you. Okay?

GLORIA: I don't think they can.

MARK CHAPMAN: Well just call them to come over, okay?

GLORIA: Mark, that's worse when they're not even calling, you know. No one knows yet.

[Given that Gloria stated earlier that "*The Advertiser* called me" this is a clear contradiction.]

MARK CHAPMAN: Well, they will. They'll bother you.

GLORIA: I won't talk. I won't go out at all.

MARK CHAPMAN: Okay, just stay in. Call your dad. Is your dad there?

GLORIA: Well, Jean's going to go over and take the kids and talk to them personally. Carol [wife's sister] called and she didn't know when she called. And I should tell her.

MARK CHAPMAN: Did they give my name out and everything?

GLORIA: No, it's not on the news. All they're saying is it's someone crazy in New York. They don't even say.

MARK CHAPMAN: All right, don't talk about it.

GLORIA: Okay.

MARK CHAPMAN: I love you and I'll talk to you again and don't worry about anything, okay?

GLORIA: Okay.

MARK CHAPMAN: You were my, you were my first concern.

GLORIA: I know.

MARK CHAPMAN: I'm just worried. You ought to call the police. You know, you know, you'd like to know what to do. And that you want somebody to come over, you know, a doctor and lawyer and whatever. Don't worry about the money. You know that lawyer that we used, what's his name?

GLORIA: Um, I don't know, but I'll figure it out.

MARK CHAPMAN: Okay, I love you.

GLORIA: I love you, darling. I really do.

MARK CHAPMAN: See you. Love you.

GLORIA: Okay. Bye.

MARK CHAPMAN: Bye.

Such a mentally exhausting conversation. But it comprised Mark advising Gloria with clear-headed precision. Her family appeared to be ready for action, as in – what to do if… And she was instructed not to worry about the money. The cost of a doctor and a lawyer should not be a hindrance. "Don't worry," he said. Unfortunately, he does not indicate where it'll come from. And the phrase… "you know that lawyer that we used, what's his name?" Why had Mark and Gloria been in touch with a lawyer? Clearly, he was a person in whom Mark held trust. Was it simply chance which stopped him speaking the lawyer's name?

Another intriguing question about this phone call is who recorded the conversation? It is possible that the NYPD did, but Officer Spiro's notes are mostly from the perspective of what Mark Chapman was saying. We know from the journalist Jim Gaines and writer Jack Jones that Gloria Chapman often recorded phone conversations between her husband and herself. Could this be one of those conversations and, if so, we must ask ourselves a pertinent question: why would a loving wife record phone conversations with her husband?

I firmly believe that the 2.55am phone call to Mark from Gloria draws a deep veil of suspicion over Gloria Chapman. If someone was desperate to get to Mark in custody and wanted to discover what he thought he did and why he did it, then his wife was the person with the best shot of achieving it. Was Gloria's call a fact-finding mission to discover her husband's state of mind? And was Gloria seeking these facts on behalf of someone else? I strongly believe she may have been.

Apart from someone recording the phone conversation, there is also film footage of Mark Chapman talking on the phone at the station after his arrest. This footage can be seen in the 1988 documentary, *The Man Who Shot John Lennon*. According to the producer of the documentary, he received this footage from the journalist Jim Gaines. The question we must ask ourselves is what was a film cameraman doing in the police station just a couple of hours after Chapman was arrested and why was this footage given to Jim Gaines? It's almost as it was staged.

In 1988, a now retired Lieutenant O'Conner, speaking then with hindsight, revealed further thoughts on Chapman to the writer Fenton Bresler:

> "It's possible Mark could have been used by somebody. I saw him the night of the murder. I studied him intensely. He looked as if he could have been programmed, and I know what use you are going to make of that word. That was the way he looked and that was the way he talked. It could have been drugs. Looking back, he could have either been drugged or programmed – or a combination of both."

We now know that Mark Chapman had three different kinds of unverified pills – 122 in total – in his hotel room, which was shamefully covered up the NYPD and New York's District Attorney's Office.

O'Connor continued:

"As far as you are trying to build up some form of conspiracy, I would support you in that line. If there is a conspiracy, it would never have been investigated and no conspiracy was investigated to my knowledge, and it would have come to my attention if it had… you've got to understand the human element involved. You're so happy to 'ground' the case, you don't want to open Pandora's box because, you know, with investigations, one thing leads to another and another and another; and you don't have resources and manpower and money involved."

"And then you have another human reaction, laziness! There could have been a conspiracy, but it was hallelujah to get this one grounded. A man acknowledges his guilt, he pleads guilty, that's it."

In September 2020, I contacted Gloria Chapman and told her that I was a writer and TV producer who wanted to discuss some anomalies surrounding her husband's prosecution. You would think that any devoted wife would want to know about my alleged anomalies and how they could help. But Gloria never asked me about the anomalies. She merely stated that she and Mark "prayed about [my] request and after MUCH prayer and discussion, I am declining your request to talk". I never asked Gloria to talk to Mark on my behalf and I took her email as a veiled inference that if I wanted to contact Mark in the future, I would have to go through her. I can confirm that this is very much the case as of 2023.

Recap

That Gloria Chapman could be told about her husband's alleged involvement within an impossible time-scale borders on fiction. His clear advice, and remember he was supposed to be mad, was to involve a lawyer to protect Gloria. His words paint him as a very caring man, albeit with something to hide. Look at the vocabulary he uses. Talk to no-one. Call the police. Get a lawyer. Money's no object. Not a word about himself. Yet, later, he did not forgive Gloria for not telling the police of his intentions.

My biggest frustration has been caused by the embellishments from dubious witnesses used in other media. But the unavoidable truth is that the NYPD literally took every step possible to close the case down. They had the killer. He had confessed. They actively did not want anyone questioning the outcome. And, as I will show, this pantomime continued when Mark Chapman was convicted and imprisoned.

CHAPTER 9 | The Hit List

Key People
Mark Chapman

Officer Stephen Spiro (NYPD)
DA Allen Sullivan

One of the more pleasant surprises I discovered when I gained access to Ron Hoffman's papers and documents was Mark Chapman's supposed "hit list". Talk of Chapman's "hit list" surfaced when Officer Steven Spiro mentioned an alternative hit list after he had first spoken to Chapman, stating:

> "Mark mentioned a hit list with Johnny Carson, Walter Cronkite, George C Scott and Jackie Kennedy names on it."

Chapman himself has never publicly spoken about having a "hit list" and Officer Spiro never officially recorded it. It is not certain when Spiro made this hit list claim, but as you can see from the names below, Spiro was accurate in his claims.

Strangely, prosecuting District Attorney Allen Sullivan tried to backtrack on the hit list claims and admitted in 1981 to *The New York Times* that:

> "Names drifted through his head. 'He didn't have a list, like a hit list'."

By 1981, DA Sullivan had access to everything associated with Chapman. He had collated all of Chapman's belongings while he was in New York. We can safely assume, therefore, that a hit list did not exist before 1981 and was not found on Chapman

Mark Chapman's alleged "Hit List" © *David Whelan*

in December 1980. Perhaps it was behind the back of a sofa in one of Chapman's hotel rooms? Though Sullivan was keen to distance the DA's office from a mythical hit list in 1981, it did not stop his assistant Kim Hogrefe speaking on numerous documentaries about Mark Chapman and a hit list over the years. He claimed that a hit list proved that Chapman was obsessed with being famous and the list also proved that Chapman would have killed another famous person if he couldn't get to Lennon.

When one of Mark Chapman's best friends, who wishes to remain anonymous, was approached by the FBI, they informed him that Mark had a "hit list" with his name and Todd Rundgren's name on it. The Bureau never provided any proof of the alleged hit list. This is the sole indication we have that the FBI may have been involved in an investigation of John Lennon's assassination. Another name often quoted as being on the hit list was David Bowie. Bowie revealed to a DJ called Redbeard, back in 1999, that New York City police told him that his name was next on a hit list of targets of John Lennon's assassin, Mark David Chapman. This shameful lie sadly meant that Bowie was in fear for his life after December 1980, for no reason at all. Bowie, as did many other rock stars at the time, beefed up his security and admitted he was paranoid about being assassinated.

At the time of John Lennon's killing, David Bowie was starring on Broadway in the play *The Elephant Man*. Bowie wrongly thought Chapman had a seat for the show, telling Redbeard:

"Chapman had a front-row ticket to 'The Elephant Man' the next night. John and Yoko were supposed to sit front-row for that show, too. So, the night after John was killed there were three empty seats in the front row. I can't tell you how difficult that was to go on. I almost didn't make it through the performance."

Bowie wasn't the only famous name that was supposedly on Chapman's hit list. Paul McCartney, Hawaii Gov. George Ariyoshi, President Ronald Reagan and Elizabeth Taylor were said to be on the list. When Chapman was interviewed on TV by Larry King in 1992, King asked:

"By the way, would you have killed someone else you think?"

Chapman replied:

"The Secret Service asked me that. If Lennon had unfortunately died a few days prior, say, in an automobile accident, would you have stalked someone else? I can't answer that question. I don't know. I was so bonded with John Lennon at that point."

If Chapman had a hit list, here was his chance to mention it on live TV to the whole world. He didn't.

In 2000, at his first parole hearing, Mark Chapman was asked about it. Chapman told the parole panel that within a month of deciding to kill John Lennon, he had apparently thought up "a substitute list" consisting of several names. "Probably, I thought he wouldn't be an attainable type of thing, and I did think of harming some people," Chapman told the board. Note that Chapman said he "thought up" a list. He did not say, and has never subsequently said, that he wrote one. If he did, then why didn't he say so at his parole hearing, or on Larry King, or whenever?

At his 2000 parole hearing, Chapman listed three names which state officials dramatically blacked out from the official transcripts and would not release. Mark said there were several others he could not remember. The always helpful journalist Jack Jones was on hand in 2000 to declare to the media that Jackie Onassis, George C. Scott and Johnny Carson were among those on his list. Mark also mentioned a possible hit list at a 2010 parole board, telling the board via a video conference call:

> "I considered shooting Johnny Carson or Elizabeth Taylor instead, but I can't remember whether I thought about targeting Jacqueline Kennedy Onassis. It wasn't about them, necessarily, it was just about me. It was all about me at the time. If it wasn't Lennon, it could have been someone else. I was going through that in my mind the other day. I knew you would probably ask that."

Elizabeth Taylor was not on Mark Chapman's alleged hit list.

I have studied Chapman's statements to several parole hearings over the years and they vary widely over time. I will cover this in more detail later. By 2010, Chapman was clearly saying whatever he was told to say to try and win his release. The theme for 2010 was very much about killing Lennon for fame and adding a hit list helped to back up this theme. According to people who have kept in contact with Mark while in prison, Mark's instructions came mainly from Gloria Chapman and one other influential figure, whose anonymity I shall unmask later.

Recap

The Mark Chapman hit list has been carefully spun into an important and iconic item in the Chapman story. If you were trying to steer people away from thinking Mark Chapman was potentially groomed or hypnotised into believing he had to kill John Lennon, then a Chapman hit list with alternative murder targets would be a useful device. Though most of what came out of Mark's mouth, post his numerous hypnotic evaluations, cannot be taken at face value or as undeniable truth, it is worth noting that he has never said he wrote a hit list. I personally don't believe he did and the people who have perpetuated the Chapman hit list myth reveal much about themselves and their motives.

CHAPTER 10 | Medical Truth and Lies

Key People

Dr Stephan Lynn (Roosevelt)

Dr Frank Veteran (Roosevelt)

Anaesthetist Eilis Egan (Roosevelt)

Dr Richard Marks (Roosevelt)

Dr Elliot Gross (New York City chief medical examiner)

Ed Koch (Mayor of New York)

Nurse Barbara Kammerer (Roosevelt)

Nurse Deartra (Dea) Sato (Roosevelt)

Dr David Halleran (Roosevelt)

Dr Stephan Lynn was in his second year as head of the Roosevelt Hospital emergency room. On the night of John Lennon's assassination, his 12-hour shift had ended at 10.30pm when Lynn returned to his New York home. His phone rang. A man with a gunshot wound to the chest was on his way to Roosevelt. The victim had no pulse, no blood pressure, and wasn't breathing. Dr Lynn rushed back to the hospital.

After John Lennon was pronounced dead in the hospital, Lynn told multiple journalists and TV reporters outside the building, that John Lennon had died and that he had "seven wounds". Dr Lynn subsequently informed the media that he opened a cavity next to John's heart and tried to massage the damaged heart with his hands, all to no avail. Lynn also stated that Lennon would have been "practically dead" the minute the first bullets entered his body outside the Dakota, and that he had lost far too much blood before reaching the hospital.

Lynn was the person who informed Yoko Ono of John's death. He gave her John's wedding ring and according to Lynn, Yoko Ono started banging her head against the floor, wailing, lost in her grief. (Ono has subsequently denied this account in 2016, stating that as a mother, she would never have behaved in a manner that might endanger her.)

Later, Lynn told *The New York Times*, "The bullets were amazingly well placed." He continued, "All the major blood vessels leaving the heart were a mush and there was no way to fix it."

At this point, record executive David Geffen arrived and escorted Ono out of the hospital through the back door – an iconic image which was carried on all the front newspaper pages across the globe. Dr Stephan Lynn formally instructed that all the medical supplies, uniforms and equipment used on Lennon be disposed of and burnt, not just for reasons of protocol, but also in case of ghoulish collectors.

In the ensuing years, Lynn made it his personal mission to be featured in as many documentaries about Lennon's murder as possible. In almost all, he claimed that he'd "held John's heart in his hand" as he tried to pump life back into the dying man with his bare hands. Very dramatic. Very heroic. The only problem was – Stephan Lynn was lying. And he wasn't the only one. Enter Frank Veteran.

Early on in my investigations, I reached out to another doctor who said he was at the Roosevelt and helped treat John Lennon on the night he was shot. Over the years, Dr Frank Veteran had spoken to magazines about his experiences and, like Stephan Lynn, had appeared in a TV documentary about the murder.

In 2010, *Guitar Legends* magazine published a special edition tribute to The Beatles and John Lennon. Inside, Dr Frank Veteran gave an interview. Veteran told how he tried to save Lennon's life. Veteran also admitted he had suffered depression after the incident, due to watching John Lennon bleed to death while he was trying to resuscitate him. Veteran confessed he was an ardent fan, and his interview with me took on a similar form to his interview with *Guitar Legends*.

"My beeper went off and when I called the hospital, they said 'we have a gunshot wound to the chest'. They [the hospital] said Dr Halleran, who was one of the younger residents, is opening his chest'. I said, well if Halleran is opening his chest, you don't need me. Opening a chest is a last resort performed when the heart has stopped and the patient is unlikely to live. But, they said, 'No, we need you now'."

Apparently, when Veteran entered the hospital, a nurse said "John Lennon" to him. But it did not register.

"I walked in and there was John Lennon, naked on the table, with all these people around him. Standing there, everything just hit me. For some reason, I thought of John Kennedy and Jesus Christ. It was a weird thing that flashed in my head. The doctors had already begun trying to resuscitate Lennon. His chest was open. They were doing everything to save him."

Veteran, who said he was used to dealing with an average of four gunshot or stab wounds per night, then gave some detail on John's wounds, stating they were all on his left side.

Veteran continued:

"Once your heart stops you have five minutes basically to resuscitate before lack of oxygen causes brain injury. So how long does it take to get from the Dakota to Roosevelt hospital, get into the emergency room, get stripped, get your chest opened? Well, it takes longer than five minutes. Lennon's heart never beat again. Had we gotten it going, he would have been brain dead. It would have been a disaster."

Veteran then allegedly had a conversation with a police officer who was on the scene at the Dakota. The officer apparently told Veteran that the last sign of life from John was a groan when they put him in the back of the police cruiser. Veteran said he was still in surgery when he heard a scream that he said was from Yoko Ono and that "it was a horrendous scream". She had been informed of her husband's death by the Head of the Emergency Room (Stephan Lynn). Veteran said he suffered depression for many months after the Lennon murder saying: "I'd feel normal and then I would wake up in the middle of the night in this deep depression. It took six months for that to go away."

After a stint as a plastic surgeon, Veteran eventually left the medical profession and went to work as a Wall Street investor and then as an artist/photographer. Veteran even went to the trouble of filming a video which he streamed online on his personal website about his alleged experiences in trying to save Lennon. When I spoke to Veteran about his experiences on the phone, he was very convincing. I was most troubled by his assertion that all of Lennon's wounds were from the left side. Chapman and the NYPD were adamant that John was shot in the back.

Before we get to perhaps the most significant doctor of all, let's quickly consider a third doctor who was on the scene at the Roosevelt, who also lied about the extent of his involvement. Dr Richard Marks was very close to the Dakota when John Lennon was shot. Upon realising what was occurring, Marks rushed to the Roosevelt to help. Dr Marks (a Vietnam War medical veteran) was, by some accounts, the first person in the ER room to confirm that the patient they were all working on was indeed John Lennon.

Like Dr Lynn, Dr Marks also claimed to be the surgeon who opened Lennon's chest. In 1990, Dr Marks told *People* magazine that he "opened up Lennon's chest but felt helpless". Dr. Halleran told me that he and his colleagues teased Marks about this embellishment at the hospital after the magazine was published.

There was only one way I was going to get to the bottom of this medical mystery, I would have to talk to Dr David Halleran who, in 2010, finally admitted that he was the surgeon who

Dr David Halleran © Roosevelt Hospital

treated John Lennon. Dr Stephan Lynn's integrity was thrown into serious doubt when, in 2010, Dr David Halleran said he was the chief resident who operated on Lennon and that he was, in fact, the one to massage Lennon's heart. Dr Halleran also had an independent witness, Nurse Dea Sato, to back him up saying very clearly "Lynn only came to help after he learned it was Lennon."

The first question I asked Dr Halleran was why Frank Veteran was not featured in the 2016 dramatic feature film, *The Lennon Report*. The film aimed to get to the bottom of the Roosevelt Hospital doctor merry-go-round once and for all. Halleran told me the reason: Veteran wasn't featured in the film because he wasn't at the hospital that night. Veteran, like Lynn, was lying.

David Halleran told me of his struggle to try and save John, placing a breathing tube inside John and preparing for a thoracotomy. There was no pulse or blood pressure at this point, so he had to try something drastic. He decided to open John Lennon's chest. The heart was intact, but empty of blood. There was a great deal of blood in his thorax. Dr Halleran used both his hands to pump John's heart but after a few unsuccessful minutes he called it. The founder of the world's greatest rock and roll band, and one of the world's most famous men, was officially dead.

Someone found John's wallet and discovered a gold American Express card and a photo of him with his son, Sean, in front of a white Rolls Royce. This confirmed the shaky whispers of the police who had brought the victim in. Dr Halleran recalled that they had worked on John for over 45 minutes. John had simply lost too much blood and was almost certainly beyond saving before he was brought into the Roosevelt.

What Doctor Halleran then told me next about the nature of John's wounds shocked me to my very core. I asked him to confirm where exactly the bullet entry wounds were. Dr Halleran confirmed, in the kind of unequivocal and direct manner one expects from a medical man, that John Lennon was hit with:

"Four entry bullet wounds that all entered his upper left chest above his heart."

He then said that three of these bullets exited directly opposite through his back in a direct line of fire. The fourth bullet was never found and must have failed to exit Lennon's body. He thought this might have been the bullet that entered through the top front left shoulder area. Halleran was certain that the shooter had to be directly in front of Lennon, no further than 4 to 6 feet away from his front left side, when he shot him.

When I told David Halleran that Chapman was at least 20 feet behind John Lennon when he allegedly shot him, Halleran said that, in his opinion, not even a Navy SEAL could achieve the accuracy of bullet strikes from that distance with a .38 handgun, even if Lennon turned around. I asked Dr Halleran how an amateur marksman like Chapman could possibly manage to place bullets in, to quote his own words, an "amazingly well-placed" configuration on John Lennon's upper left chest when – it was dark; he was at least 20 feet away; and he was standing behind Lennon. Dr Halleran had no answer: it was clearly impossible.

The 2016 dramatic feature film *The Lennon Report* correctly depicted Halleran and Marks leading the main surgical efforts. The film also shows Lynn arriving at the end of the effort predominantly to talk to Ono and the media. Halleran confirmed that the film did, indeed, get most things correct, but when speaking to me for the first time in summer 2020, he conceded that Lennon's wounds could not have been caused by Chapman because Chapman had been standing behind John and, in his opinion, the film was wrong to state that the entry wounds came from the back. I found that disturbing. Then came another bombshell.

David Halleran told me he found it strange that his ER report written that night, detailing all the above specifics regarding entry and exit wounds, illustrated on front and back human-body-outline drawings to show Lennon's wounds, had gone missing. Missing? The original drawings of the bullet wounds and their trajectory, gone? Disturbing and deeply suspicious are the kind of words that come to mind.

I asked Dr Halleran to expand further on John's wounds: "There were four over the left chest, three going out the left back. The shots came from close range." I also asked Dr. Halleran whether cracking open Lennon's chest would have made the four bullet holes in his upper left chest difficult to identify and read after that procedure. He categorically said no, stating that the chest opening and heart massage attempts did not alter the upper chest wounds. The four bullet holes in Lennon's upper left chest were intact after they pronounced him dead and sewed him up.

Despite the witness accounts, including Chapman's, it's clear that Mark Chapman could not feasibly have caused the wounds that slew John Lennon. But Dr Halleran's confirmation of the entry and exit wounds were impossible to square with the official line. John Lennon was not shot in the back as the NYPD, mainstream media and Mark Chapman have all led us to believe. It was impossible. From Chapman's position, he would have had to have been a top marksman and had the capacity to ricochet all four shots off a nearby solid object to have successfully caused Lennon's wounds as described by Dr Halleran.

Explosive stuff and crucial evidence, but it was still only one man's recollections. Dr. Halleran is a key and bona fide witness, but perhaps he became confused amidst the anxiety and high drama of that night all those years ago? David Halleran's recollections would be more powerful if they were backed up by other witnesses who also saw the wounds close-up. Enter nurse Barbara Kammerer and nurse Dea Sato.

Barbara Kammerer and Deartra (Dea) Sato were both working as nurses in the ER department at the Roosevelt Hospital on the night of the 8th December 1980. And they were working diligently by Dr Halleran's side as they all tried in vain to save John Lennon. Dea initially helped Dr Halleran and was next to Halleran's side when they cut off John's clothes and rolled his body to inspect his front and back wounds. Barbara then joined them in helping to try and save Lennon. One other woman, anaesthetist Eilis Egan was also helping to intubate John.

After John was pronounced dead, Barbara and Dea were the nurses responsible for washing John's body and for wrapping him in clean linen, a procedure that was undertaken not once, but twice. Both nurses saw all of John's wounds up close and their testimony is crucial in understanding how John Lennon died.

After hearing "a shooter" was coming in, the nurses went out to greet Officer Moran and helped bring Lennon into the emergency operating room. Dr Halleran and Dea immediately cut off all of Lennon's clothes and checked for wounds on all his body before starting IV drips. As Dr Halleran began working on the body, eventually cracking open his chest and massaging his heart, the nurses discovered they were treating John Lennon.

By coincidence (and I hate coincidences) an ABC reporter, Alan Weiss, was being treated following a traffic accident, in the hallway, just outside the operating room. One of the nurses moved him away from the emergency room in which John

Lennon was being treated to maintain his privacy. Weiss, being an experienced journalist, soon twigged what was happening and called into the ABC newsroom one of the crimes of the century. Weiss's place in the John Lennon story was secured forever.

When John was confirmed dead, it was Barbara and Dea's job to wash John's body and wrap him in linen. While they did this, they took a close-up look at John's wounds.

The nurses both confirmed to me, unequivocally and in full agreement with Dr Halleran, that John had four entrance wounds in his upper left chest – just above his heart. Three bullets exited in direct line of fire out of John's back. They both assumed that one of the bullets stayed in John and this was the one nearest his shoulder. They were convinced that the bullets did not move around and went straight through John. Barbara Kammerer also told me that anaesthetist Eilis Egan agreed with them that there were four wounds in Lennon's upper left chest. Something Egan could clearly see when she was working on Lennon. In case you have lost count, that is four people who verified that Lennon was shot four times in his chest. A doctor, two nurses and an anaesthetist. Did they all get it wrong, and in exactly the same way? I don't think so.

The nurses were aware over the years that Chapman had consistently claimed he shot John Lennon four times in the back from twenty feet away. The nurses both agreed that this would be impossible considering the tight, professional grouping of the wounds in John's chest. They both assumed that Lennon must have turned somehow and that the shooter would have been five or six feet away from him at most.

Both women, and remember they were nursing professionals, described how the dramatic movie *The Lennon Report*, a film made with the specific intention of clearing up the medical inconstancies in John Lennon's murder, had to be altered and adjusted several times as it was being shot. When the filmmakers kept insisting that John was shot back to front, the nurses were adamant that Lennon was in actual fact shot in his left anterior chest area. Depressingly, a crew-member stated that they were only following what Wikipedia said. Amusingly, Barbara told them that "no-one called Wikipedia was in the emergency room when John Lennon was being treated." I love these nurses. And I say again, they were medical professionals.

Barbara and Dea were aware that some people (including the lead Detective on the case) would accuse them of not knowing the difference between an entrance and an exit wound. They confirmed that with an entrance wound, you can visibly see the tissue being pushed in by the impact of the bullet. With an exit wound, the rupture is bigger, more jagged and a little blown out. They both knew the difference and had no doubts where John's entrance and exit wounds were.

Barbara Kammerer stated that Dr Lynn turned up near the end of their efforts to save the victim. He arrived and effected nothing. Kammerer and Lynn broke the news of John's passing to Yoko Ono and Kammerer confirmed what Ono has always insisted, that Dr Lynn was lying when he insisted over the years that Ono banged her head on the floor in grief. Kammerer confirmed that on hearing news of her husband's death, Ono cried. They then hugged. She informed Ono that her husband was not in pain when he passed. Ono did not ask to see her husband's body.

Both nurses then agreed with what Dr Halleran had previously told me. And more. All the paperwork from the night Lennon was admitted to the Roosevelt had gone missing. An ER report would have included extensive details of Lennon's wounds, including a front and back human outline drawing, clearly showing bullet entrance and exit wounds, with arrows appropriately pointing at the exact trajectories. All the copies of the notes, which had been recorded on a multiple carbon copy notepad, disappeared. Someone may have been looking for a gruesome souvenir or someone may have been trying to suppress the truth about the exact nature of John's wounds... we will probably never know for sure. Given, however, that they have never emerged on the memorabilia market, so beloved of Paul Goresh, I favour the latter suggestion.

Add the nurses' testimony to Halleran's and it amounts to further confirmation from two more professionals who witnessed John Lennon's wounds close-up, and agreed that John was shot in a tight, professional grouping in his upper left chest area. Four bullets went into his front left chest and three came out of the back in the same matching trajectory. John must have been shot by somebody standing a few feet away from him and standing directly in front of him to his left. By all official accounts, including the alleged shooter himself, Mark Chapman could not have killed John Lennon.

When, in 2010, David Halleran publicly revealed that he was the surgeon who had tried to save John Lennon at the Roosevelt Hospital, Stephen Lynn, thankfully, (mostly) disappeared from public view. Lynn was publicly humiliated in a 2015 Fox News piece called "The Untold John Lennon Story". In the piece, Dr Halleran, Nurses Kammerer and Sato and Eilis Egan all state that Lynn was not involved in helping to save John Lennon's life. When Fox presenter Howard Kurtz challenged his involvement, the squirming and back-tracking by Lynn on camera is one of the most uncomfortable things you will ever see on screen.

The nurses told me that, at around 12.30am on the 9th of December, they had a surprise visit from a man calling himself Elliot Gross. This small, pompous male said that he was the Chief Medical Examiner and he demanded to see John Lennon's body. No medical examiner had ever visited the ER before, and the nurses did not believe he was who he said he was. An argument followed but Barbara and Dea conceded he must be telling the truth. They asked Gross why he was in such a hurry to see a body that he would receive in the morning from the mortuary? Why the rush to see the wounds? Gross would not answer and demanded they unshroud Lennon's body and sit him up.

Begrudgingly, the nurses did so and as John began to bleed out, Gross silently walked around his body observing the entrance and exit wounds. As macabre and inappropriate as Gross's request was, it did give the nurses another chance to see John's wounds up close again. No one saw these wounds as closely and as often as did nurses Kammerer and Sato.

At roughly 12.45am, Nurse Deartra Sato was offered a lift home by a police officer. Since the car was passing the Dakota on its way to Deartra's home, Elliot Gross asked to accompany them. He wanted to the visit the crime scene. At roughly 1am, Gross entered the Dakota crime scene and interviewed concierge Jay Hastings. Unlike ER visits, crime scene visits by Chief Medical Examiners was not unheard of and often occurred. By the time Gross got to the Dakota, Hastings was the only witness left at the scene. José Perdomo, Joseph Many and a cab driver called Richard Peterson had all been taken down to the 20th Precinct police station. Hastings told me he didn't want to go to the station to give a statement and incredibly the NYPD were happy to leave him alone at the Dakota. When I asked Hastings what he and Gross talked about, he couldn't recall the meeting. At roughly 1am, back at the Roosevelt, a truck took Lennon's reshrouded body over to the mortuary.

The chief medical examiner for New York City, Dr Elliot Gross, duly performed an autopsy on John Lennon at 9.30am on Tuesday 9th December 1980. He told reporters that Lennon died of shock and blood loss and that no one could have survived more than a few minutes with his injuries. It was also reported that Gross said John Lennon had multiple gunshot wounds of the chest and left shoulder. He never indicated where the shots might have come from. Press reports which were issued at the same time as Gross's press conference, also suggested that John was shot twice in the back and twice in the left shoulder. There were also unconfirmed reports that Gross found one bullet lodged in Lennon's leather jacket and one bullet was lodged in his trachea.

Police officer Tony Palma, one of the officers who first found the mortally wounded Lennon in the Dakota lobby area, was given the task of going to the New York City coroner's office to observe the autopsy. Normally this task would be carried out by a detective. Palma told journalist Fenton Bresler in 1985 that Lennon was his boyhood hero and as Gross began his incisions, he could not take it and had to leave the room. Elliot Gross therefore performed John Lennon's autopsy unobserved.

I spoke to Tony Palma in March 2022 about the autopsy and he explained that he was sent along to the autopsy to collect John Lennon's clothes. He refutes Bresler's claim that he couldn't bear to watch the autopsy and he told me he did observe some of the autopsy and saw "holes in Lennon's chest" area. He could not say how many holes. Palma said that after he was given Lennon's clothes, he was told that he could leave, indicating that he may not have witnessed the whole autopsy after all. Palma also told me that he thought it was very poignant that in death we are all the same when he observed one of the most famous rock stars in the world lying naked in a room with other ordinary people, all eventually equal in death. Almost touching.

Elliot Gross became chief medical examiner for New York City in 1979, replacing Michael Baden. Baden was removed from his position by New York Mayor Ed Koch after Koch received complaints about Baden's work. Did persons unknown in the New York Mayor's office deliberately want Michael Baden out of his post before 1980? Baden later won a $100,000 in a wrongful termination suit.

History will mostly remember Baden as the chairman of the House Select Committee on Assassinations forensic pathology panel. He was a recognised expert. The committee had concluded that "there is a likelihood" that Dr Martin Luther King's assassination was the result of a conspiracy. The committee had also concluded that President Kennedy was "probably assassinated as a result of a conspiracy" and that a fourth shot came from a second assassin located on the grassy knoll, but missed. Baden, as Chairman of the HSCA forensic panel, would have certainly been earmarked as a man of integrity by many. Unfortunately, Mayor Ed Koch didn't see it that way and by the time that John Lennon was assassinated, Baden was not the New York Chief Medical Examiner. Gross was an odd choice to replace Baden. Previously he had been the chief medical examiner of Connecticut for nine years. Early in his New York career, he performed the highly controversial autopsies on graffiti artist Michael Stewart, Eleanor Bumpurs and Nicholas Bartlett, who were all killed by police officers. Gross may have appeared to some as a man who had a lenient side when it came to accusations against police officers and authority.

By returning to New York, Gross was going back to his roots. He had graduated from New York University School of Medicine and while a captain in the Air Force Reserve Command, Gross served as chief of the aerospace pathology branch of the Armed Forces Institute of Pathology. In the years after John Lennon's autopsy, Gross and his staff were accused by several defence lawyers and forensic specialists of producing misleading or inaccurate autopsy findings in various police custody cases. In January 1985, Mayor Koch ordered an investigation into Gross and his office. In July 1985, Gross took a leave of absence following eleven charges of incompetence. He was eventually cleared, but an administrative law judge ruled against the decision.

The internal investigations continued in 1986 due to an increasing number of allegations of misconduct, misleading causes of deaths and concealment of evidence of police brutality against Gross and his department. *The New York Times* reported at the time "the facilities were poorly maintained and disorganised and evidence in criminal cases were not handled in accordance with any identifiable system which assures quality control, accuracy, reliability, security, or availability."

In October 1987, Mayor Koch dismissed Gross, leading to the

pertinent question – what took him so long? Gross was a survivor and in 1990, after a five-year investigation, Gross was cleared of eleven charges of negligence, misconduct and incompetence stemming from nine autopsies, including several involving people who had died in police custody. Despite this official exoneration, Gross had to move on and his career at the top table of forensic pathology was over. Accusations of corruption kept on hounding Gross. In 2002, he was fired from his position in Atlantic County after an investigation into one of his autopsy findings concluded he had incorrectly classified a death. In 2003, Gross was barred from preforming autopsies, but (ever the bounce-back survivor) the ban was reversed the following year.

To date, the details of John Lennon's autopsy have not been publicly released. All FOI requests have been refused on the grounds that John's next of kin must give permission for the autopsy to be released. To date, Yoko Ono and John Lennon's family do not want this document to be released and that is understandable in one sense. Everyone is entitled to privacy.

I have not tried to obtain a hard copy of John's autopsy and, as it is a private medical record which contains highly personal biological details (other than John's wounds) that the family has clearly not wanted to release, I will not attempt to do so. That said, I have spoken to several credible people who have seen the autopsy and I believe it is crucial to my investigation to reveal what the Gross autopsy apparently says regarding John's wounds.

Below is the list of wounds according to the autopsy:

Wound 1 – Gunshot wound of left back (middle back). 9th intercostal space, 5th rib. Direction of track forwards and to the right. Entry and Exit.

Wound 2 – Gunshot wound of left back (lower back). 11th intercostal space, pancreas, diaphragm, 6th rib. Direction of track upwards and to the left. Entry and exit.

Note – Lead bullet recovered in leather jacket of deceased (Lennon), consistent with exit track of wound 1 or wound 2.

Wound 3 – Gunshot wound of left shoulder, left humerus, left anterior chest wall. Direction of track forwards and to the right. Entry and exit.

Wound 4 – Gunshot wound of left shoulder, scapula, 1st inter-costal space, left upper lobe (lung), left subclavian artery and trachea. Direction of track left to right and slightly forward.

Note – 38cal lead bullet recovered from subcutaneous tissues of neck adjacent to trachea and marked L/O.

In essence, what Gross is saying is that two bullets stayed in John and his clothes, and two bullets exited John. One exited his upper left chest area (wound 3) and one exited in his lower chest area/stomach.

One thing is certain, Gross's conclusion about entrance and exit wounds is entirely at variance with the evidence from the medical professionals at Roosevelt Hospital. Dr Halleran, Barbara Kammerer and Dea Sato dealt with gunshot wounds every day, often every shift. They saw the raw evidence right in front of them when they desperately tried to save John Lennon's life and again, when they washed and shrouded him afterwards. They all knew the truth of the matter.

Recap

Considering what we now know about Elliott Gross and his tainted reputation, I would personally give the autopsy report scant credence. John Lennon's Death Certificate, dated 10th December, was made available to the public. In this document, Elliot Gross contradicted what he had written in his autopsy report when matched against his initial press statement. There he said John Lennon was shot twice in the back and twice in the shoulder. That was altered on the death certificate to "multiple gunshot wounds of the left shoulder and chest." Perhaps Gross, ever the maverick career survivor, was covering his bets to accommodate every eventual assessment of his work. Elliot Gross is now in his 90s and is retired. He has refused all requests for interviews regarding his autopsy on John Lennon. I would suggest to him that that is a wise course of inaction.

My conclusion is that Gross was not, and is not, credible.

Both Dr Lynn, and to a lesser extent Dr Veteran, ensured that the truth about John Lennon's wounds stayed concealed from the public for thirty years. Like JFK and RFK's assassinations, the crucial facts regarding entrance and exit wounds remain the key to unlocking which direction the bullets came from and who may have fired them. Dr Lynn and Dr Veteran could not adequately answer these questions because they did not see John's wounds up close. Lynn arrived too late, and Veteran possibly never arrived at all.

Thankfully, Dr Halleran and Nurses Kammerer and Sato's revelations put the record straight. Their recollections made it absolutely clear that it was impossible for Mark Chapman to have caused John Lennon's fatal wounds from where he was standing. If this information had been made common knowledge in December 1980, perhaps Lennon's real killer would have been caught. Sadly, Dr Lynn's ego obstructed the facts, and the truth was buried for 30 years. Better late than never I suppose. And Chief Medical Examiner Elliot Gross's autopsy is highly problematic to say the least.

CHAPTER 11 | The Smoking Bullets

Key People
Brad Trent (photographer)
Ron Hoffman (NYPD lead detective)
Rodolfo Blake (NYPD officer)
Commissioner Ray Kelly (NYPD)

Dr Elliott Goss (Chief Medical Examiner)
Doug MacDougall (ex-FBI Bodyguard)
Nicholas Proto (Medical Officer in 1980)

When a person is shot, forensic evidence often offers the most reliable clue to the specifics of the crime. In the case of John Lennon's assassination, what I have uncovered leads to the disturbing conclusion that there was another gunman present. A marksman. A professional killer. An assassin. If this raises the probability of a conspiracy to kill John Lennon, don't flinch from the evidence which I have unearthed.

Firstly, I want to break all the issues surrounding the bullets into five separate parts.

1) Two Different Bullets
In 1989, *Life Magazine* commissioned a New York photographer called Brad Trent to photograph the gun with which John Lennon had allegedly been shot. *Life* wanted the image for a piece they were doing on infamous guns from history. I have spoken to Brad and he told me that *Life* managed to gain him access to the New York City Police Department Ballistics Department Lab. The lab then allowed Brad to photograph the gun and two accompanying bullets. He noted the nonchalant attitude of the Ballistics Department and was surprised they allowed him to shoot his pictures without the presence of anyone from the department. The gun was presented in a large brown envelope, inside which was a second small brown envelope with two

different bullet types. After *Life* printed their 1989 piece, Trent filed the photos away and forgot about them.

Thirteen years later, he was asked by Spain's *El Mundo* newspaper if they could use one of his images of the gun which was allegedly used to assassinate John Lennon. Trent agreed and decided to write a blog post about his experiences. Brad Trent's photo became a hugely important image and currently remains online for the whole world to see. I think that this image will become one of the most iconic crime photos of the twentieth century. The image, hidden in plain sight since 2012, indicated that two different types of bullets were found in John Lennon's body.

Ideally, I would have liked to have included Brad Trent's photo in my book. I did once try and license the image from him, but Brad believes my investigation into John Lennon's killing is a "conspiracy theory". I understand his reluctance to put aside the cognitive dissonance which stops many people accepting the facts simply because they were taught or believe differently. It is a difficult emotion to challenge. The Lennon assassination is a highly emotive issue and many people have completely bought into the official narrative. It has been spoon-fed to them for forty-three years. Emotions often triumph over logic.

The bullets which Trent photographed came with a helpful note from Chief Medical Examiner Elliot Gross. The note stated that one of the bullets had this specific marking:

"LG on base .38 cal semi wadcutter hollow point from jacket"

This means that Gross believed that one of the bullets came from John Lennon's leather jacket. The eagle-eyed amongst you will note that these are two different types of bullets in Brad Trent's original 1989 image. One is a .38cal semi-wadcutter (SWC) hollow bullet. A type of bullet which mushrooms at the top after firing. The other is a normal .38cal lead bullet. This is powerful evidence that other than Mark Chapman, there was a second killer who fired a different type of bullet when John Lennon was assassinated.

To corroborate this, I accessed a receipt for ballistic evidence from the New York morgue that was holding John Lennon's body. The receipt clearly specified that a NYPD detective discovered that there were two different types of bullets found from John's body and held as "evidence". These are listed as:

1 x 38cal. SWC (semi-wadcutter hollow) lead bullet

1 x 38cal. lead bullet

Though unlikely, it is possible to have different types of ammunition in a single revolver. But Chapman always insisted he was using hollow point wadcutter bullets and Chapman was familiar with guns and ammunition from his security guard days. It is also worth noting that two different bullet types in a revolver hinders the gun's accuracy, since the rounds will print differently and consequently the gun may handle poorly. The doctors and nurses who treated Lennon all said the bullet wounds in his upper left chest were in a "tight professional grouping".

Different bullet types found in John Lennon's body is explosive information. Perhaps this is one of the reasons why Lennon's autopsy has not been shared with the world and the wishes of his family to keep John's autopsy private have been respected. This was certainly not the case in President J F Kennedy's assassination. Going by Brad Trent's image and the evidence specified from the morgue receipt, the presence of a second shooter in John Lennon's murder now seems highly likely. Adding this to the other evidence I have uncovered over these past three years, I am 100% certain that this complex murder was a planned assassination.

I heard first-hand from people who have seen John Lennon's autopsy that Chief Medical Examiner Elliot Gross apparently found one bullet in John's front neck and one bullet somewhere in his leather jacket.

If we are to believe the doctor and nurses who tried to save John Lennon's life on 8th December 1980 (and why wouldn't we?), then we can confidently assert that four bullets entered Lennon's upper left chest area in a tight professional grouping, and three bullets exited his upper left back in a direct line of fire. That means Gross produced one bullet too many. If we accept the rumour from the autopsy that one bullet was found in Lennon's leather Jacket and one bullet stayed in his body, then Gross's two bullets would make some kind of sense if the bullets were the same... but they are not. The doctors and nurses who cut off John Lennon's leather jacket when he was brought into the ER, and then subsequently bagged them, did not see a bullet lodged in Lennon's jacket. They may easily have missed seeing a small bullet, but would a small bullet lodged in a leather jacket have survived the journey to the morgue after being cut from Lennon and then bagged-up and sent to Gross? Perhaps.

For me, the alleged "leather jacket bullet" does have disturbing echoes of the bullet that was conveniently found on Texas Governor Connally's stretcher in 1963 and was identified as the "magic bullet" in the Kennedy cavalcade assassination. A magic bullet that went all the way through JFK and then into Governor Connally, through numerous fanciful twists and turns. A bullet that was famously identified as Ce 399. Elliot Gross wrote in his note attached to the gun, that the hollow bullet came "from jacket". Perhaps this hollow bullet fell out of Lennon's jacket and onto the autopsy floor?

2) The Small Grey Metal Cremation object

Yoko Ono gave her Ex-FBI bodyguard, Doug MacDougall, the task of arranging the cremation of John's body which duly took place on the afternoon of 10th December, just 36 hours after his death. (More details on the cremation to follow.) While

The MacDougall Crematorium Note © David Whelan

McDougall was at the crematorium, he somehow discovered a small metal object in John's ashes. Concerned, the bodyguard rang Lead Detective Ron Hoffman and informed him of the anomaly. Hoffman noted this exchange in his notebook. He told me this object greatly concerned him, and it left him wondering "if there was a second shooter".

The police lab report request form regarding this metal object described it as a *"Metal Object, Grey in Colour"*. The lab was requested to: "Determine type of steel and/or was it a bullet, if so what cal. This object has been subject to 2000 degree Fahrenheit during cremation process."

Hoffman stated that the lab came to the unconvincing conclusion that the unidentified metal object was probably a part of the "metal basket" that collected John's ashes and it must have "broken off somehow." The NYPD clearly thought the grey metal object may have been a bullet, otherwise they would not have asked the question. We will probably never know what the unidentified metal object was.

3) The Extra Bullet

In 2005, detective Nicholas L Proto presented the London Metropolitan Police Museum at Scotland Yard with a bullet. Nicholas Proto was initially an NYPD detective, who, after finishing his training at an FBI academy in 1979, went on to work as a detective with Elliot Gross at the Medical Examiner's Office in New York.

According to Proto, the bullet was found intact in Mark Chapman's handgun. It was also apparently test fired as part of the evidence. However, the bullet looks pristine and unused to my eyes. Proto's claim flies in the face of Chapman's assertion that he shot five bullets from his five-shot .38 revolver. It also contradicts Detective Hoffman who told me that he found five empty shells in Mark Chapman's five-bullet revolver. Hoffman's assertion is also corroborated by police evidence vouchers which I have seen. Where on earth did Proto get this single bullet from?

4) The Missing Bullets

If we take the official narrative of John Lennon's assassination as fact, there is also the awkward question of where the other spent bullets allegedly fired by Mark Chapman are. According to Chapman, the NYPD and the mainstream media, he shot Lennon four times in the back and missed his target with one shot. It now appears that Chief Medical Examiner Elliott Gross found two different bullet fragments in John Lennon's body. That means at least three spent bullets should have been collected at the crime scene at the Dakota. But, according to the vouchers from the crime scene, no bullets or bullet fragments were found. When asked specifically, Detective Hoffman refused to confirm whether any spent bullets were found at the Dakota.

When I was examining the NYPD's Dakota crime scene inventory, I found a voucher for

1 x 38 Calb revolver Charter arms/Strafford Conn – Serial number 577570 – no record nyspin

5 x 38 Calb spent shells with initial R.B.

The initial "RB" almost certainly stands for Rodolfo Blake – the NYPD officer who, we have been told, collected a gun from the Dakota basement. (More details to follow.) No spent bullets were identified in the police inventory vouchers. The official gun voucher also makes the following observation:

"above weapon was recovered in basement of 1 West 72st room number 13"

It's important to remember that no gun was found on Mark Chapman when the police arrived at the Dakota.

5) Police Commissioner Ray Kelly

When I spoke to officer Peter Cullen about what it was like at the 20th Precinct station after they brought Mark Chapman in to be arrested, Cullen said the station was full of people he hadn't seen for a long time. One of these people was Raymond Kelly, the former Vietnam War colonel and New York police commissioner between 1992 to 1994 and 2002 to 2013.

Back in December 1980, Kelly was a captain in the 88th Precinct and was working for the NYPD Emergency Services. A convenient role for anyone who wanted to get access to a crime scene in a precinct where they had never worked. Cullen knew Kelly from a previous stint he'd had at the 20th and asked him what he was doing there that night. Kelly replied: "We had to come up and see if there's any more spent bullets around. It's kind of a formality."

Really? A captain of the police emergency unit doing such a menial chore. Or was it a crucial task? Kelly decided not to include this formality in his autobiography and it was neither recorded nor explained why he was drafted into the Lennon crime scene to search for spent bullets under an Emergency Services guise.

Recap

Regardless of whether you believe the official John Lennon assassination narrative, or the new contradictory evidence of the Roosevelt doctor and nurses, we simply cannot get away from the fact that morgue evidence and Brad Trent's 1989 photograph prove that there were two different types of bullets in John's body. Spent bullets that Mark Chapman allegedly fired are also missing. We know the NYPD and the DA's office concealed the fact that there were 122 unidentified pills in Mark Chapman's hotel room. We also now know how nonchalant the New York Ballistics Department were in allowing *Life* Magazine's Brad Trent to photograph the gun and two bullets. Or should we thank them? Have they also concealed how many bullets, and of what type, were found at the Dakota crime scene when John Lennon was assassinated?

CHAPTER 12 | Something Not Quite Right

Key People

Andy Peebles (BBC Radio presenter and DJ)
Elliot Mintz (Yoko Ono publicist)
Vikki Sheff (journalist)

Doug MacDougall (ex-FBI/bodyguard)
Yoko Ono
Sean Lennon (son of John & Yoko)
Fred Seaman (Lennon employee)
Michael Medeiros (Lennon gardener)

In September 2020, writer Lesley-Ann Jones published a book about John Lennon's life, in time for the upcoming 40th anniversary of his death. The biography was called *Who Killed John Lennon* and, despite its arresting title, it was basically a Lennon by-the-numbers biography, albeit a well-researched one. There is one very interesting passage near the end of the book where Jones talks to BBC presenter, Andy Peebles. Peebles was one of the last people to have interviewed Lennon just a few days before he was assassinated. He told Jones that he was very frustrated that his three-hour interview, which was due to air in mid-December 1980, had never been officially released. He then told her about an episode that he said had "haunted him for decades".

What troubled Andy Peebles was the absence of bodyguards on the night of John's assassination. Peebles had spent a few days in their company prior to his interview. Meetings had taken place at the Dakota and meals-out were laid on, with John and Yoko in attendance. Peebles therefore had a good sense of how the Lennons' world worked from the inside in the days leading up to John's assassination. Even though John had always given the impression that he could wander around New York freely without being bothered, Peebles saw a different security dynamic. Two burly, armed bodyguards were always in attendance. They were both uniformed in blue blazers and plain slacks and they were always present, 24/7. What deeply troubled Peebles is that on the night that John was assassinated, the two bodyguards were nowhere to be seen.

I briefly spoke to Andy Peebles in early 2022 about the two mysterious bodyguards and he told me they never left the Lennons' side throughout his whole time with them. They were very large and imposing individuals and both wore matching blazers. They were so prominent, Andy Peebles felt obliged to discuss security matters in his subsequent interview.

The exact identity of these two bodyguards is currently a mystery. What we do know is that Yoko took care of all the security arrangements for herself and John. Their official bodyguard in 1980 was an ex-FBI agent called Doug MacDougall, who was hired by Yoko in February 1980. MacDougall was a World War 2 veteran and a Soviet espionage expert in the New York area. I have also heard from a source who knew Doug MacDougall, and who wishes to remain anonymous, that McDougall may formerly have been part of an FBI black-ops team. MacDougall's alleged partner was another FBI agent called Richard Bates. Bates's main claim to fame was investigating the Patty Hearst kidnapping and being congratulated by FBI director J. Edgar Hoover for his work on investigating Martin Luther King's alleged assassin, James Earl Ray.

In August, Yoko had granted an interview to a magazine in which she detailed the family's whereabouts with precise timings of their daily routines. MacDougall allegedly said she was foolish to do this and advised Ono that they needed more bodyguards to protect them. Strangely, following this professional advice, Yoko put MacDougall on a temporary leave of absence.

John's assistant, Fred Seaman, said that the next time he heard from MacDougall was on the morning of the 8th December 1980 – the morning of the day John Lennon was assassinated. MacDougall was apparently calling to confirm an appointment he had previously arranged with Yoko. They were scheduled to have a meeting on 9th December to discuss "security arrangements".

In summary, according to Seaman, Yoko Ono had replaced her usual bodyguard with two unknowns sometime in late September 1980. Andy Peebles saw both bodyguards protecting the Lennons on Thursday 4th December, four days before John Lennon was assassinated. Both bodyguards were apparently given two days leave in the days leading up to John Lennon's assassination on Monday 8th December 1980. The original Lennon bodyguard (MacDougall) was then pre-booked by Yoko to be re-employed as a bodyguard on 9th December, the day after John's murder. Doug MacDougall did, in fact, return to work for Yoko on the morning of 9th December 1980 – the very morning after John Lennon was assassinated. Unfortunate bad timing or was it prearranged?

This allegation is entirely based on a claim made by Fred Seaman. And Seaman had an acrimonious relationship with Ono. Speaking to me in early 2022, Lennon insider Michael Medeiros told me that the reason Ono chose an ex-FBI agent as a bodyguard was because she wanted to use MacDougall to get information about what the FBI were thinking and doing about the Lennons. Apparently, MacDougall fulfilled this role though I very much doubt he told Ono everything his previous employers had been doing in the years leading up to the assassination.

Back to the narrative and a burning issue… John's cremation. Let's look at the chain of command. Despite John Lennon having a well-known phobia for cremations, Yoko Ono gave her ex-FBI bodyguard Doug MacDougall the task of arranging the secret cremation of his body on 10th December. To be clear, that was a mere thirty-six hours after the autopsy. Back in the fold after his two-month "suspension", MacDougall duly carried out Ono's instructions, so he was the chosen commander in the field. John's family and friends – all of them – were, at a stroke, denied the chance to say their last farewells. There was no one present at John Lennon's cremation other than Doug MacDougall, ex-FBI agent.

Like the proverbial John Doe, John Lennon was cremated alone, uncelebrated, dismissed from life without ceremony. Perhaps he would have wanted that? However, the speed of John's cremation was unusual. His cremation had to have been approved by the authorities; met all the procedural requirements, including proofs of identity and the surrender of his passport; and been booked into the crematorium, finding a space in the daily list of cremations at short notice. By the time John's first-born son Julian had flown into New York on Tuesday 9th December, his father was already booked in to be cremated on the 10th. It is unclear whether Julian was informed about John's imminent cremation when he arrived in New York. Ono decided not to attend. Her ex-FBI bodyguard was the sole representative. After years of harassing and stalking John Lennon, the FBI had one of their own on hand to oversee the cremation of John Lennon's mortal remains. Sickening really.

At 3.40pm on December 10th, Fred Seaman was asked to ring Doug MacDougall at the crematorium to ask him if he could postpone the cremation until five-year-old Sean could see his father again. (Note how the power rested with Doug MacDougall.) He informed Seaman that he was too late. John had been cremated two hours earlier. At approximately 6pm, Doug MacDougall found a grey metal object in John's ashes and informed Lead Detective Ron Hoffman. Doug MacDougall then returned John's ashes to Yoko at the Dakota in a brightly wrapped box. The box was apparently a ruse to fool the fans camped in the street outside the Dakota. When Fred Seaman asked MacDougall what was in the package, he replied "in there was one of the greatest rock stars who ever lived". Ono allegedly asked MacDougall, "How did John look before he went in?" MacDougall replied, "He looked like he was sleeping." Ono never replied. After the assassination, Doug MacDougall did not remain on Yoko Ono's payroll for much longer.

I must comment on what I would call the indecent haste to cremate John. He had repeatedly said that one of his worst fears was to be cremated. His wishes were disregarded. His close family were denied the right to share their grief and express their admiration for their friend, their dad, their employer, their professional collaborator, the man on whose shoulders other talented musicians stood. A man in a million. An inspiration. An influencer. A Working-Class Hero. There was a rush to condemn Yoko for the speedy cremation and it does seem suspicious, but to be fair, who knows what one would do when faced with the distress, grief and pain of a sudden assassination. Did someone in government give an order that there had to be a quick cremation? The authorities certainly wouldn't want the streets lined with mourners en masse. But John was rock and roll royalty. The nature of John's cremation is one of the cruellest facets of the whole case. We might yet understand the case more when the FBI and CIA records are released, unredacted and in full. Of course, if the records do contain skulduggery, they will no doubt be lost, removed, burned by accident, or otherwise disappear. What can we expect? Vital documents always remain out of reach. Ask the JFK assassination researchers. When you come to think about it, the greatest piece of evidence in the case – John's body – was destroyed *immediately*.

A ghoulish worker in the crematorium was alleged to have taken a photo of John's body before he was cremated. He then sold this to the *National Enquirer* for $10,000. A further rumour claimed that a video was made of the event but, thankfully, it has never surfaced. I have heard from a contact close to the Lennons that Doug MacDougall took the photo.

There is no evidence of this, but MacDougall was certainly there and could have done.

In September 1981, MacDougall allegedly lost sight of Sean Ono for a moment in Central Park. Ono angrily rebuked MacDougall, who was Sean's favourite bodyguard, for this mistake. Journalist Vikki Sheff claims MacDougall responded, "If you don't like the way I do my job, I quit." Ono immediately accepted MacDougall's resignation and she hired New York Police Sergeant Dan Mahoney to take his job.

Doug MacDougall subsequently contacted Yoko Ono's publicist, Elliot Mintz, and demanded some "back pay". To ensure he got it, he told Mintz he was "holding some stuff until I get my money". According to Sheff, the stuff he was holding was some electronic equipment, a dozen cassette tapes, two Swiss army knives, a pair of Lennon's glasses and a love letter from John to Yoko, including the original version of the song "Dear Yoko". McDougall was rewarded for his theft – or misappropriation. Mintz took MacDougall a bag of cash and retrieved the items. I suspect Mintz also took a very strong non-disclosure agreement with him. Doug MacDougall disappeared from the scene after this "exchange". He died 30 years later in July 2011, aged 86. Much more research is required into his association with John, Yoko and the Dakota staff, including his previous employment by the FBI before and after he worked for the Lennons.

Yoko Ono continued living in the Dakota after John's murder. This decision meant she had to walk past the scene of her husband's assassination regularly. There were changes. Vital changes. The Dakota management removed the shattered glass vestibule doors and threw them in the basement. You might think these invaluable items of evidence would have been taken away by the NYPD for forensic examination. Not so. It seems to me that evidence was treated as if it was toxic. Don't touch it, don't ask about it, shred it.

Thankfully, photographs of the doors were taken before they were replaced. These images tell their own story. And it, too, is disturbing. One of the images below of bullet holes on the Dakota vestibule door was taken from brief flash frames contained in Kevin Sim's 1988 Lennon murder TV documentary. In August 2020, Sim confirmed to me that he obtained crime-scene

Two visible bullet holes can clearly be seen in the right-side vestibule door. © NYPD

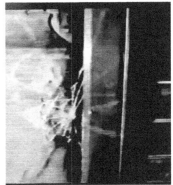

The bullet hole/damage in far vestibule door. Stairs seen on the right. © NYPD

Another angle of the right-side vestibule door from the back of the driveway © Manhattan DA Office

stills from an insider in the NYPD. Sim found the 20th Precinct station very unhelpful and suspicious of his requests to see Lennon murder-scene material. He never received any further materials from the NYPD.

Despite numerous FOI requests directed at the New York Police Department and District Attorney's office over the years, they have refused to release all the John Lennon crime scene report details. We know that an extensive crime scene report was compiled, but for some reason, NYPD and DA authorities do not want it to be released.

I wonder why.

The two visible bullet holes in the road-side vestibule door are too low to be caused by the bullets that would have gone through Lennon and then hit the glass doors. It's also highly significant that the hollow bullets Chapman thought he was using normally don't often pass through their victim. Hollow bullets are not designed to do that.

The vestibule doors were closed on the night Lennon was murdered: multiple people have confirmed to me that these doors had automatic closers attached. Taking this into account, it would only then be possible to make the three bullet holes from a gun that was fired very near to the vestibule doors or inside the vestibule doors. Various witnesses place Mark Chapman at the pavement entrance to the driveway. Chapman has also confirmed this. Knowing all we know – Chapman could not feasibly have caused these bullet holes.

If we are to believe the official murder narrative for just a moment, Lennon would have had to turn a full 180 degrees and face Chapman in the driveway, assuming Chapman called out to him (but Chapman has consistently said he never did this). If Lennon was shot four times from this position (and John would have had to stand completely still, while Chapman steadily fired his gun four times into his left chest from up to 20 feet away), John would then have had to turn back 180 degrees, open the glass panelled vestibule doors and climb some stairs up towards two further large mahogany doors that lead into the lobby (which Dakota staff say were usually closed in winter). Pushing through these doors, a mortally wounded John would have had to enter the lobby area and continue onwards through a swinging door on the immediate left, then through a front concierge office to his left and then further on and out into a back office, where he then finally collapsed on the floor. This official version of events, if true, still does not account for the three lower-positioned bullet holes in the Dakota vestibule doors.

It is important to also note that there was no blood splatter on these doors. Staff at the Dakota and the police officers who were there on the 8th of December 1980 have all confirmed to me that there was no blood on these glass doors. Therefore, the holes could only have been caused by bullets shot through the doors before they potentially hit Lennon. There were no bullets holes noted by anybody on the walls of the Dakota or the Dakota office windows. Consequently, these bullet holes on the vestibule doors could not have been caused by ricochets.

Dakota lift operator Joseph Many confirmed to me that the vestibule glass and wooden doors were taken down and placed in a basement area in the Dakota, very shortly after John Lennon was assassinated. Amazingly, the NYPD did not deem these two critical pieces of evidence worthy of further investigation and forensic analysis. Tellingly, Joe Many also told me that soon after the damaged doors were deposited in the Dakota basement, both door handles mysteriously disappeared and the two bullet-hole glass windows went missing shortly thereafter. Many assumed it must have been either workman replacing the glass or ghoulish souvenir hunters working in the Dakota. Possibly, it could have been somebody who didn't want anybody to examine vital evidence. It was becoming more and more clear to me that the NYPD simply didn't investigate John Lennon's murder because most of them thought they already had their man.

The lead detective on the case, Detective Ron Hoffman, is exactly what you would expect – a hardened New York detective. Initially suspicious of my approaches to him, Hoffman eventually softened when I told him that I wanted to cover all angles of the Lennon case, for the sake of history. Fiercely loyal to his men, his superiors and the NYPD in general, Hoffman was a somewhat tired 84-year-old when I first spoke to him in early 2022. He still had all his notebooks from the investigation and he opened these up to me throughout our conversations.

I firstly asked Ron Hoffman to describe what happened on 8th December 1980 and how he went about investigating John's shooting. His story follows:

When he discovered that he was the lead detective on a shooting case at the Dakota, he thought it was just another gun crime. Hoffman drove to the Dakota and started talking to witnesses. At that point, he learned who had been shot and realised that the case would have huge interest worldwide. He didn't yet know how badly John had been injured, so he drove to the Roosevelt Hospital to get a statement. By the time he got there, John Lennon was dead.

Hoffman then told me that he accompanied a doctor to tell Yoko Ono her husband had died. This did not happen. Nurses Kammerer and Sato both categorically stated that they did not see Detective Hoffman at the Roosevelt Hospital and Kammerer insisted Hoffman was not there when she and Dr Lynn announced the death to Yoko. There is a possibility that Hoffman went in to see Ono after Kammerer and Lynn did, but why lie about breaking the news to her?

We know that Hoffman was at the hospital after John Lennon was pronounced dead as there is news footage of him being interviewed outside the hospital by multiple journalists.

Hoffman, dressed in a light brown leather jacket, appeared angry and bemused. After confirming that they had a suspect, Hoffman then revealed a zinger for the ages, stating:

"He [Lennon] was leaving a limousine, arriving at home, and he was shot from behind in the vestibule of his apartment."

Ron Hoffman confirmed, on camera, that John Lennon was shot IN the vestibule. Not outside the vestibule, not near the vestibule, but IN the vestibule. Hoffman must not have known at that point in time that, from where he was standing, the chief suspect Mark Chapman could not have shot Lennon inside the vestibule. What Hoffman might have found out, if he bothered to talk to the medical staff who tried to save Lennon, was that John Lennon had been shot in the front.

Outside the hospital, a journalist stated to Hoffman: *"There was talk of a second suspect."*

So, barely an hour after Lennon was murdered, journalists had heard about the possible involvement of a second suspect. Hoffman's response to this was "I don't know". In the footage, he becomes visibly angry at this point, remonstrating that the journalists were "badgering" him.

After his hospital grilling, Hoffman's first theory was bizarre. He considered the possibility that there might have been some kind of link with Pearl Harbour attached to the assassination. His logic was based on the fact that Yoko Ono was Japanese, and the killing happened a day after the anniversary of the attack on Pearl Harbour in 1941. Needless to say, this crackpot theory led nowhere. An insider at the Dakota told me that he thought the NYPD went out to Hawaii to discuss a possible link between Yoko Ono and Gloria Chapman. This has never been confirmed. It's worth remembering that no journalist has ever spoken about a possible conspiracy regarding John Lennon's assassination and the 1941 Japanese attack on Pearl Harbour. This bizarre theory seems to have come from Detective Ron Hoffman's imagination.

When I interviewed Hoffman, he initially said he felt the case was straightforward. According to him, Yoko entered the Dakota first followed by John. Chapman stepped out from the shadow and stepped between John and Yoko. (Please note Chapman has never said he did this, neither has Yoko Ono.) Hoffman then thought Chapman dropped into a three-point stance and fired five shots, three of which hit John in the back. When I told Hoffman that John had four bullet wounds in his front, he couldn't explain the anomaly. When I challenged him about who entered the Dakota first, he couldn't be certain. He changed his story multiple times. Let me remind you, this was the lead detective on the case, and he apparently didn't have a clue about what happened on the night John was slain... it's staggering really.

I asked Hoffman whether forensic teams worked at the crime scene. He told me that they didn't need to do finger prints, as they already had their man. Ballistics were also not a problem, as they "found some casings". Everything was dismissed. The NYPD had their man. Full stop. The Dakota staff who were present that night and the days thereafter, told me that there were no forensic or ballistic teams working at the Dakota. Lennon's blood was mopped up early the very next morning and life at the Dakota continued as if nothing had happened.

Clearly the unexplained low bullet holes in the Dakota glass doors didn't bother Ron Hoffman or the forensics team. Or maybe it did and it was ignored. When I asked him if he remembered details about bullet holes in the glass doors, he simply replied, "No". Hoffman had never bothered to check how many entrance wounds and exit wounds there were in Lennon's body. Had he done so, he would have discovered by simple deduction that four bullet holes in the front and three out the back could not mean that John was shot in the back. Hoffman probably came to his "three in the back" conclusion from Elliot Gross's autopsy.

Hoffman decided that Chapman was a loner (which I believe is a bad judgement) with an overwhelming urge to please people. He had to admit that Chapman was non-violent and that none of his friends had a bad word to say against him. I fully concur with this fact. All Mark Chapman's friends whom I have spoken to have said the same thing... he was a lovely guy who would help anybody. Some of the comments Mark's friends have said about him include "Mark was an out-going, good humoured, optimistic guy"; "He was a gentle and compassionate man"; "Mark never lost his temper, never violent"; and "Mark could always talk easily to women. He had the chat". Marks friends struggled to believe that he could have shot John Lennon. It was so out of character.

Chapman's mother gave only one interview, which she granted to journalist Jim Gaines in 1987, where she said, "I've seen him described as being a loner. Are you kidding? He had lots of friends, I never had to tell him to go out and play." The mother of Mark's former girlfriend Jessica Blankenship once stated, "There was nothing devious about Mark. Everybody liked him." Mark's YMCA colleague Vince Smith noted Chapman's ability to get on with children: "No one was better with kids."

Ultimately, Hoffman was convinced that Chapman killed John Lennon to be famous. I disagree. Chapman, by pleading guilty, denied himself a trial – an event that would have had universal attention. Mark Chapman has only ever given the media two major interviews stretching over forty years. During one of these TV interviews, in 1992, Chapman unconvincingly revealed (for the one and only time) that he killed John Lennon to "acquire his fame". In my eyes, Chapman's *acquiring fame* statement comes across as staged. I believe at this point, after twelve years in jail, he was repeating whatever he was told to say, in the hope that it would get him out of his tiny jail cell.

Recap

The stark fact that on the very night John Lennon was assassinated, there were no bodyguards on duty (as there always had been) is troubling. People will be inclined to point an accusatory finger at the one person who organised the Lennon's security, Yoko Ono. She personally hired, suspended, and later fired the bodyguard who was a bona-fide former FBI agent, Doug MacDougall. A staggering person to hire when you consider the years of intimidation John suffered at the hands of the FBI with their constant, invasive monitoring of his activities.

John's rushed cremation, the arrangement of which Yoko

Ono inexplicably handed over to her bodyguard ex-FBI agent Doug MacDougall, was unforgivable and inexplicable for many. I would venture it was borderline illegal. Major strings must have been pulled to have the cremation arranged and conducted within thirty-six hours of John Lennon's assassination.

Why the rush? Why were John's other relatives and friends denied a say? Yoko didn't bother to attend her husband's cremation ceremony. His body was dispatched without a friendly soul in attendance. The only one present was the former FBI agent. This cold and deeply impersonal arrangement is disturbing to say the least.

The bullet holes in the glass panels of the Dakota vestibule doors are also cause for deep concern. They were simply in the wrong place. Whichever version of the official narrative you may choose to believe – John turned, John didn't turn, Chapman shot at John's back, Chapman shot John's shoulder, and so forth – the position of these bullet holes completely contradicts. The hasty disposal of the vestibule doors also leaves troubling echoes of John's cremation: Get the awkward stuff thrown away as quickly as possible. No evidence can be gleaned from evidence that has been destroyed.

CHAPTER 13 | Witness Statements: A Roll Call of Confusion

Key People

José Perdomo (doorman)
Joseph Many (lift operator)
Jay Hastings (concierge)
Franklyn Welsh (cab passenger)
Michael Medeiros (interior gardener)
Yoko Ono
Tony Cox (ex-husband of Ono)
Joe Grezik (Dakota worker)
Victor Cruz (Dakota worker)

Richard Peterson (cab driver)
Nina Rosen (dog walker)
Officer Herb Frauenberger (NYPD)
Dr Elliott Gross (Chief Medical Examiner)
Nurses Kammerer and Sato
Officer Tony Palma
Lead Detective Ron Hoffman
Mark Chapman
CIA Director Allan Dulles
Sean Strub (opportunist)
Jann Wenner (Rolling Stone Editor)

On the night of John Lennon's assassination, we know that cab driver Richard Peterson was taken by police officers to be questioned with the doorman, José Perdomo. Both were driven to the nearby police station. Joseph Many, the Dakota lift operator and sometime doorman, confirmed to me that he was also taken down to the police station to give a witness statement with Perdomo. When I asked him why Jay Hastings didn't go down to the station to give a statement, Many said Hastings had a somewhat arrogant attitude and said he didn't need to help the NYPD if he didn't want to. He simply decided not to co-operate. Incredibly, Hastings didn't go to the police station to give an official statement.

For reasons that remain unclear, the NYPD and DA's office decided the public should not be allowed to read the statements from Perdomo and a dog walker, Nina Rosen. Could this possibly be because these two key witness statements did not match the murder narrative which the NYPD and higher authorities wanted to sell to the public? I have read Nina Rosen's statement from the notebooks of Detective Ron Hoffman and can confirm that her statement most definitely fails to support the official narrative. More on that later.

Back at the Dakota, while the Police and DA's office were building their chosen case, Joseph Many continued working. He told me that he saw no police investigation taking place at the murder scene in the hours and days after the assassination. A few detectives milled around for a short while on the night of the murder and then they were gone. People in white forensic suits were not seen at the scene and no ballistic experts appeared to be working at the scene either. The glass-shattered vestibule doors were thrown in the Dakota basement and Joe Grezik was tasked to mop up John's blood that very night. Case closed.

It is clear from my interviews with Detective Hoffman and a full examination of his notebooks and files that there was not a thorough and proper investigation into John Lennon's murder.

An image from Kevin Sim's 1988 documentary showing John Lennon's blood in the Dakota back office. Jay Hastings has confirmed to me that this is definitely the back office. Hastings also confirmed to me that the floor was marble. The three police officers who found John in the back office all said he was lying face down on a rug. The rug is not shown in this image. © NYPD

Crucial evidence such as entrance and exit wounds were over-looked and, on more than one occasion, Hoffman indicated that the case was easy and "laid out" for him.

I became quite fond of Hoffman even though I knew he hadn't done his job properly and failed to investigate John Lennon's assassination in the manner it deserved; I was convinced he was only following orders and was told to focus on bolstering the "Chapman did it" narrative.

Almost as an afterthought in one of my later interviews, I asked Hoffman where in the Dakota driveway he thought Lennon was struck. I was expecting him to say what most people were told at the time and have believed ever since – that Lennon was struck just outside the glass vestibule doors in the driveway. But no, Hoffman reverted to his initial Roosevelt Hospital assertion and insisted that he was "convinced" that Lennon was struck in the stairwell, on the steps, inside the glass vestibule doors, leading up to the lobby doors. Hoffman had no doubt about this. I could have pointed out that it was impossible for Mark Chapman to shoot Lennon if Chapman was standing outside near the street and Lennon was inside the vestibule doors, walking up the stairs to the lobby area, as he would be out of sight and out of range from Chapman and his alleged gun. But I knew at this point that I would be wasting my breath. Hoffman was 84 and he had had over forty years to convince himself that Chapman was a "lone-nut gunman".

If John Lennon had been shot inside the vestibule doors, on the steps leading up to the lobby, this would have to mean that a second, concealed shooter could have been covertly positioned inside the vestibule doors, waiting in the concealed stairwell for Lennon. Or they could have shot John from behind the con-cealed vestibule door and the courtyard gate. Hidden from view, the second shooter would have been free to shoot Lennon at point-blank range.

These are mind-blowing and explosive hypotheses, which could account for the three low positioned bullet holes in the vestibule doors. It could also account for what doorman Perdomo told police officer Cullen, that the bullets "pushed Lennon through the doors". (The vestibule doors had to be pulled to open therefore the shots must have come from inside to push Lennon back through them.) I still found it hard to believe that a mortally wounded Lennon travelled up the steps, through the lobby doors and onwards into the back office with four bullet holes in his left chest area. At a later point, I discovered that Lennon might have achieved this superhuman feat with some help.

Could there be more evidence to emerge to support this mind-blowing second-shooter theory? Yes, there was. Lots of it.

Ron Hoffman insisted time and again that he and his colleagues examined every possible scenario surrounding John Lennon's killing. It didn't ring true to me. If only I could somehow get hold of Hoffman's notebooks, everything would become clearer regarding what Hoffman and the NYPD did or didn't do. I mentioned to Hoffman, almost as a casual aside, that he should consider writing a book about his time investigating the Lennon murder and that his notebooks would be a great way to do this. He told me that at 84, he felt he was too old to write a book, but he was looking to get rid of his Lennon materials – clear the decks, so to speak. With my heart racing, I asked him what he meant by this, and he told me that he wanted to sell his Lennon murder case notebooks and paperwork and he asked if I would be interested in buying them. I told him I would be very interested, and I quickly contacted my agent and media lawyer to ask him to explore buying the notebooks on my behalf. A few days later, a price was agreed with Hoffman and my lawyer flew out to Florida to acquire the notebooks. Contracts were duly exchanged and suddenly I had everything I needed to piece together what happened (and didn't happen) in the John Lennon murder investigation. I finally had in my possession the holy grail of the murder case. It was as if a bright light had suddenly been switched on in a very dark room.

Apart from the victim and the alleged shooter, only three other people verifiably witnessed the assassination of John Lennon, and one of them only heard it. The testimonies of doorman José Perdomo and John's wife Yoko Ono are especially invaluable accounts, but as you will see, they pose more questions than answers.

Witness 1: José Perdomo – Dakota doorman

José Perdomo, who was doorman at the Dakota, should be THE key witness. He should have witnessed Lennon being shot in the Dakota driveway (pictured below) first-hand. Perdomo was standing just a few yards away from the crime.

Kim Hogrefe has confirmed to me that Perdomo was interviewed by the DA's office at the time as a key witness. Other Dakota staff working on the night of the shooting have also revealed to me that Perdomo was taken to the local police station

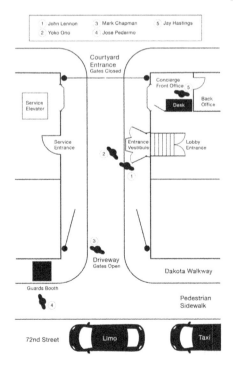

Overhead Layout of the Dakota Driveway © David Whelan

that night to give his statement. His witness statements remain sealed to this day and because he is now dead, we can only piece together, from the testimony of others, exactly what Perdomo should have seen and what he might have said and done on the night of December 8th, 1980.

The official narrative goes like this: After finishing up some late evening work at a New York recording studio, John Lennon and Yoko Ono arrived back at the Dakota in their limousine. They pulled up at the sidewalk on 72nd Street, at the entrance to the Dakota driveway at roughly 10.50pm.

The Lennons' limousine could have driven them up the driveway and dropped them off at the vestibule entrance door-way, but it didn't. The vestibule entrance doorway consisted of two wood-panel and glass doors which had to be pulled open. (During the winter months, the vestibule doors were there to keep the cold winds from blowing up into the Dakota lobby area.) Once through these doors and inside the vestibule (or small porch area), there were then six steep steps leading up to a set of mahogany doors which opened into the lobby area. To the right of the lobby area, there were stairs and lifts providing access to the apartments. Running along the left-hand side of the lobby area was the concierge's desk. Attached to this desk, there was a swinging saloon-type door which gave access into the concierge's front office. At the rear and to the right-hand side of this front office was a door leading through to the back office. The layout of the Dakota driveway, entrance, lobby area and offices are very important when you are considering John Lennon's assassination.

José Perdomo was waiting on the sidewalk and opened the door of the Lennons' limo and greeted them. They then got out. Who exited first is debatable, but for now let's accept the official story and say Yoko left the limo first. She walked towards the entrance doorway at the right end of the driveway, with John roughly ten to twenty feet behind her.

They both walked past Mark Chapman who, by most accounts,

was standing near the open, large, black gate by the street, on the left-hand side. As John walked past Chapman heading towards the vestibule's covered doorway on the far right, Chapman pulled out a .38 revolver and shot five bullets into John's back. Chapman's statements consistently say that he believed four bullets hit Lennon in the back and one missed. The NYPD said three bullets hit Lennon's back. Either way, John Lennon was mortally wounded. Once shot, John apparently staggered onwards up the driveway to the glass vestibule doors, opened them, went up some steps, opened a large mahogany door, turned an immediate left and went through a swinging saloon-type door, walked into the concierge's front office, told the concierge (Jay Hastings) that he had been shot, walked through the concierge's open-plan office and into the back-office area adjacent to it, and then he collapsed on to the floor. Moments later he was dead. What a macabre magical mystery tour.

From where he was supposed to be standing, Perdomo could not have seen much of John Lennon's extraordinary interior journey: opening doors, climbing stairs, walking through two offices – all after having been shot a minimum of three times. Perdomo was allegedly left alone in the driveway with Chapman, whom he claimed still held a gun. Accounts vary, but Perdomo allegedly walked up to Chapman crying, and said to him, "Do you know what you have just done?" Chapman calmly replied, "I just shot John Lennon". Perdomo advised Chapman, "Get out of here, just go, get out of here". Chapman apparently replied, "Where would I go?"

Perdomo said he shook the gun from Chapman's hand and kicked it to the back of the driveway. Chapman could not remember how the gun got on the ground, but he said he remembered Perdomo kicking it. A witness called Franklyn Welsh, who was exiting a cab (almost certainly Richard Peterson's cab, though Petersen denies this), said he heard shots and saw a gun on the ground, with a doorman and a man (presumably Chapman) standing next to it. Franklyn said he saw the doorman (Perdomo), kick the gun to the rear of the driveway (the area where the vestibule glass doors are).

Joseph Many, the Dakota service lift operator, heard shots and came up from his basement office in a service elevator and entered the driveway through a concealed doorway, directly opposite the vestibule entrance doors. Joe Many said he had heard three shots while in the basement and when he came up to the driveway to see what was happening, he saw Perdomo "pacing frantically", with a gun lying at his feet. Perdomo asked Joe Many to pick up the gun and take it away for safe keeping. Joe Many told me that Perdomo may have also kicked the gun over to him. That's a lot of gun kicking from Perdomo. Perdomo was apparently concerned that the gun might have more bullets in it and Chapman might pick it up again. According to Joe Many, this was unlikely, as Chapman was standing calmly in the driveway near the street, reading a book. This all begs the pertinent question, if Perdomo was so concerned that the gun may have more bullets in it, why kick it? Is this not a dangerous thing to do on a cobbled driveway?

Joe Many picked the gun up as instructed and took it down to his basement office to hide it in a drawer. When he came back up to the driveway a couple of minutes later, Perdomo was still pacing frantically, and according to Many muttering "What the f**k happened? What's going on? What did you do?"

Perdomo then left Chapman, and, with Joe Many, walked up to the lobby and into the back office behind the concierge (Jay Hastings') office, where Lennon was apparently dying, with Yoko Ono attending to him. Hastings then asked Perdomo what had happened and, according to Hastings, he replied: "Wow, the boy, oh my God, the boy, the boy shot John. The boy he's been here like all day like outside. He's outside. I don't have the gun. I kicked the gun to Many. He's got the gun downstairs".

At this point, Perdomo went back outside into the driveway with a co-worker. Both Joseph Many and Jay Hastings claim they were the co-worker who went with Perdomo. Outside, Chapman was still calmly reading a book by the driveway entrance. Two NYPD officers, Cullen and Spiro, arrived at the scene. Officer Spiro pointed his gun at Perdomo's co-worker and, thinking he was the killer, shouted at him to put his hands up (both Hastings and Many claim to be the person misidentified as Lennon's killer.) Perdomo shouted, "No. it's him, he shot John Lennon," pointing at Chapman. Some accounts state that Perdomo said "he is the only one" while pointing at Chapman. Mark Chapman was duly handcuffed and read his rights. In a later interview, Spiro claimed that Chapman had said, "I am the only one".

Officer Cullen approached Perdomo and asked him where Lennon was. Perdomo answered, "The bullets pushed him [Lennon] through the door". Perdomo then motioned over to the vestibule door entrance, "Over there," he said, "that's the father of a five-year-old kid." It's important to understand that around the time of John's assassination, Perdomo had not been working the door at the Dakota every night. Concierge Jay Hastings was mainly sharing the doorman duties with lift operator, Joseph Many. At that time, Perdomo complained that he had bad circulation in his legs and could not stand for very long so he spent most of his time in the lobby area and concierge's office. According to Hastings, this caused much confusion because of Perdomo's poor English. Hastings was constantly being called away from the front gate to manage phone calls for Perdomo. We must ask why did the Dakota put up with this? On the night of the assassination, it was unseasonably mild. This prompted Perdomo to ask Hastings if he could work the door of the Dakota on that fateful night "to take in the warm air" so to speak. This ensured that Perdomo, and not Jay Hastings or Joe Many, was close to Mark Chapman when John Lennon was assassinated.

Despite his apparently poor English, Perdomo seemed keen to explain the murder scene for anyone who spoke to him on that fateful night. Immediately after the shooting, as people started to arrive at the scene, Perdomo was quick to give his version of the story to curious by-standers who had heard shots and wanted to find out what had happened. One of these was Sean Strub. Strub was asked by first-on-the-scene reporters if there was any kind of exchange between Lennon and the suspect. Strub claimed that the doorman had told him that there was some kind of altercation or argument. But this was almost certainly not between Chapman and Lennon as neither Ono nor Chapman has ever said that there was an argument between Lennon and Chapman. The NYPD and DA's office have never mentioned an argument. Jay Hastings never heard any argument from his window facing out onto the driveway. Either Strub was confused, and it was Perdomo's argument with Chapman (which Chapman has hinted at) or he was embellishing his account. Chapman's argument with Victor Cruz also complicated the story.

After the killing, Perdomo told his employers that he no longer wished to work outside as a doorman. While the international media gazed at the Dakota gates, Perdomo made sure he was not visible. Fred Seaman, John Lennon's personal assistant, told me he spoke to Perdomo on the following day. Seaman observed that Perdomo seemed devastated by John's death. He found it incomprehensible that Chapman, with whom he had been chatting on and off in the hours leading up to the shooting, had committed such a brutal crime. Perdomo rejected the notion that Chapman was simply a crazed fan who went too far. "Chapman's not crazy," Perdomo kept saying. Fred Seaman didn't see Perdomo until a few years later when, by bizarre coincidence, he found the doorman drunk in Central Park, still apparently deeply affected by the murder.

Nothing was heard of Perdomo for years. Numerous Lennon biographies were written, and all of them referred to Perdomo as "the Doorman". Some of these books even named Jay Hastings in that context. José Perdomo the Dakota doorman slipped unnoticed from the building.

Are Dakota doorman José Perdomo and CIA "Bay of Pigs" José Perdomo the same person?

In 1983, journalist Jim Gaines was granted a prison visit with Mark Chapman and conducted a lengthy audio interview with him. Most unexpectedly, Perdomo's name resurfaced. In a subsequent 1987 *People* magazine article, Gaines wrote:

> "That evening, Chapman had only the Dakota's night doorman, José Perdomo, to keep him company. José was an anti-Castro Cuban, and they talked that night of the Bay of Pigs and the assassination of John F. Kennedy. Chapman remembered – 'I have a lithograph… of John F. Kennedy… and I hung it in our living room. Gloria [Chapman's wife] didn't want me to because it would stare down on us when we watched TV and ate and stuff, but I wanted it that way… That assassination has always meant a great deal to me.'"

*Note he used the word "assassination".

Ever since Gaines's provocative 1987 article, the internet became awash with multiple theories about the mysterious Cuban. Most assumed he was a CIA operative at the Bay of Pigs. In order to examine this theory, let's first get some historical background:

In April 1961, CIA backed anti-Castro forces were trapped and killed in the Bay of Pigs, an abortive invasion planned by the CIA and the American military to seize the country back from its elected communist leader, Fidel Castro. Two of the men who survived this shambolic and chaotic mission were called José Perdomo and Frank Sturgis. Sturgis would go on to be one of the Watergate burglars working for President Nixon.

The surviving Cuban invaders blamed President John F Kennedy for the failure of the mission by casting the blame on Kennedy's refusal to provide air cover on the day of the invasion. Kennedy (who inherited the mission from his predecessor, Dwight Eisenhower) stated he was misinformed about the mission's chances of success and had never promised military assistance. After the Bay of Pigs fiasco, Kennedy fired CIA director Allen Dulles (though it was kindly sold as Dulles stepping down) and promised to smash the CIA into a thousand pieces. Two years later, President Kennedy was assassinated in Dallas.

Part of the Bay of Pigs invasion force was made up of a group of right-wing Cubans and a legendary group of hardcore soldiers put together and led by one "José Perdomo". Operation 40 was the unofficial name for a Cuban exile intelligence and assassination team that was initially put together to accompany the Bay of Pigs invasion brigade as it advanced into Cuba. Members of OP40 were meant to identify and apprehend pro-Castro and communist sympathisers and, if necessary, execute them in a similar way to what the Nazis' much-feared Einsatzgruppen troops did, twenty years earlier in Russia.

A José "*Sanjenis*" Perdomo was tasked to run OP40 and his immediate boss was a man called David Morales. Morales, an American of Cuban-Mexican descent, was a legendary CIA assassin and intelligence officer. He was known as a ruthless killer who would do the kind of dirty jobs that nobody else wanted. Morales was also involved in several Central and South American coups for the CIA. According to close CIA associate Tom Clines, if you saw Morales walking down the street in a Latin American capital, you knew a coup was about to happen. Morales worked with this José Perdomo in Miami, which is where OP40 were based before and after the Bay of Pigs debacle. The US backed invasion was a disaster: Castro's forces were waiting for them, and many were cut down on the beaches.

Morales blamed President Kennedy for the disaster and once boasted to two friends in 1973: "I was in Dallas when we got the son of a bitch, and I was in Los Angeles when we got the little bastard." It is widely believed by many that Morales was in some way involved in the assassination of JFK and possibly Robert Kennedy's assassination as well.

Authors Warren Hinckle and William Turner have pointed out in their book *Deadly Secrets,* that members of OP40 were "assassins-for-hire". OP40 José Perdomo (also known as Joaquin Sanjenis, José Sanjenis, Sam Jenis and Carlos Blanco) first met CIA assassin Frank Sturgis in 1960 in the CIA's Miami office (covertly located on the campus of Miami University). He was busy putting Operation 40 together with a core group of Cuban assassins and mob-linked henchman. The group's sworn intention was to return Cuba back to the "good old days" of Mafia control and corporate power.

Once the Bay of Pigs debacle was over, the OP40 men maintained close contact with the CIA. It is alleged that they were often used for unilateral "off-book" operations. Sturgis and Perdomo became close associates, and Perdomo organised new mail drops and CIA phone numbers. They remained solid friends even after Sturgis was arrested and charged with being one of Richard Nixon's Watergate burglars. Perdomo spent many years collecting secret files on Cubans in the Miami area, using them for blackmail and coercion. Spy, assassin, and blackmailer, Perdomo was considered by everyone who knew him to be a very dangerous man. José Perdomo apparently retired from "official" CIA/OP40 business in 1972 and most of the Miami OP40 team was also officially disbanded at this time. In 1978, Hinckle and Turner spoke extensively to John Sturgis, who confirmed that he was a friend and associate of José Perdomo. The *Deadly Secrets* authors painted an interesting picture of Perdomo:

"On a June morning in 1972, the week after Watergate, Joaquin Sanjenis left his modest import-export office in Miami. José Joaquin Sanjenis Perdomo was a plain man of undifferentiated features, which was, in his profession, an asset: he was a professional spy. His personality suited his work in that neither encouraged close personal relationships. His was a lonely life, sweetened by habitual cups of thick Cuban coffee."

Sturgis then told Hinckley and Turner that José Joaquin Sanjenis Perdomo died in 1974 of natural causes. His family were only notified of his death after his funeral. The legendary assassin and super-spy José Perdomo had apparently passed away. Well, at least for the next fifteen years.

On the Cuban Information Archives website, a José Perdermo is listed as a "Bay of Pigs soldier" and this Perdomo is almost certainly OP40 Perdomo. He is listed as 'José Joaquin Sanjenis Perdomo' (aka Sam Jenis). There is tellingly no picture of him on the website and according to some unverified online records, Sanjenis Perdomo was born around 1912 and died in 1973 (which would roughly fit with the Frank Sturgis interview).

There is, however, one problem with Sturgis's claims regarding Sanjenis Perdomo's death in 1974. In 1989, a Bay of Pigs soldier called José Perdomo was quoted in the *LA Times*, regarding the suicide of his colleague Pepe San Roman, a prominent Cuban exile commander. If Sanjenis Perdomo died in 1973/4, who was this Bay of Pigs Perdomo quoted in the *LA Times* in 1989?

Online forums and blogs have long claimed that Dakota José Perdomo was the same man as CIA José Perdomo. Numerous images have been posted online trying to prove the fact, but most remain unverified and many are just plain wrong.

There is one Dakota Perdomo image that has been verified by people at the Dakota who knew him. The picture was taken in 1977 by a paparazzi photographer. John Lennon can be seen, as can a two-year old Sean Lennon. José Perdomo lurks in the background. The image of Perdomo is blurry, but it is clearly a picture of a man who is in his fifties, possibly even his sixties.

Below is another picture of Dakota Perdoma, which emerged in 2023, that matches the 1977 paparazzi one.

From piecing together my interviews with people who knew Dakota Perdermo, I have deduced that this Perdomo was born in Cuba in 1934 and died in Florida in 2010 and his name was indeed José Perdomo. Going by these dates, the Perdomo in

José Perdomo © Unknown

the photo above would have been 43 at the time the photo was taken. The guy in the photo seemed older to my eyes, but it was possible.

I discovered that Dakota Perdomo wasn't overtly political. He left Cuba with his wife in 1965 because he didn't feel safe. He got a job working at the Dakota in 1969 through his brother, who also worked there. Please remember that was four years before the Lennons moved into the Dakota and two years before they moved to America. No one at the Dakota still alive today remembers much about Perdomo's older brother. Like José, he is a ghost. We also know that José Perdomo's sons worked at the Dakota in the 1990s, so the Perdomos at the Dakota was very much a family affair.

In my April 2021 interview, Detective Hoffman revealed further details about Perdomo:

> "He [Perdomo] was right there. He saw them enter the building, or the vestibule, or whatever it's called. He saw the whole thing. He saw Yoko come in first, he saw Chapman the killer step behind her across the hall. He [Chapman] was on one side of the courtyard and they [Lennon and Ono] walked in through the middle and he stepped between them, between John and Yoko. Took his gun, went into a three-point stand, bang, bang, bang, bang, bang, five shots. Three of them hit John in the back. No mystery."

I felt by the Summer of 2022, I had gone as far as I could regarding José Perdomo's role, or lack thereof, in John Lennon's murder. I had managed to piece together fragmentary accounts of what he might have done and what he might have seen, but Perdomo was still a ghost to me and I knew I could never get the NYPD or DA's office to finally release his statement. I couldn't figure it out. In such an open and shut case, why were the authorities so keen to suppress Perdomo's statement? And then, as has happened so many times in my investigations into the assassination, I got lucky.

In March 2022, I conducted a lengthy interview with Michael Medeiros, the Lennon's interior gardener/house plant man and archivist. Near the end of our interview, I told Medeiros how frustrating it was that I didn't have the witness statement of the one man who should have seen everything, doorman José Perdomo. "That's OK," said Michael, "he gave a full account of what happened to me and Doug MacDougall." I was shocked and delighted in equal measure. But how did it come about?

Medeiros said that MacDougall, the ex-FBI agent and bodyguard, asked Medeiros to accompany him down to the concierge's office on the afternoon of the 9th of December. He was going to interview Perdomo and wanted Medeiros to accompany him as a witness to Perdomo's statement. Finally, I was going to get the information that I thought I would never get.

Firstly, Perdomo told MacDougall and Medeiros that he felt deeply guilty about the killing, as he thought he should have done more to stop it. After Ono and Lennon had exited their limousine, Perdomo apparently walked back to his golden doorman's booth, outside on the street. Just before he got there, he heard gunfire. When he turned back into the driveway, Chapman was there and Lennon was slumped inside the vestibule door area at the bottom of the lobby stairs.

Perdomo did not mention whether he saw Chapman with a gun or whether there was a gun on the ground at this point.

Perdomo did not see Chapman firing a gun. Perdomo did not say how he knew Lennon was inside the vestibule door area, but perhaps Lennon had been thrown back into the driveway from the force of the bullets that hit him. This would explain Perdomo saying to Officer Cullen that the bullets pushed Lennon through the door. Either way, Medeiros is certain of what Perdomo said he did next. Perdomo claimed that he immediately went over to the vestibule door area, picked Lennon up and carried him into the hotel lobby concierge area. Perdomo then came back down to the driveway area and confronted Chapman. We can only assume that this is when Perdomo might have kicked a gun to the rear of the driveway and Joe Many shortly arrived thereafter to take the gun away.

I was left reeling by this. It explained so much, but it also led to many further questions. I had never bought into the theory that a mortally wounded Lennon could get through two sets of doors and climb some steps, open some other doors and walk through offices, all unaided. It made no sense. That Lennon was carried up the lobby entrance steps by Perdomo made perfect sense. One nagging question remained. Why didn't concierge Jay Hastings say he saw Perdomo carrying Lennon into the lobby? Did Perdomo leave John just inside the lobby doors and Lennon then made his own way into Hasting's office from there? This is highly unlikely. Why didn't Jay Hastings mention any of this?

When I spoke to Medeiros, he had no idea that Perdomo's missing statement was being kept from the public. He gave me further information as if he was reading out a shopping list. It rang of truth and Medeiros had no reason to sensationalise an account that he did not even believe to be important. He thought it was common knowledge. The main problem with this information was that Jay Hastings was adamant he did not see Perdomo carry a mortally wounded Lennon through the lobby doors. Someone was clearly not telling the truth about what happened after John was shot. In his case notebooks, Lead Detective

Hoffman wrote a brief note about Perdomo and what he saw. He knew Perdomo's evidence was important, calling him "Witness 1", but Hoffman didn't write down his statement, briefly noting instead:

"He saw entire incident. Perdomo also saw the perp on previous occasion."

So, what exactly did the Dakota doorman do (or not do) when John Lennon was assassinated?

Consider the "Gun Kicking Perdomo". By some accounts, José Perdomo bravely shook the gun out of Mark Chapman's hands after Chapman allegedly shot his .38 at John Lennon. In his first statement to the police, though, Chapman said "I don't remember what happened to the gun" after he fired it. Another witness caused yet more confusion when he said he saw Chapman throw his gun to the ground. However it found its way to the ground, one thing seems to be universally accepted, and that is that Perdomo kicked a gun to the rear of the driveway. One witness clearly states he saw Perdomo do this.

No one other than Perdomo can be certain that the gun on the ground which lift operator Joseph Many saw and picked up was Mark Chapman's; we must take Perdomo's word for that. There is a significant time delay between a witness seeing Perdomo kick a gun to the back of the driveway and Joe Many arriving on the scene and seeing a gun on the ground in the driveway. Perdomo could have been alone with that gun for well over a minute. This all begs the following key five questions:

1. Why did Perdomo kick the gun to the rear of the driveway?
2. Why didn't Perdomo just pick up the gun after Chapman allegedly dropped it?
3. Why did Perdomo wait until Joe Many arrived on the scene to pick the gun up, after kicking it to the rear of the driveway?

If Perdomo was so scared that Chapman might pick up the gun and start firing it again, why didn't he pick it up and take it into the Dakota himself?

4. How did Perdomo know Joe Many would even arrive on the scene to take the gun away?

5. Why was Perdomo so keen not to get his fingerprints on Mark Chapman's gun?

In 1980, fingerprint databases were not kept by local New York police forces. Fingerprint analysis had to be sent to the FBI. Did Dakota Perdomo have cause to fear such an analysis? In fact, Perdomo had little to worry about when it came to fingerprints. Lead Detective Ron Hoffman revealed that the NYPD never took fingerprints from the gun or the driveway area. Hoffman wasn't even sure if Chapman was wearing gloves or not. Just how many instances of malpractice did the NYPD commit in this single case?

According to Dakota concierge Jay Hastings, Perdomo was a no-nonsense, bull-like figure of a man. The image we have of him in 1977 certainly backs up this claim. In the picture, he is exactly the kind of guy you would want to work at the door of an exclusive New York residence. Of course, he would have been expected to meet and greet the residents and their guests as they went about their daily business, but he was also expected to keep them safe. Security obligations must have been written into his job description. Which then begs the important question – why didn't Perdomo try to stop Chapman from firing his gun? He told Cullen he saw Chapman's bullets push Lennon through the doors, so why do nothing? Why even allow Chapman to loiter at the mouth of the driveway in the first place? Chapman said he calmly took his gun, took aim and then started firing steadily at Lennon. Chapman even claimed in a 1992 TV interview that he went into a combat stance first, before firing. (He didn't.)

What was Perdomo doing when all of this was going on?

Absolutely nothing. Perhaps he was scared or perhaps he just froze, both understandable reactions in the circumstances. But one harsh fact cannot be ignored: as a security guard, José Perdomo completely failed at his job on the night John Lennon was assassinated.

Chapman said on numerous occasions that immediately after he shot at Lennon, Perdomo came over to him with tears flowing down his face. Crying has always struck me as a strange emotion for the no-nonsense doorman to have at this precise moment. You could imagine Perdomo being shocked at what he thought he had just witnessed, but crying? To me, this doesn't make any sense. Bursting into tears seconds after witnessing gun fire seems very odd. Note that Dakota staffers such as Jay Hastings and Joseph Many never mentioned Perdomo's tears, even though they saw him only moments after Chapman. None of the police officers mentioned Perdomo's tears either. How strange.

According to Joseph Many, immediately after the shooting, Perdomo said he didn't want to work outside. Joe Many was then duly asked by the Dakota management to don the doorman's uniform to help control the thousands of mourning fans outside, while a plethora of TV cameras trained themselves on the Dakota driveway gates. If Perdomo wanted to stay anonymous, his decision was a wise one. Numerous Dakota doormen can be seen in the hundreds of hours of archive video footage from the media coverage, but not Perdomo. He made sure of it.

Journalists and TV reporters were very keen to interview secondary witnesses, such as Sean Strub. Secondary witnesses who never actually saw the shooting were all that was on offer. José Perdomo, the key witness, was never interviewed by the media. We know that the NYPD and New York DA's office told other witnesses not to talk to the media. But, as I have shown, Perdomo told secondary witnesses exactly what he thought had happened. It's incredible that no journalist or reporter managed to talk to Perdomo. Not one single person from the media mentioned

Perdomo by name. He was always referred to as the doorman. Why was Perdomo's identity kept secret from the world for seven years? For the remaining years of his employment at the Dakota, he worked mainly in the basement preforming menial tasks. Let's hope his circulation problems allowed him to sit down.

José Perdomo retired from working at the Dakota in 1994. He would have been 60 years old. He subsequently died in Florida in 2010, aged 76, taking all his secrets with him. So why have the NYPD and New York District Attorney's office kept Perdomo's witness statement from the public's gaze for over 40 years? I believe the answer is very simple and very telling. If we are to believe the account of Medeiros regarding Perdomo's alleged actions after Lennon was shot, the public would then know that John Lennon was almost certainly shot inside the glass vestibule/lobby stairwell area. This would mean that Mark Chapman could not have feasibly caused John's wounds (or the holes in the glass panels) from where he was standing. To pin the murder on and convict Chapman, the authorities had to keep Perdomo's statement hidden. What other reason could they have for concealing it for so long? The fact that Perdomo never saw Chapman fire the bullets is another major problem for the authorities. José Perdomo was a ghost by necessity.

Every famous assassination has a tagline: the "grassy knoll" for JFK's, or the "lady in the polka dot dress" for RFK's assassination. Questions also tend to float unanswered around these famous moments: why were MLK's companions pointing to the sky after he was shot and did Gavrilo Princip's desire for a sandwich really lead to Archduke Franz Ferdinand's assassination and the start of the First World War? For John Lennon's murder, it is simply: where was Yoko?

Witness 2: Yoko Ono – John Lennon's wife

Aside from Perdomo, Yoko Ono was the only other person who could have witnessed his murder. Her statements regarding that

December night are often contradictory and muddled. This is not in itself necessarily a sign of something sinister: witnessing a traumatic event can often result in strange and confused recollections. In addition, Yoko Ono was a self-confessed heroin user throughout 1980, and might have been under the influence of the drug on the night of December 8th, 1980.

Before we analyse exactly what Yoko saw that night, it might be useful to look briefly at her life and political activities with John in the run up to his death – a life in which there appear to be almost as many gaps and anomalies as there are in her husband's murder.

Ono was born into a wealthy banking family in Japan. By 1962, at the age of 29, she found herself in New York and on the receiving end of a string of bad reviews for her embryonic modern art exhibitions. She was also estranged from her husband of the previous six years, Japanese composer Toshi Ichiyanagi. When Ono returned to Tokyo to try and save her marriage, she attempted to commit suicide and was diagnosed with clinical depression. Ono was then apparently placed into a Tokyo mental institution by her family after she divorced Ichiyanagi.

This might have been the end of the Yoko Ono story but for a New York based, aspiring jazz musician called Tony Cox. According to legend, Cox was such a fan of Yoko Ono's art, he felt compelled to travel to Tokyo to try and find her. Cox discovered from Ono's family where she was being treated for depression. Once there, the story goes that he helped Ono to escape. Cox accused this unidentified Tokyo mental institution of "holding her [Ono] against her will" through the use of drugs. Despite Cox's claim that he had a deep knowledge of the type of drugs that Ono was apparently being forced to take, neither Cox nor Ono ever revealed what these mysterious drugs were. After Cox heroically sprung Ono out, a strange ménage-a-trois living arrangement occurred in Tokyo, with Cox, Ono and her ex-first husband all now living together. This bohemian living arrangement was finally curtailed when Ono fell pregnant with Tony's baby.

I have never accepted the story that Cox liberated Yoko from her confinement in Japan. I asked Dan Richter, a friend of Cox and Ono, what really happened. Richter confirmed that Ono and Cox knew each other in New York as far back as 1962, when Yoko was a new face on the modern art scene. Cox knew some of Ono's friends. Richter said Cox flew to Tokyo to meet up with Ono again. According to Richter, Cox managed to get Yoko Ono out of the mental institution by marrying her in the hospital.

Whatever the truth of their reunion, Cox and Ono were married by June 1963 and had a baby girl called "Kyoko Chan Cox" two months later. After moving to London in 1965, Cox became the full-time carer for Kyoko, while Ono focused on re-igniting her stalled career, amidst the flower-power bustle of sixties swinging London. The one thing Ono needed for her exhibitions was money.

Dan Richter has confirmed to me that Ono initially contacted John Lennon to acquire funding for her art career. This had the full backing of Tony Cox. Ono met John Lennon in November 1966 and soon after, they started their affair with the ever-compliant backing of Tony Cox. Ono says that she was completely oblivious to who John Lennon was at the time they met (despite Lennon being one of the most famous people in the music world). Ono has always claimed that Lennon romantically pursued her and that she was initially reluctant.

John's wife, Cynthia, saw things very differently. She was furious at the way Ono pursued her husband. Cynthia has also said that she thought Ono had an almost hypnotic control over her husband from the start. Beatles insider and confidante Tony Bramwell agrees with Cynthia, stating that Yoko Ono relentlessly pursued John Lennon, even hanging outside the Apple HQ like a groupie with the rest of the "Apple Scruff" obsessives desperate for a glimpse of their heroes. Bramwell told me that John once asked him to get some of his stuff back from Ono's flat, as Lennon was reluctant to go back and spend more time with her.

Tony Cox had a reputation as a bit of a grifter who became highly adept at getting money out of bank managers. Dan Richter, Cox's friend, confirmed to me that Cox often secured advances of money from gullible bank managers for films and schemes which never materialised. Cox was well known at the time as a master con-man and manipulator.

Dan Richter (who at the time was an actor, living next door to Ono and Cox in London) and Tony Bramwell (who at the time was running Apple Films) believed that in late 1966, Cox and Ono made a pact over a plan to help Yoko attract Lennon for his money. Bramwell and Richter both state that Cox made Ono sign a one-page contract, promising Cox half of Ono's income, in perpetuity. Richter told me he remembers seeing the contract and that Cox was very happy that it was agreed and signed by Yoko Ono. Richter has previously claimed that he thought the contract was for Ono's general income (though Richter has confirmed to me that he cannot remember this detail). Tony Bramwell insists the contract was for any Lennon inheritance that Ono might gain control over. Bramwell made the claim about the Ono/Cox contract in his bestselling book *My Life with the Beatles*. He believes it to be significant that Yoko Ono never sued him regarding this claim.

John Lennon finally left Cynthia in late 1968 to be with Yoko Ono. Tony Cox and Yoko Ono divorced in February 1969 and Ono married Lennon shortly thereafter, in Gibraltar. Even though Ono gained custody of Kyoko, according to Cox the child was not interested in being with her mother, and in 1970 Cox fled the UK with Kyoko and went to America to join the controversial Christian cult "Church of the Living Word" (sometimes known as "The Walk").

To help Ono retrieve her daughter, she and Lennon moved to New York in 1971. As of 2023, Kyoko Chan Cox is said to be helping to take care of her elderly mother.

Regarding the assassination of John Lennon, the official account is clear. John and Yoko arrived back at the Dakota at about 10.50pm, where a killer was lying in wait for John. What remains unclear is where exactly Ono was when John was shot. This is crucial because pinpointing where Yoko was positioned will help ascertain what she saw and what really happened.

In April 2021, NYPD Lead Detective Ron Hoffman (and information from his notebooks) gave me some new insights into where Ono might have been. Hoffman claimed he went immediately to the Roosevelt Hospital after arriving at the Dakota murder scene. He had not reached the hospital before John was declared dead but insists he was there shortly after. There is news footage from the time which shows Hoffman being interviewed outside the Hospital. When Hoffman arrived at the Roosevelt, John Lennon was already dead. According to Hoffman, while at the hospital, he asked Ono what had happened in the Dakota driveway, and she allegedly told him:

> "We got out of the car, John walked in front of me, nothing unusual. He walked in."

According to Chapman, John Lennon was 20 feet in front of him before he started shooting at Lennon. If this is true, and Ono was behind John (as Hoffman stated from Ono's initial recollection), she would have seen the shooting right in front of her eyes and would have had to walk or run past Chapman to get inside the Dakota after he had just shot her husband. None of this makes sense. Perdomo has never mentioned where Ono was when John was shot, and Chapman has consistently said Ono was ahead of John before he started shooting. From this first contact between Ono and Hoffman, we can assume Yoko Ono thought she was behind John when Chapman shot him. However, this was (allegedly) Ono's first recollection of the murder, possibly less than an hour after it happened. Her recollections would change again, and again and again. So, which was it? To help clarify this important detail, Hoffman's notes revealed a further statement given by Yoko Ono. It's unclear when exactly the statement was given. Hoffman mentions that Daniel Warmflash, Yoko's attorney, was present. So, this second Ono statement was likely taken by Hoffman in Ono's Dakota apartment, a few hours after John Lennon was assassinated. This is what he wrote down:

> "We went to the recording studio. And we just came home. We got out of the limo, heard noises, thought something was happening in the street. We didn't turn around to look at anything. We went inside the glass door and John said, 'I'm shot.'"

This is another indication that Lennon was shot inside the vestibule doors and out of sight of Chapman. Crucially, Yoko Ono clearly states that she and her husband "didn't turn around". This important detail calls into serious question the official line that Chapman called out to Lennon and he turned around. If Chapman did call out, surely Ono would have said so. To have Lennon being shot in the front, the authorities had to have the possibility of Lennon turning around. It didn't happen.

Hoffman's notebooks then describe a further statement given to him by Yoko at 12.20am in her apartment, 90 minutes after her husband's assassination.

> "Left the studio at 22:30. Esquire Limousine Service and parked at the curb. Thinks John got out of the limo first. We walked to the building and then I heard shots. John said, Christ, I'm shot. He just ran in the glass door. I think the two shots in the glass door were after he was shot. I just rushed in after him."

We can safely assume that from this point in time, 90 minutes after the murder, Yoko Ono has definitively declared that she was

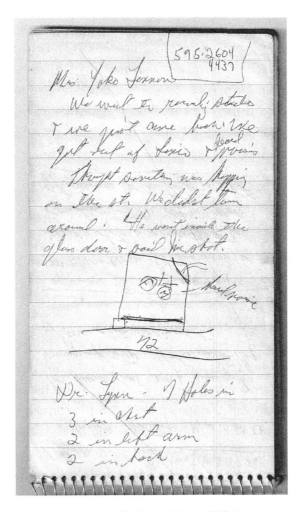

Yoko Ono early statement to Ron Hoffman © David Whelan

behind John when he got shot. Which would then lead us to ask, did Ono see Chapman shooting her husband and how did she not get in the way? If Ono was behind Chapman while he was shooting her husband, why didn't she run back out into the street? Why did she apparently run or walk past Chapman into the Dakota? Ono's inference that the bullet holes in the glass doors came after Lennon was shot, is very strange. Yoko Ono has never said she saw Chapman shoot her husband, never. None of this makes sense.

Hoffman's notes then describe Yoko as "Yoko Lennon". She

is also described as "Witness number 4". The brief but highly important note states:

"She heard the shots but did not see the shooter."

After four statements, Hoffman was still keen to talk to Ono. Clearly her variable statements must have been troubling him. 10 days later, Hoffman recorded the next Ono account:

"We went to Record Plant, stayed until 10.30. We came back. I heard shots very near. Thought it could be a tire. It did not occur to me that he was hit."

The official version of events must have John being shot in the driveway outside the vestibule doors. It is the only place Chapman could see from where he was standing. We know Ono was in the driveway after gunfire (more details on this later). Therefore, how could Ono not feasibly know her husband had been hit? None of this makes sense. Also, how can five gunshots be mistaken for a blown tire?

On 18th December, Yoko Ono changed her story again, when she gave an interview to NYPD Detective Peter Mangicavallo. Now Yoko was not just behind John, but sometimes in front as well:

"Went to Record Plant, stayed until about 10.30. We wanted to go to restaurant but did not. We normally go into the gate but did not. Got out walked past gate. John was walking past the door, he was walking faster. I heard shots, I heard shots. He walked to door upstairs. He said I'm shot. I followed him. He was standing but staggering. I told him to lay down.

Sometimes he was ahead. Sometimes I was. I saw a male by the Watchman's box. It was dark and night. He nodded at me. He was not small."

This was the last official statement Yoko Ono ever gave about her husband's killing. When I asked Hoffman why he didn't ask more questions to clarify the anomalies in her statements, he stated that he did not want to further upset a grieving widow.

This final statement makes a few things clearer. John was "walking past the door" when Ono heard shots. The only door in the driveway is the glass vestibule doors. This fits with a previous statement from her that John was shot when "he went inside the glass door". Ono said that Lennon "walked to door upstairs" which must mean the two wooden doors that lead into the lobby and concierge's area. Taking all of this into account and considering that Detective Hoffman was "certain" that Lennon was shot in the stairwell area, and that Perdomo told Medeiros and MacDougall that he helped a mortally wounded John up the stairs into the lobby, we can safely assume that John Lennon could have been shot inside the vestibule and collapsed somewhere on the six steps that lead up to the lobby area.

Yoko Ono has made it very clear that she "followed" Lennon and was behind him. Detective Hoffman is also certain of this and bizarrely thinks that Chapman stood between Lennon and Ono when he allegedly shot John, with Ono watching all of this happening in front of her eyes. One matter is crucially clear here, and I repeat it because of its importance, Yoko Ono has never said she saw Chapman shooting her husband. She had five chances to say so in the hours and days after the murder and she never mentioned it. She has also had forty-three years to reveal this important fact – but, she never has. She placed Chapman by the watchman's box, which is on the street and not in the driveway. It is completely out of the sight line of the vestibule doors and the stairway leading to the lobby. It is at least 35 feet away from the vestibule entrance.

Combining what Perdomo, Hoffman and Ono have said, we can now assume that John Lennon exited the limo first and strode towards the glass vestibule doors. It is highly likely that when he entered the vestibule area and started to climb the six steps up to the lobby doors, he was struck with four bullets in his upper left chest area. He fell backwards and possibly fell partly out of the glass vestibule doors. He almost certainly collapsed in the stairway area, moments from his death. Perdomo may have run to his aid and helped carry him up the steps and left him at the lobby doors. Ono then may (or may not) have followed on, as Lennon staggered into the concierge's area, where he eventually collapsed. So many options… such little clarity.

In September 2022, *Rolling Stone* magazine co-founder and long-standing editor, Jann Wenner, released his autobiography. Contained within, Wenner recounted a moving story of meeting Yoko Ono a few days after John's assassination. Before we delve into this, allow me to add some context. *Rolling Stone* magazine was founded by Wenner and his partner in 1968 in San Francisco, at the height of groovy hippiedom. The music and culture magazine became ever more popular when John Lennon gave it a lengthy interview in 1970. Wenner cleverly secured Lennon's participation by promising to promote Lennon and Ono's dreadful *Two Virgins* album. An album that was universally banned at the time due to nude images of its stars on the cover. Music lovers across the world owe those nude images a great debt of thanks. Wenner was the ultimate social climber who was attracted to music stars for the social cachet they would give him. He made it his mission to become friends with the most famous couple on the planet, John Lennon and his new wife Yoko Ono. Wenner's ambition and hubris eventually infuriated and alienated Lennon, when he turned his 1970 *Rolling Stone* interview into a book called *Lennon Remembers*. John never spoke to Wenner again. Wenner later admitted, "I chose the money over the friendship".

After John Lennon's death, Wenner went on NBC's *Today* show and, still racked with guilt about how he previously betrayed Lennon, opined how Lennon and JFK were "intimately connected". Wenner claims that Ono was so impressed by this

TV performance, she invited him over to see her at the Dakota. In his officially sanctioned (but subsequently disowned) biography of 2017 called *Sticky Fingers*, Wenner talked about how he met Ono and Sean alone in the Dakota and Ono "talked it [John's death] through with him, telling Wenner "what happened that night, constantly reliving it, repeating it".

Then in his autobiography of 2022, *Like a Rolling Stone*, Wenner decided to up the ante about his Dakota visit to Ono, stating:

> "She gave me an account of the killer calling out John's name and then the gun coming out, how she and John had seen him there in the afternoon when they'd left."

The big problem with this new information is that Ono, in all her interviews to the police and subsequently to the media, has never said she heard Chapman call out, or said she saw his gun, or recognised him from earlier. I can categorically confirm this as I've seen and read all the original written notes from her police interviews. You would think such crucial details would have been given to the police or the media, but there is absolutely nothing from Yoko on these issues.

There are other problems with Wenner's account. It is well documented that throughout the 90s, Wenner befriended Ono and spent some time with her in public. What is problematic about his alleged invitation to the Dakota in 1980 is that neither Ono, nor Fred Seaman, nor Michael Medeiros, nor Elliot Mintz have ever said they met or saw Wenner at the Dakota and they were all verifiably there with Ono around that time. No Lennon or Beatles biographer has mentioned the visit either; in all the hundreds of books on the subject, no mention. You would think a visit to Yoko Ono at the Dakota by the then famous editor of a very famous magazine, with the world's media on site, would have been noticed and recorded by someone. But there is nothing. Zilch.

I contacted Wenner in person. He was initially suspicious of my approach, and he stuck to his story, stating:

> "It is absolutely true, I remember it like yesterday. She was understandably in a bit of a haze."

When I told him that I had possession of all of Yoko's police statements and interviews and she had never mentioned that she heard Chapman call out, saw his gun or recognised him from earlier, Wenner, to his credit, rowed back, saying:

> "That's what I recall to the best of my ability. It was so long ago that it would be impossible for me to describe those remarks with certainty. The memory is funny. Perhaps she's right, who knows."

Ono was there. I would therefore suggest she is right. Wenner continued:

> "I was for sure there. Maybe I came to elaborate it. Sorry to be evasive."

To his credit, after I made him admit he possibly embellished important facts, Wenner said I could quote him.

For completeness, I also decided to contact Wenner's biographer Joe Hagan to try and dig deeper into the mysterious Dakota visit. Thankfully, Hagan interviewed Yoko Ono in 2016 about the book and her relationship with Wenner and being the thorough professional that he is, Hagan asked Ono about the 1980 December visit. Here's the exchange:

Hagan: But you had him [Wenner] over here [The Dakota] for the first time. Do you remember his coming to see you?
Ono: No, but I'm sure it happened.

To be honest, I'm not sure it did happen.

This whole episode neatly encapsulates how a version of a famous event can be etched into the public's conscience many decades after the event, regardless of how accurate or untruthful the narrative turns out to be. Wenner was a famous magazine editor and journalist who had decades of experience. Journalism was in his DNA, yet he still got the facts wrong, or should I charitably say, he was comfortable reporting facts that were out of the reach of his memory? He clearly felt comfortable doing so because dubious "facts" had long been included in a narrative the public had been consistently fed and therefore accepted.

I'll leave that one there.

Witness 3: Jay Hastings – Dakota concierge

So, are there any other clues leading us to the conclusion that Lennon was shot in an area of the Dakota that Chapman could not have even seen, never mind shot bullets into? Yes, there are. Enter concierge Jay Hastings.

José Perdomo's witness statement is still sealed and as Yoko Ono's recollections have been rather varied, we can perhaps try and get some clarity from one of the other key witnesses in the case – the Dakota concierge, Jay Hastings.

Jay was born in October 1953, grew up in Monroe, New York, and went to Washingtonville High School. I assumed Jay would have been drafted into military service at this point, but Jay told me he avoided the Vietnam draft by securing a lucky number in the draft lottery scheme that was introduced in 1969. Jay told me he might have stayed on at high school until 1972 and he then went to the New York School of Visual Arts from 1972 until 1978, doing a three-year course. When I asked Jay how a three-year course took six years to complete, he told me he took a year out for a bad knee. I gave up asking him about the other missing two years. It was a long time ago, to be fair, but Jay's exact whereabouts and activities between 1971 and 1978 are still somewhat unclear.

What we do know is that Jay started working at the Dakota in the summer of 1978. By December 1980, Jay was a concierge and part-time doorman. Hastings says he didn't see the shooting take place with his own eyes, but he did hear it. He was probably one of the closest to the location where John was shot. His account is key. Before we get into the details, it's important to understand where Hastings was when John was shot. Jay Hastings says he was where he should have been that night – which was in the concierge's front office. This office has a window located in the wall just beyond the vestibule door entrance. Hastings has stated that he could hear everything going on in the driveway from this window. He knew when people were coming and going. He claimed to know how to recognise the footsteps from different residents on the driveway cobbles.

As with José Perdomo, no official witness account from Jay Hastings has ever been released to the public. This may be because, as Joe Many revealed to me, Hastings did not want to give an official statement to the NYPD and wasn't forced to. Hastings told me that he gave his account to several detectives on the night of the assassination, but none of these accounts have surfaced. Hastings has, however, given his account on three separate occasions. Firstly, to *Rolling Stone* journalist Greg Katz on the night of the murder. Katz managed to bag this scoop because, coincidentally, his parents lived in the Dakota, above the very driveway that Lennon walked into. According to Joe Many, Hastings was paid for this interview. Hastings then subsequently gave a few brief words to Lennon biographer Ray Coleman in 1983. Lastly, and most relevant to my investigations, Hastings gave me numerous long and detailed accounts of what he heard and saw on the night John Lennon was assassinated. I found him laconic and surprisingly chilled about the whole incident. Some people could describe his manner as detached. Much of what Hastings told me rang true, but some details were troublingly inconsistent with what we know.

This is Hastings' statement, told on 9th December 1980 to Greg Katz, which was published in *Rolling Stone* magazine:

"Hastings was reading a magazine shortly before eleven pm when he heard several shots outside the office, and then the sound of shattering glass. He stiffened. He heard someone coming up the office steps. John Lennon stumbled in, a horrible, confused look on his face. Yoko followed, screaming, 'John's been shot, John's been shot'. At first, Hastings thought it was a crazy joke. Lennon walked several steps, then collapsed on the floor, scattering the cassette tapes of his final session that he'd been holding in his hands.

Hastings triggered an alarm that summoned the police and he rushed to John's side. The anguished doorman gently removed Lennon's glasses, which seemed to be pushing in on his contorted face. He struggled out of his blue Dakota jacket and placed it over Lennon. Then he stripped off his tie to use as a tourniquet, but there was no place to put it. Blood streamed from Lennon's chest and mouth. His eyes were open but unfocused. He gurgled once, vomiting blood and fleshy material. Yoko, frantic, screamed for a doctor and an ambulance. Hastings dialled 911 and asked for help. Then he returned to Lennon's side and said, 'It's okay, John, you'll be all right'."

There are two important points to consider here. Firstly, Hastings said he heard several shots outside his office and then the sound of broken glass. This ties in with the location of Hastings' office window and indicates that the glass doors were hit when John was shot, or shortly thereafter. Secondly, the words "Yoko followed" indicates that she was behind John, as her early statements corroborate. If this is true, then how did Ono not get in the way of Chapman or his bullets?

I initially thought the "scattering of cassette tapes" might have been an invention by Katz. But in the police inventory vouchers of property found at the "homicide crime scene" (a copy of which is reproduced below) a Sony Cassette Recorder TCM-600 and a Cassette Tape SXC-90 are clearly listed. This was one of the first embryonic "Walkmans" on the market and it had a portable speaker built into the back of it. This cassette recorder and the 90-minute tape were almost certainly what Hastings told Katz was scattered on the floor from John's hand, after he was shot. John was even seen carrying the recorder in one of the last Paul Goresh photos. His leather jacket at the time was fur-lined, with deep pouch pockets at the front. If John had the recorder and tape in this kind of pocket, it probably wouldn't have fallen out when he fell. Hastings has confirmed the tapes fell out of John's hand. I do not believe Hastings was telling the truth on this point. The voucher said the recorder and tape were recovered from the crime scene, not John's body.

Sony Tape & Recorder Inventory Voucher © David Whelan

There's another interesting angle to this. If John was carrying the Walkman or tape in his right hand, then he would have had to use his left hand to pull open the vestibule door. However, John's left hand and arm would have been completely immobilised due to his left subclavian artery being totally severed on the bullets' impact. John could not have feasibly been shot in the driveway and pulled open the vestibule door, then got himself to the lobby and concierge's office area. Alternatively, if he was carrying the Walkman or a cassette tape in his left hand, surely he would have immediately dropped them in the driveway, as he would have lost the function of his left arm.

Many months after the killing, Officer Spiro tried to play down the importance of the recorder and tapes to Lennon's assistant Mario Casciano. Spiro claimed that John only had one tape in his jacket at the time of his murder and that was a Carole King tape cassette of her *Tapestry* album. According to police voucher records which I have personally seen, John did not have a Carole King tape on him that night. Why did Spiro invent this story? Was he trying to confuse the tape and recorder issue to play down its significance?

In one of my early interviews with Hastings, he said he could not remember any tapes and John "may have had an envelope or something". In my last interview with Jay in October 2023, he admitted that the Katz account was true and lots of tapes scattered in the back office when John fell. Remember, only one tape and one tape-recorder was submitted in the police evidence vouchers.

In my first interview with Hastings, he told me:

"I'd listen out for the slam of their black limousine door. I could always tell his walk."

Hastings confirms again that he was in the best possible position to hear what happened when John Lennon was shot.

Hastings told me that he was sitting in his office, with the office window that faced out onto the Dakota driveway open. This meant Hastings could hear everything going on in the driveway. At around 10.50pm, the Lennons' limousine pulled up and Perdomo greeted the couple. Hastings then heard footsteps which he presumed where the Lennons walking towards the vestibule doors at the right end of the driveway and right next to his window. He heard the vestibule door swing open and he heard gunfire, four or five shots, close together.

Hastings then said that moments later, John entered his office/ lobby area and staggered like a drunk man. As John stumbled past, he allegedly said "*I'm shot*", and had blood running out of his mouth. John managed to lurch into a back office, which apparently was the superintendent's office. (In my October 2023 interview with Jay, he added a second "I'm shot", now claiming that John said this to him twice.)

Once in the back office, John collapsed on the floor, partly on his side. Hastings rolled John onto his back and took his glasses off. He opened John's leather jacket and saw his chest was covered in blood. He could not remember where Ono was at this point, but he did recall a few moments later that Lennon gave out a death rattle, as he coughed up blood and material. Hastings was convinced that this is the moment that John Lennon died. One crucial fact to remember here is that all the police officers who found John Lennon's body said he was face down on a rug in the back office. Hastings told me that he tuned him onto his back. Why the discrepancy? Did Hastings or Ono turn John back onto his face? When I asked Hastings about this in October 2023, he could not find an answer as to why John was left face down. Hastings remembered Yoko screaming for an ambulance. He ran out of his office and pressed a panic button.

Jay Hastings has now updated his story from 1980 and adds the new detail that John told him he had been shot. Hastings didn't say this to Katz in 1980. Hastings told Katz that he triggered an alarm. Hastings told me that the alarm was already triggered when he tried it. Hastings told me that John ran/lurched into the back office. In 1980, Hastings inferred that this did not happen and John walked several steps and collapsed.

Hastings also said that Perdomo was at the kerbside when the limousine pulled up to the Dakota driveway. If he could hear Perdomo greeting them thirty feet away by the roadside, he would also have been able to hear Chapman calling out to Lennon as Perdomo said he did. Hastings never mentioned this to Greg Katz and he never mentioned it to me forty years later. Perhaps Chapman whispered John's name or perhaps he never called out at all. I repeat again, Chapman has never said he called out to John… ever.

Hastings' testimony also reveals that John was possibly shot after he opened the vestibule door. Hastings' window was right next to the vestibule doors, so he would easily have heard them open. It's probable that John was shot when he was next to, or just inside, these doors. Hastings then tells us that John ran through his front office and collapsed in an office behind his office. This is problematic, as some accounts and witness testimony have John collapsing in Hastings' front office – again, why the discrepancy?

Jay Hastings could not remember whether the vestibule doors were open or shut that night. Lift operator Joe Many has told me that the vestibule doors and the two mahogony doors at the top of the stairs were on automated spring closers. They were always closed. Many would know that for sure.

When the police officers arrived, Hastings told me that he helped them carry John's body out to the police car. He told me that the officers made him carry the bloody "business end" of John's body (i.e. the shoulders) because AIDS was prominent in the news at this time. (This is not true as the first cases of AIDS in the USA were reported in 1981). Hastings told me that carrying John out to the police car with police officers is how he got covered in blood. Joe Many the lift operator said it was because he thought John must have collapsed in Hastings arms. Joe Many said he thought this because Hastings told him this is exactly what happened. The key point is that officers Frauenberger and Palma, the two police officers who carried John's body outside, both state unequivocally that Hastings did not help them. Officers Spiro and Cullen, who witnessed the body being carried out also have never said Hastings helped them. Other secondary witnesses also say the same thing. Hastings clearly did not help carry John's body out to Officer Moran's squad car, but Hastings wants the world to believe he did and he also wants the world to believe that this is how he got John Lennon's blood on his shirt. This is troubling.

We can now safely assume that John was shot within the vestibule door area, on the steps, in a concealed area a long way away from where Mark Chapman was standing and totally out of his sight.

In 2016, Jay Hastings sold the "blood-stained" shirt he was allegedly wearing on the night John Lennon was shot for $31,000. There is not much blood on the shirt and many criticised Hastings for the macabre sale. If Hastings did help the NYPD carry Lennon out to their squad cars, should there not perhaps be more blood on this shirt?

Two things trouble me with Jay Hastings. Firstly, why does his statement about Lennon staggering into the lobby area

Jay Hastings' "bloody" shirt sold at auction © Unknown

contradict statements that say Perdomo helped Lennon into the lobby area? When I spoke to Hastings in late April 2022, I asked him again about Perdomo allegedly helping a mortally wounded Lennon up the stairs and into the lobby area. Did he see Perdomo helping Lennon and why had he not mentioned this before? Hastings said he was certain that he did not see Perdomo helping Lennon. Secondly, his recollection that he helped the police carry Lennon's body out to the patrol car has been refuted by Mark Chapman, both police officers who carried Lennon's body and Dakota staff who were there. Why did Hastings lie about this? Is it because he wanted an excuse for having blood on his shirt?

In Detective Hoffman's notebook, the following brief notes on Hastings were made:

> "He [Hastings] heard shots, 2 or 3 and JL running up steps. Yoko said, he's been shot, call a doctor."

It is interesting that Hastings told Hoffman that he only heard 2 or 3 shots and that he heard John "running up" the steps. I'm not sure he could have heard John running up those outside steps to the lobby, as the stairs were in an enclosed area behind mahogany doors. Also, would Lennon be "running" at this point, given his critical injuries? Dr Halleran and nurses Kammerer and Sato, who treated John Lennon at the Roosevelt, had all told me that once he was shot, John could not possibly have taken more than a couple of staggered steps before dying. When I told Hastings about the doctor and nurses questioning Lennon moving – never mind walking or running – immediately after being shot, Hastings replied, "I can't answer that."

None of Hastings' statements make much sense when you consider the evidence to hand and other people's recollections. His statements need to be considered very carefully and, in my opinion, with much scepticism.

Witness 4: Richard Peterson – taxi driver

Cab driver Richard Peterson spoke to me at length in spring 2022 about what he saw at the Dakota. Before we get to his witness statement, Peterson told me about an incident that happened when he was brought in for questioning by the NYPD and DA's office. What he had to say, if true, was disturbing and frankly unbelievable.

Peterson alleged that while at the police station on the night of the murder, he was interviewed by multiple police officers in multiple rooms to see, in his words, if his story "jived" with each group. After this merry-go-round was over, Peterson was left alone in a room for over an hour. Then, suddenly, police officers brought in a bloody t-shirt with a hole in it, which Peterson assumed was the one Lennon wore. The cops then allegedly put a gun in front of Peterson. He asked them to take it away as he was afraid of guns. To ramp the improbability factor up one more notch, Peterson then alleged that the cops brought in the rest of Lennon's bloody clothes which he was wearing when he was killed. A black leather jacket, a red shirt and "shabby" boots were placed silently in front of Peterson. He claims that after a while the items were taken away and no further questions asked.

If this story of Lennon's bloody clothes and murder weapon is true, it simply beggars belief that crucial criminal evidence could be so poorly treated, almost with disdain. I don't believe this story. Both nurses Kammerer and Sato have confirmed that Lennon's clothes went with his body into the care of Elliot Gross, the chief medical examiner, just a few hours after they tried to save Lennon. They are adamant his clothes could not have gone to the police station on the night of the murder. Herb Frauenberger also told me that he never saw any blood-stained clothes at the police station and Peterson's story could not be true. Officer Tony Palma, speaking to me in March 2022, confirmed that he collected Lennon's bloodied clothes from the office of the chief medical examiner the day after the murder once Elliot Gross had completed his autopsy. Palma said the clothes were given to him in a paper bag and he remembered being hounded by the press outside Gross's office and back at his police station. Crucially, he said he arrived back at the station at lunchtime. This means Peterson's account of having Lennon's bloody clothes presented to him the night before seems highly unlikely, if not impossible.

After lengthy questioning at the 20th Precinct, Peterson was told he was free to go. The press was gathered outside, and he recalled that the police officers seemed concerned that the press might talk to him when he left the station. They apparently tried to come up with a disguise to fool the press. Peterson said that he was a nobody. Why would any of the press want to talk to him? An officer then escorted him from the station, with the threat that should he talk to the press, he would be in big trouble. He was apparently threatened many times "do not dare talk to the press".

The NYPD's alleged fear of Peterson talking to the press is hard to understand. For many years, researchers have often wondered why José Perdomo and Richard Peterson were kept out of the public's eye and didn't talk to the press. Listening to the alleged threats which Peterson had to deal with, perhaps they were simply too frightened to talk about what they saw when John Lennon was killed. Why was the NYPD so scared of witnesses talking to the press? Is it perhaps that they were concerned that their recollections wouldn't match the story they were concocting? It might very well have been.

Richard Peterson recalled that the New York District Attorney young staff spoke down to him as if he was stupid. He made several visits, and felt that they constantly patronised him, expecting that he would change his testimony to suit their own version. What irked the DA's office was the number of bullets which Peterson heard. He insisted he heard four shots, the DA's office insisted that it was five. This discrepancy was apparently discussed many times over.

Taxi Driver Richard Peterson is the witness who apparently

saw it all. Richard Peterson pulled up to the Dakota at the same time as John and Yoko. Peterson's very comprehensive witness statement was told to NYPD Detective Allen Mintz:

"On 12/9/80 at about 0020 hours I interviewed at the 20th Police Detective Unit office one Richard Peterson… employed as a taxi driver for Valeria Cab Corp. He stated that on the day of the occurrence he had picked up two passengers in Soho and that they were going to the Dakota. As he reached 72nd Street and Central Park West he was behind John Lennon's limo. As the limousine came to a halt in front of the Dakota he pulled up behind it. The passengers in his taxi stated, 'There is John Lennon and Yoko.' Yoko was in front and John Lennon behind her. The doorman and perpetrator were standing at the entrance to the Dakota. The perpetrator was wearing a black, three-quarter-length coat and a black fur hat. At this time, he pointed the gun at Lennon. The perpetrator stood in a three-point stance and fired the gun three or four times. He then threw the gun to the ground and walked around. He takes off his coat and hat and puts a red book in his hand."

Like doorman José Perdomo, concierge Jay Hastings and lift operator Joseph Many, cab driver Peterson disappeared from history after making his statement. He was never seen or heard of again. His statement pretty much follows the official line. Peterson claimed that Yoko Ono was in front of John, and Chapman and Perdomo were by the street entrance. If Chapman was at the vestibule entrance, Peterson would not have been able to see him from his cab. Peterson puts Chapman by the pavement. This means if John was struck with Chapman's bullets, Chapman would have been more than 20 feet, possibly as much as 30 feet, away from Lennon.

I tracked Peterson down in late 2021 and the testimony he gave me pretty much matched up with what he said forty-three years ago. Now in his eighties, Peterson was equally erratic and suspicious in his conversation and demeanour. He confirmed that he saw Ono get out of the limo first, followed by Lennon. He said he saw Chapman standing on a ledge before firing his gun, which probably means the kerb that surrounds the Dakota driveway (interestingly, Chapman said he stepped off the curb before firing his gun). Peterson said Lennon was out of sight when Chapman allegedly fired his gun at him. He assumed that Lennon must have been at the glass vestibule doors or inside them when Chapman's bullets struck him. After partially witnessing the shooting and seeing Chapman subsequently drop his gun, remove his coat and hat and get his Salinger book out, Peterson told me that he had then run off to get help. Peterson could not get a response from any building along 72nd. He assumed that none of the apartment blocks would let him in because he was a black man. Peterson then allegedly returned to the scene and saw the police carrying Lennon out.

When I interviewed Peterson, he added a new detail stating that he had heard Chapman calling out "John Lennon". There are some major problems with this. Firstly, how would Peterson have heard Chapman? It was winter in New York so Peterson would presumably have had his windows closed and Chapman could easily have been thirty feet away at this point. Remember the Lennon's limo was in front of Peterson's cab and Peterson told me that he didn't move forward. Peterson would have had to cope with ambient New York city noise, whilst contending with exiting passengers. Taking all this into account, how did Peterson hear Chapman say anything at all? More importantly, Peterson never told the police in 1980 that he heard Chapman calling out to Lennon. He has added this detail many years later. Adding extra details is a habit of Peterson's. As I was discussing his recollections, I asked him whether he saw Lennon interacting with Chapman. Peterson said: "Actually, now you mention it, they did nod at each other."

That was a first. I felt he was making up parts of the story as he was going along. Was he saying exactly what he saw, or was he saying what he had heard from other witnesses and subsequently read about many times since?

Richard Peterson also told me that he saw Chapman's gun on the ground under a coat when he returned to the Dakota driveway. This clearly doesn't chime with the official story. The official narrative says that Perdomo kicked Chapman's gun to the back of the driveway after Chapman dropped it. It apparently happened moments after Chapman allegedly fired the gun. According to Dakota lift operator Joseph Many, Perdomo then hovered over the gun at the back of the driveway. By the time Peterson got back to the driveway after knocking on several doors, the gun had to be either at the back of the driveway or it had been taken away by Many. So, how could Peterson see a gun?

Was there another gun or did Peterson go to the back of the driveway and talk to Perdomo about it? Both unlikely. How did Peterson know there was a gun if it was under Chapman's coat? Crucially, how could Peterson have seen all of this if he immediately went running off for help? In his witness statement to the police, Peterson states that he saw Chapman shoot, drop his gun, take off his overcoat, take out a book and start reading it. The problem is, Peterson also says he immediately ran off away from his cab after hearing gunfire, and only returned to the scene after knocking on several doors in the near vicinity. If this is so, he couldn't have seen Chapman do all those things after firing a gun. The timeline simply doesn't equate with what we know.

Witness 5: Franklyn Welsh

Peterson told me that he had picked two men up in his yellow taxi in the West Village. Both were going to a party at the Dakota. Peterson told me that he described his two passengers to the DA's office and they later informed him that they had found the two men. One of the candidates for Peterson's cab passengers is

Franklyn Welsh whose witness statement was given to a detective E. Regan on the 12th December 1980. It was revealed for the first time in the early 1990s, in Jack Jones book *Let Me Take You Down*. His version of events went as follows:

> "I pulled up in a taxicab to visit my friend in the Dakota at about 11 P.M. I saw a grey limo double parked in front. I recognised John Lennon and Yoko getting out of their limo (I've seen them several times before during other visits) and went into the building. I was paying the cab fare when I heard four gunshots coming from the courtyard. I ran to the gate and saw José, the doorman, and another man inside. I also saw a gun on the ground which José kicked to the rear of the courtyard. I then ran across the street to the Majestic to have someone call the police. When I returned, the police had arrived and had the suspect in custody."

Welsh did not see Perdomo pulling the gun out of Chapman's hand or Chapman dropping it, but he did see a gun on the ground and Perdomo kicking it away. This concurs with Chapman's recollection of events. Importantly, if his recollection is accurate, Welsh saw Perdomo kick a gun to the rear of the driveway, therefore firmly placing Chapman at the front entrance of the driveway. When I asked Peterson whether he thought Franklyn Welsh might have been one of his passengers, he angrily replied "no way". Peterson insisted his passengers stayed in his cab and it was he, and not Franklyn Welsh, who ran for help. The prospect of another witness account countering his own claims angered Peterson.

If Franklyn Welsh was one of the two cab passengers, this destroys the credibility of Peterson's statement. Peterson said his passengers were still in the back of his cab when he was looking through his windscreen and saw Chapman. Welsh says he was paying his cab fare when he heard gunfire. How could Peterson have seen the shooting if he was taking cash from Welsh when gunfire was heard? Cab drivers always put collecting fares to the fore. It is somewhat odd that Welsh said he went running off for help after hearing gunfire. Running off for help is the exact same thing that Peterson said he did. Did they both run off or is one of them not telling the truth? Welsh said that he saw the grey limo in front of the Dakota. That matches Peterson's recollections. Could two cabs have pulled up to the Dakota at the same time? It's possible, but one of these two witnesses would possibly have had two cars in the way of their view of the driveway and therefore couldn't have seen much at all. Peterson is adamant that no other taxi cabs were at the Dakota.

In Detective Hoffman's notebook, the following note is recorded. Peterson is identified as Witness 2:

"Cab driver [Peterson] pulled up behind victim's limo and saw perp [Chapman] take a ~~combat~~ [Hoffman crossed out 'combat'] 3pt stance and fire several shots."

Note the word combat has been scored through. Crucially, there is no mention of Peterson saying he heard Chapman call out to Lennon. Peterson added that detail later.

Hoffman's notebook also records that a couple in the Dakota heard four shots:

"They looked out of the window and they saw a male get into a yellow taxi and leave."

This had to be Peterson and one of his passengers, possibly Franklyn Welsh. Taking the couple's statement into account, Peterson's story simply does not stack up.

In Albert Goldman's controversial but impressively researched book, *The Lives of John Lennon*, he states:

"The only other witnesses to the shooting, a pair of men in a cab that had pulled up behind the limousine as it was discharging its passengers, had hastened back into the cab, which made a screeching U-turn on 72nd street as it took off down Central Park West."

None of the witnesses at the Dakota, nor the police on the scene, have said they saw Richard Peterson's cab outside the Dakota after John Lennon was shot.

I personally believe that after hearing gunfire, Peterson and his two passengers drove quickly away from the scene. Peterson and Welsh may have briefly seen Chapman and I'm sure they heard gunfire, but I do not accept that Peterson saw what he claimed to have seen. I believe that after driving away at top speed, he might have parked his taxi a few blocks away and returned to the crime scene a few minutes later. Once there, Peterson probably picked up what might have happened from José Perdomo (who we know was talking to secondary witnesses) and other people at the scene. Skewed facts duly collated, Peterson then embellished his story. So, too, might Franklyn Welsh have done.

The pertinent point was that Mark Chapman constantly reiterated that he shot five bullets. John Lennon had four gunshot wounds in his upper left chest area. The numbers couldn't be made to match. Peterson never had to explain his testimony in court. The authorities had no intention of presenting contrary evidence. Having spoken to the DA's office three or four times, Richard Peterson faded into obscurity. Peterson told me that he rang his partner after being questioned all night by the NYPD and his partner didn't believe his story. I'm not sure I do either.

Nevertheless, the most important takeaway for me is the fact that Peterson placed Mark Chapman at the roadside entrance of the driveway when he heard gunfire and that he did not see any bullets striking John Lennon. These are interesting insights for sure, but I regard them as insights with huge caveats attached.

Witness 6: Nina Rosen – dog walker

But what of the dog walker, Nina Rosen? Nina's witness

statement, like Perdomo's, has not been released. We first came to hear about Nina Rosen through Albert Goldman's controversial, but very well researched, 1988 book *The Lives of John Lennon*. Goldman states that Rosen walked past John and Yoko when they exited their limousine. After hearing gunfire, Rosen then doubled backed. She found Chapman standing there (no mention of Perdomo's whereabouts), and he warned her "if I were you, I'd get out of here". After he repeated this warning a couple of times, according to Goldman, Rosen left.

Albert Goldman also identified that there were two men in the back of Peterson's cab, claiming they witnessed the shooting. Goldman's passenger story is very different. He recalled that the shooting started as the two men were exiting Peterson's cab and on hearing gunfire, they jumped back into the cab and Peterson made a "screeching U-turn on 72nd street and took off down Central Park West".

Speaking to me in December 2021, Peterson elaborated on the mysterious Nina Rosen:

> "There's a lady with her dog [Rosen] who saw the murder. She was walking by. I guess she was starstruck. She stood to watch him go in, and there was a doorman, and me. There was only three of us there. And they corralled us up on the ledge and told us to stay there. And that's what I did. I stayed there until they said, 'We got to take you to the police station'. I said, 'You can't, my cab is right there'. My cab was still in the same spot I left it, right by the archway."

> "They took her [Rosen] to the police station. I don't know. She's just an old lady, she's probably dead by now. But she was not young. And I heard that the doorman's dead also. And I'm the only one alive that saw it."

Nina Rosen may have seen the whole incident, or maybe she didn't. What is certain is the fact that her witness statement, like Perdomo's, has never been shown to the public… until now. Having taken possession of Detective Hoffman's case notebooks, Rosen's witness statement can finally be revealed to the world. It's in the basic note form Detective Hoffman used, but it is highly revealing:

> "I walked down the street and saw John and Yoko get out of the limo. I passed the gates and heard the shots. I turned up the block. I went back to gate. I saw doorman and heavy man. I didn't see a gun but I heard Yoko screaming. Yoko was in courtyard. I didn't think it was him that got hit (JL). Doorman was talking to guy. I didn't remember what was said, except doorman said 'police will be here in two minutes'. Heavy set man said I should leave if I were you.
>
> After I saw he is the same man whose photo was in the papers. Doorman was in uniform. He was middle-aged and had a Spanish accent. Person that told me to leave was calm, no glasses. 5.8 or 5.9. He was taller than me (5.6). About 3 feet away, very dark and dim. After he spoke to me I left.
>
> I heard 5 shots, all in succession, evenly spaced. I got caught up in a conversation with the news reader so I didn't go to the police station. I gave the press my name. Yoko arrived 5 minutes after they carried Lennon out. Lennon was wearing jeans and leather brown jacket. Yoko was wearing pants. I left at about 12.30."

So, there we have it. Given that Perdomo's statement remains withheld from public scrutiny and Ono's wildly varying accounts are short on detail, this is the most insightful and important statement of what actually occurred when John Lennon was murdered. It is infuriating that Hoffman did not ask Rosen how much time passed between turning back and the gunfire. We can assume from Yoko's scream in the courtyard, hardly any time at all passed. Yet Yoko screaming in the courtyard remains a problem. Yoko and Jay Hastings have both said that she followed John immediately into the Dakota after he was shot. Rosen saw no Lennon in the driveway, but she did see Yoko in the "courtyard". Ono has never intimated that she made it as far as the courtyard (which is beyond the driveway and accessed through an iron gate). Nina Rosen was a regular local dog walker, who probably knew exactly where the courtyard was in the Dakota layout. Rosen puts Ono in the courtyard and not the driveway, where the official narrative says she should be. Why the anomaly and why would Yoko and Jay Hastings lie about Ono following John into the lobby immediately after he entered the area?

The next problem is why didn't Rosen see a gun. The official narrative from Chapman and the police is that after the shots were fired, Perdomo walked up to Chapman crying, asking him if he knew what he had done. Then, either Chapman dropped the gun or Perdomo shook it out of his hand, depending on which account you choose to believe. Rosen inferred that Ono was screaming in the courtyard... screaming when she arrived on the scene, which must have happened mere seconds after shots were fired. Yet there was no gun. It should have been on the ground at this point, but Rosen didn't see it. This is a troubling detail.

We then have Perdomo's odd behaviour in warning Chapman that the police were about to arrive. Why was Perdomo warning Chapman that he was going to be arrested in two minutes. Remember, too, that according to Chapman, Perdomo had said "just get out of here". Did Perdomo want Mark Chapman to run away?

It is clear to me that the main reason the authorities kept Rosen's witness statement hidden for forty years is because what she saw that night casts doubt on the official narrative. No gun, Yoko in the wrong place and Perdomo apparently warning Chapman to run away. Does Perdomo's hidden statement contain the same anomalies as Rosen's? I believe it almost certainly does. His statement can't be suppressed for security reasons, so why has it been hidden from the public? As with this entire investigation, it is so often one step forward and then two steps back. So, let's keep going. On to the other witnesses, less important in many ways but sometimes far more revealing.

Witness 7: Joseph Many – Dakota lift operator

Joseph Many was primarily responsible for operating a service lift at the Dakota. This elevator could be accessed via a partially concealed alcove and doorway on the left side of the Dakota driveway. Opposite this concealed doorway was the vestibule doors where John Lennon was shot.

Joseph Many's witness statement from 1980 was belatedly released to the public when it was published in a 1992 book. This is what he said:

> "I saw the perpetrator for the past two or three days. When I arrived at work at 3.30pm, I saw him [Chapman] talking to a female named Jerri. At 9.30pm to 10pm, I saw him [Chapman] still outside the building and I said why are you still hanging around here, you already got his autograph. I went downstairs at about 10.45. I relieved a clerk in the office for five minutes who needed to go the men's room [Jay Hastings]. I then went downstairs again. Five minutes later I heard three shots. I got my coat and went upstairs with Victor Cruz and Joe Grezik, who are employees. I saw José [Perdomo] who was motioning towards the gun and saying 'get this out of here'. I picked up the gun and brought it downstairs. I hid the gun in the bottom drawer of an armoire, which was in the storage closet. Approximately five minutes later, I took the police officers down to the storage room and opened the drawer where I put the gun. I lifted up a few pictures I put on top of the gun and officer Blake removed it."

In my interviews with him, Joseph Many revealed much more. Joe allegedly saw Chapman hanging around the Dakota driveway entrance earlier in the day. In the evening, while working on the driveway security when Perdomo was on a break, Many said he asked Chapman why he was still hanging around, after getting Lennon's autograph earlier in the day. Apparently, Chapman told Many that he wanted to get Yoko's autograph. When Perdomo returned, Many went back down to the Dakota basement. Two other employees, Victor Cruz and Joseph Grezik, were with Many in the basement.

At roughly 10.50pm, Many heard three shots and came up to the Dakota driveway via the lift he operated. Many told me that Cruz and Grezik stayed in the basement – this is not what he said to the NYPD in 1980. When I told Many that I had written statements from Grezik and Cruz in Hoffman's notebooks, stating they came up with Many when he collected the gun, Many refuted these statements. Many wanted history to record that he was the only person who came up and took the gun.

Joseph Many told me he entered the Dakota driveway through the entrance exactly opposite the vestibule doors. He firstly observed a gun on the floor, near the back gate. Perdomo was pacing frantically around the gun, muttering to himself. Many presumed Perdomo was hovering around the gun to stop Chapman using it. He vaguely remembered Perdomo kicking the gun over to him when he first arrived in the driveway. Did Perdomo perhaps kick the gun twice?

Many could not see Yoko in the driveway and assumed Lennon must be "in Jay's arms". Later Many would tell me that he thought Lennon had collapsed into Jay's arms.

Perdomo then asked Many to take the gun away and Many picked it up and went down to the basement, where he hid the gun in a drawer. He returned via a different route and entered Jay Hasting's office. This took place at least five minutes after John was shot. Many said he saw Hastings "covered in blood" and Yoko with John's head in her lap in the back office – not the concierge's front office. Many couldn't figure out how a mortally wounded Lennon made it all the way up the steps and into the back office.

When Many returned to the driveway, he placed Chapman near the street, reading a book under a lamp, which is exactly what various witnesses said. I asked Many where exactly Chapman was when he first arrived in the driveway. He confirmed that Mark Chapman was standing on the right side of the driveway, on the same side as the doorman's golden booth, standing near the street, reading a book intently. This is where all witnesses have placed Chapman. He was nowhere near the glass vestibule doors, where Lennon was allegedly shot. Joseph Many confirmed that José Perdomo might have kicked a gun to the rear of the drive-way and that when Many arrived in the driveway, Perdomo was walking around the gun, near the glass doors where Lennon was shot. Many does not mention that Chapman was near the gun, so we can safely assume that Chapman was by the street end of the driveway immediately after the shooting as several witnesses, including Many, stated.

Jay Hastings has questioned Joe Many's recollections, telling me that he cannot recall seeing Many until after Lennon's body was taken to the hospital. Many could have feasibly slipped past Hastings view to observe John's stricken body in the back office, but Hastings doubts that happened.

Joe Many confirmed to me that he saw a "huge" pool of blood in concierge Hastings' front office. I asked him to confirm whether John's pool of blood was in the front office or the back office. Many was adamant that it was in the front office, but John's body and Yoko were in the back office when he got there. Many also mentioned that Lennon's blood was collected in a hollow long dent in the marble floor of the front office. A hol-lowed-out area had been caused by heavy wear and tear on the front office marble floor directly behind the main lobby desk. Jay has confirmed to me that this hollowed out floor observational detail from Joe Many was true, and that the front office did have a worn out hollow area in the marble floor. This would mean John almost certainly collapsed in the front office to cause a pool of blood to form there, and somehow, he ended up in the back office. Many told me that he thought Ono and Hastings probably dragged John into the back office to be safe from Chapman. Hastings said John did not collapse in the front office; he was adamant that John ran past him in the front office and collapsed in the back office. All police officers said they found John's body, face down, in the back office. This is a deeply disturbing anomaly. How did so much of John's blood accumulate in the front office?

Many then told me that when the police arrived, he was standing in the driveway and the police misidentified him as the shooter. This contradicts Jay Hastings' claim that the police had actually misidentified him as the shooter. One of them must be lying. Joseph Many told me that Jay Hastings' assertion that he helped carry John's body outside with the police officers to a squad car is untrue. The police also denied the claim. Both Officer Frauenberger and Officer Palma told me that Hastings did not help them carry John's body out of the Dakota. Hastings had insisted to me that he did help carry the body and that he was given the bloody "business end" to carry. Something was clearly wrong with his statement. Was Hastings inventing this story to explain why he was covered in blood?

Joe Many has attracted much negative attention over the years as the man responsible for hiding Mark Chapman's gun, for his potential motives for doing so, and for refusing to give any interviews after the murder. I found him composed and precise throughout our conversations, despite lying about Cruz and Grezik's involvement.

Joe Many thought John must have initially collapsed in the front office. This is crucial. Hastings put forward a different version of where Lennon fell.

Witnesses 8 & 9: Victor Cruz and Joe Grezik – Dakota workmen

Victor Cruz and Joe Grezik were both in the Dakota basement with Joe Many when they heard gunfire. According to a statement given to Ron Hoffman, Joe Grezik said he "came up" with Joe Many. He saw a gun on the floor. (No mention of Perdomo). He said he didn't approach Chapman.

In his police statement, Victor Cruz also said all three were in the elevator going up to see what was going on. Hoffman noted: "He [Cruz] opened the door. Saw gun on floor. José kicked it and said take that down". This is further evidence that José kicked the gun (possibly for a second time) over to the three workers when they arrived on the scene. Victor admitted to Hoffman: "I was afraid. Many picked it up. We all went to the basement and Many put the gun in the drawer. I didn't look at person that shot gun."

When Victor Cruz came back up to the driveway, he almost certainly must have been the Hispanic person who Officer Cullen had said was arguing with Chapman. Even though Joe Many has recently tried to erase Grezik and Cruz from the narrative, they were with him when he picked up the gun and when he returned to the driveway after hiding it.

Recap

The three main eyewitnesses were José Perdomo, Yoko Ono and Nina Rosen. All their statements are troublesome. Concierge Jay Hasting's aural recollections are certainly insightful and cab-driver Richard Peterson seemed to have had a front row seat to the whole crime. Joe Many only witnessed the aftermath of the murder – albeit, while playing a key role in hiding Chapman's alleged gun and verifying where Lennon might have fallen. If the "official" eyewitness statements are all either incomplete, sketchy or untrue, what can we glean from the witnesses to John Lennon's murder who were not in or near the Dakota driveway when the shooting took place? Perhaps some of these people can shine some light on what happened.

Life would have been so much simpler for the NYPD if the key witnesses had given similar statements. But they didn't. Perdomo's evidence is littered with problems often caused by what he doesn't say. His witness statement has been withheld by the police for more than 40 years and we don't know why. What of Yoko Ono? Clearly, she was there but her statements differ and her precise location is thrown into doubt by inconsistencies from others. She above all had cause to be utterly shattered and shocked by the events which happened in front of, or behind, her. I completely understand this and readers should not jump to conclusions. Crucially, Ono has never said she saw Mark Chapman kill John. Hastings offers really interesting facts but also worrying inconsistencies. In particular, his persistent claim to have carried John with the police officers appears to be non-sense. Richard Peterson's story lacks credibility and may well have been pieced together from other accounts. And poor Nina Rosen – out for a late-night walk with her dog and she ends up being a partial witness to a major crime. Her testimony though is invaluable.

CHAPTER 14 | Minor Witnesses: With a Story to Tell

Key People

Jack Henderson (Dakota resident)

Guy Louthan (eyewitness)

Bill Christian (limo driver)

Ellen Chesler (Dakota resident)

Maury Solomon (Dakota resident)

Charles De Leon (dog walker)

Sean Strub (publicity seeker)

Minor witness 1: Jack Henderson – Dakota resident

Statement given to Ron Hoffman NYPD and recorded in his notebook:

> "I was out for the evening and returned at approx 10:45. I heard the shots— don't remember how many. I ran down the stairs and found Jay [Hastings] and Yoko. Jay had Lennon in the back office. Yoko said please, someone get him a doctor. I called our office and told the person there to get an ambulance here as quickly as possible. I never saw the person that shot him. After shots maybe 15 to 20 seconds and I was at the office."

Please remember that Joe Many said he saw a pool of blood in Hastings' front office, yet Hastings said Lennon collapsed in the back office after running through the front office. In Hoffman's notes, Henderson describes seeing "Jay and Lennon in the back office". I have been told by Jay Hastings and Joe Many that it is not easy for residents to see into the back office from the lobby because it is concealed behind the front office, which you would have to go through to get to it. (See Dakota layout diagram below) I believe Henderson may have confused the terms front office and back office: did he actually mean the concierge's office (which was known as the "front office" by Dakota staff) when he described Jay and Lennon being in the back office? An office behind a front desk in the lobby would, I believe, often be described as a back office by a resident – who would not have access beyond it. I don't believe Henderson from his position in the lobby would be able to see the part of the superintendent's back office where John was found by the NYPD. From an image we have of exactly where Lennon was found in the back office, we can see that Lennon's blood on the floor is behind a door. Jay Hastings has confirmed to me that the dark gap in the top left of the image is the open back office doorway which he says Lennon ran through to get into the back office before collapsing. Joe Many has told me that the back office, which was used by the superintendent of the building, was nearly always locked when the superintendent was not using it. The superintendent was not working on the night John Lennon was assassinated. Joe Many therefore assumed that Hastings and Ono must have "broken into" the back office somehow to get Lennon's body into that space. I personally suspect Jay had a key.

Henderson places Lennon's body in an office, apparently 15 to 20 seconds after hearing gun shots. Henderson getting to the lobby area in such a short time after hearing gunfire is highly suspect. Henderson was described to me by people who knew him as a "bit of drinker". If he had been drinking on the night in question, his timings may have been a little off. To hear gunfire and then decide to leave your apartment and make your way downstairs into the lobby area in such a short space of time is highly unlikely. Henderson was not a young man. I'm not sure even a young man could sprint to the lobby in such a short space of time. Nevertheless, Henderson's recollections are vital to understanding what happened to John after he was shot.

Minor witness 2: Maury Solomon – Dakota resident

Interview as recalled by NYPD Detective William Lundon:

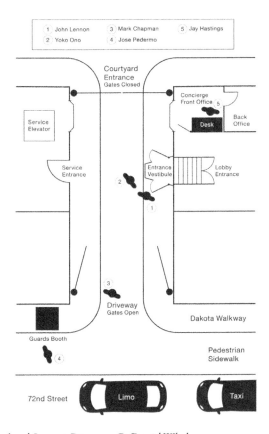

Dakota Overhead Layout Diagram © David Whelan

The Superintendent's back office area photo © NYPD

"On 12/8/80, while at the scene of occurrence, I interviewed one Maury Solomon. Mr. Solomon was about to go to bed when he heard five shots being fired in rapid succession. He brought it to the attention of his mother and informed her he was going downstairs to investigate. After running down the stairs he entered the front office and as he entered he heard José the doorman shout something. Then he exited the office and as he was coming out he noticed for the first time that there were holes in the glass on the door. He began to go out to the street and as he did he observed a male white on the west side of the enclosed entrance. The man appeared to have a smile on his face and was just turning around."

Minor witness 3: Guy Louthan – local resident

In December 1980, Guy Louthan was a struggling actor living in a building called The Majestic opposite the Dakota. On the night of the murder, he was in bed with a girlfriend. Suddenly Louthan heard gunfire coming from the direction of the Dakota. He and his girlfriend immediately jumped out of bed and ran to their window. Louthan said he looked across to the Dakota from his tenth-floor apartment across the street. He told writer Fenton Bresler what he saw:

"I saw two people standing there, the doorman and this other guy. The first police car had not yet arrived. There were just two men. That was all I could see. I was slightly to the right of the building and could not see up the stairs and into the entrance office where I now know Lennon was. All I could see was these two men on the street outside. The doorman and Chapman. For a long time afterwards I wondered whether I had really seen Chapman. I was actually under the impression that he must have run away. But I realise now that it was him alright. He just stood there, it was incredible."

Louthan does not say that he saw Richard Peterson's yellow taxicab parked next to the Dakota driveway. Louthan mentions a police car hadn't arrived, so surely he would have mentioned if he had seen a yellow taxi car? I do not believe Richard Peterson's car was there.

Albert Goldman says in his book that immediately after gunfire, people heard the screeching of car wheels driving off. I'm certain this was Richard Peterson's cab.

Minor witness 4: Charles De Leon – the mysterious dog walker

Studying Detective Hoffman's Lennon murder notebook, I read a statement he took from another dog walker (who was in addition to Nina Rosen). Hoffman wrote, "The guy's name, Charles De-Leon and he's a self-employed operator at the Sugarman and Berger for African art."

Hoffman then gives this dog walker's account:

"My little Toby always urinates on the wall of the Dakota. On Saturday at approximately 10:30, we were giving him his favourite spot, to wee at the Dakota. I was talking to the doorman. He [the witness] describes the doorman as light complexion, black guy [Perdomo was white Cuban] tall, 6'2", light hair, three people besides the doorman, two males and one female. Doorman was talking to a couple and male was by himself. My dog was trying to do his thing. There was an album with a pen stuck in it. He [Chapman] looked like he was looking for trouble or an argument. I dismissed it easily that day. His eyes were glassy. He stared with an unblinking facial look and a direct glare, right at me, sandy or blondish hair. He did have light color, brown hair, no hat, roundish, rimmed glasses, no cross bar on the glasses. Light brown, plastic frames. Cherubic boyish face, waspish, at least 6'1". I'm five nine and a half. His build was stocky, footballish, wearing a trench coat, a beer belly, nearly 200 pounds, at least three-quarter, light button, navy blue jacket. His coat was closed. He was collegiate, not a businessman, a leisure look. The incident took 10 to 15 seconds. Album had Yoko and Lennon on front. Album was flat on sidewalk."

Hoffman's "Charles De-Leon" account tells us something about what was happening outside the Dakota approximately 20 minutes before John Lennon was shot. This is the only account we have, thus far, about how Chapman was behaving in the minutes before John Lennon was shot. The description of a black doorman is confusing. What does ring true is the description of a Yoko and John album (*Double Fantasy*), with a pen in it, lying "flat on the sidewalk". This must be the album Chapman had signed by Lennon nearly six hours earlier. But how was it found later up in a plant pot? The male and female couple talking to the doorman is interesting – did the police manage to locate them? But the most interesting detail is the description of Chapman staring at the dog walker with a direct, unblinking glare and most especially, with eyes that were "glassy". It sounds like Chapman could have been in some kind of a hypnotic state before he allegedly shot John Lennon.

(Potential) minor witness 5: The (unidentified) Lennons' limousine driver

One individual who continually gets overlooked is the Lennons' limousine driver from that night. We know (from his notebooks) that Detective Hoffman thought the car was from Esquire Limousine services but Joe Many told me the limousine company was called Farrells. Someone must have called for a car to take the Lennons home from the recording studios on that fateful night, but we do not currently know who. We know from many sources that the grey limo did not drive the Lennons right up the driveway, but dropped them off in front of the driveway, on 72nd Street.

According to Richard Peterson, the limo drove off before Chapman started shooting. What did the limo driver potentially see and, more importantly, why was he not identified and questioned by the police? Like Perdomo, Peterson's two passengers and many others, the Lennon's limo driver drifted into obscurity immediately after. The limo driver who had turned up late on the afternoon of the 8th of December had been identified in Hoffman's notebook as Bill Christian. Was Bill Christian the limo driver who took the Lennons home in the evening? This is still unclear.

Joe Many has confirmed to me that when he came up to collect Chapman's gun, the Lennons' limo was nowhere to be seen. He also said he could not see Richard Peterson's yellow cab. He did, though, admit that he could not see all the street from where he was standing, but he was certain there was no yellow taxi in his view. When Many saw Lennon being carried out to a squad car, he confirmed that the street outside the Dakota was awash with police cars. He did not see Richard Peterson's yellow taxi and doubts it was ever there.

Minor witness 6: unidentified woman

An unidentified female eyewitness was heavily featured on the early new bulletins. She didn't see the actual shooting, but observed:

> "I heard Yoko Ono screaming moments later. They stepped out of
> the limousine, and they went inside of the gate there. Then all of
> a sudden, I heard five, six shots, and that was it."

This is helpful, as it implies Yoko was screaming "moments" after she heard shots. Meaning Nina Rosen hearing Ono scream in the courtyard, must also have been moments after shots were fired. This helps us place Rosen at the crime scene, just moments after the shots were fired and increases the importance of her recollections of Lennon not being in her view, no gun in sight and Chapman and Perdomo alone together in the driveway, conversing with each other.

Minor witness 7: Sean Strub – the eyewitness who never was

Sean Strub was identified as one of the most prominent witnesses by the TV News coverage after John's assassination. The photogenic young man said he was walking south near 72nd Street when he heard four shots coming from the Dakota. He then subsequently said: "Some people say they heard six shots and said John Lennon was hit. Police said he was hit in the back twice." Others told him the assailant had been: "Crouching in the archway of the Dakota. Lennon arrived in the company of his wife and the assailant fired". Strub said he saw six police officers carrying John Lennon out to a police car and that Lennon still had on his iconic glasses.

It is noteworthy that TV news crews on the night of the murder seemed only interested in talking to Sean Strub. By his own admission, Strub arrived at the Dakota when the body was being carried out, which could have been, by some estimates, about ten minutes after shots were first heard. Yet Strub was the guy who first laid down details to the world about John Lennon's murder. He wasn't there when Lennon was actually shot but became the main witness. He was on TV, you see.

Strub was next seen at the Roosevelt Hospital and was interviewed there by Jeanne Downey, of Channel 2, CBS, minutes after Lennon was pronounced dead. It was almost as if Strub was being used as a media prop to fill in missing details about the murder. Strub's Roosevelt Hospital interview went as follows:

STRUB: I kind of waited for a minute and started to walk on; a police car drove by very fast. And so I followed it on down, I thought it was something in the park, but it was at the Dakota on Seventy-Second Street and Central Park West. As I got there, there were about a half-dozen people there, and very shortly there were that many squad cars.

JD: Did you see Mr. Lennon at that time?

STRUB: Yeah, they were just bringing Lennon out of the, sort of an entryway, the driveway between the sidewalk and the court-yard, and he was limp; there were about six officers carrying him. He had a little bit of blood coming out of his mouth.

JD: And Police tell us they do have a suspect. Did you see anyone?

STRUB: Yeah, they scuffled with a guy and arrested him; he was about thirty-five, he was white, brown hair.

JD: Was he alone?

STRUB: He was the only person I saw. Yoko was there.

JD: She was?

STRUB: And they put him in a squad car and took off.

JD: Was there any kind of an exchange, do you know, between Lennon and the suspect?

STRUB: That's what the doorman [José Perdomo] said that there had been some sort of altercation or argument; I heard the cops say that Lennon was hit twice in the back. I heard someone else say that the guy had apparently been hanging around all evening, and another person said he'd been there all week, and he was just kind of like waiting for him.

JD: Thank-you very much, Sean.

An unspecified News Crew also interviewed Strub outside the Roosevelt Hospital and he revealed a highly useful bit of information that he must have picked up from José Perdomo:

> "I saw there were about five police cars there. He got shot at least four times. One police officer said two times and other people were saying six. I heard four shots. He was shot going into the vestibule of the Dakota".

Strub has always said that he heard four shots when he was nearby. Chapman had always insisted he fired five shots. Strub does not mention seeing Peterson's taxi cab, which Peterson said was parked right next to the driveway entrance. Strub's recollection of six officers carrying Lennon's body does not tally with what the officers on the scene told me happened. Officers Palma and Frauenberger insisted they were the only officers who carried Lennon out.

Strub's claim that the doorman told him that there was some kind of altercation or argument is highly debatable. Neither Ono nor Chapman have said that there was an argument between Lennon and Chapman. The NYPD and DA's office have also never mentioned this. Jay Hastings didn't hear an argument from his window facing out onto the driveway. Either Strub was getting confused about Perdomo possibly arguing with Chapman to leave (which Chapman has confirmed), or Perdomo was possibly embellishing his account which was repeated by Strub. Yoko Ono did once mention hearing "noises'" in the street, but she clearly stated that she and John never turned around after hearing this. Surely if Chapman and her husband had an argument, Ono would have mentioned it.

I believe the argument Perdomo must have been referring to was either between Chapman and Dakota worker Victor Cruz, or possibly between Perdomo and Chapman, regarding Chapman's remaining at the scene before the police arrived. Chapman's argument with Lennon almost certainly didn't happen, yet Strub repeated it as a fact on television. Either way, it appears that Perdomo, with his apparent poor English, was setting the murder scene for anyone who cared to speak to him on that fateful night. This is probably how cab driver Richard Peterson also picked up his version of the events. The media wasn't finished with Sean Strub. They conducted a studio interview with him which came across like a mini-press conference.

He started with his well-worn *facts* about hearing shots and proceeded to repeat all of the fictitious ramblings. Much of what Strub repeated at this staged interview has been verifiably discredited by other police witnesses who were at the scene before him. Only two officers carried Lennon out and he was not wearing glasses. Strub muddled up the timelines: Chapman was already in a squad car when Lennon was carried and when Ono came out. And, by all accounts, Mark Chapman did not scuffle with anyone.

Strub said he saw a Rolls Royce in the driveway when he first arrived at the scene. Nobody, and I mean nobody, said a Rolls was in the driveway. Anyone who knows John Lennon's fabled history will know that he owned a Rolls Royce in the sixties and over many years embellished it with modern gadgets and psychedelic paint. Lennon even imported his cherished Rolls Royce into America in 1970. I believe Strub was familiar with John's past association with a Rolls Royce and assumed that John and Ono would have been driven to the Dakota in their famous Rolls. Balderdash. A complete fantasy. The man's ego stomped across the TV coverage.

I can confidently say that Strub was lying. He was certainly in demand from the TV news crews but his testimony is of no value in helping us understand the actual events of the night John Lennon was murdered. But the media latched onto Strub like a leech. Live TV has its drawbacks. The morning news created the first-hand witness who never was. Sean Strub wasn't a sinister agent working for shadowy organisations to create a false narrative. He was merely a young man who took his fifteen minutes of fame. The lazy media were the main culprits in the Sean Strub story. Who cares about truth when you need an eye-witness to push up the ratings. Inadvertently or not, he confused the issue, and officialdom did not interfere.

Minor witness 8: Ellen Chesler – Dakota resident

Ellen Chesler and her lawyer husband Matthew Mallow lived in apartment number 25 on the second floor of the Dakota. From her kitchen window, Ellen could see the full sweep of the Dakota courtyard and, beyond the iron gates, some of the Dakota driveway. John and Yoko regularly used this route to access the lobby through the vestibule door entrance. Ellen's kitchen window sat to the left of the courtyard, as you look at it from the driveway. Consequently, Ellen's line of vision was impaired because she could not see clearly all the way to the far-right of the driveway by the street, which is precisely where Mark Chapman was standing on the night of 8th December 1980.

When news got out about John Lennon's assassination on 8th December 1980, George Arzt, the chief political writer for the *New York Post,* was brainstorming how best to cover this seismic event with colleagues at a bar in Greenwich Village, when he remembered that Ellen Chesler lived at the Dakota. George had often spoken to Ellen in his professional capacity for the *Post* as she was the chief of staff for New York city council president, Carol Bellamy. George called Ellen from the bar and she confirmed that she had heard gunshots. Furthermore, her husband had called 911. She thought she'd seen the gunman hanging out in front of the building, waiting for John Lennon, for days before. How she knew the guy was the gunman, was not explored. George sent his story to the *Post* as quickly as possible. It was an interesting account, but other people had heard gunfire and other witnesses had spotted Chapman hanging around before and after the assassination. So, no big deal.

In 2020, Keith Greenberg wrote a book called *December 8th, 1980: The Day John Lennon Died.* He had tracked down Ellen Chesler and she shared her recollections of the incident which had happened forty years before. Greenberg stated that:

> "From Ellen Chesler's second-story apartment, on the seventy-third side of the Dakota, the sound of gun-fire echoed so loudly that she knew it was close. She had been warming a bottle of milk for her six-month old daughter. Now she grabbed the baby and ran out of the room. Her husband called the concierge for details. Remarkably, Jay Hastings picked up and said that John Lennon had been shot. 'Please,' Hastings said, 'call the police'."

How interesting. Chesler's husband Mathew Mallow had called Jay Hastings, who – amazingly, given the absolute chaos of the moment – picked up the phone. But again, this was not a mind-blowing revelation. We also learned that Ellen was in her kitchen warming baby milk. Fearing danger close by she allegedly grabbed her baby and ran into the safety of the apartment. What else would any caring mother do? Therefore, Ellen's second on-the-record version claimed she had seen nothing.

Something jarred. Looking through Ron Hoffman's notes and paperwork, I discovered his notes on an interview he conducted with Ellen Chesler on 25th December 1980. I expected the usual narrative, "*I heard gunfire and we called 911/Jay Hastings*" stuff, but no. Ellen had had much more to say to Detective Hoffman. His diary notes read as follows:

> "Ellen Chesler 12.25.80. Apartment 25. She heard the shots and looked though her window. She could see Lennon stumble, but could not see his face. She did recognize him. She saw the shooter but not his face. Her husband called 911. She then called the office of Dakota and found out that Lennon was shot."

It's an entirely different account. Initially, according to Hoffman's notes, Ellen seems to have been an onlooker, a vital eyewitness, offering important, albeit vague, evidence. What is incredible is that this testimony given to Hoffman was not only concealed by the NYPD and DA's office for over 42 years, but also by Ellen Chesler herself. Why?

If Chesler saw Lennon stumble up to the vestibule doors after hearing gunfire, Chapman would had to have struck Lennon with his bullets just as John passed him in the driveway. Lennon then would have continued to have stumbled onwards to the vestibule doors and then have been spotted by Chesler, who strangely couldn't see his face, but somehow knew it was him. However, we know from statements from Chapman, Ono and

Richard Peterson that John Lennon was near the vestibule doors when he was struck (and this is the area the NYPD concentred on in their investigation). But if Lennon was hit at the vestibule doors, it would then have given Chesler no time to see Lennon "stumble" after hearing gunfire. Furthermore, if John was already stumbling after being shot in the driveway, then how on earth could he have the strength to continue on his amazing journey through the vestibule doors, into the vestibule, up some stairs and through two office areas before collapsing?

As for Chesler seeing "the shooter" but not his face? Virtually impossible. Chapman was standing on the left-hand side of the driveway (looking at it from the pavement side) by the street and near the doorman's booth. Key witnesses placed him there just before and immediately after gunfire. Chesler's view across the courtyard from her kitchen window was not directly opposite the driveway. It is doubtful that she could see the extreme far right-hand side of the driveway as she looked at it, and yet she apparently saw a "shooter". Does this sound likely? There are other key factors which make her claim unlikely. Ellen Chesler was possibly 100 feet away from the driveway when she heard gunfire. The courtyard in front of her was poorly lit. Nina Rosen recalled that the driveway was "very dark and dim" moments after gunfire. Images of the driveway from 1980 mostly show a black area in shadows, with a few dim lights close by and this is in daytime. There was also an iron gate between Chesler and the very dark driveway. So how could Ellen Chesler possibly see what she initially said she saw? Did she simply want to be one of the eyewitnesses who had a good story to tell at dinner parties? We might piece together several scenarios which offer different levels of possibility, but they quickly dissolve into speculation.

Interestingly, Ellen Chesler and her husband became wildly successful establishment figures in the interim years. Ellen was a UN Commissioner and is a member of the Council for Foreign Relations. She also became a senior fellow at The Open Society

Institute, the international foundation started by George Soros. From 1997 through 2004, she directed the foundation's $35 million programme in reproductive health. As for her husband Matthew Mallow, he became Vice Chairman of Black Rock – the world's largest money "management" firm, with more than $10 trillion in assets, a large proportion of which are in the global arms industry so detested by John Lennon. Matthew Mallow was personally appointed by his good friend, the billionaire Black Rock co-founder, Larry Fink.

In 2022, Chesler and Mallow sold their Dakota apartment for $4,700,000. They were and are clearly members of upper middle-class American society, and if the first version of Ellen's account to the police department raised any concerns, her second in 2020 washed them away.

Ellen Chesler has refused to acknowledge my requests for an interview.

Recap

Nina Rosen, cabdriver Richard Peterson, Franklyn Welsh and Guy Louthan are the only confirmed witnesses to have seen Chapman and Perdomo immediately after the shots were fired and subsequently to have given a statement about what they saw. All four of them place Chapman at the roadside entrance to the driveway when gunfire was heard. When I asked Peterson to point out where Chapman was standing in the Dakota driveway, he instantly indicated that it was on the left side of the entrance, by the street, on the doorman's booth side. This matches Joe Many's account of where Chapman was standing, less than a minute after gunfire was heard. Chapman's own accounts of his position also allow us to be certain that he was close to the street on the left-hand side of the Dakota driveway when he allegedly shot John Lennon. Lennon was positioned, by most accounts, near or within the vestibule glass doors, which are to the far right of the driveway, when he was shot. This is a distance of at least twenty feet from

Chapman's position. Mark Chapman could not feasibly have shot John Lennon in the chest from this position, particularly because Lennon was walking away from, and with his back to, Chapman.

Then we have the newly uncovered recollections of Ellen Chesler from Hoffman's notes. The official narrative has Lennon being struck by Chapman's bullets as he gets to the vestibule doors. If this is so, where exactly did Chesler see Lennon stumbling? Also, from Chesler's second floor apartment window, she could not have feasibly seen Chapman from where he was standing in the dark driveway. Finally, why has Chesler concealed this information for over forty years? She had a chance to tell George Azrt from the *New York Post* on the night of the murder and another chance to tell Keith Greenburg in 2010. But it seems she chose to withhold what she told Hoffman she saw, from them. Or did they not write everything she told them?

The truth has been compromised by so many different and contradictory accounts. I am concerned that we won't ever have access to all the witness statements withheld by the NYPD which might offer some much-needed clarity.

CHAPTER 15 | Lawyers and Pastors

Key People

Herbert Adlerberg (lawyer)
Jonathan Marks (lawyer)
Special Agent Charles McGowan
CIA Director John Deutch

Dr. Naomi Goldstein (psychiatrist)
Dr Bernard Diamond (psychiatrist & hypnotist)
Preacher Stephen Olford
Evangelist Billy Graham

Mark Chapman had many unauthorised visitors while he was held for sentencing, and he was allowed numerous unmonitored phone calls. He was, therefore, liable to the influence of others. Did one of these calls or visitors instigate Mark's erratic behaviour? After four days of assessments in a secure hospital, Mark was transferred to Rikers Island, a remote jail on the outskirts of New York. He went on a four-day hunger strike to force the prison to have a civilian cook make his meals. Death threats aimed at him in the prison drove Mark to be paranoid that the prison's cooks might try to poison him.

All the time Mark was in prison awaiting sentence, six months in total, he was allowed open contact with the outside world. Numerous calls came in for him and Mark was permitted to make outgoing telephone calls, as long as they were collect calls. None of these were monitored or recorded. Writer Fenton Bresler stated in his 1989 book: "It was practically open house. A prisoner should be isolated from the outside world so they cannot be 'got at' in any way. Who might have told him what to say or what to do or given him fresh instructions? The means of access were there." Bresler was 100% right. Chapman was vulnerable to any amount of coercion and manipulation and he was moved constantly between Bellevue and Riker before his sentencing.

Chapman Lawyer #1: Herbert Adlerberg

Mark Chapman was given a state-funded lawyer to defend him at trial and the next on the list was fifty-year-old Harold Adlerberg. Harold didn't want the job. Apparently his first reaction to being allocated the case was "oh shit". Adlerberg was particularly concerned about all the "lonely fans" he saw at a vigil outside the Dakota.

Unfortunately, the nervous Adlerberg helped give birth life to an enduring myth regarding Mark Chapman's alleged obsession with John Lennon. Just before Adlerberg saw a judge, he was given twenty-five minutes to speak alone with Chapman outside the courtroom. One account states that Adlerberg thought Chapman spoke very well, but when it came to questions relating to the incident, Chapman was "all over the place". "I honestly cannot tell you what his motivation was," Adlerberg remarked. "I thought the guy was a nut, he was crazy." When Harold Adlerberg stood in front of the judge, he said Chapman had not been "coherent and his answers were not connected with the questions in any way". He then added an impromptu aside, stating, *"Chapman admired the Beatles very much. He doesn't value himself too much."* Outside the courtroom, Adlerberg was set upon by a posse of reporters. In the bedlam, Adlerberg embellished his story and told the throng, "He [Chapman] told me he admired Lennon very much since he was ten years old. My impression was of a very confused character."

Despite all the evidence to the contrary, Chapman was labelled hereafter as a lifelong Lennon obsessive. By 1989, talking to writer Fenton Bresler, Harold Adlerberg could not remember whether he had specifically asked Mark whether he was a fan of John Lennon or whether Mark had volunteered the information.

The press quickly picked up on Adlerberg's comment that Chapman "admired Lennon". On 10th December 1980, the *LA Times* headlined: "Fan of Lennon stalked him". On 22nd December 1980, *Newsweek* called Chapman "Lennon's alter ego".

Later in December, newspapers as far apart as the *Honolulu Star Bulletin* and London's *Daily Telegraph* both said the same thing, describing Chapman as "a devout Lennon fan". Over 8 years later, in a 1988 *60 Minutes* trailer for a new Lennon film, Chapman was still described as a "deranged fan". When Adlerberg quit at the end of the day on December 10th, he had been in the job for just one day. He decided to give an interview on 12th December to Mike Pearl at the *New York Post*. What Adlerberg said was deeply disturbing. The piece was titled "Marked for Death – Lawyer Who Quit: If he goes free, all are in peril."

Harold Adlerberg was described as white-faced and trembling and was quoted as saying: "Everyone in the case will be marked for death if he is found not guilty by reasons of insanity." He insinuated that there was a death list organised by Lennon fans and he somehow "knew he was on the list unless he withdrew from the case." He then stated that none of the hundreds of calls he received after taking on Chapman's defence contained death threats. "I'm not scared of phone calls," he said, but a clearly spooked Adlerberg added, "I'm scared of people who don't call'. Then Adlerberg went even further, stating: "This is a cult thing. It has international ramifications. I'm scared that I and my family will be killed."

The twenty-five-minute chat Adlerberg had had with Chapman in which he allegedly professed to "admire" the Beatles and John Lennon, then took another dark twist. Adlerberg refused to comment further to the *New York Post* about the chat, but he did whisper "if you knew what he told me, you'd be shocked'. Unfortunately, Mike Pearl at the *Post* didn't pursue the shocking nature of Adlerberg's claim, but it does leave you wondering if this led to Adlerberg's decision to abandon the case.

Chapman Lawyer #2: Jonathan Marks

Next in line for the job of legally representing Chapman was Jonathan Marks. Marks was 37 years old, Harvard educated and

Jonathan Marks © Unknown

keen to make his name as the man who defended John Lennon's killer. Death threats or sinister cults did not seem to bother him. On his first day in the job on 12th December 1980, Marks declared that he would enter a plea of temporary insanity. This ensured that the NYPD and DA's office would only have to be concerned about whether Mark Chapman was insane, and not whether he committed a crime or not. Marks apparently found Chapman co-operative and told the press that "Mark Chapman desperately needs a friend." Marks had an assistant helping him throughout the case, David Suggs.

Jonathan Marks was an odd choice. He had embarked on the standard Harvard Law School route that took him to graduation in 1968. Then he had a strange and unexplained gap in his résumé from 1968 to 1974. Perhaps military service in Vietnam, perhaps not. It's a mystery. What we do know is that Marks became an assistant United States attorney in the Eastern District of New York for four years, from 1974 until the end of 1978. By December 1980, Marks had barely two years' experience as a trial lawyer. And yet he was given one of the greatest legal defence gigs of the twentieth century. Marks operated a private practice at the time. It is unclear whether he offered his services for a fee or not and if a fee was involved, who was paying him. If the authorities had not wanted Jonathon Marks as Chapman's court lawyer, it would have been simplicity itself to rearrange the appointment. Perhaps the list was skewed to ensure Marks got the job. Perhaps certain people knew that Marks was a man with whom they could work.

Nevertheless, as a lawyer, Marks failed to defend his client properly and all the evidence that has been laid out in this book thus far was wholly ignored by Marks. Just a couple of days after being arrested, Mark Chapman was sent to Bellevue psychiatric hospital for evaluation. While there, Chapman was interviewed by two court-appointed psychiatrists, who both found him in a daze and state of shock. He allegedly slept most of the day and was disinterested in reading the newspapers or watching television.

Psychiatrist Dr Naomi Goldstein was asked to assess Mark Chapman when he was at that hospital. Though only in her second year of training at the time, Goldstein recommended he be charged with second-degree murder. In her report, she wrote he was not insane but had "grandiose visions of himself".

In the interim period, at Riker's Island prison before his sentencing, Chapman started acting very erratically. He cut off all his hair, and in mid-August went berserk, destroying a television set and screaming at his fellow inmates that he would be "tortured in hell for his vicious crime". When guards threw him back in his cell, he tore off all his clothing and began screeching and jumping up and down like a monkey. He tore up his bible and blocked up his toilet with the pages. He was eventually subdued by six guards and sent back to Bellevue mental hospital. There, he eventually quietened down, but he began to speak to doctors in two different voices completely unlike his own. He claimed they were his two personal demons, Lila and Dobar, sent by Satan to torment him.

In Walter Bowart's seminal book called *Operation Mind Control,* he relates how Dr. Bernard Diamond (who was one of the first psychiatrists to officially interview Chapman after he was arrested) had previously made Sirhan Sirhan climb the bars of his cell like a monkey in a hypnotic trance.

Preacher Stephen Olford

While in Rikers Island prison, Chapman met with Special Agent Charles McGowan. Chapman's old pastor flew over a thousand miles from his ministry in Alabama to see Mark, to apparently give him "comfort". Back in the mid 1980s, McGowan had explained to writer Fenton Brelser that he had all his trip expenses paid for by an anonymous benefactor, who was worried about "Chapman's well-being"— a very Christian act at a time when most of the world hated him. The trip was even more strange as Mark hadn't seen McGowan for many years, and he wasn't his current pastor.

It didn't take me long to find out that evangelist preaching superstar, Stephen Olford, was McGowan's benevolent benefactor. Olford, now deceased, ran the New York church next to the Salisbury Hotel in the 1960s and early 1970s. He was a widely recognised evangelical preacher whose main claim to fame was inspiring the firebrand preacher, Billy Graham. Olford had an even more impressive visitor – the future President of the USA (and John Lennon's bette noire) Richard Nixon. An image of Nixon, Graham and Olford together was once taken, but rarely seen. A collection of individuals who all despised John Lennon.

Olford was *inspired* to send McGowan on his long trip to see Chapman following reports of Lennon's assassination on the evening of 8th December 1980. Had Olford ever met Chapman before, and if so in what context? As far as we are aware, Chapman never attended Olford's church in New York. Yet Olford was very keen to get somebody in to see Mark Chapman just hours after John Lennon's assassination. Olford and McGowan planned to put one of their pastor *friends* in Chapman's cell. They acted quickly. Suspiciously so. McGowan flew out to New York on Wednesday 10th and before he set off to see Chapman at Rikers, McGowan managed to put a call through to Chapman to let him know he was coming to see him.

Speaking in 1985, McGowan said he found Chapman "lucid

and very rational" with Mark stating, "I understand what I have done and although it was planned by me, I do not understand why I did it… It was a struggle, and I went through a torment for the last two or three months. It's been a struggle between good and evil and right and wrong, and I just gave in. It was almost as if I was on some kind of special mission that I could not avoid." What a telling choice of words. A special mission?

McGowan revealed to Bresler in 1985 that one of the most important things Chapman asked him to do on his first visit to Rikers Island was to communicate with Dana Reeves and tell him that he (Chapman) was "alright". McGowan told Bresler that he contacted Reeves, but Reeves didn't want to talk to him for fear of being implicated. How interesting. Mark was very keen to let his old friend know that he was alright. Had that been prearranged? Dana Reeves, the policeman, didn't want to be linked to Mark the alleged assassin in any manner. Why? What lay on his conscience?

McGowan wanted to link Chapman up with a New York pastor who could visit him regularly. The ever-helpful Stephen Olford happened to know a good pastor friend whom he recommended to Special Agent McGowan. This chosen pastor was operating out of the upper east side of New York. He was also a member of the Christian and Missionary Alliance Church. It will probably not surprise you at this point in the book that there are confirmed reports of CIA involvement in the Christian and Missionary Alliance Church. Intelligence infiltration of Christian missionary groups was (and I'm sure still is) very common and obviously useful for undercover surveillance. As if that wasn't bad enough, one other seriously embarrassing episode for the Christian and Missionary Alliance Church is the fact that one of their flock, David Berg, set up the notorious Children of God – a controversial religious cult accused of child sex abuse.

Suspicion about CIA involvement with U.S. foreign missionaries has a long history. Fausto Vasconcelos, evangelism director for the Baptist World Alliance and a former pastor in Brazil, said in an interview in 2013 at the Baptist World Alliance in Falls Church that he remembered hearing speculation about whether a particular Southern Baptist missionary worked for the CIA in the 1960s. I wonder who that could be? In the late 1960s, reports appeared in the press of "systematic use of American missionaries by the CIA".

In 1975, President Gerald Ford admitted that the CIA had used missionaries as agents in the past and might do so again. "In many countries of the world representatives of the clergy, foreign and local, play a significant role and can be of assistance to the U.S. through the CIA with no reflection upon the integrity of their mission." This became such a problem that in 1977, the CIA was prohibited from the recruitment of journalists, academics, clergy, and missionaries. However, speaking before a Senate Intelligence Committee in the mid 1990s, CIA director John Deutch testified that the spy agency could waive this ban in cases of "unique and special threats to national security."

Some religious leaders were not happy with this cosy missionary/CIA relationship and tried to do something about it. In 1996, the National Association of Evangelicals (NAE) adopted a resolution at its convention condemning (note, not banning) collaboration between missionaries and intelligence agency employees. The NAE requested that President Clinton and Congress "correct this intolerable situation" of soliciting religious workers for covert activity. "For intelligence agencies to seek any relationship whatsoever with our religious workers must be unequivocally prohibited," said NAE president Don Argue. Allowing such a loophole, Argue said, endangered missionaries as well as church, relief, community development and refugee workers in politically sensitive areas. They probably branded him a left-wing agitator and opened an FBI file.

Gloria Chapman and a group called All About Jesus Ministries have subsequently set up a global prison newsletter that purports to be from Mark and Gloria Chapman. This newsletter is aimed at inspiring incarcerated people all around the world with a short story from Mark called "The Prisoner's Letter" and a mini biography called "The Man Who Shot John Lennon (The Inside Story of Mark David Chapman)". The final pamphlet is called "John Lennon's killer" (the word "killer" is in a font that can only be described as frenzied). This pamphlet is bizarrely based on Mark's 2012 parole hearing transcript. A dubious marketing tool for Jesus. Looking at these pamphlets, crass is the only word that comes to my mind. They are allegedly sent free, but there is a funding component built into the website that allows you to order them. Charles McGowan funds this pamphlet operation. The pamphlets appear to be sent from a PO Box in Kailua in Hawaii, with the exact same zip code as the old Castle Memorial Hospital. But I'm sure that is just a coincidence.

Recap

Stephen Olford contacting Pastor Charles McGowan – on the very night John Lennon was assassinated and urging the (former?) counter-intelligence agent to immediately visit Chapman in his cell – is highly suspicious. Firstly, how did Olford know his friend McGowan knew Chapman? Chapman was a nobody who hadn't been in McGowan's congregation for at least three years. Why would McGowan talk to "superstar" New York preacher Olford about Chapman? Secondly, how did Olford even know that Chapman was the alleged murderer of John Lennon at such an early hour? The press didn't release Chapman's name until roughly 3am. The morning papers were not yet printed with Chapman's name on them. How did Olford know it was Chapman being held for John Lennon's murder?

It is also deeply troubling to observe the way Chapman's initial public defence lawyer, Herbert Adlerberg, was coerced out of his position through anonymous, threatening phone calls. Calls so threatening that Adlerberg initially denied they even existed. Adlerberg's replacement, the inexperienced Jonathan Marks, worked out of a building and with a legal assistant, both of which were connected to the CIA. Marks also sent self-confessed CIA mind control hypnotists, such as Milton Kline, into Mark Chapman's cell. Many people may assume that Marks was naive and was played. Others may assume he was a willing participant in an intelligence operation to get nefarious agents into Mark Chapman's cell. Jonathan Marks still has a lot of questions to answer.

CHAPTER 16 | Catcher vs The Demons

Key People

Dr Milton Kline (CIA consultant)
Dr Bernard Diamond (hypnotist)
Dr Richard Bloom (hypnotist)
Professor Dorothy Lewis (psychiatrist)

Jim Gaines (journalist)

Mark Chapman

Every specialist who subsequently came into contact with Chapman at Rikers and Bellevue tried to persuade him that there were other reasons for him killing John Lennon, not the J.D. Salinger book. *The Catcher in The Rye* had to be lost down the historical memory hole in the John Lennon murder narrative.

His deprogramming was difficult. From the 27th of January onwards, Chapman was convinced that he killed Lennon to promote *The Catcher in the Rye*. All he wanted to talk about was the Salinger book and how the world was full of "phoneys" like John Lennon. The *Catcher* fixation reached its height on 1st February 1981 when Chapman sent a letter to the *New York Times* stating that he wanted the whole world to read the book to find "answers". Throughout the following few months, Chapman was visited by several psychiatrists with side hustles in hypnotism and intelligence work. Mark was also visited by numerous preachers and lawyers. These visits were not monitored by independent assessors. It was open house for messing with Mark Chapman's mind and slowly, as the months rolled by, Mark began to perceive "demons" as another potential cause for his killing of John Lennon, although *Catcher in the Rye* wasn't out of his system yet.

In a 1987 *People* magazine article, journalist Jim Gaines revealed the following about CIA consultant Milton Kline and Sirhan Sirhan expert Bernard Diamond when they visited Chapman in his cell: Gaines wrote:

"In an interview with Dr. Milton Kline, Chapman talked about promoting Catcher in the Rye across the world. Chapman apparently saw himself riding a chariot into an arena with millions of people cheering as Mark held the book up. In early February, Dr. Bernard Diamond had an interview with Mark where they discussed 40 parallels between Mark's life and Holden Caulfield's life in *Catcher in the Rye*. I am the Catcher in the Rye of this generation."

After his meeting with Diamond, Chapman told his lawyer:

"To remain true to the book, I must not talk to doctors or anybody about myself, because then people will say, 'He felt so strongly about the book and he wants us to read it so much that he sacrificed his own defence for the book….' I mean, wouldn't that be something? It's just like [Christians] being thrown to the lions. They wouldn't betray what they believed in…. They didn't get up and try to defend themselves. And [shouting] that's all I'm doing. Jesus Christ did not say a word. He didn't have to. The fact was there. He didn't have to defend Himself and I don't have to defend myself."

This sounds like the by-product of a very confused and manipulated mind.

Jim Gaines wrote in his article that Milton Kline was highly regarded and widely published, and he probably had the best relationship with Chapman out of all the experts, perhaps in part because he seemed to share Chapman's belief that a trial would be a boon to *The Catcher in the Rye*. In his interview with Milton Kline, Mark Chapman sought confirmation: "This is going to be the biggest trial of the decade, and the book will be read by millions. Wouldn't you say that was right?" You can feel his enthusiasm, his excitement. Like a child in the early years of learning, Mark was repeating what he had been primed to believe. They were playing with his mind. Milton Kline is reported as replying:

> "I'd go one step further, Mark. Everybody will read *The Catcher in the Rye*. *The Catcher in the Rye* will become the No. 1 best-seller and will probably become one of the biggest motion pictures in the history of literature."

No one in full command of their faculties would have swallowed this claim. But if the subject is vulnerable, desperate for vindication, trusting of his doctor and pastor, the situation changes. Kline and Diamond were clearly encouraging Chapman's obsession with *The Catcher*.

It's important to recognise that journalist Jim Gaines was given audio tapes of discussions Diamond and Kline had with Mark Chapman. These were the conversations that the two hypnotists wanted the world to believe they were having with Mark Chapman. It is highly likely that Kline and Diamond didn't always press the tape record button when they were engaged in other interactions with Chapman. Interactions that they wanted to keep secret. They had Chapman all to themselves. They totally controlled the narrative.

There are some reports that an unnamed psychiatric expert brought in a suitcase full of *Catcher in the Rye* books to Chapman's cell. The expert then asked Chapman to sign them all and promised he would use the signed copies to help promote the book. No proof of these signed books has ever been offered up. The main suspect for the multiple book signings is Dr Richard Bloom, who can be seen reading a copy of *Catcher* in a 1988 TV documentary.

In subsequent years, Chapman had to endure numerous

demon exorcisms by persons known and unknown. This demon gaslighting went on for many years, and I believe its purpose was to successfully expunge all thoughts of the Salinger book from his mind. However, Mark's obsession with *Catcher* was initially allowed to flourish throughout January and February 1981. If it kept Mark from thinking too deeply about what might have really compelled him to try and shoot John Lennon, what was the harm? But on March 30th, 1981, John Hinckley tried to assassinate US President Ronald Reagan. A copy of *The Catcher in the Rye* was found in Hinckley's hotel room. That was clearly a powerful and disturbing connection too far. *Catcher* was now linked to two world-famous assassination attempts in less than four months. A decision must have been made to try to expunge the Salinger book connection from Chapman's addled mind, and to stop promoting it publicly. From that moment on, "Project Demon" peddling began.

The Demon peddlers were eventually highly successful in their mission: Mark's old, imagined demons were going to be put in charge soon. But more on that in Chapter 23. For now, the Mark Chapman "Catcher-made-me-do-it Project" was officially dead and buried.

This successful erasure of *Catcher* from the Mark Chapman story didn't quite mean the subject would disappear forever. In a 2014 article on Gloria Chapman by the *Daily Mail*, she refused to discuss her husband's previous obsession with the Salinger book. According to Gloria, Chapman killed Lennon for the "bright light of fame". A hollow claim when you consider that Chapman has only given two filmed media interviews in the last 43 years; and considering that he deliberately decided to forgo the trial of the century, which would have placed him at its epicentre – in the spotlight, where he would have received all the public attention he *apparently desired.*

Clearly, when Mark Chapman picked up *The Catcher in the Rye* after John Lennon was shot, it appeared, even to the casual observer, that this was an involuntary programmed response. The concerted effort to expunge the book from the Mark Chapman narrative is very telling and shines a harsh and suspicious light on the people who have tried so hard to erase *Catcher* from Mark Chapman's backstory – in my opinion. The book's Intelligence background is impossible to gloss over, and for many, it was a connection that was too dangerous to be allowed to stand as an enduring historical signpost. The Chapman and *Catcher* link will never completely go away, but if you tell enough people enough times that a quest for "glory" and "demons" made Chapman try to kill John Lennon, *Catcher in the Rye* will inevitably fade from view as a contributing factor. This has now come to pass. It had to. No one in authority wanted a signpost to Intelligence being linked to Mark's actions.

Chapman's lawyer Jonathan Marks met Charles McGowan for dinner one evening, and Marks informed McGowan that the defence team had little money to get the experts they needed to counter the claims of the experts that the prosecution could afford. Marks asked McGowan if he would start up a defence fund for Chapman to help raise some funds. The first, and apparently only, donor for Chapman's defence costs was the ever-helpful Stephen Olford. Did Olford then choose the psychiatric experts for Chapman's defence?

One of the defence team's psychiatric experts to first examine Chapman was Dorothy Lewis, a research professor of psychiatry at New York University's school of medicine. She was also associated with a research programme at Bellevue Hospital, on violent young adults. It was in this research capacity that she obtained Jonathan Marks' permission to interview his client on condition that she provided Marks with a report. Some of Lewis's report has thankfully leaked out over the years.

Jonathan Marks has always steadfastly refused to be interviewed about his legal defence of Mark Chapman. It is also worth mentioning at this juncture that no full defence psychiatric reports on Chapman have ever been authorised to be released to the public, by order of Mark Chapman and Jonathan Marks.

Some brief extracts of Chapman's psychiatric reports were made available to the writer Fenton Bresler. In these, Dorothy Lewis said that she thought Mark harboured ideas that could be considered psychotic, and therefore, in ordinary language, mad, but, she then added that Chapman "might have been acting in response to a command hallucination on the day of the shooting."

This assessment, coming as it does from an independent source, is doubly valuable and highly significant. Lewis had no agenda. This is what she really thought. I wholeheartedly agree with her. Between 7th January 1981 and 17th June 1981, Chapman endured over 150 hours of taped interviews from nine (known) psychiatric experts or psychologists. Six for the defence and three for the prosecution. Chapman also undertook a CAT scan, a glucose tolerance test and two EEG's.

The district attorney's psychiatric experts all, predictably, came up with the same diagnosis to support the prosecution's case – that Chapman was not insane. All three psychiatrists (Dr A. Louis McGarry, Dr Emmanuel F. Hammer and Dr Martin L. Lubin) said Chapman was not mentally ill or psychotic but was suffering from a narcissistic personality disorder.

Recap

The Intelligence-linked "experts" that were sent into Mark Chapman's cell were initially willing to go along with Chapman's belief that he killed John Lennon to promote the *The Catcher in the Rye* novel. They actively encouraged this fantasy. After Ronald Reagan's would-be-assassin, John Hinckley Jr was found to have a copy of the Salinger novel in his hotel room, clearly a decision was made to convince Chapman that *Catcher* was no longer his main driver to kill John Lennon. A new reason had to be concocted. The new reason would be "Demons." The demon peddlers would reveal much about themselves and their nefarious motives when this new "demons made me do it" idea was carefully planted into Chapman's fractured and vulnerable mind.

CHAPTER 17 | Team Hypnosis

Key People

Jonathan Marks (lawyer)

Dr Jules Bernhardt (hypnotist)

Dr Richard Bloom (hypnotist

Milton Kline (CIA hypnotist)

Dr Bernard Diamond (hypnotist)

Dr Daniel Schwartz (expert in demons)

Dr Emanuel Hammer (hypnotist)

Dr Jules Bernhardt

We know that Mark Chapman had seen psychiatric "experts" in Hawaii. We have a good idea who one of these was, from a *National Enquirer* article on John Lennon's assassination (it was of course called murder) from the 30th of December 1980. In the article, Dr Jules Bernhardt, a so-called Chapman family friend and psychological counsellor, talked about his experiences with Mark. Also in the article, another – unnamed – "close friend" said that Chapman saw Lennon as the "anti-Christ" and a "demonic figure" whose comeback would "lead people away from God".

Dr Bernhardt has been described by some of his disciples as a man with an "innate capacity to connect with nature and unseen realms". The mysterious Bernhardt described himself as an author, lecturer, human relation counsellor and founder of the Institute for Dynamic Living. Bernhardt claimed that he had served in the field of human behaviour and the spiritual nature of men for over 25 years. He released a self-hypnosis album in the 1960s, which demonstrated how the listener could use their life energy as the keys to the kingdom within themselves. Bernhardt promised that his "programme" would help people "experience and know the perfect source of their own inner self" and they would know that "GOD IS WELL... AND SO ARE YOU!".

Bernhardt also released a self-hypnosis book in 1968 called *Self Hypnosis — The Miracle of the Mind*.

Yet again, Mark Chapman found himself entwined with a psychiatrist who had a side-line in hypnosis. When Bernhardt spoke to the *National Enquirer* in late 1980, he stated that "Chapman would never have killed Lennon had the rock star stayed in retirement. It was only when Lennon's comeback convinced Chapman that the former Beatle would again be in a position to rival Christ, that a death **plot** was **triggered** [emphasis my own] by his tortured mind." Bernhardt also thought that Chapman saw himself as an "avenging angel". Did Chapman really see himself as some a kind of Christian assassin or had this idea been implanted in his mind?

Bernhardt is a mysterious character about whom little is known. What we do know is that he started his career as a chiropractor, and after leading a childbirth team where the unfortunate expectant mother died shortly after giving birth, he was charged with medical negligence and manslaughter and eventually ended up in prison. When he was released on appeal, Bernhardt understandably erased his past and set himself up as a human relations counsellor with a side-line in self-hypnosis.

I have spoken to people who knew Bernhardt when he was lecturing in Hawaii in 1980 and they were of the view that he seemed to be a new-age thinker who was asking people to look within themselves for answers and not to rely on organised religion. He was aware of the benefits and the dangers of hypnosis, and I suspect he may have gained some insight into Chapman being part of a "plot" to kill the "anti-Christ" Lennon. There is, of course, the possibility that Bernhardt was actually involved in this plot to hypnotise Chapman to kill Lennon. He certainly had the hypnotic skills. One advocate of Bernhardt recalls the hypnotist placing a lighter's flame under her hand and hypnotising her so she could not feel the burn of the flame. After he took her out of her trance, she saw her left hand was covered in black from the flame. Bernhardt clearly was a highly skilled hypnotist. It is interesting to note that Bernhardt has been written out of the Mark Chapman story. After he had spoken to the *Enquirer* on the last day of 1980, it seems he was erased from history.

Dr Bernard Diamond

One of the early defence psychiatric experts who diagnosed Chapman was a Dr Bernard Diamond. Incredibly, Diamond was a psychiatrist who spent time in 1968 with Sirhan Sirhan, the man accused of assassinating Robert Kennedy. What are the chances of that? Dr Diamond was rumoured to be working for the CIA throughout his long career. He pronounced a matching diagnosis for both Sirhan Sirhan and Mark Chapman. Sirhan hated Diamond. He said that he misspoke for him in court. Diamond was an avid exponent of hypnosis and its uses in assisting criminal trials. He hypnotised Sirhan on more than one occasion. (More later regarding the mercurial Diamond and what he got up to.)

Dr Daniel Schwartz

Next up was Dr Daniel Schwartz, a prominent "expert" for Chapman, who often spoke on his behalf in court. Schwartz was very much in the "demons were involved" camp. He had previously examined the notorious "Son of Sam" serial killer, David Berkowitz. Schwartz thought that Berkowitz had been commanded by "demons" to kill. Continuing his well-worn demonic theme, Schwartz stated in court that Chapman had been pushed by the demons of his dementia to shoot John Lennon. He added that Chapman told him that: "I can feel their [demons] thoughts. I can hear their thoughts. I can hear them talking, but not from the outside, from the inside". Schwartz became so well-known for mentioning "demons" as a cause of insanity that in a case where he was defending a police officer for shooting a civilian, the prosecutor quipped that he thought Schwartz "only talked to demons". Dr Daniel Schwartz's assessments of "Son of Sam" Berkowitz and Mark Chapman were almost identical.

Dr Richard Bloom

Dr Richard Bloom was another "expert" who claimed Chapman was primarily a paranoid schizophrenic. Bloom, like so many other people connected to Chapman, had a previous career in Intelligence and the military. Bloom was also a strong exponent and advocate of hypnosis. He furthered his career in this field by becoming the Director of Research and Development at the Institute for Research in Hypnosis and Psychotherapy.

Milton Kline

Even more incredible than Bloom spending quality time with Chapman and Bernard Diamond making an appearance in the aftermath of an infamous murder was the fact that Milton Kline was invited into Mark Chapman's cell. Kline, like his friend and colleague Bloom, became a signed-up member of the Institute for Research in Hypnosis and Psychotherapy. Chillingly, Kline was also the man who, in a 1979 TV documentary, had once described himself as a CIA's hypnosis consultant and had worked on project MK-Ultra. The huge importance of that will be thoroughly considered in the next chapter. Kline was a former president of the American Society for Clinical and Experimental Hypnosis and was brought in as an expert witness for the defence, specifically by Jonathan Marks.

Jonathan Marks was not reticent about the reason he brought in Kline. Immediately after being appointed to the Chapman case, Marks spoke to the *New York Post* on the 12th December and told them that he was planning to hypnotise Chapman to help him re-enact the killing. Marks told the *Post* that he would be asking Kline to unlock Chapman's "thoughts and feelings" about Lennon.

Johnathan Marks had used Kline's capabilities with hypnosis

in a previous murder trial. He succeeded in gaining the acquittal of a man accused of pushing a young woman, Renee Katz, under a subway train, partly through Kline's assessment. According to the defendant, Allen Lewis, Kline had managed – through hypnosis – to dredge up memories in his subconscious where police forced him to "say things against [his] will". These "things" included a confession and a previous admission that he pushed the female student under a subway train. It appears that Kline's hypnotic skills helped get Lewis acquitted. Kline commented at the time that "a person under hypnosis, cannot lie". Marks wanted to use these hypnotic skills on Chapman. Tape recordings of the Kline hypnotic session would, according to Marks, provide "a rare glimpse into the mind of an accused killer [including] feelings that Chapman may not even know lurk in his subconscious".

Kline was one of the first psychiatrists to see Chapman in custody. He never submitted an official report as his qualifications were found to be suspect. Tapes do exist of Kline's conversations with Mark Chapman. Tapes that were used by the journalist Jim Gaines in his 1987 *People* magazine piece. Gaines and Marks were reputed to be intending to writing a book together. The book fell through for reasons unknown, but this is almost certainly how Gaines accessed Mark Chapman's psychiatric tapes. I'm sure these tapes were useful to Jonathan Marks on one level, but we must ask ourselves whether any of the hypnotists and psychiatrists would have willingly pressed the record button if there was malpractice afoot.

Kline later served four months in a prison in Florida on a perjury charge.

Dr Emanuel Hammer

It wasn't just defence-appointed hypnotists who gained access to Chapman in his cell. The prosecution also used a psychologist, Dr Hammer, who had previously published a book called *Post*

Hypnotic Suggestion. People with skills in post hypnotic suggestion can make somebody do something against their will, while they are not in a hypnotic state. This happens because the suggestion has been implanted while the subject was under hypnosis. Once free from the hypnotic state, they are not aware of the implanted suggestion. Once embedded, the suggestion can be activated by a simple command, such as a word or a phrase. For example – "shoot John Lennon".

Recap

Take a look at this group of mind-manipulators, the "experts" who were given access to a vulnerable man. These sharks who fed on Mark Chapman's insecurities were deeply involved in hypnosis and some had strong ties to the military and links to the CIA. A coincidence? I don't think so.

If we accept that people who are vulnerable to hypnotic suggestions are easily manipulated and often completely unaware of their susceptibility, then Mark Chapman ticked all the boxes. This fact was well known on the Hawaii circuit. He had been constantly abused by these "mind doctors" from his late teenage years. Of equal importance is the links to the CIA: Diamond was accused of it; Kline even boasted about it.

CHAPTER 18 | Project MK-Ultra: A Weapon of War

Key People & Institutions

Frank Olson (MK-Ultra victim)

Sidney Gottlieb (CIA Technical Services)

Allen Dulles (CIA Director)

George Estabrooks (Hypnotist and CIA agent)

Sheffield Edwards (CIA officer)

Dr Louis Jolyon (Jolly) West (CIA)

Richard Helms (CIA)

James McCord (CIA)

Sirhan Sirhan (alleged assassin RFK)

Prof John F. Kihlstrom (Professor in Psychology at University of California, Berkeley)

Thomas Narut (Lieutenant Commander US Navy)

Milton Kline (Society for Clinical and Experimental Hypnosis co-founder and CIA consultant)

Project MK-Ultra, the CIA's "program of research into behavioral modification" officially began in 1953. But what exactly is this MK-Ultra programme, which Milton Kline worked on for the CIA? To answer this question, we must go back to 1945 and the end of the Second World War. In 1945, at Fort Dietrich in Maryland, a secret US biological laboratory began work on aerosol technologies, focusing on ways to spray germs and toxins on enemies and to defend against such attacks. Two US scientists, Harold Abramson and Frank Olson were assigned to work with ex-Nazi scientists brought over to the USA through a secret programme called Operation Paperclip. It is estimated that over 1,600 Nazi scientists were permitted to work in the United States under Operation Paperclip. What influence this large group of Nazi scientists had on the American military and intelligence communities can only be guessed at with trepidation and dread.

Rumours began to circulate that American Intelligence officers had experimented with "truth drugs" in Europe in the last years of the Second World War. In 1949, at the Nuremberg trials which judged the war crimes of World War Two, the United States adopted the International Code for Human Experimentation: "A person must give full and informed consent before being used as a subject." After 1953, Project MK-Ultra scientists flouted this code remorselessly. Their work encompassed everything from electronic brain stimulation to sensory deprivation to "induced pain" and "psychosis". They sought ways to cause heart attacks, severe twitching, and intense cluster headaches. If drugs didn't do the trick, they'd try to master ESP, ultrasonic vibrations, and radiation poisoning. One project even tried to harness the power of magnetic fields. Hypnosis lay at the heart of this evil project. The CIA, then in its infancy, launched Project Bluebird: a mind-control programme that tested drugs on American citizens, mainly in federal penitentiaries or on military bases. Most didn't know about, let alone consent to, the battery of procedures they underwent.

This abusive research into mind-control found further justification when, in 1952, captured American pilots confessed on Peking radio that they had sprayed the North Korean countryside with biological weapons. It was a confession so beyond the pale that the CIA blamed the communists, asserting that the POWs must have been "brainwashed" into confessing. This theory articulated a set of growing fears that a new class of chemicals could rewire and automate the human mind. When the American POWs returned home, the US Army brought in a team of scientists to "deprogram" them. Among those scientists was a Dr Louis Jolyon West. Born in Brooklyn in 1924, West had enlisted in the Air Force during World War II, eventually rising to the rank of colonel. His friends called him "Jolly." Back on civvy-street, Jolly researched methods of controlling human behaviour at Cornell University. He would later claim to have studied 83 prisoners of war, 56 of whom had been forced to make false confessions. He and his colleagues were credited with reintegrating the American POWs into Western society and, more importantly, getting them to renounce their claims about having used biological weapons.

West's success with the POWs gained him entrance to the upper echelons of the Intelligence community. Sidney Gottlieb, the poisons expert who headed the chemical division of the CIA's Technical Services Staff, along with Richard Helms, the CIA's chief of operations for the Directorate of Plans, had convinced the agency's then director, Allen Dulles, that mind control operations were the future. Initially, the agency wanted only to prevent further potential brainwashing by the Soviets. But the defensive programme quickly became an offensive one. Operation Bluebird morphed into Operation Artichoke and a search for an all-purpose truth serum was on. In a speech at Princeton University, Dulles warned that communist spies could turn the American mind into "a phonograph playing a disc put on its spindle by an outside genius." Just days after those remarks, on April 13, 1953, Dulles officially set Project MK-Ultra into motion.

In 1952, the CIA set up a centre in Beirut, Lebanon, as a Middle Eastern base of operations. This base was to remain active throughout the 50s, 60s and 70s. By 1953, Project MK-Ultra was in full swing. Using drugs and hypnosis, the CIA's director Allan Dulles hoped the programme would unlock new interrogation techniques as well as techniques to train and order unwitting assassins to kill under hypnosis. When the secret operation was uncovered in the mid 1970s (despite most MK-Ultra documents being shredded after Watergate) surviving evidence showed Project MK-Ultra had over 100 off-shoot projects and that many unwitting people had been experimented on, and that some had died.

One project concerned the ability to control mass populations, basically for cheap labour. Dr Delgado, a pioneer of electric brain simulation, told the American Congress that he hoped for a future where technology would control workers in the field and troops at war through electronic remote signals. He found it hard to understand why people would complain about electrodes implanted in their brains to make them "both happy and productive." Many observers, including myself, believe this statement to be one of many indicators that demonstrate that the 1978 Jonestown disaster in Guyana, for example, could have been a CIA experiment in mass mind-control and hypnotic coercion.

Experts disagree somewhat on a definition of hypnosis. Some believe it represents enhanced concentration. Others describe it as a partial sleep state. The common understanding is that hypnosis is a state in which people are more susceptible to suggestion, but the level of suggestibility varies widely from person to person. Someone who has only been lightly hypnotised can remember almost everything that happened to them under hypnosis. Someone in a deep trance, however, may not remember anything that happened to them under hypnosis. Experts agree that roughly twenty-five per cent of the population are so susceptible to suggestions under hypnosis that they perform incredible acts which the other seventy-five percent would never consider.

Sometimes people in hypnotic states look half asleep, or in some other way "out of it" as is often the case in staged hypnosis demonstrations. But not all hypnotised subjects look sleepy, dazed, or unnatural. Some, even when under hypnosis, will appear normal.

According to George Estabrooks (a lifelong hypnosis experimenter whose prolific contributions on the subject caused others to call him "the father of modern hypnosis"):

"We can coach the subject so that in the trance he will behave exactly as in the waking state. Under these circumstances we could defy anyone, even a skilled psychologist, to tell whether the subject was 'asleep' or 'awake'. There are tests which will tell the story but in warfare we cannot run around sticking pins into everyone we meet just to see if he is normal. Is hypnosis dangerous? It can be. Under certain circumstances, it is dangerous in the extreme. It has even been known to lead to murder. Given the right combination of hypnotist and subject, hypnosis can be a lethal weapon. We know that dual, and even multiple, personality can be both caused and cured by hypnotism. Moreover, the Dr. Jekyll and Mr. Hyde combination, is a very real one once it is established. The key to creating an effective spy or assassin rests in splitting a man's personality, or creating multi-personality, with the aid of hypnotism…. This is not science fiction. … I have done it."

When Sirhan Sirhan shot Robert F. Kennedy in 1968, his defence team brought in the hypnosis expert Dr Bernard Diamond to get him to recall what happened. The problem was that Diamond believed Sirhan *had* killed Kennedy, and all his questions, therefore, had that as a built-in assumption. As a result, Diamond's work on Sirhan was designed to produce a specific result. He wasn't interested in an open-ended investigation into what might have been in Sirhan's mind during the period of the shooting. In 1980, Diamond said:

"I believe that once a potential witness has been hypnotised for the purposes of enhancing memory, his recollections have been so contaminated that he is rendered effectively incompetent to testify. Hypnotised persons, being extremely suggestible, graft onto their memories fantasies or suggestions deliberately or unwittingly communicated by the hypnotist. After hypnosis the subject cannot differentiate between a true recollection and a fantasy or a suggested detail. Neither can any expert trier of fact. This risk is so great, in my view, that the use of hypnosis by police on a potential witness is tantamount to the destruction or fabrication of evidence."

Unfortunately, Bernard Diamond's meetings with Mark Chapman were not officially recorded or revealed. So, we do not know what this alleged CIA agent suggested to Mark.

Professor John F. Kihlstrom of the University of California at Berkeley noted that:

"Among those individuals who are most highly hypnotisable, these alterations in consciousness are associated with subjective conviction bordering on delusion, and an experience of involuntariness bordering on compulsion. And this compulsion doesn't just persist in the hypnotic state. The compulsion happens even when the subject is awake, after having received a post-hypnotic command or trigger."

Be mindful that Mark Chapman said that he felt "compelled" to assassinate John Lennon.

George Estabrooks, wrote in his 1947 book *Spiritism* about how difficult it is for subjects to resist post-hypnotic suggestions, even when the subject suspects the origin. Estabrooks described an experiment which demonstrated this effect:

"One peculiar thing about these post-hypnotic suggestions is their compulsive force. One of our greatest modern authorities tried the following experiment. He suggested to a subject that after he awoke [from hypnosis] and on a given signal he would go to the window, cut a pack of cards which was placed there, select the ace of spades and give it to the hypnotist. He was then awakened and the signal was given. Now, as it happened, the subject was a graduate student in psychology at one of our large universities and so was perfectly familiar with every phase of hypnotism. On the signal, he started for the pack of cards and then suddenly stopped 'You know,' he said, 'I believe that's a post-hypnotic suggestion.'

'What do you want to do?' asked the operator.

'I want to go to that pack of cards, select the ace of spades, and give it to you.'

'You are right. It is a post-hypnotic suggestion. What are you doing to do about it?'

'I'm not going to carry it out.'"

The hypnotist then bet the subject 50 cents he would not be able to resist the post-hypnotic suggestion. For the next two hours, the subject found himself wandering over to the deck, realising what he was doing, and stopping himself. By the end of the afternoon, he found himself unable to concentrate on anything else. He went back to the deck, pulled out the ace of spades, and gave it to his hypnotist along with a dollar.

"He could obtain no peace of mind," Estabrooks said, "until he had obeyed the suggestion."

This experiment was on someone who was fully aware that he had been hypnotised and recognised the source of his compulsion. How much more quickly and willingly would an unsuspecting subject have given in to any suggestion? It has often been noted that a disturbing phenomenon of hypnosis is how few people, unlike the trained psychological student in the example above, will be unable to attribute their compulsions and actions to the actual cause, because the conscious mind is unaware of suggestion made under hypnosis, as Estabrooks explained:

"One of the most astounding things about the post-hypnotic suggestion is the subject's conviction that he is acting of his own free will. For instance, I tell a subject that he will repeat the alphabet to me backwards on a given signal after awakening. Then I say to him, 'Allen, why did you repeat the alphabet to me?' For a moment he is puzzled and then he replies, 'Why, as a matter of fact I heard you say about a month ago to someone that the average person couldn't do it backwards and I just wanted to show you I could.'"

Bernard Diamond demonstrated to Sirhan's defence team how easily he could hypnotise Sirhan through suggestion. After putting Sirhan in a hypnotic state, Diamond told him that he would climb his prison cell bars "like a monkey" when Diamond blew his nose with a handkerchief. After Sirhan was taken out of his hypnotic spell, the pre-suggested signal for Sirhan to act was instigated by Diamond blowing his nose. In front of Sirhan's amazed defence team, Sirhan began to climb the bars of his prison cell. When Sirhan was asked what he was doing, he tried to explain his bizarre actions by saying that he was just taking some exercise. Diamond had not only demonstrated that Sirhan's actions were totally under the hypnotist's control, but that Sirhan's conscious mind had no recollection of the suggestion made under hypnosis, as he thought he was acting of his own free will.

Twelve years later, Diamond (with his amazing hypnotic skills) had – unmonitored – access to Mark Chapman in his prison cell.

Estabrooks described in his book *Hypnosis* how he could create multiple personality states in an individual through hypnosis. He'd then programme the two states such that one personality wouldn't know what the other one was doing. Mark Chapman often said he had a big person and a little person inside him fighting for control of his actions. Estabrooks asked in his book if it was unethical to split personalities in this manner and answered his own question "perhaps," but he felt that anything was justified in war. In later years, Estabrooks speculated that the assassination of John F. Kennedy by Lee Harvey Oswald, as well as the actions of Jack Ruby, were likely the result of hypnotic mind control. Thanks to the work of Tom O'Neill, we now know that Dr Jolly West, an MK-Ultra linked psychiatrist, visited Jack Ruby when he was awaiting trial.

In 1979, a documentary on MK-Ultra was produced by ABC in America. In it, Dr Milton Kline was interviewed – the very same Milton Kline who met Mark Chapman in his police cell.

In the documentary, Kline was billed as a psychologist, a clinical and experimental hypnotist and lastly, an unpaid consultant to the CIA. Kline said to the interviewer, "If you're asking whether an individual under hypnosis can be influenced, coerced, persuaded, shaped to perform an anti-social act or a destructive act or an act of violence – then my answer is yes." Furthermore, in a CIA FOI document published in 1980 (and released in 2010) about Kline's campaign to legally restrict the use of hypnosis to health professionals, he says one of the goals of the early 1960s "experiments to create a hypnotized, remote-control assassin… was entirely possible." He goes on to claim that given the proper subject and circumstances, by using hypnosis he could produce such a killer (a Manchurian candidate killer) in three to six weeks.

The unfettered expansion of MK-Ultra would go on to shock American society when it was exposed in the mid 1970s. In the 1950s and 1960s, the psychologists and hypnotists had been unleashed.

Frank Olsen

In Manhattan, November 1953, at the sinister looking Statelier Hotel, Frank Olson, a father of three, apparently threw himself from his hotel room 1018a onto the street below. When the police arrived at the room, Olson's roommate Robert Lashbrook was sitting on the toilet with his head in his hands. Lashbrook told the police that he heard a noise while sleeping and when he woke up, he discovered that Olson had jumped out of the window. That night, the police discovered that a phone call was made from Olson's room to Dr Harold Abramson, a physician and, at that time, one of the CIA's "medical consultants". The switchboard operator overheard the conversation: "well he's gone" the caller said. Abramson replied: "well that's too bad".

Olson's family were informed that their father and husband had committed suicide. Olson's wife Alice was also told that, given the condition of her husband's body, family members should not view it. The funeral was held with a closed casket. Decades later, disturbing stories about Olson's involvement with MK-Ultra started to emerge. First it was revealed that Olson told his wife that he had made "a terrible mistake" getting involved with the CIA. This followed an episode where one of Olson's colleagues lured him to a retreat and secretly fed him and others LSD. This episode deeply disturbed Olson. Worse was to follow. He witnessed terrible acts of inhumanity.

It started with monkeys being gassed and poisoned and continued with suspected spies or moles interrogated to death with the combination of drugs, hypnosis and torture. The torturers, according to one study, were also attempting to "master brainwashing techniques and memory erasing" through these sessions. By the time he had been there for ten years, Olson literally knew where all the dead bodies were buried – monkey or otherwise. In the spring of 1953, matters got worse. Olson visited a CIA safe house near Stuttgart and saw men dying in agony from the weapons he had helped to create. On his return to the US, Olson confided in CIA psychiatrist William Sargent that he was deeply disturbed about his work. He was hospitalised at a Maryland sanatorium before being taken to Manhattan where he allegedly took his own life via a tenth storey window. The investigating police detective concluded that Olson had died from multiple fractures "subsequent upon a jump or fall". This became the official narrative.

CIA officer Sheffield Edwards was brought in to clean up the mess. The New York Police were persuaded not to investigate and to co-operate in misleading the press. Lashbrook was given a fake career and, finally, a CIA officer called James McCord was brought in to clean up the room. McCord had previously been an FBI agent specialising in counterintelligence. Making police investigations evaporate was one of his specialities. McCord, with Frank Sturgis, went on to be Watergate burglars 20 years later. In June 1975, the *Washington Post* ran a story about an army scientist who had been drugged with LSD by the CIA. The Olson family quickly realised the story referred to their father. They called a press conference in their back garden and said they were seeking several million dollars in damages. President Ford's chief of staff Donald Rumsfeld and his deputy Dick Cheney were concerned that a lawsuit might force the CIA to "disclose highly classified national security information". Ford was encouraged to meet the Olsons and publicly apologise for "a terrible thing that never should have happened". President Gerald Ford further explained: "Some of our people were out of control in those days. They went too far. There were problems of supervision and administration." The Olsons accepted a $750,000 pay-off and a handshake from the President for dropping their lawsuit.

Frank Olson's son waited another decade after his mother had died before having his father's body exhumed. Pathologist James Starr discovered that there were no glass shards on Olson's head or neck, and although he had landed on his back, the skull above his left eye was disfigured. Starr concluded that Olson was struck with a stunning blow to the head by someone prior to his exiting through the window of room 1018a. Later, Starr was convinced that Frank Olson was deliberately thrown out of that window. All in the name of national security.

John F. Kennedy

In November 1963, President Kennedy had been assassinated in Dallas. While being transferred by the Dallas police, the chief suspect in JFK's assassination, Lee Harvey Oswald, was assassinated by Dallas mobster, Jack Ruby. The famous attorney Melvin Belli represented Jack Ruby at his trial. One of Belli's friends, an attorney named Leonard Steinman, suggested in a letter to Belli that he thought Jack Ruby had been acting out a post-hypnotic command when he killed Oswald.

When in April 1964, Jack Ruby started claiming from his jail cell that a "cabal" was responsible for JFK's murder, Dr

Louis Jolyon West showed up to examine Oswald's assassin. After meeting Ruby in private, Jolly West claimed that in the last forty-eight hours, Oswald's murderer experienced an "acute psychotic break". He believed Ruby was a man who was "completely unhinged, who hallucinated and heard voices". From that day forward, every doctor to examine Ruby concluded the same – that Ruby was delusional. Prior to Jolly's visit, a half-dozen psychiatrists found Ruby "essentially compos mentis". In 1967, Jack Ruby died of cancer while still in prison. In his final days, he claimed that drugs given to him prior to his death had made him terminally ill.

Martin Luther King

On April 4th, 1968, James Earl Ray, a down-and-out petty thief whose criminal career was littered with petty offences such as taxi-cab hold-ups and grocery store robberies, for which he usually got caught, allegedly assassinated Martin Luther King. As well as pulling off a complicated crime such as a sniper assassination, Ray also somehow made his getaway to London via Atlanta, Toronto and Portugal. How he afforded the travel expenses, much less planned this convoluted getaway, has never been explained. Ray concocted an elaborate assassination scheme, yet was still careless enough to leave the murder weapon at the scene of the crime with his fingerprints on it. These stark facts bring everything into disrepute. This same claim involving fingerprints on the murder weapon at the scene of the crime also blighted Lee Harvey Oswald and Sirhan Sirhan and possibly Mark Chapman. Interestingly, like Ray, Mark Chapman also went on a round-the-world trip that he could not possibly afford. In 1967, while he was trying to get a job in Los Angeles, Earl Ray consulted no fewer than eight different psychiatrists, hypnotists and Scientologists, trying to find "relief from his depressions and feelings of inadequacy".

Robert F. Kennedy

Almost exactly two months after Martin Luther King was murdered, Robert Kennedy was assassinated in a hotel kitchen in Los Angeles, on the night he was nominated as the Democratic candidate for the Presidency of the United States. It is widely reported that a polka-dressed lady was seen whispering into a blank-faced Sirhan Sirhan's ear, seconds before the so-called assassin pulled the trigger of his gun.

Sirhan did not remember shooting Robert Kennedy. All he could remember was having a few drinks with a woman and then waking up with various men's knees bearing down on his face. On his arrest, Sirhan did not fully understand what they said he had done. He could not recall if he had a wife or not. He had a cool and detached demeanour which witnesses noticed after his arrest. They stated that Sirhan had a sickly smile, and it was noted that he also had unnatural strength, being able to hold off six men while keeping the gun from professional football player Rosey Grier after RFK was shot.

Some witnesses commented that Mark Chapman had a strange smirk on his face after shooting John Lennon.

Thirteen bullets were allegedly fired when Robert Kennedy was murdered – Sirhan only had eight bullets in his gun. A journal of Sirhan was found after RFK's murder. In it he repeats the following lines:

"RFK must die, RFK must die, RFK must die.

RFK must be Assassinated, RFK must be Assassinated, RFK must be Assassinated. Please pay to the order of of of of of of of of this or that, please pay to the order of."

Psychiatrist Dr Bernard Diamond put Sirhan under hypnosis six times. He declared that Sirhan was happier answering questions in writing when interviewed under hypnosis. Sirhan couldn't remember writing in his notebooks. Diamond showed Sirhan an example from one of the notebooks. This is the exchange:

Diamond: Is this crazy writing?
Sirhan: Yes, Yes, Yes (Sirhan wrote)
Diamond: Are you crazy?
Sirhan: No, No (Sirhan wrote)
Diamond: Well, why are you writing crazy?
Sirhan: PRACTICE PRACTICE PRACTICE (Sirhan wrote)
Diamond: Practice for what?
Sirhan: MIND CONTROL MIND CONTROL MIND CONTROL (Sirhan wrote)

Sirhan complained that he was "outraged" over Diamond's testimony in court, accusing him of "saying things about me that were grossly untrue. Nor did I give him permission to testify on my behalf in court."

Again, remember that twelve years later, Bernard Diamond analysed Mark Chapman in his prison cell.

Many modern investigators, such as Lisa Pease, believe that there were four important factors in the Robert Kennedy assassination. Firstly, you had a brainwashed Manchurian candidate who did not remember pulling the trigger. Secondly, you had a handler standing close to the brainwashed candidate triggering him to commit the act. Thirdly, you had a concealed second shooter on-site, ensuring the assassination target is killed with additional shots fired by a trained marksman. Lastly, you had a local police force who did not investigate the murder properly and covered up any further investigation attempts. It is now widely believed that all these elements were in place when Robert Kennedy was assassinated.

Herbert Spiegel, the Columbia psychiatrist and author of one of the standard texts of clinical hypnosis, concluded that Sirhan was hypnotically programmed to shoot RFK. As of 2023, Robert Kennedy Jr is pushing for a new investigation into his father's murder. He has met Sirhan Sirhan in prison and is convinced all the four above elements were factors in his father's murder.

The Manson Family

In 1969, the infamous Tate–LaBianca murders were perpetrated by members of the Charles Manson "family" in Los Angeles, California.

Once they were caught and incarcerated, most of the Manson family said they were encouraged to take enormous amounts of LSD under instruction from Charles Manson. They also said Manson had a strange hypnotic affect over them and many could not recall committing the murders for which they were charged.

Journalist Tom O'Neill believes that Dr Jolly West was deeply connected with the Manson case. He believed that it was highly probable that West, through Manson, controlled the Manson family and through massive LSD ingestion and mind-control techniques, used them to attack and destroy symbols of the "counterculture" socialist utopia, that the west coast hippies were now spreading around America and the world.

Watergate Aftermath

In 1972, CIA operative Frank Sturgis and some other CIA "burglars" broke into the Democratic Party campaign offices in Washington DC to photograph documents and install listening devices. The ensuing Watergate scandal destroyed Republican President Nixon's presidency. By 1973, a panic-stricken Richard Helms, the then head of the CIA, concerned that the CIA's more unsavoury activities would be uncovered in the post-Watergate witch-hunt, instructed his CIA staff to destroy all MK-Ultra files. The shredders did a poor job and 20,000 MK-Ultra documents survived and were found four years later.

In 1975, The Church Committee, a US Senate Select

Committee, was set up to investigate government wrong-doing and abuses by the CIA, NSA, FBI and IRS. As well as releasing a report titled "Alleged Assassination Plots Involving Foreign Leaders", the Committee revealed Project MK-Ultra to a shocked public for the first time. MK-Ultra chief Sidney Gottlieb testified that the purpose of these programmes was "to investigate whether and how it was possible to modify an individual's behaviour by covert means". The Church Committee was told that MK-Ultra ceased operations in 1973. However, in 1977, a FOI Act request uncovered the remaining 20,000 documents which led to the Senate Select Committee on Intelligence hearings which further investigated Project MK-Ultra, and the world was horrified to discover the full extent of the atrocities of MK-Ultra programme.

One of the early classified MK-Ultra off-shoot projects, which was revealed after the Church Committee, was Operation Spellbinder. The purpose of Spellbinder was to create an effective sleeper assassin, such as a Manchurian Candidate. Initially this was to assassinate Fidel Castro. The programmed killer would be hypnotised, drugged, and conditioned through a combination of mind-control techniques to assassinate someone without being aware of their lethal programming.

To carry out this nefarious project, the CIA required a suitable candidate. The American Society of Clinical and Experimental Hypnosis helped nominate a candidate. The very same society that had as its president, Milton Kline. The same hypnotist chosen to "assess" Mark Chapman after his arrest.

Having been sensationally uncovered in 1975, the CIA's MK-Uktra project faded into obscurity and was all but forgotten by the world's mainstream media. It was assumed that the use of hypnosis for nefarious means by American intelligence agencies was a thing of the past. But the deeply disturbing question always remained, how far did the intelligence agencies continue to use hypnosis for black ops after 1973? It was a secret weapon whose dismemberment was unlike ballistic missiles or nuclear bombs. You might order the military agencies to stop using physical weapons or dispose of them, but mind control lay exclusively in the hands of practitioners. Of those who still controlled the dark arts, the key question is, who controlled them?

At a NATO conference in Oslo in 1975, a US Navy Intelligence Psychologist, called Lieutenant Commander Thomas Narut, startled the assembled psychologists by revealing that he was involved in teaching "combat readiness units" to cope with the stress of killing. He then had a private session with a small group, which thankfully included the London *Sunday Times* journalist, Peter Watson.

Narut expanded on the units under his control by revealing that some of them where men programmed to kill. They were, to use his own exact words, "Hit Men and Assassins" made ready to kill in selected countries should the need arise. He also told Watson that US Naval intelligence had also taken convicted murderers from military prisons and conditioned them as political assassins who were placed in American embassies around the world.

Narut claimed that he was personally involved with such programmes in both Naples, Italy and San Diego. When the story ran in the *Sunday Times*, the US navy published an official denial explaining that Narut had been talking in "theoretical and not practical terms".

Cleary, MK-Ultra had not ended in 1973 and US Navy intelligence were one of the main drivers of the programme. Coincidentally, this was same US Navy intelligence community in which Pastor Charles McGowan operated.

CHAPTER 19 | Men From the CIA

Key People

Milton Kline (CIA consultant/hypnotherapist)	David Suggs (lawyer)
Jonathan Marks (lawyer)	
William J. "Wild Bill" Donovan (founder of the CIA)	Paul Helliwell (CIA)

We know that CIA consultant Milton Kline was one of the first psychologists to see Mark Chapman in custody. We also know that hypnosis experts Bernard Diamond and Richard Bloom also had full and private access to Chapman and his fragile psyche. What I just couldn't figure out was why Chapman's legal defence team would place all these hypnotists in Mark Chapman's cell. Jonathan Marks was apparently just a run of the mill lawyer. He had no known links to the CIA. Marks had used Milton Kline's unique hypnotism skills in another case in 1979. As Kline was a CIA consultant, the CIA would surely have been aware of Marks using their man. But how could the CIA possibly wangle it to make sure Kline, and others, got into Mark Chapman's cell? If that's what they intended to do. How could the CIA also know what was going on in Chapman's defence case? Did Jonathan Marks work for the CIA?

Then I discovered that Jonathan Marks' assistant on the Chapman case was a young lawyer called David Suggs. The prestigious New York law firm that Suggs worked for back in 1980 was called "Donovan, Leisure, Newton and Irvine". The founder of this prestigious law firm was William Joseph Donovan – the same William J. "Wild Bill" Donovan considered to be the founding father of the CIA.

Donovan's law firm was so full of ex-CIA men that the firm

was basically known as the CIA's very own law firm. Donovan was a decorated First World War veteran, who, during the Second World War, was responsible for setting up the OSS (Office of Strategic Services), the precursor to the CIA. A statue of Donovan stands in the lobby of the CIA's headquarters in Langley, Virginia.

Donovan set up his New York law firm in 1929. One of its earliest recorded famous recruits was William Colby, who joined the firm in 1947 and re-joined the firm again in 1987. In the interim years, Colby was a Second World War hero and major CIA operative in Cold War Europe and Vietnam. Between 1973 and 1976, Colby was the CIA Director. His main claim to fame was testifying at the Church Committee, where he had to explain all the CIA's nefarious activities such as assassinations and heart attack guns. Colby officially left the CIA in 1976, and by some accounts, was keen to reform his old agency while he was there. The footage of him explaining the dark activities of his agency to congress makes very uncomfortable viewing. Colby died in suspicious circumstances while out in his canoe at night. The official report suggested a heart attack brought on by exposure to cold water.

Many suspected foul play, while Colby's son Carl suggested, in a documentary film he made about his father, that he committed suicide due to the guilt of his work in the CIA. It is also

Wild Bill Donovan© Unknown

worth noting that Colby was investigating the Franklin child sex scandal just before he died. Anyone familiar with this scandal will know that many people who got close to that case died in mysterious circumstances.

"Wild Bill" Donovan's law firm had lots of blue chip clients, including the likes of General Electric, Mobil Oil, Pfizer and Walt Disney. There is no hard evidence or reason to believe that either Jonathan Marks or David Suggs was involved with the CIA, though Suggs clearly worked for a law firm with very close ties to the CIA. Marks had used Kline in 1979. Marks must have known Kline had previously worked for the CIA: Kline had even boasted about his CIA involvement in a TV documentary in 1979. It is worth noting that Jonathan Marks was working as a one-man law firm in an office building at 30, Rockefeller Plaza when he was chosen to defend Chapman. The same expensive office building that the "Donovan..." law firm was operating from. It's a big building for sure, but Marks must have been aware of the CIA-connected law firm in his building. He was surely introduced to Milton Kline and David Suggs in this building. Perhaps that's why he moved in?

Recap

The Donovan, Leisure, Newton and Irvine law firm was practically bursting at the seams with CIA operatives – they even had a CIA Director working at the firm. Suggs teaming up with Marks gave the CIA, through their association with the Donovan law firm, a clear path to get MK-Ultra consultant Milton Kline and other hypnosis experts into Mark Chapman's cell and, therefore, his mind. Is this all just a coincidence? I don't think so.

Donovan, Leisure, Newton and Irvine eventually closed its doors in 1998. One of its staffers, Lloyd Blankfein, eventually went on to work as CEO of Goldman Sachs and was globally known as one of the most well-paid men in the world. I'm sure "Wild Bill" would have been very proud of him.

CHAPTER 20 | The (Non) Trial of the Century

Key People

Mark Chapman

Justice Dennis Edwards (Judge)

Daniel Schwartz (demon expert)

Jim Gaines (journalist)

Barbara Walters (TV presenter)

After six months of psychotherapy tests (some on the record – and many of them not), Mark Chapman had one final surprise up his sleeve for the world. On 13th May 1981, it was ruled that all pre-trial legal procedures had been completed. The case was transferred to the Supreme Court's trial division. The "trial of the century", as some people were now calling it, was set for 22nd June 1981. Justice Dennis Edwards would be the presiding judge.

On 2nd June 1981, Chapman's lawyer, Jonathan Marks, told reporters that he was seriously worried about how he was going to find an unbiased jury for his client. Journalist Jim Gaines's 1981 *People Magazine* article/hit piece (more on that in the next chapter) was syndicated out into the public domain and Chapman was probably the most hated man in the world at that point.

Nevertheless, Mark Chapman, the man who shot John Lennon "to become famous/or become like Lennon/or become a character in a book" – take your pick – was now set to be front and centre on a global stage of millions in the trial of the century. Then Chapman dropped a bombshell.

On Monday 8th June 1981, Mark telephoned Jonathan Marks to tell him that God had visited him in his cell the previous night and told him to plead guilty. The public were later told that Chapman had been lying down in his cell when God apparently came to him. Chapman allegedly said that he had "heard a small voice in my heart… a very small male voice. I could not hear it, but I could feel it. It was the voice of God. He said I was to give up this trial for Him. It would be a Circus!"

Marks apparently tried to talk his client out of his new decision, but Chapman would not budge. When Chapman phoned his lawyer back soon after, he was more forceful saying "I'm not going to talk to any more phoney doctors. You're all fakes. You're a bunch of phoneys" before hanging up.

Prosecution and Defence psychiatrists were dispatched to find out more about Mark's "visit from God". Predictably, the defence doctors said it was all a hallucination, brought on by Mark's paranoid schizophrenia, while the prosecution doctors said it was no more than a fanciful representation of Mark struggling with his conscience.

It is very important to realise that at this point, in the summer of 1981, Mark Chapman believed there was no such thing as mental illness. He declared to his legal team that he thought that people who were considered mentally ill, were really possessed by "demons". By being sent to mental hospital, Chapman thought he would be surrounded by demons, everywhere. His skewed thinking regarding demons and mental hospitals led him to openly co-operate with the prosecution team and their psychiatric experts. He repeatedly admitted that "yes, I murdered Lennon" and actively participated in his own prosecution. Did Chapman's belief that mental illness was actually demon possession come from his time, ten years earlier, with charismatic Fred Krauss? Or did it possibly come from the new pastor whom Stephen Olford and Charles McGowan planted in his cell? Could it have come from McGowan himself, who has said on multiple occasions that he thought Chapman was possessed by demons? Could McGowan and whatever pastor he introduced Chapman to from New York have influenced Chapman to reject the insanity plea to protect himself from a demon-infested mental hospital? One thing seems certain, Chapman's belief in demons helped get him convicted by ensuring he aided the prosecution's experts.

One other potential factor in Chapman deciding to plead guilty was revealed by Jonathan Marks in a mid 1990s documentary for A&E called *American Justice*. Marks revealed that Chapman "was afraid that the witnesses that would have come into the court to testify on his behalf, would be at risk. That they would be vilified. The many hundreds of thousands of people who were grieving John Lennon's death, would come after them." Marks never declared whether this paranoid idea came from Chapman or from himself. Marks also never said that he tried to alleviate Chapman of this concern.

A "guilty by insanity" verdict leading to incarceration in a mental hospital was later passed down to Ronald Reagan's attempted assassin, John Hinckley. Hinckley was sent to a secure mental hospital in 1981 for attempting to kill the American president. Thirty-five years later, Hinckley was released in 2016. TV interviews with John Hinkley after his release are uncomfortable viewing. Heavily medicated, Hinckley can remember next to nothing of his alleged assassination attempt from 1981.

On 22nd June 1981, Chapman entered the Manhattan Supreme Court and was put in front of Justice Edwards:

Edwards: We understand that you wish to withdraw your prior 'not guilty' and to plead 'guilty'.
Chapman: Yes sir, your honour.
[The judge then read out the murder charge to Chapman.]
Edwards: Do you understand the indictment sir?
Chapman: Yes, your honour.
Edwards: By waiving and giving up your right to trial, you give up your right to have a trial by judge and jury. Do you understand?
Chapman: Yes, your honour.
[Judge Edwards then took Chapman through the essential facts

of his alleged crime. Below is a summary]

Edwards: We (State County of New York) accuse Mark David Chapman of the crime of murder in the second degree on or about 8th December 1980, with intent to cause the death of John Winston Lennon by shooting him about the chest and body with a pistol. Do you understand the indictment?

Chapman: Yes, your honour.

Edwards: If you wish, tell the court in your own words, what you did on 8th December 1980 in the area of the Dakota at about 11pm.

Chapman: I intended to kill John Lennon and that night I drew a pistol from my pocket, proceeded to shoot him with intent to kill him.

Edwards: Do you recall how many shots you fired from the pistol?

Chapman: Five shots.

Edwards: Did you know at the time of the five shots, how many actually struck John Lennon?

Chapman: No, your honour, I didn't.

Edwards: Do you now know how many shots struck the victim?

Chapman: Yes, your honour I do.

Edwards: How many were there?

Chapman: Four.

Chapman confirmed, yet again, that he thought he fired five shots, and that he didn't immediately know at that time how many of those struck Lennon. Therefore, he must have subsequently been told that Lennon was hit four times. Why did he not know at the time and who later told him? Also, he does not mention getting into a combat stance and he does not say he called out to John Lennon, confirming that he did not "say anything". We can only deduce that this false information must have come later from José Perdomo. Although Chapman did tell Barbara Walters in 1992 that he crouched into a "combat stance", by this time, he seemed to be repeating claims about himself and the Lennon murder that he had repeatedly heard from others for 11 years. Or did he perhaps hear some of these details from one of his many, unrecorded visitors to his prison cell? Did one of them plant this thought in his mind?

Edwards: How far away were you from the victim, Mr Lennon, when you started firing the shots?

Chapman: I am not quite sure, but I think it is around twenty feet.

Edwards: At any time during the firing of the shots, did the distance between you and Mr Lennon change or did you remain?

Chapman: I don't believe so no.

Edwards: You remained approximately in the same area?

Chapman: Yes, your honour.

Edwards: What was Mr Lennon doing just before you started to fire the shots at him?

Chapman: He was approaching the door that would lead up to the security area.

Edwards: What were you doing just before you fired the shot?

Chapman: A second before?

Edwards: Yes, or a moment before. As you were standing. Did you stand and wait for him?

Chapman: Yes. As he passed me, I stepped off the curb and walked a few steps over, turned, withdrew my pistol and aimed at him in the direction and fired off five shots in quick succession.

Edwards: Did you say anything at or about that time?

Chapman: No, your honour.

Edwards: You were there to cause the death of John Lennon and you fired five shots from your pistol with the intent to cause the death of John Lennon?

Chapman: Yes, your honour.

Importantly, Chapman had also confirmed that he was "around twenty feet" away from Lennon when he shot him and that the distance did not change. He also confirmed that he was standing on the curb (all witnesses state that Chapman was on the left-hand side curb) before stepping off, as Lennon passed, and walking "a few steps over" (presumably to the right) before he started shooting.

District Attorney Allen Sullivan then asked further questions of Chapman:

Sullivan: What kind of bullets did you use?

Chapman: They were .38 calibre hollow points.

Sullivan: What was the reason for using the hollow points?

Chapman: To ensure John Lennon's death.

(Ballistic evidence now indicates that John Lennon had a non-hollow bullet in his body.)

Sullivan: Why did you change your plea?

Chapman: It's my decision and God's decision.

Sullivan: When you say it's God's decision, did you hear any voices in your ears?

Chapman: Any audible voices?

Sullivan: Any audible voices

Chapman: No, sir.

Sullivan: Before you made the decision, did you indulge in any prayer?

Chapman: Yes, there were a number of prayers.

Sullivan: After you prayed to God, did you come to the realisation that you should plead guilty?

Chapman: Yes that is his directive, command.

Sullivan: Is that a realisation you came to within yourself inspired perhaps by God?

Chapman: No, I felt that it was God telling me to plead guilty and then probing with my own decision whether to do what God wanted me to do, whether to do what I wanted to do and I decided to follow God's directive.

Sullivan: So would you say at this time that this plea is a result of your own free will?

Chapman: Yes.

Chapman was due to be sentenced on 24th August 1981. In the meantime, he was to be held in Rikers Island jail. After Mark's decision to plead guilty and forgo a trial, the New York Coroner's office called Yoko Ono and informed her that she should collect her husband's clothes: the clothes John was wearing when he was shot. They were no longer needed as evidence. There was no trial. A carrier bag containing her husband's bloody clothes, all apparently neatly folded inside, was collected. A label on the bag said "patient's belongings".

Yoko Ono subsequently displayed the bag of her husband's clothes in an anti-gun violence exhibition. It can only be hoped that she kept the bag and its belongings safe. Its contents could potentially be used as vital evidence in any future reappraisal and investigation into John Lennon's assassination.

On Monday 24th August 1981, Mark Chapman arrived at court for his sentencing. He wore dark slacks and a light blue t-shirt with no jacket. Under the t-shirt was a visible bullet-proof vest. Chapman also carried with him a copy of *The Catcher in the Rye*. The judge ruled against Jonathan Marks' attempts to get Mark re-examined for plea competency. Jonathan Marks then played a final, futile card —he brought in an "expert" witness to talk about Mark and he chose "demon-loving" Daniel Schwartz.

Dr Daniel Schwartz claimed:

"He [Chapman] doesn't just believe in Satan, he knows that Satan is here on Earth. Right or wrong is decided in his life by a struggle between God's angels and Satan's demons, who both struggle for possession of his will. He tells me that he can feel the presence of Satan's demons around him – 'I can feel their thoughts, I hear their thoughts. I can hear them talking, but not from the outside, from the inside'. He tells me that is was Satan's demons that gave him the strength and the opportunity for the present offence. He told me that he 'prayed to God for strength to resist'. Even up to the last minute, he believed that external forces, supernatural or otherwise determined his behaviour. I think that he is a chronic paranoid schizophrenic and he also has a narcissistic personality disorder. I believe that he became perilously close to losing his own identity."

Mark was then asked if he had anything to say before sentencing. Mark asked if he could read a brief passage from *The Catcher in the Rye* which he said would be "his final spoken words." He opened his book and read the passage, appearing to equate himself with the titular "Catcher" who "saves" little children from the "cliff's edge".

Despite the book-reading antics, the judge stated that he thought Chapman was not insane and had carried out an intentional crime. The judge also had no problem with Chapman being guided by the voice of God. The crime, the judge said, was contemplated, planned and executed by an individual fully aware of the situation and consequences of his conduct. Mark Chapman ought to have been sentenced to a state correctional facility for a minimum jail sentence of 25 years and a maximum jail sentence of life. Judge Edwards, however, decided that he would in fact hand down a lesser sentence of 20 years to life because Mark had entered his guilty plea voluntarily. It had no effect whatsoever. Chapman has been behind bars ever since.

On 2nd June 1988, journalist Fenton Bresler wrote Chapman a letter stating that he thought Mark had been under the influence of someone else to commit the crime. Mark replied five months later, denying that he had been part of a conspiracy. Mark cryptically wrote:

"The reasons for Mr. Lennon's death are very complex and I'm still trying to sort them out emotionally myself."

Recap

Mark's decision to plead guilty was accepted by the New York court. We will probably never know for sure whether a hypnotist, a psychiatrist or a pastor convinced him to do so. I suspect it might have been a combination of all of them. Mark was manipulated into thinking that small voices from God were directing his decisions. Mark was manipulated into pleading guilty because somebody convinced him that by doing so, he would avoid being sent to a "demon-infested" mental hospital. Mark was manipulated into thinking that by pleading guilty he would be protecting his loved ones from reprisals. Mark was manipulated at every turn while he was awaiting his trial. The manipulation worked. The trial was avoided. Justice for John Lennon and Mark Chapman was snuffed out. Mark Chapman was duly sent to prison. Forty-two years on, he remains there.

CHAPTER 21 | Assassinating Mark Chapman Part 1: Jim Gaines

Key People

Jim Gaines (journalist)
Mark Chapman
Gloria Chapman (Mark's wife)

Milton Kline (psychologist
and CIA consultant)
Reverend Charles McGowan

One of the initial published attempts to get to the facts surrounding Mark Chapman and John Lennon's murder came from Jim Gaines, a prominent mainstream journalist, in his June 1981 *People Magazine* article. Gaines had no access to Chapman while he was in police custody at this time, so we can assume that he probably got most of his "information" from José Perdomo, various witness statements, Mark's friends and associates, and possibly some police insiders that he may have known.

Jim Gaines's 1981 *People Magazine* piece was published before Mark Chapman's trial was due to begin. He was an experienced journalist, as well as being a member of the Council of Foreign Relations. He firstly took to describing an apparent nightmare that a Chapman "friend" had:

> "Mark is smiling and walking up to me, then all of a sudden he
> has a knife and he stabs me. It takes 10 of us to hold him off, and
> we put him in a cage, but he breaks free. We run after him and
> catch him and cage him again. But I'm still scared to death he's
> going to get out."

Gaines didn't identify his nightmare story source and this brief dream sequence neatly sums up the angle I think Gaines was going for. An angle that went more for the emotional rather than the thoughtful mind.

The official Chapman narrative written by Gaines in his 1981 article, and then subsequently picked up and run with by every other journalist around the globe, is listed below. However, Chapman in his police statement on the night of the murder, and his subsequent statement to the court, never mentioned any of these events. Likewise, Mark's family, friends and ex-girlfriends failed to recognise the dark character traits and past events that Gaines wrote about.

Jim Gaines's main observations and assertions from 1981 are in bold below. My observations are noted after each one:

1. Chapman crouched in a combat stance when shooting Lennon. Chapman only once said he did this, in a 1992 TV interview which appeared staged to my eyes. And, as discussed earlier, he made no mention of this "stance" in his 1981 court plea hearing. The combat stance has often been used as an indicator of Chapman's callousness and professionalism. It is, of course, irrelevant how he held his gun, and there was nothing professional about an assassin who could not remember what he had just done and one who got out a book after committing his alleged crime.

2. Chapman called out "Mr Lennon" to John Lennon before shooting him. This is untrue. Chapman has never claimed he said this. Interestingly, Jay Hastings told me that this was a greeting José Perdomo often used to greet Lennon.

3. Lennon turned to acknowledge Chapman's "greeting". Untrue. In an early witness statement, Yoko Ono clearly specified that neither she nor John turned around.

4. Chapman told Perdomo "I just shot John Lennon."

Unverified. Chapman has never claimed he said this. Perhaps this came from Perdomo?

5. The New York police thought he was a "wacko". Probably true.

6. Chapman took LSD five days in a row and heroin was his favourite drug. Untrue. I have it on authority from the people who regularly took drugs with Mark Chapman that he never took heroin.

7. Mark became obsessed with the "McCartney is dead myth" in 1969. Unverified and irrelevant.

8. The Beatles pictures papered Chapman's room at his home. Unverified and unlikely. None of Chapman's friends have ever claimed to have seen pictures of the Beatles in Mark's home or bedroom.

9. Mark told his friends that "on the first day, God created the Beatles". Unverified and nonsensical.

10. Mark "believed" in John Lennon. Unverified.

11. Mark took his bedroom door off its hinges when his mother grounded him for drug use. This has been verified, but it was achieved with a screwdriver as a premeditated protest, not in anger.

12. Mark told his friends he wanted to burn down his parents' home. Unverified.

13. When Mark found God, he turned "against John Lennon". This appears to be true.

14. Mark's prayer group sang, in imitation of Lennon's hit, "Imagine, if John Lennon was dead". This morphed later into Mark singing the song solo. The prayer group leader later denied ever hearing the group sing the song. Therefore, unverified and denied.

15. Mark kept telling workers about Lennon's arrogance about his "bigger than Jesus" statement. Unverified but possibly true.

16. Mark thought that guitar playing "took him away from God and had some kind of control over him". Unverified, but it is likely his pastor friends may have inspired this nonsensical thought.

17. While working at Castle Memorial Hospital, Mark sold all his Beatles records. Unverified.

18. Mark thought he was a "Security Guard of Righteousness". Unverified and frankly ridiculous.

Most of Gaines's 1981 article is based on hearsay and conjecture. Gaines never revealed his sources and much of what he claimed could never be proven. But, as character assassinations go, he left absolutely nothing to chance.

Chapman was probably unaware of this 1981 article by Gaines when he allowed Gaines to conduct interviews in prison with him in 1984 and 1985. Chapman had endured three years of incarceration at this point and may have told Gaines what he wanted to hear rather than the actual truth. Or perhaps Chapman had started to believe what he was being told. Gaines then took two further years to collate all his interviews and to talk to people including Mark's mother and his wife Gloria, to enable him to write three long articles for *People Magazine*, all published in 1987.

Three 1987 *People Magazine* articles by Gaines claimed the following:

1. Chapman insisted he did not kill John Lennon to become famous. This is clearly true. Chapman did not give any media interviews up to 1984, nor did he allow his picture to be taken. By pleading guilty, he avoided the world media's constant attention for many months. It is very clear that Chapman did not kill John Lennon to seek fame. Five years later, Mark changed his mind yet again on this issue and stated (highly unconvincingly), in a 1992 TV interview, that he killed Lennon "to acquire his fame." In 2020 he claimed he killed Lennon "for glory".

2. Chapman claimed John Lennon's murder was "meant to be… from before time". What does this mean?

3. Chapman wrote a letter to the state attorney office in Hawaii, trying to change his name to Holden Caulfield. There is absolutely no evidence that this letter was ever sent.

4. Chapman said to his lawyer, "I think I have problems and I don't know what some of them are. Things that happened to me 10 or 15 years ago still haunt me, things people did to me. I still can't figure it out, why they would do these things." I strongly believe Chapman is referring to the demon exorcisms he suffered at the hands of Fred Krauss when he was 15. A crucial moment in his conditioning.

5. After discussing the tight security around him, Chapman said, "I'm not afraid of dying. I'm tired of all the struggle, the bother and worry and maybe that's the best thing, if someone out there knew what they were doing and would just shoot me and it wouldn't hurt."

6. Chapman had a list of other people he wanted to kill apart from Lennon. Chapman didn't write a "hit list". It was clearly invented to demonise him.

7. Mark was a devoted Beatles fan. He used to invite his friends into his garage to see him lip-synch "She Loves You". Not so.

8. In an interview with a psychological expert for the defence, Milton Kline, Chapman described for the first time a vivid fantasy he harboured. Other boys called him names and, feeling helpless to fight back, he retreated into a world in which he was admired. "I used to fantasise that I was a king," he told Kline, "and I had all these little people around me and that they lived in the walls…. And that I was their hero and was in the paper every day and I was on TV, their TV, and that I was important…. And I'd give concerts for them, and… I got these army men and cut off their rifles and [glued on] little guitars… and set them… right in the middle of the [living room] floor when my parents would go away. When we'd go on trips, I'd be in the car and I'd be rocking and the hand crank for the window was the volume control and I'd turn up the signal to send back this music that was in my head to the people in the kingdom. They all kinda worshipped me, you know, it was like I could do no wrong. And sometimes when I'd get mad, I'd blow some of them up. I'd have this push-button thing, part of the [sofa] and I'd like get mad and blow out part of the wall and a lot of them would die. But the people would still forgive me for that, and, you know, everything got back to normal. That's a fantasy I had for many years." Gaines revealed for the first time what MK-Ultra consultant Milton Kline likely discussed with Chapman in their interview a month after Lennon's murder. Chapman's statement on the night of the murder mentioned "large and small parts" of him that constantly vied for dominance within him, with the "small part" making Chapman do bad things. Now we discover that a month after John Lennon's murder, CIA consultant Milton Kline discussed the concept of Chapman having an inner kingdom of "little people" he could rule. If this testimony was truthful, and we must remember that Kline was later imprisoned for perjury, then this sounds like an extension of the "small part made me do it" scenario, that Chapman cited as one of the possible reasons for having a compulsion to murder John. It is also very important that this concept came from the mouth of a man who was known to work on a CIA project which tried to hypnotise people into doing actions against their will. Chapman's friends and family never mentioned Mark ever discussing an "inner kingdom of little people". This strange concept only surfaced after a discussion with Milton Kline in 1981 and was subsequently reported by Gaines in 1987.

Milton Kline and his "little people kingdom" concept is a very important factor in the Mark Chapman story. More later.

9. In his interview with Milton Kline, Chapman apparently revealed that he feared that he might have gotten too close to his young charges he looked after in his YMCA days. Chapman allegedly said "I have always loved children. I think maybe I loved them so much, identified with them so much, that it became a confused kind of thing." I have heard other reports that Chapman confessed to Kline that he might have had sexual thoughts regarding the children in his care. I have seen no proof of this. That said, Chapman's friend Dana Reeves was later convicted of child molestation, so this cannot be ruled out as a possibility.

Looking after children seemed to have been one of the happiest and most fulfilling periods in Chapman's life. He was constantly praised for his abilities with children and many commented how he was the nicest person they had ever known. Somehow, Milton

Kline managed to interpret Chapman's fulfilment as something sinister. More research is needed in this area.

10. After finding God, Chapman refused to play songs on his guitar anymore because John Lennon had once said the Beatles were more popular than Jesus.

11. In 1975, Mark sent a letter to his ex-girlfriend stating: "I'm so sinful and filthy. I'm constantly struggling with my identity… My ship is nearly sinking."

12. Gloria Chapman said she heard Mark in the middle of the night, when he thought she was asleep, making anonymous and threatening phone calls to various people including a doctor at Castle Hospital and a manager of a TV repair shop. How did Chapman manage to get through to a doctor and a TV repair man in the middle of the night? If this story is untrue, and it sounds very dubious to me, why would Gloria Chapman lie about her husband's nocturnal activities to Jim Gaines?

13. Gloria said Mark began to paint watercolours. He started with bright colours and then it became darker and darker until he crushed it and threw it away. This clichéd painting story seems like a pathetic parody of a man going insane.

14. Late at night, Mark listened to Beatles records through headphones when Gloria had gone to bed. It was apparently so loud that Gloria could hear the music in their bedroom. Gloria also said that Mark became physically abusive towards her. Though he apparently never struck her hard enough to leave bruises. Soon the marriage became a torment for her. She stayed with him only out of pride. Chapman had no Beatles music in his collection in Hawaii. A security guard colleague and Gloria's lawyer both confirmed this. No one in Hawaii has ever

said Mark often talked about the Beatles. This 1987 interview is
the first and only time Gloria Chapman mentioned being physically abused by Mark. Despite suffering alleged beatings, despite
him being accused of John Lennon's murder, despite the allegation he hired a prostitute in New York, despite years of negative
press coverage and Mark's refusal to see her after he was first
incarcerated, Gloria Chapman is still married to Mark and goes
to see him regularly. She even still apparently shares a bed with
him during alleged conjugal visits. This does not make any sense.

In 1987, Gloria blamed pride as the main reason for staying
married to Mark. In 2014, she told a British newspaper that God
told her to stay with Mark. In 2017, she gave an interview to a
Christian group and revealed that Mark had asked her to divorce
him but she refused. Today, Gloria is now adamant that the devil
made Mark kill Lennon. All mention of *The Catcher in the Rye*
is ignored and erased. Mark has become more devout in recent
years, no doubt due to Gloria's influence, and often states "all I
need is Jesus". Gloria currently handles all of Mark Chapman's
affairs.

**15. To help him in his various projects, Mark began receiv-
ing the advice and counsel of an imaginary population of
little people like those he had ruled as a king in his childhood. By this time, they had advanced beyond monarchy to
a representative government, with a House and a Senate and
numerous committees, but they were still ruled absolutely
by President Chapman. Gloria knew of the little people who
had inhabited the walls of his home in Decatur, and his ref-
erences to them now let her know they were back. She made
light of his tiny subjects sometimes, asking him what they
thought of this or that household decision, but Mark made it
clear he took them seriously. Gloria thought it odd, but nothing to worry about.** The "little people" concept only came to
light after Jim Gaines gained access to Milton Kline's audio tapes

in 1987 (which were almost certainly supplied by Mark's lawyer, Jonathan Marks) and was expanded by Jack Jones in 1992. It is very strange that Gloria Chapman, speaking to Jim Gaines in 1987, talks about Mark's "little people" at that point in time. It's almost as if Gloria Chapman and Milton Kline were somehow comparing notes.

16. Late Summer 1980, Mark apparently remembered something meaningful. "I remembered being caught up in these fits of anger and euphoria at the same time. Looking at a picture of Lennon and saying 'you phoney, I'm going to get you'. And then I would pray for demons to enter my body, to give me strength to pull that gun out.... I was praying for Satan to send me his more experienced demons. Not a little one: This is a big thing, I need a big demon.... My face got all red and fiery, and teeth like this, and I felt like I was very powerful, you know, and John was going to die. Nobody knew in the whole world what was going on in that room, [that] I was going to kill him". After 1981, Mark often cited the devil being responsible for making him murder John Lennon. This developed from his original confession that the "small part of him" caused him to kill Lennon and his promotion of *Catcher* as the cause. The common denominator is that Chapman always felt an unseen force was driving him to murder.

17. At the Dakota, Chapman had only the Dakota's night doorman, José Perdomo, to keep him company. José was an anti-Castro Cuban, and they talked that night of the Bay of Pigs and the assassination of John F. Kennedy. Chapman remembered – "I have a lithograph... of John F. Kennedy... and I hung it in our living room. Gloria didn't want me to because it would stare down on us when we watched TV and ate and stuff, but I wanted it that way.... That assassination has always meant a great deal to me". This is the comment that initiated the myth that Dakota José Perdomo was the same as Bay of Pigs José Perdomo.

18. Waiting for Lennon on the night of the 8th December, Chapman prayed to God to help him from killing Lennon. "I was also praying to the devil to give me the opportunity. Cause I knew I wouldn't have the strength on my own. I remember thinking, I can't kill a rabbit on my own". If Chapman didn't have the strength to kill "on his own", was there someone else with him on the 8th December to help him?

19. Chapman reflected: "As the night wore on, it seemed calling on God was futile. It's like… the actors were there for me, José, the girl and Paul [Goresh] and one by one it was their turn to exit, although I wanted them to stay. And [then] it started getting darker and the wind was whipping up that street. It was very eerie. I knew it was going to happen."

20. "The limousine appeared. I knew it was his, I knew it. I felt it. My soul reached out to that car and I knew he was out there. I said,'This is it'. So, I got up, and the car rolled up, and the door opened and Yoko got out…. Yoko was about 30 or 40 feet in front of him-weird. It was all meant to be. If they were together, I don't know if I could have shot him or not. But see, he was alone…. He looked right at me, and I didn't say anything to him. And he walked by me. I know he remembered me because I had this hat… and I had my coat on, you know, I looked the same. I'm sure he [remembered me], but he didn't say anything. And he walked past me, and then I heard [a voice] in my head say 'Do it do it do it' over and over again, just like that. 'Do it do it do it do it do it….' He walked a few feet. I turned, pulled the gun out of my pocket…. I don't remember aiming. I must have, but I don't remember drawing a bead…. I just pulled the trigger

steady five times". What was going through his mind, and the only answer he ever had was: "I remember thinking, 'The bullets are working'. I thought the humidity in the plane might have gotten to them. I think I felt a little regret that they were working, but I'm not sure. I just remember thinking, 'The bullets are working.'" Could the voice in Chapman's head saying "Do it" over and over come from someone standing next to Chapman? Could the fact that Chapman can't remember aiming the gun or pulling the bead, or the fact that he was surprised "the bullets were working" be due to the fact that he didn't actually fire any real bullets, and the real bullets that were hitting Lennon came from another shooter in a different location.

21. On the night of the murder, Gloria was watching TV – "anyway, on the bottom of the screen it ran across, like ticker tape, JOHN LENNON SHOT or something.... After that I didn't know for sure it was Mark, but I thought it could be and I kind of went through a state of semi-shock. I just went around the apartment going 'Oh, my God, oh, my God.' Then I thought maybe it wasn't him. I was getting kind of hopeful maybe it wasn't him, so I was turning on the radio…. I wasn't supposed to know where he was, but on the pad next to the phone he had written these numbers and it said YMCA… I called there and he wasn't in, so that wasn't good. It was later, as the evening progressed, that I started to get calls and stuff." Gloria had a second reaction as well, one that came that night before Mark's mother and everyone else had started arriving and she was still alone with her thoughts and her fears. "I felt a kind of joy for him," she says. "A happiness. Just for like a fleeting thought, you know, I felt relief for him, like 'Hooray.' I mean, I know it sounds crazy, but… I just felt kind of relief for him, that he had accomplished something he set out to do." Wait a second. In her telephone conversation to the NYPD, which was recorded on the night of the assassination, Gloria

swore to Mark that she hadn't been called by anyone other than a journalist. Her claims not to know where Mark had gone were surely shot down by her admission that she had three telephone numbers to call. And one was the YMCA in New York.

Gloria Chapman's reaction of "joy" and "happiness" for her husband "accomplishing something he set out to do" is very hard to comprehend or forgive. It does also leave us with the disturbing conclusion that she knew he was setting out to "do something" and that that something may have involved murdering John Lennon. It is worth remembering that Gloria Chapman booked her husband's plane tickets and personally drove him to the airport when he went back to New York in early December 1980. This came after the incident a month earlier, when Mark had laid out a gun and bullets in front of his wife and told her that he went to New York in late October 1980 to kill John Lennon. Was Gloria Chapman an accessory to murder? Many could understandably argue so. At the very least, Gloria must have suspected her husband had intentions to kill John Lennon again in early December 1980. Why did she not call the police? Why did she help with his travel arrangements? She was a travel agent when she first met Mark, but by December 1980 she was working full-time for the Castle Memorial Hospital of all places! According to Jim Gaines, Gloria has taped all her telephone calls with her husband after John Lennon's murder. Why would a devoted wife do this?

22. Shortly after the murder, Chapman saw Rev. Charles McGowan, who convinced Mark that there were 'spiritual matters' behind Lennon's murder. He also convinced Chapman to 'embrace his old religion'. McGowan rang Gloria shortly after the meeting with Mark and told her: 'There is a dimension to this case that the secular psychiatrist world would never understand. I believe there was a demonic power at work'. From his arrest on 8th December 1980 to his sentencing in August 1981, Mark Chapman's stance morphed from blaming his compulsion to murder John Lennon on *The Catcher in the Rye*, to a small, evil part inside of him, and finally to a more straightforward and clichéd battle between God and Satan. This was all clearly designed and manufactured by the small army of hypnotists and "experts" who camped out, unmonitored, in Mark Chapman's cell for nearly six months.

23. In an interview with Dr. Milton Kline, Chapman talked about promoting *Catcher in the Rye* across the world. Chapman apparently saw himself riding a chariot into and arena with millions of people cheering as Mark held the book up. In early February, Dr. Bernard Diamond had an interview with Mark where they discussed 40 parallels between Mark's life and Holden Caulfield's life in *Catcher in the Rye*. Milton Kline, who was also highly regarded and widely published, probably had the best relationship with Chapman of all the experts—perhaps in part because he seemed to share Chapman's belief that a trial would be a boon to *The Catcher in the Rye*. It is very interesting to note that the two psychiatrists who are historically related to MK-Ultra, hypnotism and mind-control were the keenest to talk to Mark and encourage his initial fascination with *Catcher in the Rye*. Gaines also forgets to talk about the two mind-control doctors' previous work, and even goes as far as to praise Kline as "highly regarded", while failing to remind his readers that Kline was a convicted criminal.

Mark Chapman subsequently said he regretted the interviews he gave to Jim Gaines in 1984 and 1985 and never allowed Gaines to visit him again. Gaines turns up from time to time on various Chapman TV documentaries over the years, sometimes holding a 1980 calendar that belonged to Mark Chapman. One can only assume that Gaines got the calendar from the ever-compliant and helpful Gloria. Jim Gaines and Chapman's lawyer, Jonathan

Marks, were allegedly writing a book together in the mid 1980s. The book fell through, for reasons unknown, but this is almost certainly how Gaines got access to some of Chapman's psychiatric tapes.

Recap

Mark was the victim of many intrusions as charlatans and opportunists took advantage of his mental fragility. Jim Gaines's articles did not look beyond the official version of events and made no attempt to ask deeper questions like: Where did you first get the idea to kill John Lennon? Who were your associates? Have you ever been hypnotised? Gaines started the misinformation media train – every subsequent article was another nail in the prison-coffin, in which the authorities wanted Chapman to stay.

CHAPTER 22 | Assassinating Mark Chapman
Part 2: Jack Jones

Key People
Jack Jones (journalist, with a background in Naval Intelligence)
Larry King (TV host)
Mark Chapman

After Jim Gaines's final meeting with Chapman in 1986, the mysterious 'journalist' Jack Jones began to write to Mark Chapman and slowly gain his confidence through the Attica Cephas prison friends group, run by a man called Harold Steele. Jones somehow befriended Steele and when Chapman asked Steele if he could have somebody to talk to, Steele suggested Jones. They apparently hit it off quickly, but Jones did not initially tell Chapman that he was a 'journalist'. Jones has subsequently often stated that he first heard from Chapman via a letter Mark wrote him in 1982. I can find no proof of this letter or Jones knowing Chapman in 1982.

Jack Jones's writing career is as much a puzzle as Mark Chapman's mind. Jones has claimed to have undertaken journalistic work with Vietnam veterans. He has also called himself a "top crime journalist" who has been the "winner of numerous Journalistic awards". He apparently conducted the first prison interview with the serial killer David Berkowitz, known as the "Son of Sam". His short paperback bio claims he secured the Berkowitz interview after "working undercover" inside Attica to produce and investigate a series of stories on crime and mental health. Jones has also claimed that he has interviewed E. Howard Hunt from Watergate and CIA fame and has been nominated three times for the Pulitzer prize.

I can find no evidence whatsoever of Jack Jones's award-winning journalism or three Pulitzer nominations. I'm not doubting they exist, but the absence of any record of this seems odd. It is worth noting that anyone can nominate themselves for a Pulitzer prize. A Pulitzer nomination is meaningless, but it sounds impressive.

Chapman has revealed that he discovered that Jones was probably working "undercover" after he first met him. Jack's duplicity apparently angered Mark, but this didn't stop Jack Jones from conducting an alleged 200 hours of interviews over a five-year period, from around 1986 to 1991. Jones even managed to get Gloria Chapman and a sanctioned friend of Yoko Ono on board. Jack Jones has subsequently called Gloria Chapman "a dear friend". Quite why Gloria wanted to befriend journalists who continually published negative stories about her husband is baffling – or is it perhaps revealing?

In 1992, Jones used his alleged 200 hours of taped interview sessions with Mark to write a bizarre book on the Lennon murder called *Let Me Take You Down*. The book quoted Chapman's interviews with Jones extensively and was very much an affirmation of the Chapman was a Lennon/Beatles/*Catcher in the Rye* obsessive, who shot John Lennon for fame.

One other important detail about journalist Jack Jones which he didn't share with Mark Chapman, or his readers, was the fact that he was a Vietnam veteran who served in the U.S. Navy and supervised security communications and intelligence gathering in support of combat operations. He also trained U.S. Army and U.S. Air Force troops at communication bases in Southeast Asia. Jack was a code breaker during his military service gathering intelligence in Vietnam and Communist China. To put it in more simple terms, Jack Jones was a spy working for the intelligence agencies.

Jones first revealed his past association with military and intelligence agencies when he successfully ran for the office of local town supervisor in Plattsburgh. He used his military service as a vote-catcher and played the "oldest son of poor Alabama labourers" card, claiming that he struggled through adversity and lifted himself from poverty through hard work. I can't help wondering whether some of that hard work was used gathering 'intelligence' when he was undercover in Attica, befriending Mark Chapman?

Jack Jones made a substantial amount of money from his association and interviews with Mark Chapman. His book sold well and he appears regularly on TV documentaries about John's killing, always sticking to and sometimes enhancing the official narrative. He has continued to sell his Chapman audio tapes to TV broadcasters right up until the present day. Going undercover and inserting himself into Mark Chapman's life has been a very lucrative endeavour for Jack Jones.

Mark Chapman went public in 1992. It was a big year for Chapman and the media. Almost certainly instigated by Jones and under his influence, Mark gave two television interviews. On December 4, 1992, *20/20* aired an interview that Chapman gave to Barbara Walters, his first television interview since the shooting. Then on December 17, 1992, Larry King interviewed Chapman on his programme *Larry King Live*. Both interviews appear stage-managed and therefore awkward in the extreme.

Below are the interesting extracts from the Larry King interview:

KING: "Are you saying, Mark, that the young man who shot John Lennon was not you? What are you saying?"
CHAPMAN: "It was me, Larry, and I accept full responsibility for what I did. I've seen places where I'm blaming the devil, and I hope that that isn't kept going after this interview. I'm not blaming the devil, I'm blaming myself. But in the major sense, it wasn't me, because I'm better now. I'm normal, I'm functioning, I have a lovely wife, and we have a great marriage, as much as, you know, can be had from here, from Attica. But I'm not the same person in the major sense, because back then

I was lost and I didn't know who I was. But now I do."

KING: "By the way, would you have killed someone else you think? Would Mark David have done that if it weren't Lennon?"

CHAPMAN: "The Secret Service asked me that. If Lennon would have unfortunately died a few days prior, say, in an automobile accident, would you have stalked someone else? I can't answer that question. I don't know. I was so bonded with John Lennon at that point."

Mark never mentioned the "hit list" that has been attributed to him. Surely if it had been genuine, Chapman would have said so at this point. This was the first time that Chapman said he was "bonded" with John Lennon.

KING: "Therefore, you have to have daily regrets."

CHAPMAN: "I have regrets. I'm sorry for what I did. I realise now that I really ended a man's life. Then, he was an album cover to me. He didn't exist, even when I met him earlier that day when he signed the album for me, which he did very graciously. And he was not a phoney, by the way. He was very patient, and he was very cordial and he asked me if there was anything else. So if that didn't register – and I also met his son that day. If that didn't register that he was a human being, then I wasn't perceiving him as such. I just saw him as a two-dimensional celebrity with no real feelings."

KING: "OK, why did Mark David Chapman want to shoot the album cover?"

CHAPMAN: "Mark David Chapman at that point was a walking shell who didn't ever learn how to let out his feelings of anger, of rage, of disappointment. Mark David Chapman was a failure in his own mind. He wanted to become somebody important, Larry. He didn't know how to handle being a nobody. He tried to be a somebody through his years, but as he progressively got worse – and I believe I was schizophrenic at the time. Nobody can tell me I wasn't – although I was responsible, Mark David Chapman struck out at something he perceived to be phoney, something he was angry at, to become something he wasn't, to become somebody."

This was the first time Mark said he killed Lennon to "be somebody". Since John Lennon's death, the media had run with the story that Chapman murdered John for fame, but up to this point, Mark had always said he had no idea why he wanted to kill John Lennon. Armies of psychiatrists couldn't find a motive. Chapman also told Barbara Walters that he killed John Lennon to acquire his fame. In my eyes, this is an unconvincing statement and I believe that Chapman was persuaded to make this excuse as a bid for future release. As of 2023, Chapman is blaming "demonic forces" and "glory" for making him kill John Lennon.

CHAPMAN: "Well, the photographer [Paul Goresh] left. I – in all fairness I have to say I tried to get him to stay."
KING: "Because?"
CHAPMAN: "Because there were those that felt I wanted him to shoot pictures of the shooting, which is not true."
KING: "Why, then, did you want him to stay?"
CHAPMAN: "I wanted him to stay because I wanted out of there. There was a part – a great part of me that didn't want to be there. I asked Jude the fan before she left for a date that night. She said no. If she'd have said yes, I would have been on date with her."
KING: "The circumstances of the killing, what happened?"
CHAPMAN: "I was sitting on the inside of the arch of the Dakota Building. And it was dark. It as windy. José, the doorman, was out along the sidewalk. And here's another odd thing that happened. I was at an angle where I could see Central Park West and 72nd and I see this limousine pull up and, as you know, there are probably hundreds of limousines

that turn up Central Park West in the evening, but I knew that was his. And I said, this is it, and I stood up. The limousine pulled up, the door opened, the rear left door opened. Yoko got out. John was far behind, say 20 feet, when he got out. I nodded to Yoko when she walked by me."

KING: "Did she nod back?"

CHAPMAN: "No, she didn't. And I don't mean to be so clinical about this, but I've told it a number of times. I hope you understand. John came out, and he looked at me, and I think he recognised, here's the fellow that I signed the album earlier, and he walked past me. I took five steps toward the street, turned, withdrew my Charter Arms .38 and fired five shots into his back."

KING: "All in his back?"

CHAPMAN: "All in his back."

Twelve years after allegedly shooting John Lennon, Mark Chapman still thought he shot Lennon in a manner disproved by medical evidence. Chapman's mind envisaged things that clearly were not happening. As if Chapman was under some kind of hypnotic spell. This was the first and only time that Mark mentioned that he took five steps "towards the street" before shooting Lennon. This would mean that he was easily 20 feet away from Lennon when he started shooting him in the dark Dakota entrance-way (a distance that Mark confirmed in his court hearing in 1981). Again, there is no mention of talking to Lennon before he shot him.

KING: "Never saw it coming?"

CHAPMAN: "He never saw anything coming, Larry. It was a very quick – it was a rough thing."

This is yet more proof that Mark Chapman was convinced that he thought he shot John Lennon in his back, and that John didn't turn around or see it coming.

KING: "What do you make of all the conspiracy theories that have come up in the last 12 years, CIA, mind control, et cetera?"
CHAPMAN: "Against the death of John Lennon?"
KING: "Yes."
CHAPMAN: "Hogwash."
KING: "No one asked you to do it? No one prompted you to do it? No cabal, nothing?"
CHAPMAN: "No, they probably wished they would have had me, Larry, but they didn't. It was me doing it, it wasn't them."

This was the only time on record that someone had spoken to Chapman about CIA/mind control involvement. The first thing to note is that if Chapman thought he had been brainwashed into committing the murder, he might have brought this up before Larry King asked him about it twelve years after the Lennon murder. Of course, the whole point of a hypnotised MK-Ultra subject is that they are programmed **not** to remember their actions or what induced them to act in a certain way. What did Mark mean by the statement "they would have had me"? Is he perhaps inadvertently inferring that "they" tried to "have him" in the past and he now possibly can't remember whether "they" did or not?

CHAPMAN: "So, if you have nothing to start with, and your life consists of fantasising about celebrities or being with them, that can become very dangerous. And that is a phenomenon in this country that has to be addressed. That's why the Secret Service has been talking with me and other people to try and find out what was ticking in this thing here on that night and before. I'm meeting with them Friday, by the way."
KING: "With the Secret Service?"
CHAPMAN: "Friday."
KING: "Are they going to talk to you about protecting Clinton?"
CHAPMAN: "They've asked me about presidential candidates. If

there are so many bodyguards, would that have prevented you? And my answer to that is no. I still would have probably struck out at John Lennon if he had 20 bodyguards. I was that desperate."

This is clear confirmation that the American Secret Service visited Chapman in prison. We shall almost certainly never know how often this happened. And what were the Secret Services trying to elicit? Twelve years after the assassination, the Secret Service were back interrogating Mark in prison. Were they afraid that he was about to change his story? Were they present to find out if the effects of the trauma which he undoubtedly experienced were wearing off? Wow. On live TV, we hear that the CIA or FBI were still directly involved. Where are their reports? Note too, another inconsistency. Chapman had repeatedly said that if only Paul Goresh had stayed with him, he probably would not have "shot" John Lennon. But here he claims that 20 bodyguards could not have stopped him because he was so desperate. As well as the word "desperate", Mark has also often used the word "compelled" to describe his need to kill Lennon.

KING: "Might it have been anger then at a president? Did it have to be…"
CHAPMAN: "It could have been anger at a president."
KING: "Or a broadcaster?"
CHAPMAN: "It could have been anger at a broadcaster. It could have happened that way very easily, but I think because it was Lennon, because my past – Jack [Jones] gets into this in the book deeply. My past was very rooted in Lennon. I believed in the things he was saying, and I believe he did too, by the way. I don't think he's phoney anymore."

Up until this reference about Mark's past being apparently "rooted with Lennon" Chapman has never said he was a massive Lennon fan or cared about the "things" he [Lennon] was saying".

Chapman made his thoughts on Lennon very clear in his statement immediately after the murder, stating:

> "I have nothing against John Lennon or anything he has done in the way of music or personal beliefs."

Somehow in the interim 12 years after saying this, and after talking with Jim Gaines and Jack Jones, the secret services and god knows who else, Chapman now saw himself "rooted in Lennon". After the live satellite link to Mark Chapman was closed, Larry King introduced Jack Jones, who was sitting nervously in the studio beside King.

KING: "We're back. Journalist Jack Jones has made a habit of probing the criminal mind. His latest subject is John Lennon's assassin, Mark David Chapman, who we just spent most of this program with."

Despite Jones's claims to the contrary, there appears to be no evidence, that I can find, that shows Jack Jones had been involved in any other work probing criminal minds.

KING: "Now you've looked at criminals a long time, right, written about them extensively."
JONES: "Fifteen years in and out of Attica prison."
KING: "You call him a sociopath. As I remember the definition of sociopath, they don't know. They just – they don't have a moral – they don't have a conscience. Is that still true, do you think? Is he conning us?"
JONES: "I think Mark cons himself, still. I think that his mind is capable of almost infinite self-deception. I believe that unlike a lot of people, he tries very hard to empathise with other people. He tries to sense that other people have pain also, but it's mostly intellectual sort of knowledge. He doesn't really feel it."

Countless witnesses from Chapman's time working with children said he was one of the most empathetic people they had ever met. One mother tells a story of Mark crying in empathy when her young daughter was receiving medical treatment.

KING: "Our guest is Jack Jones. He did a lot of extensive interviews with the Son of Sam, David Berkowitz – they're very different, right."

JONES: "Different in some ways, but actually both acts, or both men were carrying out acts of rage against the world."

Again, there is no record or evidence that I can find that Jack Jones ever spoke to or wrote about David Berkowitz.

KING: "And who was Chapman killing?"

JONES: "Some psychologists say he was killing his father but, I think, on a much more relevant level he was killing a part of all of us. He wanted to hurt the world."

There is no evidence for this assertion. Chapman has never publicly said he was killing his father through the Lennon murder. The same applies to the claim that he wanted to "hurt the world".

JONES: "Chapman told me at one point that he fantasised about getting his hands on nuclear devices and maybe blowing up a small city, injuring or killing thousands, if not millions, of people – and reasoned that, by killing someone that most of the people in the world identified with or had been touched by in one way or the other he could hurt us all, and he did."

There is no evidence for this. It may have been said in one of Jones's "off the record" conversations?

KING: "He says he'll never get out, even though it's 20 to life. Do you agree?"

JONES: "I don't think he wants to get out. I think the more relevant question here is, would he accept parole if it were offered? And I don't think, particularly if it were offered today or tomorrow, he would get out."

From the year 2000 onwards, Mark Chapman has applied for parole thirteen times. He clearly wants to get out. His friends who have spoken to him in prison have told me that he desperately wants to get out and will say anything he is advised to say to achieve this goal.

KING: "He told me, at the end of the program, after the show, that he was a big fan of mine – I'm not saying this for gratuitous things – and that he listened and watched all the time; and he told that to you, too, right?"

JONES: "Right."

KING: "You compared him to Hannibal Lecter?"

JONES: "Well, actually he compared himself to Hannibal Lecter in a couple of instances. He talked of having almost hypnotised a fellow in a cell next to him in a previous institution where the guy was cursing him, yelling at him; and the fellow went into an epileptic seizure after Mark had talked to him in this slow voice about a cobra that was under his bunk and was crawling up the bunk."

If this "hypnotising a cell mate" story is true, where did Mark Chapman learn these techniques? A Jack Jones taped interview surfaced in a 2005 Channel 4 documentary called *I killed John Lennon*. In the taped monologue, Chapman states:

"It was like a train, a runaway train. There was no stopping it. Nothing could have stopped me. I was under total compulsion.

I'm thoroughly convinced in my conscience and in my heart, that there was nothing I could do beyond that point to help myself".

Is "under total compulsion" another term for brainwashed?

Mark Chapman did not engage in another long-form interview with the media after 1992. His previous experience with Gaines and Jones was probably sufficient proof for Mark that not all journalists are interested in reporting the facts objectively. Mark did agree to talk to Jones once again briefly in 2020 for a "by-the-numbers" Lennon murder documentary for Sky TV in the UK. As usual, Chapman sounds rehearsed as he briefly tells Jones on a mobile call that he killed John "for glory", with Chapman then tellingly saying he must get off the call to check in with Gloria.

At this point in his lucrative 30-year media evolution, Jones wants to be the star of the show. His access to Chapman in prison, albeit more recently limited, appears to be a device to get Jones on screen as much as possible. In the 2020 documentary, Jones went for a tough guy look, but with a sensitive caring side underneath the cool dark shades and baseball cap. We first see Jones wandering through the lonely woods to his remote cabin with a big axe over his shoulder, talking about how he heroically "stood his watch in the Vietnam war". Jones then starts to chop some wood in slow motion. A pathetic parody of the virtues of the all-American homesteader.

Jones also comes across as a somewhat tragic figure. He invokes the sympathy of the viewer by talking about the death of his wife and the struggles he had as a single parent after her death, but he ruins the moment by solemnly quoting a Sting lyric from the Police song "Murder by Numbers", as if it was a moving Biblical passage. At this point, the name "David Brent" started to fixate in my mind. The full David Brent metamorphosis for Jones is complete by the end of the 2020 documentary, when he gets out his guitar and starts to jam with his friends. The lyrics to the song are thus:

New York, New York, December 8th, near midnight outside Dakota's gate. A man who couldn't pull his weight, raised on religion, fear and hate. A man whose name shall not be spoken, since a child that man's been broken. A creature of his own invention, not need for love, he craves attention. But when you play the devils game, you lose.
I'm sorry John,
I'm sorry John,
I'm sorry John,
I'm sorry John,

Copyright – Jack Jones

Jack Jones now describes himself as a friend of Mark Chapman for over 40 years. Some *friend*.

Recap

While it is easy to laugh at Jack Jones's unbounded ego and to wonder aghast at how a journalist as experienced as Jim Gaines could ignore details as vital as entry and exit wounds, we must never forget the deeply disturbing fact that two men managed to control the narrative of John Lennon's assassination, unchallenged for 42 years, without any reaction from their journalist peers. Peers who wilfully ignored crucial facts regarding John Lennon's murder. This head-in-the-sand approach regarding the crime still continues today. Shameful.

Between the two of them, Jones and Gaines gave the world a myriad of salacious tales of *Catcher in the Rye* and *little people* and *demons* swirling around in Mark Chapman's head mixed with a loser's quest for fame. What they never noticed was the shadowy people and institutions that shaped Mark Chapman's life and addled his vulnerable mind. They never gave a credible and detailed account of what really happened in the Dakota driveway when John Lennon was assassinated. Pertinently, Gaines and Jones stayed away from the medical experts who saw the truth of the wounds as they tried desperately to fix the unfixable. In the world of Gaines and Jones, the important details regarding the "how" is always missing, and the "why" is ever-changing and often nonsensical. Jones and Gaines solely focus on the who, where and when.

Insightful analysis was never part of their remit. They played on people's emotions and encouraged them to ignore reason and detail. This is a modern malaise across all media. The mantra is simple: don't think, just feel. People are encouraged to see the world in a binary way. Nuance is frowned upon. If you ask questions, you will be dismissed as a "Conspiracy Theorist". The problem is that no one is encouraged to ask, "Who organised this highly nuanced affair?" Conspirators lurk in every dark corner of John's murder.

Now that the nuanced truth is finally emerging from under the dark crevices which Jones and Gaines constructed, the establishment will double-down on their position and continue to peddle their well-worn Mark Chapman sideshows. Gaines and Jones have had a great run with their Lennon fantasies, unchallenged and happily supplying the rich fodder which the lazier mainstream media have lapped up. Their time is thankfully up.

CHAPTER 23 | Demons

Key People

Jonathan Marks (lawyer)   William Hellerstein (lawyer)
Gerald McKelvey (DA spokesman)   Ken Babington (Southern Baptist pastor)
Charles McGowan (Southern Baptist pastor)   Gloria Chapman (Mark's wife)
Don Dickerman (Southern Baptist minister/International Ministry to prisons/exorcist)

Once sentenced, Mark Chapman was sent back to Rikers. He told Jonathan Marks after his sentencing that he was going to take a vow of silence forever. The vow lasted two days. Mark found his voice again when he was moved to Fishkill Prison, where he was evaluated by prison psychiatrists to assess which institution he was going to spend at least the next twenty years of his life in. Mark fully co-operated probably in the hope that if he played the game, he might not be sent to a tough jail such as New York's Attica, where ten years earlier, 37 men had been killed in a four-day riot. Chapman was sent to Attica.

And then came an episode that most of the official Lennon murder barrow-boys carefully omitted from their versions of Chapman's "God told me to plead guilty and go to prison" narrative. Jim Gaines failed to mention it his three *People Magazine* 1987 articles. Jack Jones failed to mention it in his 1992 book and good old Wikipedia of course doesn't go there. Mark Chapman, after finally understanding perhaps how much he might have been played, decided to appeal against his sentence.

With the cold light of day seeping into his tiny prison cell, Chapman decided to allow his lawyer to argue that he was mentally impaired after all. If successful, he would end up in a mental hospital with lots of privileges and not a harsh prison. Chapman wisely decided that a lifetime in prison was not worth embracing, even if it meant going against the specific instructions of God whom, a few months earlier, he claimed to have heard or felt inside his head.

Jonathan Marks lodged his formal appeal for Chapman on 10th September 1981. It was lodged in the appellate division of New York's Supreme Court. Tellingly, Marks wasn't looking for a trial, he requested that Chapman's guilty plea be vacated and he hoped for a fresh court psychiatric examination to be ordered which would reveal that Chapman was unfit to stand trial. If this happened, Chapman would, most likely, have been sent to Marcy Hospital, the state mental institution.

Jonathan Marks decided he didn't want to carry through Chapman's appeal request personally and he handed over the appeal request to one of his friends, William Hellerstein. On 17th November 1981, Hellerstein was named as Mark's new legal aid attorney. The appeal dragged on for three years and eventually on 1st May 1984, a five-member panel of the appellate division decided that Mark had not been denied due process when his guilty plea was accepted. The writer and barrister Fenton Bresler asked for a copy of the court's judgment, but New York district attorney spokesman Gerald McKelvey said he could not find a copy and thought no detailed judgement was produced. What? No copy or detailed judgement covering the most publicised of criminal cases? Ridiculous. Truly unbelievable. But the detail is even worse.

One other crucial piece of information came from Mark Chapman's appeal fiasco. I have explained how Milton Kline implanted the "little people kingdom" concept into Mark's troubled head when he visited him in his cell. This "vision" had never been raised before. Kline had a specific reason to concoct this seemingly benign fiction. At his appeal hearing, Mark revealed that he was visited by two armies of little people in his cell. One army was fighting for God and one army was fighting for the devil. Mark envisaged a battle between the two armies on his cell floor. God's army won the battle. Mark picked up the winning general and put him to his ear. The little holy general duly told Mark – "God wants you to plead guilty". Mark obeyed the command and rang up his lawyer and declared that he wanted to plead guilty and forego a trial. But the victory went to Kline and his backers. A catastrophic trial was averted and the truth about John Lennon's assassination was buried... until now. The official line at the time was that God told Mark to plead guilty. The little people scenario had to be concealed, because it led back to the nefarious CIA consultant who exclusively implanted this idea. You could almost admire the clever subterfuge, if it wasn't so evil in its intent.

In 1982, while awaiting his appeal, Chapman began to grapple with his demons again, usually with an obliging exorcist preacher at his side. The demon slayers weren't always men of the cloth though. Chapman told Jack Jones that back in 1981, he refused to co-operate with exorcisms that were attempted by a Christian guard at Rikers Island. Chapman also told Jones that he refused an exorcism with a hometown minister who visited him in jail. This was almost certainly Charles McGowan, though he has never suggested he has ever performed exorcisms on Chapman or anybody else. Perhaps he learnt some demon casting skills from Fred Krauss? Chapman also revealed that a chaplain visited his prison cell and tried an exorcism. It seems that from the very moment of his incarceration, a whole slew of exorcists, chaplains, pastors and even prison guards were very keen to cast demons from Mark Chapman.

Ken Babington

Another Southern Baptist pastor called Ken Babington entered the Mark Chapman story at this point. Babington wrote a letter to Chapman in December 1980 with lots of appealing scriptural quotes and mentions of salvation. The letter worked a treat and in 1982, Babington became a confidant of Chapman and

346 | MIND GAMES: THE ASSASSINATION OF JOHN LENNON

eventually gained access to Chapman's cell and Gloria's life. Ken Babington's main gig was writing letters to prisoners and visiting them in prison. Babington was a car salesman in the early 1970s and converted to Christianity in 1976, where he appeared to practise the same kind of "charismatic" teachings as Fred Krauss.

What has not been so widely reported is that Babington, like special agent Charles McGowan, and "journalist" Jack Jones, served in the United States Navy in the 1960s as a navy diver on the USS Atule. He received an honourable discharge in 1972.

In 2014, according to Babington, Mark Chapman suggested that he write an autobiographical book about himself. Babington duly obliged. The book was called *Not My God: My Life as The Pastor of the Man Who Murdered John Lennon*. Clearly the book was not going to focus on Babington. The book is a dull Chapman biography by-numbers, very much in the same vein as Jim Gaines and his *People Magazine* articles and the Jack Jones book. It does reveal a few interesting details about what Chapman might have got up to in his early life, but it is a very dull read.

While Chapman awaited his transport to Attica, a correction department chaplain asked to visit him in his cell. The chaplain told Chapman that he would be protected from angry Beatles-fan convicts who threatened to avenge Lennon's death. He would be confined with other notorious murderers in protective custody. The chaplain also told Chapman he sensed "a demonic presence" about him and prayed that the demons would come out. Mark accepted the chaplain's offer of solitary confinement. Chapman has now been locked up in solitary confinement for over forty years. Handily for some, this meant Chapman could not discuss with fellow prisoners his confused mind and his scrambled reasons for feeling "compelled" to allegedly kill John Lennon. How convenient.

Chapman told Jones how he felt about the attempted exorcisms from 1982 and how angry they made him feel, stating:

"I was a Christian. I believed that it wasn't possible for a Christian to be really possessed. Even though I was the one that did the inviting, I didn't believe there could be really demons inside me. It made me angry when these people were commanding demons to come out of me. When an officer with a Bible commanded Satan to come out of me, I didn't believe it. I didn't believe these things were inside of me at the time. Not really. Not really. Not deep in my heart. I could summon them and use them, but they had to stay outside. When the officer said, 'I command you, in Jesus's name, come out, you demons! You demons, I know you, Satan' He made me angry by saying these things."

Hearing these words from Chapman, one can only conclude that the men who repeatedly told him he was possessed by demons — Krauss, McGowan, Schwartz, Babington and unknown others — were all guilty of mental cruelty and abuse. The fact that a prison guard could perform a side-hustle in exorcisms is simply beyond belief. Where were the safeguards to stop these evil acts being performed on Chapman. Evil acts that were ironically described as expunging evil? Worse was to follow.

Gloria Chapman

For the first twelve months of his incarceration in prison, Mark would not see Gloria and he urged her to divorce him. By some accounts, Mark was angry with Gloria for not contacting the police when he first told her, in early November, that he went to New York to try and murder John Lennon. Gloria still wanted to handle Mark's affairs for him when he was in prison, so in June 1982 Gloria moved from Hawaii to New York and started working as a night-time salesclerk so she could be available to see Mark if he ever forgave her. Despite Gloria's geographical efforts to be nearby, Mark still refused to see her in his, apparently, "demon-filled" cell. Gloria, taking the lead from her friend, agent McGowan, warned her husband in a letter that

Gloria Chapman © Unknown

she believed that "creatures from the dark side" of his spirit were again taking possession of his mind. Despite not having access to her husband, Gloria could apparently *see* it in his eyes and "hear demons playing in the random, unguarded words that slipped from the corners of his conversation". Apparently with her Bible in her hand, Gloria told Jack Jones that she closed her eyes and rebuked the demonic forces that were controlling her husband with all the power she could muster within her soul and mind. In full keeping with the demon-obsessed individuals who were constantly trying to influence Mark, Gloria was attempting to exorcise her husband remotely.

The constant gaslighting about personal demons worked. Chapman began burning red lamp bulbs in his cell and claimed to have started praying to Satan again. I suppose if you continually gaslight somebody by telling them that they are possessed by demons, it is only logical that they might start believing it. Around this time, Mark went on hunger-strike for thirty days. He was transferred to Marcy Correctional Facility for treatment at their mental health unit. The state correction authorities took out a court order which permitted the starving prisoner to be force-fed through intravenous tubes. Gloria took this opportunity to visit her incapacitated husband – no doubt to tell him again about his inner demons while he was strapped down and forced-fed liquids. Mark Chapman continually refused to agree to meet Gloria in prison. According to Jack Jones, he refused to come out of the prison cell where he "held himself as a hostage to the devil". For eighteen months, Chapman allegedly burned his red lamp, invoking the name of Satan at all hours of the day and night. He allegedly composed hymns to his demons which he sang and played on the guitar he kept in his cell. Gloria didn't hear from her husband throughout the remainder of 1982, and in February 1983, she returned to Hawaii and began working again at Castle Memorial Hospital. I'm sure they were keen to know how their old employee/patient was doing.

Chapman told Jack Jones about why he asked Gloria to go home:

> "I got scared and told her [Gloria] to go back home. I invited the devil into me again and went through an eighteen-month period where I couldn't communicate with her. I was lost; I was gone, a bag of chaos."

I would suggest Chapman was a "bag of chaos" because of constant, what we would now recognise as, gaslighting from the "godly" people around him, who repeatedly told him that he was possessed by demons.

Through an extensive letter-writing campaign and monthly flights out to New York, Gloria eventually got back into Mark's life. With Charles McGowan's heavenly guidance, Gloria now handles all contact that Mark has with the outside world. If anybody wishes to contact Mark, they must go through Gloria and Charles McGowan. Mark believes everything his gatekeepers say and they handle all his needs.

By 1985, the exorcists were not yet finished with Mark. Remote exorcisms were the next mind trick they played on Mark. He revealed that he undertook a series of prison exorcisms which he performed by himself with the help of an unnamed "minister", who agreed to pray outside the prison at prearranged times. The exorcisms were conducted late at night when the prison was quiet and guards weren't likely to find Chapman writhing on the floor of his cell. Mark remembered fluids pouring from the corner of his mouth as he vomited out "seven evil spirits, snarling and cursing". According to Jack Jones, "the creatures evaporated through the walls of the prison before his mind began to feel restored". Chapman gave this very graphic account of an exorcism:

> "When they're [demons] are coming out, there's a grinding inside you. When you really feel them is when they're coming out, with these squelched screams and cries and languages and cursings. You just feel this filthiness. It's like a shower when you're covered in filth, with filth in your nose, your hair, your ears. Filth caked to your skin. Imagine how you would feel if the dirt was inside you. That's what it's like.... You feel the demons' personalities as they're coming out. Some of them are nasty. Some of them are weak. Some are filthy mouthed. Some are very, very strong and don't want to let go. They hang on as they're being pulled out of you. Sometimes it takes an hour and a half to get one of them out. You're exhausted at the end of one of these sessions."

Don Dickerman

One of the main suspects responsible for the exorcisms Chapman endured is called Don Dickerman. According to his brief online biography, Dickerman has directed an international ministry to prisons since 1974 and has personally ministered in more than 850 different prison facilities in North America, the Caribbean and Europe. In 1995, he claims to have received a powerful anointing for healing and deliverance and that is apparently now the focus of his ministry. Dickerman uses the word *deliverance* as a substitute for exorcism, probably to distinguish his Southern

Baptist demon-casting identity and skills from the Catholic exorcists. Dickerman has written a series of bizarre books in which he claimed almost every human ailment could be blamed on demons.

In Dickerman's books, he promoted the idea that people must vomit up a demon during exorcism. He also claimed that a person must have initially invited an evil spirit in, and that people needed to diagnose and name their demons. Mark Chapman did name his alleged demons; he has allegedly vomited up his demons; and has often referred to "inviting his demons in". He had clearly been heavily influenced by Don Dickerman and his snake-oil-demon-casting activities.

Before Dickerman performs his demon casting, he asks the prospective, "possessed" customer to fill out a form on his website. Much of the form covers questions on mental ailments such as depression and anxiety. But Don also wants to know if people were born out of wedlock, have divorced parents, or have had sex out of marriage – all potential social situations and activities which, according to Don, allow demons to enter a person. He helpfully lays out some more generic "symptoms of demonic attacks" which include:

- Deep feelings of bitterness and hatred toward others without reason: Jews, other races, the church, strong Christian leaders
- Choking sensations
- Pains that seem to move around.
- Feelings of tightness about the head or eyes
- Abnormal or perverted sexual desires
- Rebellion and hatred for authority
- Constant confusion in thinking (sometimes great difficulty in remembering things)
- Inability to believe (even when the person wants to)
- Irrational laughter or crying
- Pain (without justifiable explanation – especially in head and/or stomach)

Should the reader tick any of the above boxes, they can assume they may have been "possessed" by demons.

Don also asks if the potentially possessed person has any homosexual tendencies or if they have a predilection for Harry Potter books, horoscopes or Pokémon cards. Going by Don's thinking, the whole world is clearly possessed by demons. Don doesn't want others to miss out on the opportunity to earn from his deliverance skills. He has offered to train people in the ways of his deliverance methods for just $125 a person or the bargain price of $175 for a couple. DVDs and training books are all included. Ghostbusting clearly comes at a price.

It is easy to cast a humorous eye over Dickerman's medieval demon beliefs, but we must remember that Dickerman was permitted to visit Mark Chapman in prison, and film him on camera talking about John Lennon's death, whenever he wished. Don once optimistically called one of his Chapman videos *Mark Chapman TV Show*. Thankfully, this particular television show never got off the ground and Chapman appears to have not allowed Dickerman to film him again. In the video, Chapman reeled out the usual official murder narrative that he must have heard repeated many times. However, there is one very telling moment: Dickerman asked Chapman what happened immediately after he shot Lennon five times in the back – enquiring whether Lennon fell immediately to the ground. Chapman appeared confused and paused before replying no because "he [Lennon] still had some composure and he went into the door and the security booth and up some stairs and then collapsed". But Chapman says "I didn't see any of that... I must have turned around." So, he admits again that he did not actually *see his* bullets hit John Lennon. If Lennon had enough "composure" to continue along the driveway and through the vestibule doors, perhaps it was because he wasn't actually hit in the driveway at all.

The twisted and exploitive exorcisms which were sold to Chapman demonstrate how easy it was to manipulate him and convince him that there were demons inside him, and that it was these demons who made him want to shoot John Lennon. To pull off the illusion and validity of remote exorcisms, Chapman would have had to have been groomed for many months and, I strongly suspect, given drugs to elicit the hallucinatory images of demons leaving his body. People may rightly ask why these pantomime exorcisms were performed on Mark, especially after he was locked up and the case was closed. I strongly believe that those who obsessively tried to convince Mark that he was possessed by demons were doing so to explicitly reinforce the narrative that demons made him kill John Lennon – not some other nefarious mind-control activity that was performed on his drug-damaged, malleable mind by shadowy, nefarious entities that hated John Lennon and wanted him dead. Nefarious entities – a shadowy cabal we could say – that set up Mark Chapman as a patsy to take the fall for John Lennon's assassination.

Recap

It is often said that you can tell the most about a conspiratorial crime from the extent of the cover-up afterwards. As I see it, Chapman was constantly gaslit into believing he was possessed by demons, as part of a cover-up operation. I believe it tells us a lot about who might have been behind John Lennon's murder.

I am not saying that Olford, Krauss, Dickerman, Babington, McGowan and Anderson are all part of a Baptist plot to kill John Lennon through religious grooming or mind-control techniques. But clearly their religious teachings and practices seriously messed with Mark Chapman's already damaged mind, which in turn may have left him open to other plotters and influences. The remote exorcisms eventually did their job. Chapman told the writer Jack Jones, in 1992, that he believed:

"The demonic world was the real world. The demons were real. And of course the Little People were not real. We're talking about a very scrambled mind in a person and that's the way I was in the final months before I became a murderer. No person who is healthy summons demons wanting to kill somebody."

Chapman clearly believed, and probably still believes to this very day, that demons made him kill John Lennon. Mission accomplished for the demon peddlers you might say.

CHAPTER 24 | Parole Hearings

Mark Chapman first became eligible for parole in 2000 and is entitled to a hearing every two years thereafter. Since that time, Mark has been denied parole multiple times. Shortly before his first parole hearing, Yoko Ono sent a letter to the board opposing his release from prison. Ono's letter stated that Chapman would not be safe outside of prison. The board reported that its first decision to not release Mark was based on their interview with Mark, a review of records and deliberation.

By the early 2000s, Mark was allowed one conjugal visit a year with Gloria because he accepted solitary confinement. The programme allowed him to spend up to 42 hours alone with his wife in a specially built prison home. He worked occasionally in the prison as a legal clerk and kitchen helper. He was barred from participating in the Cephas Attica support workshops. He was also prohibited from attending the prison's violence and anger management classes due to concern for his safety. Chapman reportedly liked to read and write short stories. At his parole board hearing in 2004, he described his future hopes and plans; "I would immediately try to find a job, and I really want to go from place to place, at least in the state, church to church, and tell people what happened to me and point them the way to Christ." He also said that he thought that there was a possibility he could find work as a farmhand or return to his previous trade as a printer.

In October 2006, the parole board held a 16-minute hearing and concluded that Mark's release would not be in the best interest of the community or his own personal safety. On 8th December 2006, the 26th anniversary of John's death, Yoko

Ono published a one-page advertisement in several newspapers stating that December 8 should be a "day of forgiveness" and then, in a contradictory flourish, that she was not yet sure if she was ready to forgive Chapman. Chapman's fifth hearing was on 12th August 2008. He was denied parole "due to concern for the public safety and welfare." On 27th July 2010, in advance of Chapman's scheduled sixth parole hearing, Ono said that she would again oppose parole for Chapman stating that her safety, that of John's sons, and Chapman's safety would be at risk. She added, "I am afraid it will bring back the nightmare, the chaos and confusion [of that night] once again."

How interesting that Yoko used the word "*confusion*".

Chapman's seventh parole hearing was held before a three-member board on 22nd August 2012. The following day, the denial of his application was announced, with the board stating: "Despite your positive efforts while incarcerated, your release at this time would greatly undermine respect for the law and tend to trivialise the tragic loss of life which you caused as a result of this heinous, unprovoked, violent, cold and calculated crime."

Chapman's eighth parole application was denied in August 2014. At the hearing, Chapman said, "I am sorry for being such an idiot and choosing the wrong way for glory. I have peace now in Jesus." He continued, "He has forgiven me and loves me. He has helped me in my life like you wouldn't believe."

Well, Jesus might have forgiven Mark, but others clearly had not. Chapman tried again for parole in 2016, 2018 and 2020. All three requests were denied.

In September 2020, Chapman's parole board released a statement, apparently from Mark:

> "I assassinated him, to use your word earlier, because he was very, very, very famous and that's the only reason and I was very, very, very, very much seeking self-glory, very selfish. I want to add that and emphasise that greatly. It was an extremely selfish act. I'm

sorry for the pain that I caused to her [Ono]. I think about it all of the time."

It is very interesting to note that, in 2020, Mark was using the same kind of repeat word phrasing that Sirhan Sirhan did 55 years ago, while under hypnosis.

Chapman also stated in 2020 that as he was older, he could see it was a "despicable act" and "pretty creepy". He described himself as being deeply religious and a "devoted Christian". He again discussed his fascination with the book *The Catcher in The Rye* at the time of the murder and said he identified with the main character's "isolation, loneliness". What was happening inside his mind to resuscitate the Catcher? Yet again I am left feeling that he was being coached for these parole hearings.

Also in 2020, when asked if justice had been served, Chapman apparently said "I deserve zero, nothing" adding that he should have been given the death penalty following the killing:

> "When you knowingly plot someone's murder and know it's wrong and you do it for yourself, that's a death penalty right there in my opinion. Some people disagree with me, but everybody gets a second chance now… The view on the death penalty for me is a little up and down at times but for me I deserve that. I know I'm speaking for myself. I know what I did. I know who was in those shoes at that time. I know my thoughts. They were not thinking of him at all, his wife, his child, the fans, nobody. I was just thinking of me. That deserves a death penalty."

Why did Mark say this at his 2020 parole hearing? Why was a man who was asking for parole then *also* suggesting that he should get the death penalty? This was a ridiculous contradiction – if it is true. The released transcripts of his 2020 parole hearing also quote him as saying:

"He [Lennon] was a human being and I knew I was going to kill him. That alone says you deserve nothing and if the law and you choose to leave me in here for the rest of my life, I have no complaint whatsoever."

Why would a prisoner who applies for a parole hearing every two years (so clearly wants to get out of prison) say that he would "have no complaint whatsoever" if the board decided to leave him in prison for the rest his life? Another contradiction.

In August 2022, Chapman was yet again up for parole (for the twelfth time). In his short hearing, he stated that: "This was evil in my heart. I wanted to be somebody and nobody was going to stop that." He apparently went on to say that he had a "selfish disregard for human life of global consequence" and thought killing Lennon was "my big answer to everything. I wasn't going to be a nobody anymore". To my eyes, the phrase "selfish disregard for human life of global consequence" (which the parole board cited as one of their reasons for again denying parole) sounds more like a press release statement than the words of Mark Chapman. These parole hearing details were provided to the media via New York State officials, responding to a freedom of information request. Chapman has not verified he has said any of the above statements in 2022, or before then. We have to take the word of New York "officials" for that. Are these the same "officials" who covered up contents in Chapman's hotel room and are still withholding Nina Rosen and José Perdomo's witness statements? If so, I'm somewhat inclined to doubt their word.

It's very hard at this point to take anything Mark says without considering that he has had forty-three long years to reflect on his alleged crime and absorb how it has been portrayed and perceived by the world's media. It is also worth remembering that Mark has probably had hundreds of unrecorded visitors and phone calls over these years. Milton Kline and Bernard Diamond are both now long dead, but we know the secret services have visited Mark in the past and who knows who else has been talking to him and influencing his thought processes.

The stark contrast between Mark's 2022 statement and the confused one he issued on the night of the Lennon murder in 1980 (see below) are startling in the extreme. They are clearly from two entirely different mind sets from different eras.

1980: I did not want to kill anybody and I really don't know why I did it.

2022: I was too desperate for fame. I knew what I was doing, and I knew it was evil. I knew it was wrong. But I wanted the fame so much that I was willing to give everything and take a human life.

Mark's various parole hearings lend themselves to the suspicion of a rehearsed performance. Scripted theatre carefully thought out in advance. I have been told by one of Mark's friends, who writes to him in prison, that Mark is repeating what he believes will give him the best chance of parole. I suspect, though, that the people advising Mark about what to say at his parole hearings do not want him out of prison. I would suggest that they want the exact opposite.

According to a friend of Chapman's who regularly writes to him in prison, Chapman is very distrustful of anyone who wishes to contact him and his health in 2021 and 2022 was very poor. Chapman has not had an infraction behind bars since 1994. He is kept in a restricted block of the prison, where he was placed for his own safety. Contrary to media reporting of his parole hearings, Mark Chapman is very keen to be released from prison. He is currently housed at Green Haven Correctional Facility in New York's Hudson Valley where he spends most of his time in prison in a cell that is ten feet by seven – the size of an average bathroom. For most of his sentence, Mark has had to stay in his cell for twenty three out of every twenty fours in a day. Seven burly guards allegedly watch him night and day, though apparently not when he was having his remote exorcisms. He is not allowed to eat or watch television with other prisoners and from his tiny cell window, the only view he has is of a grey, thirty-six feet wall.

I believe Mark Chapman has more than served his sentence, and with the overwhelming evidence that this book lays out, it is certainly hard to see how a court would convict him today. That said, the world has had forty-three years of believing that Chapman is one of the most evil men who ever lived. I would suggest he is probably far safer staying in prison than being on the outside.

CHAPTER 25 | Life After Lennon: Yoko Ono

Key People

Fred Seaman (Lennon assistant)	David Geffen (record executive)
Yoko Ono	Richard Nicastro (NYPD borough commander)
Michael Medeiros (Lennon gardener)	Doug MacDougall (Former FBI/Bodyguard)
Jack Douglas (record producer)	John Green (Ono's tarot card reader)
Dan Mahoney (Ono's minder/cop)	Elliott Mintz (Ono's publicist)

According to Fred Seaman, the Lennons' assistant, when Ono had returned from the Roosevelt Hospital with David Geffen, she was interviewed by the NYPD's borough commander, Richard Nicastro. The commander seemed to be having the same problems as Detective Hoffman when it came to getting a coherent statement from Ono. She simply told Nicastro: "the shock is too great, I can't do this now." Given the circumstances, it seems a reasonable reaction. But I have one question. Would the NYPD accept that reasoning from any member of the public?

Michael Medeiros was also shocked on hearing the news about his employer's murder, and after trying to get news outside the Roosevelt Hospital, he returned to the Dakota in the early hours of 9th December, smoking a joint as he walked along the drizzly streets of New York. Arriving at the Dakota, Medeiros noticed three bullet holes in the vestibule doors leading into the Dakota. Two in one glass pane and one in the other. Just a few hours after the murder of one of the world's most famous men, Medeiros saw no sign of a police investigation at the Dakota. No Forensic teams, no men in white coats, nothing. Other employees at the Dakota have also confirmed the absence of an active investigation at the Dakota in the hours (and days) after the murder.

Medeiros found the Lennons' apartment eerily quiet. Yoko

was ensconced in her bedroom. Medeiros was immediately tasked, with Richie De Palma (Yoko's business manager and accountant) and Fred Seaman, to answer the phones and deal with all the telegrams and messages flooding into the Dakota. Medeiros also noticed an individual in the apartment's kitchen with an Uzi type small machine gun. Bodyguard Doug McDougall suddenly reappeared, apparently back in full employment after his mysterious three-month break. McDougall declared to everyone that he had hired armed Pinkerton guards to patrol the apartment and the halls of the Lennons' abode. Pinkerton's National Detective Agency is considered the precursor to the CIA and FBI. In 1861, Abraham Lincoln hired the firm as his "secret service" hence the origin of the term. It's still a largely unknown and seldom talked about institution that operates in a highly clandestine way. In 1980, when FBI operative McDougall used the firm for Yoko, its corporate headquarters were in New York.

McDougall then asked Medeiros to sit outside the bedroom and while doing so, he noticed Ono walking Geffen to the exit door. This was the only time Medeiros had ever seen Yoko walk someone out of her apartments.

Fred Seaman also confirmed to me that ex-FBI agent Doug MacDougall did leave his employment with the Lennons for a few months and was then re-employed the morning after John Lennon's murder. We must ask ourselves two important questions here. Firstly, why did Ono hire an ex-FBI agent as a bodyguard in the first place, when the agency had been monitoring and harassing her husband for years? And secondly, would MacDougall have protected Lennon if he was still employed as his bodyguard a day earlier than he returned?

By the following evening, 48 hours after the murder, Medeiros was given a task to watch Yoko. Ono surprised Medeiros by asking him to bring VHS videos of the Beatles to her bedroom. Medeiros duly delivered tapes and was then asked to sit with Ono on the bed and watch them. She invited Medeiros to sit on the bed by patting one side of it. Scared and apprehensive, Medeiros was amazed that Ono laughed at some of the footage playing on the monitor he set up. Ono also asked Medeiros to record all news bulletins about her husband's murder. Tapes she allegedly listened to over and over again in the days after the assassination.

Midway through the bizarre Beatles video viewing session, she apparently took out a cigarette and asked Medeiros to get her a lighter. Medeiros was directed to a cabinet with drawers. Ono then directed Medeiros to look in another drawer. Inside the drawer, Medeiros allegedly saw a Magnum 44 hand gun lying on its side. Medeiros believed it was a game played by a manipulative "chess player" like Ono. Messing with his mind for her own amusement.

Fred Seaman, writing in his book *The Last Days of John Lennon*, observed Yoko Ono on the morning of December 9th, consulting with her lawyers and financial advisers regarding John's Will. The Will was sent to the district court that very afternoon and speedily probated that very same day. Ono was now totally in charge of the Lennon estate. The Will was a short, four-page document which Lennon had made and signed a year earlier on 12th November 1979. Yoko was given fifty per cent of the estate and the other fifty per cent was put into trust for Sean. Julian, John's first-born son from his first marriage, was not included in the Will. Julian subsequently had to endure a long legal fight to gain access to some of his father's large fortune. Ringo and his partner, the actress Barbara Bach, then arrived at the Dakota and spent a few hours with Yoko. It is rumoured that Yoko did not want Barbara to come into the Dakota, but Starr insisted, allegedly saying "you started this". What Starr meant by this can only be guessed. Had Yoko stirred some animosity here?

With the Will duly finalised, Ono apparently had dinner that evening with record company boss David Geffen, Calvin Klein and Studio 54 boss Steve Rubell, who had been released from prison for tax evasion. Yoko Ono was now super rich; Geffen was also now going to be even richer than he was before; and Rubell was no doubt just glad to be a free man. I'm sure they all left a big tip in the Little Italy restaurant they were rumoured to have visited that evening. When Ono returned to the Dakota, her stepson Julian had arrived from England. We will never know if Julian knew about his father's upcoming cremation. He certainly did not attend.

The morning after Lennon's assassination, Ono told Sean about his father's death and later morbidly decided to show Sean and Julian the exact spot where John was shot. Whether this "spot" was outside in the driveway, outside in the courtyard, inside the vestibule, in the stairwell, or in the concierge's front or back office remains unclear.

In 1981, Ono decided to crassly refer to her husband's death alongside her music when she released an album called *Season of Glass*. On the front cover, she used the blood-spattered glasses which John had been wearing on the night he was killed. The record company tried to dissuade her, correctly citing bad taste and the fact that record stores wouldn't stock the album. She wouldn't budge and decided to put the sound of gun shots on one of the tracks. Her final music-related "tribute" to her dead husband was to superimpose a ghostlike image of John onto an image of herself and Sean standing in Central Park. This garish collage was placed on the back cover of another "flop" Ono album in 1984. In 1993, Ono created a sculpture of John's bloody shirt. The shirt had four bullets wounds around the heart area. Was she trying to tell us something?

In 2009, Yoko Ono exhibited a new art exhibition called *A Hole*. The exhibition consisted of panes of glass which had bullet holes in them. On being interviewed about the exhibition, Ono declared she was suddenly surprised, when near the completion of her installation, she remembered that she had somehow seen bullet holes in windows like this before. Implying that she started the work without her husband's murder in mind. I'm simply not buying that. Yoko Ono was either yet again exploiting her husband's murder to her own gain, or she was trying to send a message to the public that bullet-hole glass windows were an important feature in her husband's assassination. Was she subliminally leading a trail to the truth about her husband's murder. I strongly believe she might have been.

In the mid 1970s, Yoko Ono had hired a tarot card reader called John Green. He became a constant presence in the Lennons' lives, and they rarely made a big decision without first consulting Green's cards. By most accounts, John was ambivalent about Green's abilities, but Ono was so enamoured with Green's skills that she allowed him to live rent-free in a loft building she used to store artifacts. Some of these artifacts were in the shape of original Beatles acetates and Lennon artwork. At some point in Autumn 1981, Ono heard that Green was charging people admission for "events" in the loft: these events probably involved viewings of Beatles treasure with some esoteric card readings thrown in.

Ono instructed a lawyer to kick Green out of the loft and he immediately sued her. Ono eventually paid off Green with a $30,000 settlement. She obviously forgot to include an NDA in the settlement because Green later published a book called *Dakota Days* about his time with the Lennons. In the poorly written book, Green accused Ono of being interested in the black arts, being a neurotic and a destroyer of John's artistic spirit. He failed to mention how his magic cards didn't predict John's murder. Despite Green taking a lot of critical flak, Michael Medeiros has informed me that every word in Green's book is factual.

By November 1981, Mark Chapman decided that he wanted to write his memoirs and he thought it might be a good idea to ask Yoko Ono's permission. Chapman had found himself a new lawyer to represent him, and his lawyer agreed that it might be a good idea to send Yoko Ono a letter about his new literary ambitions. The letter said:

"My new attorney, Marshall Beil, may have contacted you concerning a possible agreement that would consist of seeking to use any funds—earned by the release of certain materials—toward charitable (child relief organisations) purposes.

Yoko, if you feel that what I might enter into (even though all funds would be given to charity) is against your wishes, I would honour this completely."

Chapman began his letter reminding Ono that he had earlier written to her to "apologise" for murdering her husband and ends the letter by saying that if she does not want him to proceed with the release of his story, she can be assured of his "cooperation in this delicate matter". The implication was clear to Ono: her husband's alleged assassin was proposing that she assent to his participation in a book. Chapman assured her that all funds would go to charity, but at that time it was virtually impossible in America for a criminal to profit from his crime by law.

It is not known if Yoko ever responded to Chapman in 1981, but I sincerely doubt she did. Chapman's 1981 book was never written, which is a shame as I'm sure it would be a very enlightening read. In 1987, Mark also discussed writing a book with journalist Jim Gaines and his lawyer Jonathan Marks. It, too, never saw the light of day.

In July 1983, Dan Mahoney (Yoko's moonlighting NYPD Cop and new "head of security") examined some files and a particular folder labelled "DERANGED". It contained all the letters received by Ono from crank writers. Mahoney pulled out a letter addressed to a man in Italy which had the Dakota as the home address. It had been returned to sender when the addressee could not be found. The name of the sender was "Mark David Chapman". What was odd was the postmark date of August 1980 – four months before Chapman allegedly murdered Lennon. Evidence, at the very least, of premeditation if it was, indeed, Chapman who wrote the letter, using the Dakota as his home address. The letter inside was chatty and innocuous, except for mention of the writer's "mission" in New York City.

Mahoney told Ono about the letter. One evening sometime later, in the Dakota kitchen, Elliot Mintz (Ono's publicist), Yoko Ono and Sam Havadtoy (Ono's alleged gay boyfriend who she apparently moved into the Dakota a few days after the murder) discussed the "Chapman letter". As they inspected the letter again, the postmark that used to clearly show 1980 as the date was now showing 1981. The letter inside, though similar in appearance and tone, was also different: There was no mention of the writer's mission in New York. If some kind of switch was made, it could only have been to make it seem as if some crank had written a letter to Italy in 1981 and, with Lennon long dead, had used Chapman's name and the Dakota address as some sort of bad joke. The implications were discussed and everyone became extremely agitated. Sitting around the kitchen table, they asked who could have switched the letter and the envelope. Was it someone in the inner circle? "Who is it?" Ono demanded. "I want to know?" Mintz and Havadtoy had no answer. The mysterious Dakota Chapman letter remains unexplained to this day.

In 1982, Fred Seaman may have been given a clue about the possible identity of the two mysterious bodyguards who Andy Peebles said he had seen with the Lennons in the week before John's murder. Some background is needed, first, in what is a fascinating sidebar to John Lennon's assassination.

Two months after Doug MacDougall left Yoko's employment in autumn 1981, Fred Seaman departed from the Dakota in December 1981. He said the main reason was because he thought Yoko was cashing in on John's death and sullying his legacy with her attempts to promote "brand Lennon" too soon after the murder. Prior to Seaman's departure, Ono hired a new "chief of security" called Dan Mahoney in September 1981. Mahoney was a New York Police officer and part-time novelist of pulp crime fiction books. When Seaman left the Dakota, he took some of John's journals with him. His excuse for doing this was that John had asked him to make sure his son Julian got his journals if anything happened to him. Fred's credibility regarding this story took a major blow when he apparently gave the journals to a writer friend of his, Robert Rosen, for "safe keeping". Rosen then informed Yoko Ono that Seaman had asked to write a book with him on the Lennon Journals. According to Rosen, Seaman called their venture "Project Walrus". Seaman has always strongly denied this.

Ono's version of why Seaman had left was that she had fired him for driving (and apparently crashing) the Lennon Mercedes. The final straw was when Ono, apparently, caught Seaman taking a bath in her private bathroom. In August 1982, Mahoney called Fred Seaman to arrange the recovery of John's journals. Mahoney was still an active 20th Precinct NYPD police officer and a special sergeant, assigned to what was called "an undercover career criminal apprehension unit". According to Seaman, Mahoney was illegally moonlighting for Ono as her security advisor. Dan Mahoney arranged to meet Seaman and informed him that one of Rosen's associates had returned most of the stolen materials to Ono (for a $60,000 finder's fee), but John's 1980 diary was, apparently, still missing. Seaman denied he had the diary. Mahoney apparently responded – "I like you Freddie and I wouldn't want to see you get hurt." According to Dan Mahoney, Seaman called Yoko Ono and allegedly said, "If you don't do anything rash, the 1980 journal might find its way back." The conversation, recorded by Mahoney, then allegedly ended with Seaman threatening "I wouldn't want anything to happen to you and Sean."

Seaman then claimed he was abducted a month later by two of Mahoney's men, Bob Greve and Barry Goldblatt. They were two 20th Precinct NYPD cops, allegedly moonlighting as Yoko's bodyguards. (Could Greve and Goldblatt be the two mysterious armed bodyguards who Andy Peebles said he saw in early December 1980, who then subsequently disappeared on the night of John's assassination?) According to Seaman, Greve and Goldblatt "beat him up" in late August 1982 and pointed a gun to his head. They then took the keys to his apartment and drove Seaman to the NYPD 20th Precinct station. The same police station that provided the arresting officers at the scene of the Lennon murder and "investigated" the Lennon murder crime scene. Waiting for Seaman at the 20th was a Detective Lt Robert Gibbons. Gibbons was not interested in Seaman's accusations against his officers and after 12 hours of videotaped interviews, they gained access and searched Seaman's apartment. According to Seaman, personal items of his which were given to him by John Lennon were taken. Seaman was eventually released after 72 hours.

After months of subsequent legal threats between Seaman and Ono, Seaman blinked and decided to take the advice of his lawyers, that it probably wasn't in his best interest to legally take on a woman who had an enormous fortune at her disposal. After spending nearly $30,000 of his own money taking on Yoko Ono, Seaman halted his lawsuit and pleaded guilty to one count of grand larceny. He was sentenced to five years' probation.

I have spoken to Fred Seaman many times and I believe he is a good man at heart who got carried away with a get-rich scheme. He knows he did wrong, and I personally believe he was close to John and (mostly) had his best interests at heart while John was alive.

Ono's publicist Elliot Mintz has defended her employment of moonlighting police officers, recalling:

"Some of Yoko's bodyguards were at the time New York City police officers. This is not unusual because New York has the Sullivan Law, which is the strictest anti-gun law in the United States. In New York City, it is very difficult for a private citizen to [legally] possess a weapon and keep it on his or her person secretly. Those who are allowed to do it are off-duty New York City police officers. So, it's not unusual for a number of very well-known celebrities in New York to have this [bodyguard] arrangement."

In a final twist, one of Yoko Ono's bodyguards called Sgt Barry Goldblatt was, in March 1991 (along with four other police officers) indicted by a grand jury on murder charges in connection with the death of Frederico Pereira, a 21-year-old found sleeping in a stolen car who was allegedly beaten and choked to death while in police custody.

To date, Yoko Ono has donated hundreds of thousands of dollars to the New York Police union. According to Fred Seaman, her overall contribution to the NYPD over the past forty years is well over two million dollars. Why Yoko did this – when it appears the NYPD never properly investigated her husband's murder, and perhaps hastened his death by irresponsibly moving him from the Dakota building before an ambulance could arrive – puzzles many, including me.

Shortly after Chapman's 1981 letter was sent to Ono, two men were stopped inside the Dakota. They said they had business with Yoko. When pressed, they began to run. One got away, but the other was tackled by a bodyguard. Before he was taken away by police, the deranged man shouted out that he had come to "get" Yoko and Sean. The identity of the captured man has never been revealed. Then, in February 1983, Dan Mahoney, Yoko's new head of security, opened a letter for Ono from a group calling themselves "The Mark Chapman Fan Club". In the letter, a man stated "Death to Ono" before writing that he was coming to New York with his brother to kill her. Mahoney tightened security and, apparently, a few days later the "Mark Chapman Fan Club" brothers were spotted in New York. It is not clear how Mahoney or his men knew what the brothers looked like. Later, a man fitting the description of one of the brothers was spotted outside the Dakota. Elliot Mintz (Ono's ever faithful, orange-faced publicist) apparently put on a bulletproof vest and went out into the street and asked the man the time. When the man looked at his watch, Mintz spotted the butt of a gun sticking out of his belt. Mintz returned and called the police. The man was apparently arrested and admitted to the police that he intended to "get" Ono. He was later released. Some weeks later, Ono received an anonymous phone call telling her that one of her bodyguards was secretly working against her. A couple of weeks after that, Mahoney's home was burgled. The only thing that was stolen were his files on the brotherly gunmen. Security was further tightened at the Dakota.

By the Spring of 1983, paranoia and distrust were rampant at the Dakota. Ono, up to this time, had endured two years of death threats and malicious phone calls. Security was tight and everyone was on edge. Elliot Mintz discussed the possibility of a conspiracy against Ono through threatening phone calls and letters. Ono allegedly found her assistant Rich De Palma sitting outside her bedroom door with a handgun tucked into his trousers. De Palma told Ono that he was at his "post" and exclaimed, "You don't know how big this thing is. The people who are doing this are too big to fight." Mysterious break-ins then occurred at the Dakota, causing Ono to order Dan Mahoney to sweep her Dakota apartments for bugs. Mahoney allegedly found some listening devices. Whoever planted these alleged devices was not known. Elliot Mintz believed at the time that the recent death threats, break-ins and listening devices were all part of a plot to discredit Ono and John's memory. Mintz had his suspicions about who may have been behind all the intrusions and surveillance, but he would not divulge any names, only stating that he thought Ono's enemies were "extremely powerful".

After a flop album in 1985 and a disastrous world tour, Yoko Ono thankfully gave up trying to be a music star. She spent the next few decades building up "brand Lennon" and accruing a large property portfolio that, by some accounts, has allowed her to amass a fortune of over $1 billion dollars.

In 1998, a 25-year-old Sean Lennon was promoting a new album, doing the normal rounds of press interviews. Sean decided to come off-script when his father's murder came up, stating:

> "He was as a countercultural revolutionary, and the government takes that shit really seriously historically... He was dangerous to the government... These pacifist revolutionaries are historically killed by the government, and anybody who thinks that Mark Chapman was just some crazy guy who killed my dad for his personal interests is insane, I think, or very naïve, or hasn't thought about it clearly. It was in the best interests of the United States to have my dad killed, definitely. And, you know, that worked against them, to be honest, because once he died his powers grew. So, I mean, fuck them. They didn't get what they wanted."

Sean's older, half-brother Julian advised caution to his younger sibling, saying his remarks were "ill-advised and if you're going to say something like that, you need to have your facts."

Sean back-pedalled and said that he regretted saying what he had previously said. Hopefully Sean can glean some facts and insights from this book.

Recap

Life after John's death was complicated for Yoko. Though an exceedingly rich woman, her creative ventures in music and art failed to resuscitate her career. Paranoia clearly prevailed in fortress Dakota. It must have been a horrible place to be after 8th December 1980. Why did Yoko continue to live in the building and walk past the spot where her husband was so horrifically slain, for the next forty years?

Yoko associating with rogue elements within the NYPD is troubling. I'm sure the NYPD are a fantastic police force today, but back in December 1980 corruption was rife and they failed to properly investigate her husband's murder. The reward for the NYPD's inaction was substantial funding from Yoko Ono. None of this make sense. Was Yoko scared of the NYPD? Was her previous heroin addiction a factor? As usual with Yoko Ono, so many questions yet so few answers.

A seismic wake-up call to the world from the Lennon family came when Sean, in 1998, bravely stated: "It was in the best interests of the United States to have my dad killed, definitely." It is not recorded how Yoko reacted to this incendiary comment from her only son. She certainly never went on the record to refute Sean's claims. I believe that is very telling.

CHAPTER 26 | Life After Lennon: Ronald Reagan

Speaking of Lennon's death being "in the best interests of the United States government" as Sean had put it, let us now consider the political world without John Lennon. His tragic assassination meant he was not around to witness or comment on any of the tumultuous political events beyond his death. Events shaped by war and political corruption.

In the immediate aftermath of John's murder, many respectful political tributes were paid. British Prime Minister Harold Wilson said, "It was a great shock to my wife and myself." Outgoing American President Jimmy Carter paid a moving tribute, praising the spirit of the Beatles and equating them to the spirit of a whole generation. President-elect Ronald Reagan was more succinct and political in his tribute. The day after John Lennon's assassination, on 9th December 1980, Reagan entered New York City of all places. He was accompanied by William J. Casey, his campaign manager. (Casey was subsequently appointed by Reagan to be CIA director between 1981 and 1987. Was his promotion a reward for something?) When asked, Reagan described John Lennon's assassination as "a great tragedy and just further evidence of something we've got to stop". Did he mean stopping gun violence or rebellious thinkers?

Reagan and Casey met Roman Catholic Archbishop Cardinal Terence Cooke. They all spoke in private for over an hour. Cooke was a pro-Vietnam War, intolerant bigot. He despised communism and supported having nuclear weapons as a deterrent, stating they were morally "tolerable". I'm sure Jesus would have approved. Cooke was also an outspoken opponent of LGB rights and abortion rights for women, which he called the "slaughter of the innocent unborn". Most interestingly, Cardinal Cooke was also a supporter of the Catholic Charismatic Renewal (CCR): a Catholic/Protestant fusion movement supporting the kind of charismatic theatrics, much beloved by many of the Southern Baptist preachers who circled around Mark Chapman throughout his life. Reagan said he and Casey had discussed "the world and everything" with Cardinal Cooke, including the situations in Poland and El Salvador. One wonders if the subject of John Lennon's murder ever came up.

The disgraced former president Richard Nixon never officially commented on Lennon's death and apparently was never asked. One can safely assume that Nixon was probably not too upset about hearing the tragic news of his constant bête noire's demise.

Many people have speculated over the years that John Lennon's death was organised to stop him from protesting against Ronald Reagan's right-wing conservative government. There is no proof, of course, that Reagan or his supporters had anything to do with John's murder. However, there is an interesting link from the Reagan government to Mark Chapman because Reagan's chief financier Joe Rodgers was connected to Agent Charles McGowan. The list of controversial foreign and domestic policies that Reagan instigated, and which Lennon surely would have strongly opposed, is a very long one indeed. Let's explore just a few.

Reagan authorized funding to the Afghanistan rebels who were fighting against the DRA government and their Soviet Union backers. Amongst these rebel fighters was Ayman Al-Zawahiri and Osama Bin Laden, two men accused of being behind the 9/11 atrocities.

Reagan also supported Nicaraguan rebel fighters called the Contras with arms and training. The aim was for the rebel army to overthrow the socialist government and install a leader who was more akin to Western capitalist ideals. When the Nicaraguan government fought back against the Contras,

Reagan's proxy army began kidnapping and torturing civilians. Women were raped and innocents executed. The Contras even killed children and murdered health care workers. When the Reagan-backed Contra violence was over, as many as 50,000 innocent people had been killed. Reagan and his government were tried in the International Court of Justice and convicted of violating Nicaragua's sovereignty and encouraging crimes against humanity. Contras had been given a helpful CIA manual titled "Psychological Operations in Guerrilla warfare". The give-away lines in the manual, as to its ultimate evil intent, were when it recommended "selective use of violence for propagandistic efforts" and "provoke riots, shootings or mass murder so that it can be used as a propaganda tool." Reagan claimed the Contra fighters were the moral equivalent of America's founding fathers. The International Court demanded the United States pay Nicaragua $17 billion in damages. Reagan refused to pay the penalty.

Ronald Reagan was also deeply involved in El Salvador's civil war, giving over $4 billion to their far-right military dictatorship. When four American nuns were murdered by Salvadorian soldiers, Reagan's secretary of state defended the soldiers by suggesting the nuns might have been shot while trying to get through a military roadblock. The fact that the nuns were raped before they were murdered was not commented upon.

Reagan also supported and financed the brutal Guatemalan dictator, Efrain Rios Montt, who, it has been said, was responsible for killing as many as 200,000 Guatemalans. He initially supported the Panamanian dictator Manuel Noriega, but when he became too close to Cuba's Fidel Castro, Reagan had him removed from power. Reagan was also a big supporter of Philippine dictator Ferdinand Marcos, even after it became clear that Marcos had a habit of killing his political rivals and rigging his own elections. The same affection was shown to Chile's mass murdering far-right leader, General Pinochet.

Most of the Central American atrocities were kept hidden

from the American public, but one Reagan scandal blew up publicly in the media. The Iran-Contra affair involved weapons being sold to Iran, who were at the time fighting Iraq – a country that was being led by Saddam Hussein, who had also been armed by America. The Iran weapon sales were used as a bribe to release some American hostages held in Lebanon. The profits from the weapon sales were then given to the Nicaraguan rebels, which in turn helped them commit further atrocities. Reagan was accused of turning a blind eye to Saddam Hussein's use of chemical weapons. Hussein seemed to have a free pass to do as he pleased from Reagan and his administration. This was clearly illustrated when the United States failed to respond to one of Hussein's fighter jets firing a missile at a US Navy ship in 1987, killing 37 men. Iraq is the only non-allied country to attack a US warship without suffering any form of retaliation.

In South Africa, racist apartheid was brutally enforced throughout the 1980s. A white minority population repressed the black majority and even denied them the right to vote. To their credit, the US Congress passed the Anti-Apartheid Act of 1986, to help apply pressure to South Africa to end apartheid. Reagan opposed any sanctions on South Africa and vetoed the bill.

Nearly 140 Reagan government and administration officials were investigated and indicted for corruption – the largest amount in US history. Most were pardoned by Reagan and President Bush Snr before they could even stand trial. Ronald Reagan has been posthumously sold to the world as a kind and folksy throwback to a notional time when America was confident and free. The truth was the exact opposite. The regime that he and his vice-president George Bush Snr headed up was one of the most blood-thirsty and corrupt in modern history.

Recap

John Lennon would surely have strongly protested against Ronald Reagan's government from 1981 onwards. Had he lived, his voice would have commanded the respect of many younger Americans. I don't think there is much doubt about that. Lennon hated war, and Reagan had his bloody hands in countless conflicts. It was very fortunate for Reagan that John Lennon was assassinated when he was. John had made it his mission to expose and ridicule Reagan's close friend, President Nixon, whenever he possibly could. Reagan would have known this all too well. With Lennon out of the way, the Republican government had conveniently lost one of its fiercest critics. It is logical to add together all the government agencies which would have considered John Lennon an enemy of state. I believe that when the White House is concerned that its foreign policies may be ridiculed and reviled, it will take steps to silence protest. From the White House to Congress, bolstered by the long arm of the FBI and the CIA, secret agents and assassins are known to have intervened abroad over many decades since the Second World War. Closer to home, the planning may have had to have been better concealed, but as Sean Lennon bravely stated in 1998:

"Pacifist revolutionaries are historically killed by the government, and anybody who thinks that Mark Chapman was just some crazy guy who killed my dad for his personal interests is insane, I think, or very naïve…"

Have we all been very naïve? Have we been deluded into believing and accepting the official version of the murder of John Lennon, and into not imagining that covert elements within the US government machine could have been involved?

CHAPTER 27 | Summary

As promised at the start of this book, I will now discuss my thoughts and theories on what I believe may have happened at the Dakota building on 8th December 1980, and on who may have been behind a conspiracy when John Lennon was assassinated. Firstly, I must say that my theories are just that – *theories*. I cannot categorically say what happened on that fateful 1980 December night because I do not have all the evidence needed: some of the potential evidence has been either destroyed or withheld and some of the crucial witnesses are no longer alive. But I have researched and studied this murder for over three years; I have acquired and studied the lead detective's case notebooks and paperwork; and I have spoken to most of the people connected to the case, often on numerous occasions.

The Entrance and Exit Wounds

According to the official version, Mark Chapman shot John Lennon four times in the back and left shoulder. However, the first red flag we need to consider is that the medically verified account of John's bullet wounds (according to the actual surgeon and nurses who treated John in the emergency room and washed his body immediately after) prove that John Lennon was shot from the front. When I spoke to Dr Halleran and nurses Kammerar and Sato, they were adamant that John had four entrance wounds in his upper left chest and three exit wounds, exiting in an identical trajectory, out of his upper left back – meaning the bullets must have come from a direction in front of Lennon. This means that Chapman could not feasibly have caused these wounds from where he was standing in the

Dakota driveway as Lennon was walking away from him, with his back to him. When Chapman fired his gun, most credible witness accounts (along with Chapman himself) have placed him standing by the left-hand side of the entrance to the driveway, on or just off the curb of the sidewalk, whilst Lennon was positioned near the vestibule glass-panelled doors, on the right-hand side of the driveway, at an approximate distance of at least twenty feet away from Chapman. From that distance, direction and angle, Chapman could not feasibly have caused John's gunshot wounds. Some might suggest that perhaps John may have turned around to face Chapman (which I believe is extremely unlikely) but even if he did, there are other factors which make it impossible for Chapman to have caused John's wounds. To accept the "John turned around" claim, we are being asked to believe that John, having heard his name called out by a stranger, turned around a full 180 degrees and stood totally still, to allow Chapman to steadily hit him with four bullets above his heart in a tight grouping (the kind of tight grouping that Dr Halleran said a navy SEAL could not achieve). What makes this even less likely is that it was dark and the driveway was very poorly lit, so poor visibility would also have been a factor. Furthermore, Chapman's .38 revolver was not an automatic gun. Presumably, John would have moved (to some degree, even if only slightly) with the force of each bullet's impact, as Chapman had to pull the trigger each time to fire off each of the four shots. However, John's wounds were very tightly grouped together which suggests he would have had to be extremely still for this to be achieved. Even if we suspend our disbelief for a moment and accept that Chapman's marksman skills were that professional from such a distance in that poor light; and we accept the tiny possibility that John might have turned and stood totally still while being shot four times — we are then being asked to believe that after receiving these four fatal gunshot wounds, John turned back around, got to the vestibule, pulled opened the vestibule doors, climbed six steps, opened another mahogany door into the lobby, then turned sharp left through a swinging door and walked into Jay Hastings front office, before having the composure to tell Jay Hastings (twice according to Jay) that he had been shot, before stumbling further on into a back office and finally collapsing face down onto the floor. This is impossible – and frankly ridiculous.

It is also crucial, at this point, to remember that Dr Halleran and the emergency room nurses told me that, in their opinion, after thoroughly assessing John's catastrophic wounds up close, they are utterly convinced that John would have collapsed instantly and died moments after being shot. The damage to the vital arteries around his heart was too severe. Even Elliot Gross admitted publicly that "death occurred within a very short time". ER chief Stephen Lynn may not have treated John at the Roosevelt, but he was in the room and had a chance to observe John's wounds close up. Lynn has been quoted as saying, "I am sure he was dead when he was shot. He never stood a chance, the first bullet killed him, even if he was shot in the middle of a cardiac department, we could never have saved him."

If you believe the official narrative, John was shot in the back in the Dakota driveway as he approached the vestibule doors. And yet, John somehow ended up face down in the superintendent's back office behind the Dakota lobby area after a super-human journey – with four fatal bullet wounds which had all entered his chest from the front.

The Bullets

According to the official narrative, Mark Chapman, the NYPD and the DA's office all insisted that Chapman only used hollow-point bullets. Why, then, does the morgue report, which I found in Hoffman's papers, state that one hollow-point bullet and one non-hollow-point bullet was found in Lennon's body and clothing? Brad Trent's 1989 photograph of these same bullets confirms that they are two different types of bullets. Could this point to a second shooter?

The total lack of any record of spent bullets found at the crime scene also points to a possible cover-up. And it is highly suspicious that an officer from a different precinct (not the 20th) was sent to the Dakota crime scene to search for spent bullets – especially considering that this officer, Sergeant Ray Kelly, swiftly ascended through the ranks to become the New York City Police Commissioner just twelve years later. There must have been spent bullets at the scene – so where are they and why has no information about them ever been released?

The position of the bullet holes in the glass vestibule doors are also impossible to tally with the fact that John was shot in his upper chest area. Even if John turned around before getting to the vestibule doors, and was hit by Chapman's bullets, why are the bullet holes so low down in the glass panels on these doors? We know from the new medical evidence and testimony from Dr Halleran and the nurses that three of the bullets passed through John's back at the same height and trajectory as they went in, so why aren't the bullet holes in the glass doors at upper chest height? We are being asked to believe that two of the three bullets that passed through John's back, immediately changed direction (once through his body) to travel downwards at a

The bullet holes in the glass panel vestibule doors © Manhattan DA Office

different angle before hitting the glass door. Bullets simply do not do this. Furthermore, what happened to the other bullet? The only way Chapman's bullets could have hit John and caused these holes is if John not only turned around 180 degrees to face Chapman, but also stooped or bent down low. However, there were no blood splatters on the doors or glass panels. The official narrative is that two bullets exited John's front (one in his upper left chest and one in his lower left chest area). For this to square with the position of the two bullets holes in the near vestibule door (and the other bullet hole on the far vestibule door, which potentially could have been caused by one of the bullets continuing onwards through one door and then the other) John would still have had to have been stooping low or bending downwards before he got to the vestibule doors. This seems very unlikely. Even Chapman himself stated that Lennon had "some composure" after he started firing and if Lennon was hit in the back (as the official version goes) he would not have seen Chapman with a gun so would have no warning or time to duck down.

Another crucial point is that Jay Hastings said he heard gunfire after hearing someone open the vestibule door. If true, this is a vital piece of evidence. In addition to this, during one of our many conversations, Ron Hoffman – the lead detective in the case – told me he was convinced that Lennon was shot in the "stairs area". Remember, too, that Hoffman had stated (just one hour after Lennon's murder while talking to the press outside the Roosevelt Hospital) that Lennon was shot inside the vestibule doors. Chapman's bullets could not possibly have hit Lennon if he was already inside the Dakota building.

A Second Shooter

I believe there is a very strong possibility that there was a second shooter who was standing in wait either near the top of the stairs that lead up to the Dakota lobby or near the bottom of the stairs just inside the vestibule doors. In this area, a second shooter would have been concealed from anyone in the Dakota building or on the street. With John taken by surprise and trapped inside the vestibule or lobby stairs area, the assassin could have got close enough to shoot him four times, in a tight grouping on his upper left chest, at point blank range using a silencer or modified bullets. The scenario where a shooter is on the stairs could explain the position of the low bullet holes in the vestibule doors: the shooter would be higher than John and firing a gun at a downwards angle. John may have tilted backwards and to the side as the bullets went through him, which could potentially account for the low bullet holes in the doors. If there was a second shooter inside who actually hit Lennon, and caused the fatal wounds, there is still a possibility that the bullet holes in the glass doors *were* caused by Chapman's bullets which missed his target (if they were real bullets and not blanks) though I feel this is unlikely. There is no report from the NYPD regarding any recovered spent bullets from the scene, so we will probably never know the truth about this.

There is another theory that a second shooter could have been standing on the far left-hand side of the driveway, in the service elevator alcove or bay window, opposite the vestibule doors. Or another that a second shooter may have shot John from the courtyard area. From either of these positions, a shooter would be close enough to shoot at point-blank range, causing a tight grouping of shots in John's chest. However, there are several problems with this theory. Firstly, the shooter would have to be facing John to cause his front entry wounds, and although they could have shot John as he walked up the driveway towards them, the idea that a dying John could complete such an epic "journey" to the back office after being fatally wounded is still difficult to believe. Secondly, Jay Hastings said he heard gunfire after John opened the vestibule doors. And finally, the bullet holes in the glass doors do not easily account for the killer being positioned in the left alcove or courtyard. The angle of the vestibule doors means it is almost impossible for somebody to have made those three bullet holes. They are interesting theories, but I don't personally believe a second shooter was in either of those positions.

But where was Yoko when all this was happening? I believe when John was shot, Yoko could have run out of the far vestibule door and exited into the gated courtyard behind the driveway. This is where Nina Rosen said she saw her. There is a possibility that Yoko might have felt somewhat ashamed about running away, and hence failed to mention this in any of her witness statements – but who could blame her: that would be a natural reaction. If she was hiding in the courtyard area, she would not have seen a second shooter in the stairs area.

Second Shooter Getaway

I believe after shooting John, the killer could have gone up the stairs and into the Dakota and then entered one of the apartments, in that part of the building, which could be accessed from stairs leading from the lobby. The assassin would almost certainly have to have been allowed into this area by concierge Jay Hastings, who controlled access to it via remote control. The assassin could have stayed hidden inside a Dakota apartment for many days after shooting Lennon, and then made a discrete exit at their time of choosing. Or the killer could have walked past John, exited through the glass doors, and walked out into the back courtyard. From the courtyard, there were a myriad of exit doors and windows they could have used to get away. Or they could have exited the driveway and onto the street, but no witnesses mentioned seeing anyone else on or leaving the driveway. Mark Chapman certainly didn't mention seeing anyone else leaving but, then again, Chapman was delusional and thought he had killed John Lennon by shooting him four times in the back.

José Perdomo

Another major problem with the assassin exiting via the street is that Perdomo would have seen a second shooter walking across the driveway or running away, and he made no mention of this. Perdomo had told Officer Cullen that "the bullets pushed Lennon through the doors". My theory about a second shooter hiding at the top of the stairs, shooting at John as he was just inside the vestibule doors, could potentially account for this as John may have been pushed back through the doors by the force of the bullets. (The doors had to be pulled from the outside and pushed from the inside to open). That said, the rest of Perdomo's alleged testimony, via various third-hand recollections, does not make a lot of sense. As Michael Medeiros told me, José Perdomo may have gone to his watchman's golden booth and seen nothing, subsequently telling the police what he thought they wanted to hear. Or, Perdomo may have seen more than he was willing to say. We probably will never know what Perdomo saw and did on the night of 8th December 1980. It is worth restating that, as of November 2023, Perdomo's official witness statement has not been released to the public. Ask yourself why? The New York's DA's office has all the files on the John Lennon murder case. Despite an avalanche of freedom of information requests sent their way, they have steadfastly refused to release any files on Perdomo.

I personally believe it is possible that Perdomo was involved in John's murder somehow. His anti-Castro past would have put him in direct opposition to Lennon's anti-Christian and pro-Socialism stance. Perdomo's past is also very murky and his mysterious brother, who worked at the Dakota before him, still needs further investigation. If Chapman was under some form of mind-control, a trigger person on site at the Dakota (like the infamous "lady in the polka dot dress" who was seen at RFK's assassination) would have been very useful. Perdomo could have been that person. Also, why did Perdomo kick the gun away and wait to ask Joe Many to pick it up and take it away? Why not pick it up himself and get it out of the way immediately? Did he not want his fingerprints on it? His request for Chapman to leave and just "get out of here" was also very strange and suspicious. Perdomo even warned Chapman that he should leave because the "cops would be here in a couple of minutes". According to Nina Rosen, Chapman had no gun on him when Perdomo said this, so why was Perdomo urging Chapman to leave? Surely, most people would want an alleged killer to be caught by the police. Perdomo clearly didn't want this to happen.

Jay Hastings

The varying testimonies of Jay Hastings deeply trouble me. Though there is no proof that he was a second shooter, we cannot ignore the fact that he was in the best position to potentially be one. People may, therefore, claim that he could have been a second shooter who could have assassinated John Lennon.

According to Hastings, John Lennon (after being fatally wounded) came running up from the stairs, through the large mahogany doors, turned left through a swinging saloon door, and ran past him (Hastings was apparently in the front concierge's office), telling him twice that he had been shot, before continuing onwards into a back office, where he collapsed face down. Quite the journey with large bullet holes in his chest and a major artery completely severed. Key medical staff believe Lennon was practically dead seconds after he was struck with four bullets, so Hastings' account seems implausible. If John was shot inside the vestibule area, how did he get from there to the back office? Michael Medeiros claims that Perdomo, the following day, had told him that he had moved John's body from the stairs into the lobby area. Hastings refutes seeing Perdomo carrying John in.

When I told Hastings, in October 2023, that all the medical experts who saw John's wounds were certain that John would have died almost instantly after being struck, he initially agreed, seemingly forgetting for a moment about the "fantastical" journey he had claimed John went on after being mortally wounded. I pointed out to Hastings that the doctors and nurses were sure

Lennon would have dropped down almost instantly after being shot because his left subclavian artery was completely severed when they assessed his wounds. After a few moments of thinking this over, Hastings declared that John's subclavian artery might have been severed by one of John's bones which he said he heard "cracking" when he allegedly carried him out to a police car – something we know Hastings did not do.

Hastings says John collapsed in the superintendent's back office. Yet Joe Many says he saw a pool of blood in the front office, and that Hastings was "covered in blood". This made Joe Many assume John must have fallen into Hastings' arms, and that Yoko and Hastings must have moved John's body into the back office, from the front office, to "feel safer". Joe Many claimed Hastings told him, on the night of the murder, that John collapsed into his arms – accounting for Hastings being, as Joe Many also described it to me, "full of blood". Jay Hastings refutes this claim and says Joe Many never saw John's body in his office. Dakota resident Jack Henderson did state that he saw Jay with Lennon in the "back office", but I am sceptical about whether residents would be able to see into the superintendent's office from the lobby or understand what the staff meant by front and back office: perhaps Henderson was just describing the office at the back of (i.e. behind) the concierge's desk.

The white shirt that Jay Hastings sold at auction in 2016 (which he said was the actual John-Lennon-blood-splattered Dakota uniform shirt he wore on the night of the assassination) is not *covered* in blood. It only has a few spots of blood stained on it (along with sweat mark stains under the arms). I personally do not believe that the shirt Hastings sold at auction was the shirt he was wearing on the night as it makes no sense – both Hastings and Joe Many had told me his shirt was "covered" in blood. Hastings had explained to me that he became covered in blood while carrying John's body out to the police car, complaining to me that the police gave him the "bloody business end" to carry. However, that is a lie: multiple witnesses, and the two officers who did carry John out of the Dakota, all state unequivocally that Hastings was not involved in carrying John's body out. John Lennon's "bloody business end", as Hastings so crudely put it, was actually carried by Officer Tony Palma. Palma has confirmed this to me, saying he swore at Chapman, who was sitting in a police car, as they carried John's body past. The fact that Chapman told Barbara Walters in a 1992 TV interview that the officer carrying John's head and arms swore at him corroborates this. That Hastings has lied about this is very disturbing. I wonder why he wants us to believe that the reason his shirt was "covered in blood" was because he carried John's body out to the car? I can confidently say that Jay Hastings did not do this, so his shirt getting covered in blood must have come from Hastings doing something else with John's body. Could it have come from Hastings moving John's body from the front office to the back office? Or could it have come from Hastings moving John's body from another location – the stairs maybe?

There is also the matter of a strange seven-year gap, between 1971 and 1978, in Jay Hasting's biography, before he started working at the Dakota. It's hard to imagine a three-year art course lasting seven years, even with busted knees, but that is what Hastings claims he did between 1971 and 1978.

That Hastings was not questioned by the police at the 20th Precinct station after the killing is also very odd. We know they officially took statements at this station from José Perdomo and Joe Many, but not Hastings. Hastings potentially saw more than Joe Many and was with Lennon, possibly alone, immediately after he was shot, yet he was not taken to the 20th Precinct. When Joe Many asked Hastings why he wasn't coming down to the station, Hastings replied he didn't want to help the cops and didn't have to go down if he didn't want to. Surely, he should have been required, by law, to go down to the station, answer questions and give an official statement. For an unspecified reason, the NYPD did not talk to Jay Hastings officially or take an official witness statement at the station. Hastings said numerous detectives questioned him at the Dakota on the night of Lennon's assassination, but no official record of these interviews has been released or proven to exist. Ron Hoffman's notebook is sparse and unhelpful. One person who was interested in talking to Jay Hastings was Chief Medical Examiner Elliot Gross. Gross deliberately sought out Hastings when he visited the Dakota and spoke with him privately. Gross was not interested in talking to anybody else at the Dakota. Hastings does not recall the Gross conversation today.

Finally, Jay Hastings' speedy departure from the Dakota after John's murder deeply troubles me. Just two weeks after the murder, a "security person" who lived in the Dakota persuaded the building's managers to incorporate a more thorough photo-card security card arrangement with more background checks built into the system. Hastings described this new regime to me as "security theatre" and stated it as one of the reasons he left. He also told me he was "fired" a couple of weeks after the murder for being late to work on just one occasion. The less than convincing reason he gave was that he was told, unexpectedly, to cover someone who was absent, and he couldn't get to work on time. Like most of Hastings' testimony, this makes little sense. Hastings told me he spent the next four decades after the Dakota working as a graphic artist for lots of different companies. During those decades, Hastings seems to have kept his head down, not appearing in any media or press to talk about Lennon's murder until he sold his shirt in 2016.

Many people might surmise that there is a possibility that Jay Hastings could have shot Lennon either on the stairway or in his front office using a silencer and modified bullets. In this scenario, Lennon might have either collapsed in the stairway or in a pool of blood in Hastings' front office. Hastings might have then moved John's body into the back office, and in doing so, ended up with his shirt "covered in blood" as described by Joe Many who arrived on the scene to also see a pool of blood in the front office, and Ono in the back office with John's body. Though there is no concrete evidence for any of this, it is one possible scenario on which others will surely speculate. However, if true, this could then implicate Yoko Ono.

When I last spoke to Jay Hastings in October 2023, I told him that I was concerned that the evidence I have uncovered might lead people to think he could have had something to do with John Lennon's assassination. I told him that the testimony of Joseph Many was especially troubling in the differences to Hastings own accounts. There were also huge problems regarding his bloody shirt and the fact that no one saw him help police officers carry John Lennon's body out of the Dakota. Hastings seemed surprisingly unbothered by my concerns, claiming that Many and Henderson's statements were "just another witness with just another story" and "all NYPD cops lie." He then finished with the repeated declaration, "It doesn't bother me". I personally think it should bother him.

Yoko Ono

As for Ono and her widely varying witness statements, if we were being kind, we could say that she was so far behind John that she saw very little of her husband's murder. If she was ahead of John, she could possibly have seen a second shooter. Again, until we have a full and coherent statement from Ono on what she did and what she saw on the night her husband was murdered, we can only speculate. Were Perdomo and Ono involved in a second shooter plot? It is possible, but I believe it is unlikely Ono was involved. Perdomo's witness statement would be helpful and a full and detailed account of Yoko's real position, movements and recollections in the moments before and after her husband's murder, would also be helpful. But I do not think we are ever going to get these important details, so a veil of suspicion will always be cast over these two individuals, possibly forever.

For the record, I think Yoko Ono may have seen more on the night of her husband's murder than she has so far revealed. Shock, possible drug use and almost certainly PTSD, may have caused any repressed memories to stay hidden, and that makes perfect sense to me. Ono may also have been frightened of reprisals if she said too much. A rushed cremation and her refusal to release John's autopsy have both caused many to harbour suspicions, but Ono was frankly a very strange lady and there is merit in her assertion that a traditional funeral for John would have meant his graveside be turned into a ghoulish fan circus, as happened with Jim Morrison in Paris. Releasing John Lennon's autopsy would be useful, but I personally do not have much faith in an autopsy conducted by Elliot Gross, a medical examiner who has been accused multiple times of falsifying autopsies in the past.

There are a few troubling assertions about Yoko Ono. If there was a plot to kill Lennon with a second shooter, it would be essential to have Yoko Ono on board to deliver him at a certain time at the Dakota. Ono did not get hit with Chapman's alleged bullets, or a second shooter's bullets, and she did not see Chapman shoot her husband. This is very hard to square with whatever position she was in. If Ono was in front of John, she potentially could have seen a second shooter. If she was behind, she should have seen Chapman shoot his gun towards her husband. She miraculously avoided any bullets and saw nothing of any significance according to her varying testimonies in the days following the murder. To be fair, she could have shut her eyes to the horror and been genuinely confused.

Ono also has said, on more than one occasion, that John spoke to her after being shot and that she then immediately followed him into the lobby. Medical evidence suggests it would not be easy for John to speak or move immediately after he was struck. Also, we know that she probably did not follow her husband into the Dakota lobby immediately, as Nina Rosen places her in the courtyard after the gunfire. Interestingly, Ono has repeated the same story as Jay Hastings. None of this adds up and unfortunately this means suspicion will almost certainly always be cast over her.

One last thing to consider is that Yoko Ono has never said she saw Chapman shoot her husband. It would have been very easy for her to claim she had and she would have been believed without question. If Yoko Ono was involved in her husband's assassination, she surely would have said that she saw Chapman shoot him. That's why, on balance, I don't believe that Ono was involved in an assassination plot to murder her husband. I can, however, understand why people might believe the contrary.

Dana Reeves and Gloria Chapman

Two characters who had a profound influence over Mark Chapman's life and "handled" many of his needs, Dana Reeves and Gloria Chapman, need further investigation. Reeves was a tough, "Rambo" type guy hence it seems strange for him to befriend the meek and mild Christian Mark Chapman. A few years older and seemingly much wiser than Chapman, Dana Reeves offered Mark a room in his own home and drove him hundreds of miles when required. Reeves, who had worked as a police officer and security guard, was the first person to familiarise Chapman with guns and violence. Reeves was the man who gave Chapman the hollow point bullets which were allegedly used on 8th December 1980 for "protection against muggers". Incredibly, Reeves did this when he was a serving police officer. The New York phone calls Mark Chapman made with Reeves before he flew to Atlanta to pick up his hollow bullets, surely meant there was a strong possibility that Reeves was all too aware of exactly why Chapman wanted them. Yet Dana Reeves was never charged with anything in relation to John Lennon's murder. He was given pseudonyms and blanket anonymity. To this day, the name Dana Reeves is protected by former senior members of the NYPD. Ask yourself why?

Dana Reeves was later incarcerated for child molestation offences. Perhaps he had a history of this type of crime, which may have left him open to coercion by others. Perhaps Reeves was blackmailed into becoming involved with Chapman and then blackmailed into keeping quiet.

Up until Chapman's move to Hawaii, Reeves was an important presence in Chapman's life and handled many affairs for him. It is very telling that, after his arrest, Chapman wanted pastor Charles McGowan to let Dana Reeves know he was ok. As for Gloria Chapman, after Mark had met her in Hawaii, she then became the most influential person in his life, taking over the baton of handling his affairs. As she was a travel agent, she was the one to arrange his amazing round the world trip. She also ensured that she worked closely with her new husband at Castle Memorial Hospital. She never left his side, and like Reeves, she was older and far more experienced than him.

Gloria had, admittedly, led a promiscuous life, and had even dabbled in the occult before she met Mark. This could have left her open to exploitation. Like Reeves, Gloria could be implicated in John Lennon's murder: she was fully aware of Mark's first attempt to take the ex-Beatle's life in New York in early November 1980. Mark had told her everything and showed her his gun and bullets, and yet Gloria did nothing to stop him. When her husband wanted to return to New York, Gloria booked the plane tickets and drove him to the airport. In the days after Lennon's assassination, she claimed she was happy that her husband had "accomplished something he set out to do" and she was sad that Lennon "had to die". Her bizarre and baffling phone call to the 20th Precinct on the night of John's assassination understandably caused many to suspect she was involved in a conspiracy. After Chapman's imprisonment, Gloria actively participated in the despicable demon gaslighting that was conducted on him. She consistently helped Jim Gaines and Jack Jones to demonise her husband in the media for over forty years. To this day, Gloria controls all access to Mark and still "handles" his affairs, in conjunction with pastor Charles McGowan (a former Special Agent in counterintelligence). Gloria isn't interested in hearing about anomalies in her husband's criminal case. Gloria demands to be Mark's gatekeeper, with Charles McGowan's guidance (and cash) always on hand. Gloria apparently visits her husband in prison often and sometimes has conjugal visits with him. Gloria Chapman, like Dana Reeves, is, in my considered opinion, an accessory to John Lennon's assassination. One Chapman remains in prison. Some might suggest it is the wrong Chapman who is currently locked up.

Chapman's Psychotic False Memory

We are left with the troubling conclusion that Mark Chapman (and disgracefully, the NYPD) to this very day, thought he was guilty of something that he couldn't have possibly done. Chapman has consistently said that he shot his .38 handgun five times, with four bullets hitting John Lennon in his back. Expert medical testimony proves he could not have possibly done this. The lead detective is also convinced Lennon was shot inside the vestibule, an area Mark could not see, never mind aim a gun at. Therefore, the only conclusion we can come to is that Chapman was experiencing some kind of psychotic episode and did not have fully functioning mental capacity when John Lennon was shot. He was imagining things that were simply not happening.

I always found it very strange that Mark Chapman said he could not remember pulling the bead of his gun and was amazed that the bullets were working. He also seemed puzzled that Lennon wasn't visible after he fired the gun. To me, this sounds as if he was not firing a working gun at all. Perhaps he was firing blanks. If Chapman was a patsy, the people who set him up to be the fall guy may not have wanted to risk real bullets hitting anybody else. Blank bullets swapped for real bullets would solve this problem. Lisa Pease, the highly respected author, and expert on Robert Kennedy's assassination, believes Sirhan Sirhan was a hypnotised Manchurian candidate patsy firing blanks. I believe Mark Chapman was also a hypnotised Manchurian candidate patsy, programmed to believe he had to murder John Lennon and to believe he succeeded. Do we have any evidence of Chapman being linked to hypnotism and the CIA's MK-Ultra mind control programme? Yes indeed. So much that it seems incredible that it has never been widely considered or talked about.

CIA Law Firm

Chapman's defence lawyer, Jonathan Marks, worked in 30 Rockefeller Plaza, the same building that also housed Donovan, Leisure, Irvine and Newton a law firm that was awash with CIA personnel. This law firm had an ex-CIA director on its books, in William Colby. We know this CIA-loaded law firm had substantial influence on Chapman's case because Jonathan Marks worked with one of their staff, David Suggs, as his assistant. It is therefore not a stretch to imagine that CIA-approved psychiatrists would be able to get into Mark Chapman's cell. This is exactly what happened.

CIA Experts

Jonathan Marks and David Suggs employed four psychiatrists to assess Chapman. Three of them have dubious links to hypnosis, intelligence agencies and previous controversial assassinations. Sirhan Sirhan's psychiatrist Bernard Diamond was one of the first "experts" to visit Mark Chapman while he was in custody awaiting trial. Diamond was well known as the psychiatrist who hypnotised Sirhan while assessing him. Diamond also worked out of the University of California in Berkeley. A location well known for its MK-Ultra programmes in the past. Sirhan bitterly complained about Diamond's involvement in his case. MK-Ultra hypnotist Milton Kline was a self-confessed CIA consultant and a former president of the American Society for

Clinical and Experimental Hypnosis. Kline had even featured in a 1979 MK-Ultra TV documentary, where he boldly stated that intelligent agencies were using hypnosis to enable operatives to carry out mission objectives, including murder. Kline spent time alone with Chapman and, by most accounts, had a good rapport with him. Is it just a coincidence that MK-Ultra consultant Kline turned up in Chapman's cell? I don't think so. Another psychiatrist sent in to assess Chapman by Marks and Suggs was Richard Bloom, a psychiatrist with an intelligence and military background who was also a hypnosis expert and advocate. Is it just a coincidence that Bloom, Diamond and Kline were all linked to hypnosis and intelligence, and all were hired by lawyers linked to a CIA law firm? I personally don't think so.

Milton Kline and the Little People

Milton Kline was a CIA consultant specifically tasked to spend time alone in Mark Chapman's cell throughout the early months of 1981. The fact that Kline, in a 1979 TV documentary, had boasted that he could create a Manchurian candidate killer seems to have been totally disregarded by the lawyers who placed this evil man into Mark Chapman's cell. Kline did his work in plain sight. In fact, Kline was announced to the world as the hypnotist who would discover "feelings" that were "lurking" in Mark's subconscious. I believe Kline, and others like him, were sent into Chapman's cell for two specific reasons. Firstly, to see if Chapman could recall why he suddenly felt compelled to kill John Lennon in the summer of 1979, and whether this had anything to do with *The Catcher in the Rye* being used as a trigger device to make that happen. I'm sure if Chapman did recall anything suspicious, Kline would have been able to expunge that from his mind, with his honed and highly-regarded hypnotic skills.

Secondly, I believe Kline was sent into Chapman's cell to make him believe in an imaginary "kingdom of little people" who were driving his life. These little people would eventually elect a godly general who would ask Mark Chapman to plead guilty and forego a trial. A trial that I'm convinced, if allowed to examine *all* the evidence, would have exonerated Mark. A trial would have opened the eyes of the world to the presence of a second shooter who assassinated John Lennon. The powers behind the conspiracy could not have allowed that to happen. A trial would have been a disaster. The conspirators risked being uncovered. Kline and his "little people" invention ensured this did not happen. Kline's mission was clear and his mission was successful. But the fact that it was instigated in the first place clearly shows that a conspiracy was at work. "Operation No Trial" is easy to unpick once you have all the hidden facts to hand. It is often the case that the cover-up of a conspiracy reveals most about its hidden operatives and their methods.

Hypnotized, Drugged and Groomed

I am now convinced that Chapman was hypnotised, drugged, and groomed over many years to set him up as the patsy in the assassination of John Lennon. Three very particular agencies ensured that "madness" was inserted into Chapman's fragile, drug-damaged thought processes: psychologists, religious preachers and (I believe) unseen intelligence entities worked on Chapman to achieve this goal. All the "Christians" in his life were determined to blame "demons" for Chapman's murderous compulsions. The psychiatrists mostly blamed schizophrenia and his internal "little people". And I believe, in Hawaii, as-yet-unknown operatives implanted *The Catcher in the Rye* as a trigger to murder.

Program Malfunction

Though many years of planning must have gone into Chapman's grooming process and programming, I do not believe the operation went exactly as planned. I think Mark Chapman, like Sirhan before him, was firing blanks. The signal to fire his blanks was given (possibly by Perdomo) as Lennon was entering the glass-panel-doored vestibule area. Once inside that area, the real killer did his work in sync with Chapman, who thought it was his bullets which killed John. So far so good. However, it is my belief that Mark Chapman was then meant to run away from the scene and disappear into Central Park across the street. Perdomo told him to run before the police arrived. I believe it was a pre-arranged command. To what purpose though? Could there have been, waiting in the park or on the street, a second hit-team ready to shoot down a fleeing Chapman. A crooked cop or a Jack Ruby type character could have taken him out in an alleged shoot-out. There is also a possibility that Chapman was programmed to kill himself after thinking he shot Lennon. A loaded gun could easily have been placed into his hands. Mark's immediate compulsion to read *The Catcher in the Rye* after the assassination seems, to me, like a trigger device. It might possibly have been a trigger to run or to kill himself. Certainly, the personal display which he left in his hotel room earlier does appear to suggest the behaviour of a person about to commit suicide. Chapman has even admitted this himself. One thing is for certain: if Mark Chapman was programmed to kill John Lennon (but was not supposed to live to tell the tale) then those who took part in the programming would have been horrified that he stayed on the scene and didn't run away or kill himself. What were they to do? Like Lee Harvey Oswald, Mark Chapman was a loose thread that had to be tied up.

Hypnotists

If Chapman was hypnotised to murder John Lennon, he certainly had plenty of "experts" in his life to help him. Prior to the assassination, we know he had contact with Jules Bernhardt, a self-described close family friend and psychological counsellor. Bernhardt wrote a book in 1972 called *Self-Hypnosis: The Miracle of the Mind*. By revealing, in a December 1980 article, a possible "plot" behind Chapman's "murder" of Lennon was Bernhardt trying to alert people to the fact that Chapman was groomed to kill Lennon. Hypnotism could also have been used by the various psychiatrists and institutions who had been part of Mark's life, especially while Mark was at Castle Memorial Hospital in Hawaii. It could be argued that the "charismatic" Christian/psychology sessions Chapman had with Fred Krauss could have had a negative hypnotising effect. Fred Krauss was a practising hypnotist. One thing is certain, after Chapman was arrested and was awaiting trial, he was visited by four psychiatrists who all had side-lines in hypnotism: Emanuel Hammer, Bernard Diamond, Richard Bloom and Milton Kline.

Shadowy Christian Presence

It deeply troubles me that there was a cabal of evangelical Christian preachers with deep ties to intelligence and the military who all had a strong influence over Mark Chapman. Charles McGowan, David Moore, Peter Anderson and Fred Krauss spent a great deal of time with Chapman, and most were ex-military or intelligence. McGowan and Krauss were both very keen to tell Mark, time and again, that he was possessed by demons; with McGowan, Ken Babbington and Don Dickerman especially keen to stress to Chapman that his inner demons were responsible for his desire to murder John Lennon – inner demons that Fred Krauss tried to exorcise from him when Mark was only fifteen. When Krauss started to work on Chapman in 1975, many of Mark's friends commented that he was "gone for two or three months", but when he returned, he was a born-again Christian. I would counter that he was a born-again Christian fanatic wholly by design.

Charles McGowan and his friend Stephen Olford were keen to get into Mark Chapman's cell as quickly as possible, immediately after he was arrested. Olford was willing to fund McGowan's trip. Olford was even prepared to pay for some of Chapman's legal costs. Stephen Olford was great friends with Billy Graham and, through him, President Richard Nixon. Nixon hated John Lennon and the feeling was mutual. Did Nixon somehow influence Olford to arrange a plot to kill John Lennon? When Lennon first arrived in New York, Olford was a star preacher in one of New York's biggest protestant churches. He even had his own Christian radio show. When Christian-bashing Lennon turned up on his patch, Olford would not have been happy. We know Nixon went to Olford's church in New York and we know that evangelist preaching superstar Billy Graham was a protégée and long-standing friend of Stephen Olford. Billy Graham was one of the first people that President Nixon turned to when the Watergate fiasco brought down his presidency. Could Graham have informed Olford about the disgraced ex-President's possible desire to gain revenge on Lennon? I have no concrete proof for this but, in my estimation, it is all too possible.

As for Special Agent McGowan of Navy Intelligence, to this day, he is still communicating with Mark Chapman while he is in prison and still helping to handle his needs. McGowan's "dear, dear friend" was Cortez Cooper, a pastor and former director of the Rand Group, a think-tank that works for the pentagon, and therefore the CIA and FBI. McGowan's close friendship with Ronald Reagan's chief financial guru, Joe Rodgers, also deeply troubles me. Rodgers was a Reagan loyalist. A man who spent many years of his life raising millions of dollars to get Reagan and George Bush Snr initially into power and then to keep them there. Olford, Rodgers and Cooper were all connected to Nixon, Reagan and the Pentagon. All were close friends with Special Agent Charles McGowan – the man who guided Mark Chapman throughout his life. These connections deeply trouble me. When McGowan retired from being a pastor, in 2003, the right-wing Senator Marsha Blackburn gave him a congressional farewell eulogy.

I am not for one minute saying that Charles McGowan, or any of the other religious and military men he knew, instigated or oversaw the programming of Mark Chapman to think he was killing John Lennon. But some of their associates may have done so, and all of them would probably have hated John Lennon for his anti-Christian and pro left-wing views. We have clear evidence from FBI files that John Lennon was seen as a thorn in the side of the American establishment. Could one of these men have inadvertently alerted an intelligence colleague to Chapman – a heavy LSD user who believed he was possessed by demons and who felt betrayed by John Lennon – as a potential candidate who could be manipulated and programmed to think he was killing Lennon? One thing is certain: all the "godly" men connected to Chapman would have deeply disliked John Lennon for what I'm sure they perceived as a constant spiritual and political corruption of their flock.

Secretive Christian Organisations

The military/intelligence/Christian links do not stop at McGowan, Olford, Krauss, Babbington and Anderson. Secretive Christian organisations constantly feature in Mark Chapman's life. Mark spent a long time at Castle Memorial Hospital in Hawaii, which was run by the Seventh Day Adventists. Chapman's alleged brainwashing by Dr Gursahani is a clear indication that Chapman was almost certainly on a Manchurian candidate type programme in Hawaii. The Adventists have had previous alliances with the American military, providing human Guinea pigs for them in the past. When the Adventists were asked to release account record details on Chapman, they refused on a confidentiality basis. Speaking shortly after Lennon's assassination, Mark's father commented that Mark's "build-up" to becoming seriously troubled came in the last three years of his life before Lennon was assassinated. These years were Mark's Hawaii years, and a large part of that time was spent with the Adventists and Dr Gursahani.

Chapman was also entangled for many years with the YMCA.

Again, like the Adventists, when the YMCA were asked to release their files on Chapman, they said they had lost them. Chapman was also apparently entangled with the military-linked Christian Navigators, and we know the Southern Baptist network had him on their radar from the time he was a young boy. Christian organisations abounded in Chapman's life: he was constantly monitored, treated, engaged, and guided by them.

The Patsy

I am often asked, why bother with a patsy like Chapman? Why not just arrange for a professional assassin to do the job and leave it at that? Imagine for a moment that Chapman was not standing bewildered at the Dakota driveway, totally confused about what he had supposedly done. Imagine the police had turned up and found no suspect. Then what would have happened is – one of the biggest manhunts and investigations in criminal history would have taken place. Details like the entrance and exit wounds would have been properly investigated and questioned. Forensics would have been properly analysed and checked. Motives and potential suspects would have been sought. None of these crucial investigations happened because the NYPD already had their perpetrator waiting in situ at the crime scene. Conspiracy was totally out of the question in such circumstances. They had their guy; he'd confessed to the killing; and Christmas was coming up fast. What a wonderful present: a pre-cooked turkey, oven-ready. Nothing further to see here. Case closed.

Motive

As for a nefarious motive for Lennon's assassination, I believe there are many. It is a mistake to seek a single perpetrator or motive when trying to uncover or solve a possible conspiracy. Lennon was anti-religion. Lennon was anti-war. Lennon was anti-capitalist. He surely would have been hated for these very reasons by Richard Nixon, Billy Graham, Stephen Olford,

Joe Rodgers, Charles McGowan, Cortez Cooper, Fred Krauss, Don Dickerman, Ken Babbington and Peter Anderson. It is very troubling to note that most of these men are connected by their Southern Christian faith and their political, military, and intelligence ties. There is no concrete evidence to definitively connect any of these men to the assassination of John Lennon, but I believe Chapman's association with these men, and others who might have been covertly involved, is at the heart of this conspiracy.

Final Thoughts

I do not think we will ever be certain who was behind the plot to assassinate John Lennon. It may have been official or unofficial elements within the American intelligence agencies. We know that Lennon wasn't popular with far-right Christians and Republicans. We also know that the FBI and CIA were tracking him while he was in New York. It could have been a combination of various people and groups who wanted Lennon dead. The actual assassin who pulled the trigger may have been connected to organised crime. We know Lennon had a legal run-in with a mob-linked record boss called Morris Levy in the mid-seventies. Did Levy help arrange for a second shooter? We must also remember that there is evidence linking the CIA and the FBI with mafia-linked individuals, and the intelligence agencies were known to hire professional criminals to do their dirty business. Lennon's real killer could have been hired by numerous organisations. Like I said, I doubt we will ever know the whole truth. I am satisfied that this book will, hopefully, change the conversation around John Lennon's assassination now that the many anomalies surrounding the case have been brought out into the open. But we have a long way to go.

I am aware that many people who read this book will consider me as anti-religion or anti-right wing. As far as politics go, my position is simple: I mostly distrust all political parties and a significant proportion of the people who operate within them. There are, of course, good politicians and political activists around the world, but most of the good ones don't get very far; and the very good ones who do get to hold influence or power – such as JFK, RFK, MLK and Malcolm X – are likely to be eliminated. I don't believe politicians are elected; I believe they are selected. And the people selecting them are not the public. I believe western democracy is an illusion. We don't live in democracies. We live in bureaucracies.

As for religion, I was brought up as a Catholic, but by the time I became a teenager, I knew organised religion wasn't for me. The endless guilt-trips and obsession with sin ground me down as a youngster. I now consider myself agnostic. I briefly saw myself as an atheist in the early noughties when brilliant writers such as Richard Dawkins and Christopher Hitchens inspired me to criticise religion without feeling guilty or somehow disloyal. I then realised that these "new-atheists" preached their doctrine with the same fundamental zeal and intolerance as the fundamental religious types whom they criticised. How can anyone possibly know for certain whether God exists? I personally believe it is highly unlikely, but nobody can say for sure. Anything is possible.

John Lennon often sailed close to the wind in his tumultuous and magnificent life, and as one of his friends once confided to me, he was consistently reckless in his attitude to life.

He took risks and paid the ultimate price. Though this is my conclusion so far, I sincerely hope that this book will encourage the start of a process that will reopen John Lennon's murder case, so that true justice can be served. Be mindful that Mark Chapman has served over forty years in prison. If the evidence that I have laid out in this book had been presented in a criminal trial back in 1981, I am certain Mark Chapman would not have been convicted. This is not a case of reasonable doubt I put to you: there is overwhelming doubt.

New evidence will almost certainly emerge in the aftermath of this book. A new Apple TV series on Lennon's assassination, scheduled for release in December 2023, will bring many of the people I talk about in this book into the public's consciousness. This can only be a good thing. People will hopefully look at the case with fresh eyes and, as with the JFK, RFK and MLK assassinations, new theories and suspects will emerge. I will of course welcome all of this but, as with JFK, I do not believe we will ever definitively know who really killed John Lennon. I sincerely hope the US authorities will eventually reinvestigate and release all of the files, unredacted, regarding John Lennon and his murder. Let us read the files hidden in the bowels of the CIA, FBI, MI5, MI6, the NYPD and the Manhattan DA's office. Let us see all the notes and dairies which may have survived. Order any agency which has refused to give evidence requested from them to do so in the name of justice. I would also like the US authorities to address his murder as an assassination. A political killing. A deliberate attempt to remove a critic in order to protect the powerful. A thorough investigation into his assassination is the least that John Lennon deserves. Lennon, during his extraordinary life, was almost obsessed with getting to the truth of things. I hope this book will go some way towards uncovering the truth about his horrific assassination.

Through his music and art, John Lennon gave so much joy and wonder to the world. He was also, most importantly, a staunch advocate of peace in a time of needless bloody war. The needless bloody wars are still going on as I write this in the winter of 2023. The world could really do with a John Lennon right now.

David Whelan – November 2023

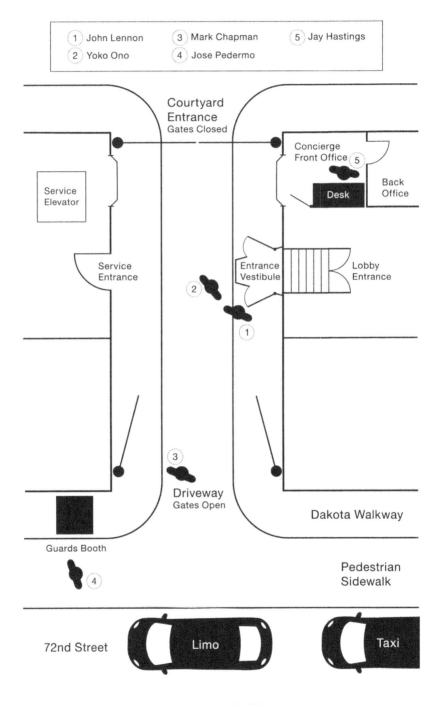

1. John Lennon 3. Mark Chapman 5. Jay Hastings
2. Yoko Ono 4. Jose Pedermo

Courtyard
Entrance
Gates Closed

Concierge
Front Office 5

Service
Elevator

Back
Office

Desk

Service
Entrance

Entrance
Vestibule

Lobby
Entrance

2

1

3

Driveway
Gates Open

Dakota Walkway

Guards Booth

Pedestrian
Sidewalk

4

72nd Street

Limo

Taxi

Dakota Overhead Layout Diagram © David Whelan

Acknowledgements

During the last three years, I have received invaluable support from numerous people.

I must start with my wife Louise, the love of my life, and my two wonderful daughters. Thank you all for putting up with my "Lennon Project" for these past three years. Without your love and support, this book could never have been produced. Special mention to Louise's brilliant proofreading and editing work, which has immeasurably helped this to become a better book.

Simon Clegg, my friend and business partner, has given me immense support from the start of this project and throughout my career. Powerful entities tried to stop me releasing this book. Without Simon and his legal skills, those entities would have succeeded. Simon is an exceptional media lawyer and a cherished and loyal friend.

I am also indebted to Kevin, Robert and Gerry. All three have been patient and insightful sounding boards for me on this project. Also, thank you to Lisa Pease and Tom O'Neil for their encouragement and inspiring work.

Credit must also be given to Ron Hoffman, for allowing me to gain access to his notebooks and paperwork. Ron may have failed to investigate John Lennon's assassination properly at the time, but future generations will surely thank him for releasing his materials.

Finally, I would like to thank all the people who have granted me interviews for this project. You know who you are. Your patience and time has greatly contributed to the historical record of what is certainly one of the most significant, and previously misunderstood, assassinations of all time.

Bibliography

The following books have been invaluable for research in helping me write this book. I recommend all these publications for further research into the subject:

Bresler, Fenton – *Who Killed John Lennon*
Pease, Lisa – *A Lie Too Big to Fail*
Seaman, Fred – *The Last Days of John Lennon*
Turner, Steve – *The Gospel According to the Beatles*
Greenberg, Keith Elliot – *The Day John Lennon Died*
Bramwell, Tony – *Magical Mystery Tours*
Wiener, Jon – *Gimme Some Truth – The John Lennon Files*
Goldman, Albert – *The Lives of John Lennon*
Pang, May – *Loving John*
Coleman, Ray – *Lennon*
Green, John – *Dakota Days*
Rogan, Johnny – *Lennon*
Jones, Jack – *Let Me Take You Down*
Kinzer, Stephen – *Poisoner in Chief – Sidney Gottlieb and the CIA Search for Mind Control*
O'Neil, Tom – *Chaos*
Jones, Lesley-Ann – *Who Killed John Lennon?*
Womack, Kenneth – *John Lennon 1980*
Hinckle, Warren & Turner, William – *Deadly Secrets*
Streatfeild, Dominic – *Brainwash – The Secret History of Mind Control*
Sheff, David – *All We are Saying*
Hopkins, Jerry – *Yoko Ono a Biography*

All significant sources have been cited in the book. Where not, the information was garnered from my own interviews or anonymous sources.

Index

Made in United States
Orlando, FL
11 March 2024